TRANSLATION REVISIO
AND POST-EDITING

Translation Revision and Post-editing looks at the apparently dissolving boundary between correcting translations generated by human brains and those generated by machines. It presents new research on post-editing and revision in government and corporate translation departments, translation agencies, the literary publishing sector and the volunteer sector, as well as on training in both types of translation checking work.

This collection includes empirical studies based on surveys, interviews and keystroke logging, as well as more theoretical contributions questioning such traditional distinctions as translating versus editing. The chapters discuss revision and post-editing involving eight languages: Afrikaans, Catalan, Dutch, English, Finnish, French, German and Spanish. Among the topics covered are translator/reviser relations and revising/post-editing by non-professionals.

The book is key reading for researchers, instructors and advanced students in Translation Studies as well as for professional translators with a special interest in checking translations.

Maarit Koponen is a Lecturer at the University of Turku, Finland, where her research and teaching focus on translation technology, post-editing and translation processes. In 2019–2020, she worked as a postdoctoral researcher in the EU-funded research project MeMAD (Methods for Managing Audiovisual Data) at the University of Helsinki, researching machine translation and post-editing for television subtitling.

Brian Mossop was a Canadian government French-English translator, reviser and trainer from 1974 to 2014. He teaches revision to BA and MA students at York University in Toronto and leads revision workshops for professional translators. He holds an MA in linguistics and is the author of *Revising and Editing for Translators*, 4th edition (Routledge 2020).

Isabelle S. Robert is a Lecturer in French in the Department of Applied Linguistics, Translation and Interpreting, University of Antwerp, Belgium, where she teaches undergraduate courses in French text production and Translation Studies, and graduate courses in Dutch–French translation, revision and translation technology. Her main research interests are audiovisual translation, translation (revision) processes and sight translation.

Giovanna Scocchera has been a literary translator from English to Italian since 2000, working for major Italian publishers both as translator and reviser. She has taught translation and revision for publishing purposes at several institutions. She earned a PhD on revision in the publishing sector in 2015 and has pursued her research interest in revision training and education.

TRANSLATION REVISION AND POST-EDITING

Industry Practices and Cognitive Processes

Edited by Maarit Koponen, Brian Mossop,
Isabelle S. Robert and Giovanna Scocchera

LONDON AND NEW YORK

First published 2021
by Routledge
2 Park Square, Milton Park, Abingdon, Oxon OX14 4RN

and by Routledge
52 Vanderbilt Avenue, New York, NY 10017

Routledge is an imprint of the Taylor & Francis Group, an informa business

British Library Cataloguing-in-Publication Data
A catalogue record for this book is available from the British Library

Library of Congress Cataloging-in-Publication Data
Names: Koponen, Maarit, editor. | Mossop, Brian, editor. | Robert, Isabelle, 1972– editor. | Scocchera, Giovanna, editor.
Title: Translation revision and post-editing : industry practices and cognitive processes / edited by Maarit Koponen, Brian Mossop, Isabelle S. Robert, and Giovanna Scocchera.
Description: London ; New York : Rutledge, 2020. | Includes bibliographical references and index.
Identifiers: LCCN 2020020054 | ISBN 9781138549708 (hardback) | ISBN 9781138549715 (paperback) | ISBN 9781003096962 (ebook)
Subjects: LCSH: Editing. | Translating and interpreting.
Classification: LCC PN162 .T73 2020 | DDC 418/.02—dc23
LC record available at https://lccn.loc.gov/2020020054

ISBN: 978-1-138-54970-8 (hbk)
ISBN: 978-1-138-54971-5 (pbk)
ISBN: 978-1-003-09696-2 (ebk)

Typeset in Bembo
by Apex CoVantage, LLC

CONTENTS

List of contributors   *vii*

Introduction   1

PART I
Post-editing versus revision   **19**

1 Preferential changes in revision and post-editing   21
   Jean Nitzke and Anne-Kathrin Gros

2 Differentiating editing, post-editing and revision   35
   Félix do Carmo and Joss Moorkens

3 Post-editing human translations and revising machine
   translations: impact on efficiency and quality   50
   Joke Daems and Lieve Macken

PART II
Non-professional revision and post-editing   **71**

4 Non-professional editing in the workplace: examples from
   the Canadian context   73
   Matthieu LeBlanc

5 When the post-editor is not a translator: can machine translation be post-edited by academics to prepare their publications in English? 89
Carla Parra Escartín and Marie-Josée Goulet

PART III
Professional revision in various contexts 107

6 Revision and quality standards: do translation service providers follow recommendations in practice? 109
Madeleine Schnierer

7 From language check to creative editing: exploring variation in the revision stage of the LSP workflow 131
Annamari Korhonen

8 Exploring a two-way street: revisers' and translators' attitudes and expectations about each other in biomedical translation 148
Susana Valdez and Sonia Vandepitte

9 Another look at revision in literary translation 165
Ilse Feinauer and Amanda Lourens

PART IV
Training 185

10 Revision and post-editing competences in translator education 187
Kalle Konttinen, Leena Salmi and Maarit Koponen

11 Improving revision quality in translator training with translationQ 203
Gys-Walt van Egdom

12 The MT post-editing skill set: course descriptions and educators' thoughts 226
Clara Ginovart Cid and Carme Colominas Ventura

Bibliography 247
Index 273

CONTRIBUTORS

Félix do Carmo is a Senior Lecturer in translation and natural language processing at the University of Surrey. After completing his PhD at the University of Porto, where he was a guest Lecturer, he worked as a post-doctoral researcher at Dublin City University. For more than 20 years, he was a translator and a translation company owner in Portugal.

Clara Ginovart Cid is a PhD student in the framework of Doctorats Industrials (Generalitat de Catalunya) in the Department of Translation and Language Sciences, Pompeu Fabra University, Spain. She is also a CAT and MT Tool Consultant at Datawords, France. Her main research interests are machine translation post-editing, and translation and terminology technologies and processes.

Joke Daems is a postdoctoral research assistant at Ghent University. As a member of the Language and Translation Technology Team, she conducts research in the field of machine translation and human-computer interaction.

Carla Parra Escartín, PhD in computational linguistics, is Global Program Manager at Iconic Translation Machines. She was previously a Marie Skłodowska-Curie Fellow in the ADAPT Research Centre at Dublin City University, Ireland. Her research focuses on human factors in machine translation and associated technologies, translation quality frameworks and multiword expressions. She has also been involved in ethics research applied to translation and machine translation.

Ilse Feinauer is Professor at the University of Stellenbosch, South Africa, where she teaches Translation Studies and Afrikaans linguistics. Her research focus is socio-cognitive Translation Studies: processes and networks. She is a founding member and board member of the Association for Translation Studies in Africa, and a member of the executive board of the European Society for Translation Studies.

Marie-Josée Goulet, PhD in linguistics, is an Associate Professor in the Department of Education at the Université du Québec en Outaouais, Canada, where she teaches technical and scientific writing. In addition to her interest in the use of machine translation for scientific writing in English as a second language, she conducts research in the field of digital university pedagogy, in particular mediated feedback.

Anne-Kathrin Gros is a PhD student, research assistant and Lecturer at the Center for Translation and Cognition, University of Mainz/Germersheim, Germany. Her research interests include cognitive Translation Studies, translation process research and psycholinguistics.

Kalle Konttinen is a Senior Lecturer in the Department of German, University of Turku, Finland. His research interests include translation pedagogy, translation workflows and translation quality assessment. His teaching focuses on practical translation (German-Finnish), translation technology and translation company simulation.

Annamari Korhonen has worked as an in-house translator since 1999, most of that time at one of Finland's largest language service providers. She holds an MA in English language and is currently working on her PhD in Translation Studies at Tampere University, focusing on translation production processes and editing of translations.

Matthieu LeBlanc is Professor of Translation in the Department of Translation and Modern Languages and Associate Dean of the Faculty of Arts and Social Sciences at the Université de Moncton, Canada. His research fields include Translation Studies and sociolinguistics. He has conducted research on language technologies, translators' social and professional status and the evolution of the translation profession.

Amanda Lourens is a Lecturer in the Postgraduate Translation Programmes of the Department of Afrikaans and Dutch at Stellenbosch University (South Africa). For her 1997 PhD, she studied the canonisation of women's literature in the Afrikaans literary system. Her research is focused on editing procedures, and she has undertaken a few projects on revision in literary translation in collaboration with Ilse Feinauer.

Lieve Macken is an Assistant Professor in the Department of Translation, Interpreting and Communication at Ghent University, Belgium. Her research focuses on the impact of translation technology and machine translation on the process and product of translation. She is the operational head of the language technology section of the department, where she also teaches translation technology, machine translation and localization.

Joss Moorkens is a Lecturer in the School of Applied Language and Intercultural Studies at Dublin City University, Ireland. He has authored over 50 articles and chapters on translation technology, machine translation post-editing, translation evaluation, translator precarity and ethics in translation. He has co-edited a number of books and special issues, and is general co-editor of the journal *Translation Spaces*.

Jean Nitzke is a postdoc and instructor at the Center for Translation and Cognition, University of Mainz, Germany. In her PhD studies, she focused on post-editing, which she also teaches to students, trainers and professional translators. Other research interests include translation process research, translation tools and technologies as well as cognitive aspects of translation.

Leena Salmi is a Senior Lecturer in French at the University of Turku, Finland. Her research interests include post-editing, translation quality assessment, information-seeking as part of translator work and themes related to the production of legally valid translations. Her teaching focuses on practical translation (French-Finnish), translation technology, post-editing and translation company simulation, as well as supervision of MA and PhD theses.

Madeleine Schnierer teaches translation, revision and German language and culture in the Faculty of Translation and Interpreting, University of Geneva, Switzerland, and leads revision workshops for professional translators. She has a PhD in Translation Studies and is the author of *Qualitätssicherung—Die Praxis der Übersetzungsrevision im Zusammenhang mit EN 15038 und ISO 17100*, about revision in relation to standards for translation service providers.

Susana Valdez is an Assistant Professor of Translation Studies at the Centre for Linguistics, Leiden University, Netherlands. Her 2019 doctoral thesis was on translation norms and expectations in biomedical translation. She is currently continuing her research on translators' decision-making processes, and she is particularly interested in how these are influenced by the expectations of the language community.

Gys-Walt van Egdom holds a PhD in linguistics and literary studies and a master's degree in Translation Studies. He lectures on translation and Translation Studies at Utrecht University, the Netherlands. His research interests include translation didactics, translation evaluation, translation ethics, translation processes and human-computer interaction.

Sonia Vandepitte is a full Professor at Ghent University, Belgium, and Director of the Master of Translation programme. She teaches Translation Studies, English-Dutch and Dutch-English translation and has experience coaching student translation companies. Publication topics include translation problem-solving, quality and competences, post-editing and translation training in collaborative learning contexts such as the International Network of Simulated Translation Bureaus.

Carme Colominas Ventura is a Lecturer in German and translation technology in the Department of Translation and Language Sciences, Pompeu Fabra University, Spain, where she teaches undergraduate courses in German-Spanish translation, computer aided translation and natural language processing and graduate courses in translation technology. Her main research interests are machine aided translation, machine translation and automatic text classification.

INTRODUCTION

Revision of translations is an old activity in Europe and probably dates back to Saint Jerome, who was commissioned by Pope Damasus I to revise existing versions of the Bible in the late 4th century. However, in the book publishing industry and in translation departments and agencies, translation revision became common practice only in the course of the 20th century. The earliest publications were practical and pedagogical: in-house manuals for institutional revisers and an article on evaluating the work of such revisers (Arthern 1983); a textbook for revision courses at Canadian translation schools (Horguelin 1978) and a book chapter on the role of such courses (Thaon 1984); advice on self-revision for professional translators (Mossop 1982). Then came the early work by translation researchers: a dissertation (Brunette 1995, published 1997) and a study of literary self-revision (Toury 1995).

In large institutions such as the UN or the EU, the function of reviser has been institutionalized for a few decades now, but in translation agencies, this development is probably more recent and has been encouraged by the publication of the European standard for Translation Services EN 15038 (European Committee for Standardization 2006a) and its successor, ISO 17100 (International Organization for Standardization 2015a). According to these standards, revision is compulsory, has to be carried out by somebody other than the translator and consists of a "bilingual examination of target language content against source language content for its suitability for the agreed purpose" (International Organization for Standardization 2015a: 2).

Although clear definitions of revision in that particular sense can be found in the literature, different terms continue to circulate to refer to the same activity and a consistent (multilingual) revision terminology within Translation Studies (TS) is still lacking. Briefly, translation revision can be defined as the act of examining a translation and making those changes which are necessary to achieve compliance with recognized linguistic and functional criteria. The term 'revision' is sometimes restricted to the examination by one translator of another translator's work (other-revision), but it is also used to denote self-revision, where translators check their own work. Revision involves checking the translation against the source text whether with occasional glances at the source ('unilingual revision') or regular checking ('comparative revision'). It is therefore distinct from proofreading or editing, both of which involve work on a text in one language only. Technology is also affecting the definition and practice of revision. Ever since translation memories came into widespread use, translators have had to assess and perhaps adjust wordings recycled from a memory, and what is that if not revision?

As for post-editing[1] of machine-translation outputs, the first mentions appear in the literature in the 1950s, around the same time as the first proposals for machine (or "mechanical") translation (MT) systems (Garcia 2012: 294). Early adopters of MT and post-editing workflows were large organizations such as the European Commission and the Pan-American Health Organization. As MT quality improved, first with the adoption of phrase-based statistical systems, and then in the 2010s with machine-learning approaches using neural networks, post-editing became more widespread. The publication of an international standard for post-editing (ISO 18587) in 2017 reflects this increasing use. In 2014, van der Meer and Ruopp (2014: 46) even predicted that post-editing would become "the primary production process in translation" by 2020. However, a Language Industry Survey published in 2019 indicates that less than 20% of translation companies and around 10% of freelancers report using MT frequently (ELIA et al. 2019). Post-editing has been used mainly in the context of localization, although more recently studies have started to investigate post-editing of literary texts or audiovisual material like subtitles, voice-overs and audio description. In practice and in research, post-editing appears to be mostly carried out by bilingual individuals utilizing both the source text and MT output. However, some research has also explored the feasibility of monolingual post-editing, where the person performing the post-editing either does not understand the source language or otherwise does not have access to the source text (Koponen and Salmi 2015).

Broadly, post-editing can be defined as editing and correcting machine-translation output, according to the International Standard ISO 17100 (term 2.2.4). However, it is not always clear which practices are covered by the term. ISO 17100 limits its use with a note stating that the term is not applied when "a translator sees and uses a suggestion from a machine-translation engine within a CAT (computer-aided translation) tool", although the reasoning for this is not clarified. In contrast to this limitation, some authors have used the term post-editing for correcting not only MT output but also segments from translation memories (TM) (Silva 2014: 27; Bundgaard and Christensen 2019: 15). Other authors draw further distinctions based on how the user interacts with the MT system. In what is sometimes called 'traditional' post-editing (Alves et al. 2016: 80), the MT system provides the translations as complete suggestions without any actual human-computer interaction. In contrast, interactive MT systems operate more like an autocompletion mode, where the suggestion generated by the system changes based on edits made by the user, which some authors do not consider post-editing as such.

While technology appears central to the practice of post-editing, an interesting feature of revision is that there are very few machine aids specific to this aspect of translation work. No software can help the reviser detect unidiomatic word combinations, language that is too formal or technical for the intended readership, nonsense, deficiencies in inter-sentence connections, or most errors in transfer of meaning or in the focus structure of sentences. For the time being, revision seems to remain largely an activity of human minds unassisted by machines (it is even sometimes done on paper rather than on screen), while the drafting work of translators is on the contrary increasingly machine-assisted. Post-editing, on the other hand, is carried out mostly in CAT tools (see Moorkens and O'Brien 2017). Machine translation and translation memories are also increasingly integrated in the same tools in the form of 'MT assisted TM' (Bundgaard and Christensen 2019), and they are used in parallel during a given translation project. As more translators are finding themselves checking not only human translation but also machine outputs, traditional boundaries between the functions of translators, revisers and post-editors are starting to blur, as are boundaries between professionals and non-professionals.

1. Research into revision and post-editing—the state of the art

Research interest in revision and post-editing has been gaining momentum in recent years, with a growing number of publications. Some are theoretical/conceptual (often personal reflections about specific aspects of revision or post-editing) and are based on a literature search or rely on argumentation. Others are empirical, involving one or more of the following: studies of the revision product, process, participants or environment (where the study is carried out). Empirical studies are based on experiments or observations and draw on qualitative and/or quantitative methods. Product-based methodologies include error analyses, quality assessment and corpus approaches, and, in the case of post-editing, automatic metrics that compare the MT output and its post-edited version and calculate the edit rate, or the number and type of changes (see Snover et al. 2006). Process-based methods generally involve the use of keylogging software, which records the user's keystrokes and mouse clicks; eyetracking, where specialized cameras are used to collect data about the user's gaze movements and fixations, or introspective methods like think-aloud protocols, where the participants verbalize their thoughts during the task or retrospectively. Participant-oriented methods include observation, interviews and surveys. Studies often combine product and process methods, making it sometimes difficult to clearly delineate product-oriented and process-oriented studies. Similarly, product or process studies may also involve participant-oriented methods, and participant-oriented studies may also involve the analysis of product and process data. Contexts for studies can be professional environments like language service providers (companies and freelancers) or in-house translation departments, translator training environments, or contexts where 'non-professionals' or 'lay people' (not working in a translation profession) carry out revision or post-editing.

2. Theoretical publications on revision

Theoretical publications are of three kinds. First, there are overviews of the field. The most complete is Robert (2018), in French, which combines a review of the literature (on which sections 1 to 3 of this introduction are based) with an analysis of bibliometric data on revision. Robert draws on Künzli's (2014) work in German, the most complete at the time, where the author looked at the concept of revision, the state of research and desiderata for future work. An interesting overview with a focus on revision in literary translation is also provided in Scocchera (2017a). A few older overviews are presented by Mossop (2007a, 2011), and by Garcia (2008) on revising for localization. In this first group of publications, we also find an enlightening theoretical reflection on the boundaries between translation, revision and post-editing (Jakobsen 2019). The author explains that in much professional translation where technologies are ubiquitous, "there is less writing and less translation from scratch, than editing and post-editing of text suggested by TM/MT systems" (76), thus making the distinction between the three activities increasingly blurred, but still useful.

Second, there are articles on specific aspects of revision, such as revision terminology (Scocchera 2013; Brunette 2000), key concepts for revision (Tardáguila 2009), revision parameters (Lee 2006), methodological aspects of revision and revision as a method of quality assurance (Parra-Galiano 2016), risk management when deciding whether to revise (Martin 2007), the place of revision in the translation process, the importance of mentoring and of didactic revision in training future translators (Rochard 2004), revisers as guardians of translation rather than censors (Brunette 2002), interventions by publishers' editors that make revised translations worse (Pergnier 1990), briefs for revisers (Allman 2007) and the need to incorporate unilingual and bilingual revision into translation quality assessment models (Mellinger 2018). Nord (2018) provides some thoughts on revision based on her experience as a professional reviser, looking at revision criteria, procedures, principles and competence, the notion of error, and relationships among those involved in revision. She also explains how the manufacturing principle of 'quality at the source' (the notion that quality must be measured at every step of a production process, not just at the end) could be applied to translation revision.

A third type of theoretical publication concerns revision teaching and the acquisition of revision competence. Rodríguez (2012) describes a constructivist approach to revision teaching. Brunette (1998) looks at revision as a translator training exercise, while Brunette (2003) considers the role of the linguistic code in teaching revision, with a focus on interference from the source language. Parra-Galiano (2001) makes the case that learning to revise will create self-confidence and thus prepare translators for professional life, while Parra-Galiano (2015) looks at the causes of defective revision. Mossop (1992) describes three possible goals of a revision course. Chakhachiro (2005) sets out a list of competences, which is expanded upon in Scocchera (2017a). Mendoza García and Ponce Márquez (2013) propose instruction in revision as a key to developing other aspects of translation competence. Robert et al. (2017a) provide a model of revision competence.

3.   Empirical studies of revision

Studies of the product

Studies that focus on the revised translation as a product are recent and still fairly rare. They generally involve analysis of a corpus, sometimes limited in scope and thus more like case studies. In a few cases, the product analysis is based on data collected through an experiment. Bisiada (2018) draws on a parallel corpus of English source texts (business articles), their unrevised German translations and the published (revised) German, in order to examine revisers' interventions, in particular with regard to nominalizations. He finds that revisers have a significant and systematic impact on translations, and that what some people see as literal translations are not necessarily the result of the translator's work, but rather the reviser's. McDonough (2015) analyses a corpus of translations of Wikipedia entries, and the revisions made to these translations, in order to discover the frequency of transfer problems on the one hand and language-and-style problems on the other, as well as the revisers' solutions. She finds that both types of problem are nearly always present, that half of them remain typically undetected by the revisers, and that language-and-style problems are revised more frequently than transfer problems. Popič (2014) analyses a DIY corpus of translated and revised (popular) scientific texts to check application of the European standard EN 15038 in Slovenia. She finds that revision is very often unilingual rather than comparative and that the reviser has not necessarily been trained as a translator.

Some corpora consist of literary texts. Solum (2018) analyses a corpus of novels translated from English to Norwegian in order to identify which of the revisers' proposed changes are accepted by the translators. While revisers are hardly ever mentioned in the acknowledgements of the published books, they are found to have a definite influence on those parts of the translations where they suggest changes. The translators accept a considerable number of the revisers' suggestions, and Norwegian literary translators expect their publishers to provide a high standard of revision work. Robin (2014) analyses a corpus of fiction translated from English to Hungarian and the revised versions in order to discover what happens to 'translation universals' during the revision phase. She finds that while explicitation and implicitation are usually deemed to be the work of translators, they can be the result of revision or editing strategies (2019). She also suggests (Robin 2018) a typology of reviser interventions based on linguistic and translational rules, norms and strategies.

As already mentioned, some product studies are based on a restricted corpus or on the analysis of a small number of texts, sometimes one. Magris (1999) analyses the revised translation of a nursing handbook in order to investigate the reviser's task definition and tolerance for the translator's choices. Rega (1999) analyses the revisions of three German-to-Italian translations, giving examples of subjective changes, necessary stylistic changes and necessary changes made by a subject-matter expert. She finds numerous changes of the second type and says that style should receive more attention in university translation courses. Notaristefano

(2010) analyses the revised translation of a macroeconomics textbook from English to Italian, classifies and quantifies the changes, and presents an ideal professional profile for a reviser. Lemaire (2018) reflects on her own revision of a corpus of museum and exhibition panels. She suggests a redefinition of the multilingual editorial process of these panels, and calls for changes in mentality and working conditions to ensure editorial quality.

Finally, some researchers set up an experiment to collect data that they analyse mainly from a product point of view. This is the case of Van Rensburg (2012), who sought to determine the impact of the work done by various revisers on the quality of the draft translation, and also to compare the impact with the time spent on revision in order to determine the cost-effectiveness of the procedure. Four revisers revised two English-to-Afrikaans translations: an unspecialized text translated by a translation student and a specialized text translated by an experienced professional translator. For each text, three evaluators rated the unrevised translation and the four revised translations. Van Rensburg found that revision had less impact on the quality of the translation produced by the professional, leading to the question of whether it is necessary to revise the work of experienced translators. The results also showed that there is not necessarily a positive correlation between revision quality and revision experience. More recently, Pontrandolfo (2017) investigated the revision of one legal translation by four different types of professionals (legal linguists, professional translators with a specialization in legal translation, professional translators without that specialization, and lawyers without translation and/or revision experience) to determine whether translation competence suffices to revise complex legal translations and what the importance of subject-matter knowledge is. Although she acknowledges that her research is a case study and that generalizations are difficult to make, her hypothesis is confirmed: professional translators with experience in translation and revision but without training in legal translation do not seem to be well prepared to revise a complex legal translation.

Studies of revision competence and teaching

The first study of revision competence (Lorenzo 2002) uses keystroke logging to compare students' self-revision and other-revision competence when working with translations into their second language. She finds that the students were not successful because they lacked strategies for detecting and evaluating errors, and that they were better at revising others than revising themselves. The second study, by Künzli (2006b), analyses think-aloud protocols from ten professional revisers with a view to discovering the components of revision competence and formulating an outline for a revision course. He suggests a module focused on strategic, interpersonal and instrumental competences. Next comes a longitudinal study (Hansen 2009) carried out in Denmark from 2003 to 2007 with 71 students and 28 professionals. Its purpose was to compare translation competence with revision competence based on both product and process analyses using keystroke logging, questionnaires and interviews. One of the main findings was that experienced translators are not necessarily good revisers, and vice versa; revision competence requires additional aptitudes and attitudes.

More recently, a group of researchers at the University of Antwerp sought to validate their model of revision competence (Robert et al. 2018). The initial results appeared in three publications (Rigouts Terryn et al. 2017; Robert et al. 2017b; Robert et al. 2018). The researchers conducted an experiment with 21 students divided into an experimental group, who had taken a module on revision, and a control group, who had no revision training. The students first performed a set of revision tasks, recorded with keystroke logging, and then filled out an online questionnaire. One finding was that the experimental group used the same search tools as the control group, but more frequently; they performed more searches in order to be able to justify their changes, and their searches were more meticulous. The experimental group was also more tolerant of wording choices and made fewer pointless changes. However the researchers were not able to demonstrate that the students in the experimental group revised better, in the sense of making more necessary changes (an indicator of strategic competence). Their explanation was that the revision training had been brief and that a pilot study has inherent limitations (such as the number of participants).

The literature also includes three experimental studies of revision teaching. In the first (Shreve et al. 2014), the researchers compare the efficacy of screen recording data with that of Integrated Problem and Decision Reporting (Gile 2004) in assisting other-revision by 12 students. They found that the students performed better when they had access to screen recording data on the translation process. The second study (Robert and Brunette 2016) looks at the relationship between think-aloud, revision quality and ability to detect errors with 16 professional revisers, to see whether think-aloud would help learners. The researchers found that the more the revisers verbalized detailed diagnoses of error, the better their detection and correction work, but the longer they took to complete the task. Applying this to pedagogy, the researchers concluded that it might be useful to ask revision students to think aloud when revising at home. Finally, drawing from previous research on revision pedagogy and didactics (Scocchera 2014) and based on a multi-component view of revision competence (2017a), the third study (Scocchera 2019) investigates the general attitudes towards revision and the background skills of revision students taking part in a short-term course, as well as their progress in the acquisition of revision competence. By comparing the students' output on different revision assignments, the study also tests the validity and efficacy of the teaching contents and methods and provides insights and practical suggestions for revision-specific education and training based on quantitative and qualitative data obtained through an end-of-study questionnaire.

Relationship between the process and the quality of the product

Among the many publications about the relationship between the revision process and the quality of the product, a set of experimental studies focus on the revision procedure and/or revision instructions. For example, in an experimental study using think-aloud for three revision tasks performed by ten professionals, Künzli (2006c) found that a lack of clear instructions (a revision brief) had a negative effect on the revised translation. Künzli (2007b) also looked at changes made by revisers, changes which should have been made but were not and the task definition for revision (revision brief), and found that defective revision could be due to the reviser not having a clear definition of the task as well as a lack of well-structured procedures. Later, Künzli (2009) found that quality takes time, and that it did not seem to matter whether the reviser read a wording of the translation first or a wording of the source text first when comparing source text and translation.

As far as revision procedures are concerned, the first study was probably that of the GREVIS research group (Brunette et al. 2005), which looked at the revision interventions by 14 professional revisers, first with the source text, then without. Analysis of the result led to the conclusion that unilingual revision is inadvisable. Robert (2013, 2014b; Robert and Van Waes 2014) looked at how revision procedure is related to the quality of the product, the error detection potential and the duration of the task. Sixteen professional revisers had to each revise four translations, each time using a different procedure. Data collection was by think-aloud, keystroke logging and a questionnaire. She found that procedure did indeed have an impact, and she formulated recommendations. Marashi and Okhowat (2013) compared revision with and without the source text by 40 professional revisers, with a focus on the linguistic quality of the revision and the revisers' profiles. The results were rated by professors of the target language. The finding was that recourse to the source had no effect on quality with this type of purely linguistic revision. Finally, Huang (2018) investigated the self-revision, other-revision and post-editing processes of translation trainees through eyetracking, keystroke logging and retrospection. Drawing on an analysis of the students' reading and typing activities, together with the corresponding cognitive activities and purposes, she observed three working phases in the processes (planning, drafting and final check) and was able to identify four types of working styles, which roughly correspond to different revision procedures. One example is the Micro processing working style, which means one or two run-throughs of bilingual reading and detailed revision. She also found three types of reviser (habit-oriented, task-oriented and habit/task-oriented). By comparing the observed students' working styles with those of professionals in the existing literature, she hoped "to offer insight into the behaviour of pre-career translators and contribute to translation pedagogy" (176).

Another set of studies pays more attention to the revisers and/or their profiles or expertise. Künzli (2005), for example, asked what principles guide translation revision, and he also looked at the quality of the product and the duration of the process. He found that revisers did not always apply the principles they had verbalized, such as "revising is not retranslating". He then considered the sense of loyalty in decision-making (2006a) and concluded that revisers are faced with a dilemma: loyalty to self versus loyalty to other actors such as the client and the reader.

With regard to profiles, Van Rensburg (2017) designed instruments to measure the quality of revision in order to find a possible link between revision quality and certain variables in the reviser's profile. With 30 revisers and 3 language experts, she found a significant correlation between years of translation experience and just one of the indicators in her measuring instrument, namely necessary corrections to the target language. Scocchera (2017a) conducted a survey in the Italian publishing sector, and the findings enabled her to outline a profile of the reviser in terms of age, gender, expertise, education/training and work practices, providing a valuable contribution to higher visibility for this professional figure. Schaeffer et al. (2019a) used eyetracking and key logging to compare the revision behaviour of translation students and professional translators. The aim was to investigate the effect of error type on error recognition, the relation between eye-movement patterns and error detection, and the relation between translation expertise and error recognition behaviour. They concluded that professional translators are more strategic in terms of cost/benefit in their revision behaviour.

A last group of studies take into account the ubiquity of technologies in the translation and revision workflow and were thus carried out within a CAT tool environment. This is the case for Mellinger and Shreve (2016), who observed revision by nine professional translators using keylogging software. They found a tendency to make unnecessary changes. Ipsen and Dam (2016) had nine students perform a revision task in the CAT tool MemSource. Data were gathered using screen capture, interviews and retrospective think-aloud. The researchers found that regardless of the procedure, participants obtained better results when they read the translation before the source during comparison. However, the order of reading was established after completion of the task, through retrospective interviews, rather than during the task using eyetracking. Ciobanu et al. (2019) looked at the embedding of speech technologies in the revision workflow in order to determine their effect on the revisers' preferences, viewing behaviour and revision quality. Five professional translators and six translation trainees were asked to revise the English translation of a French text in a CAT tool, with and without source text sound (via speech synthesis). Their eye movements were tracked and they had to fill in a post-eyetracking questionnaire. The authors found an improvement in revision quality, especially regarding accuracy errors, when sound was present.

Participant-based studies

Studies of participants in the revision process are based on surveys. Scocchera (2015) looked at revision by literary publishers in Italy from two points of view: first, she investigated the relationship between translator and reviser using a survey with 80 respondents; second, she considered the role of computer-based revision in the genesis of translations.[2] She found that 43.6% of the translators surveyed always had contacts with their reviser, but the same proportion never had contact; the remaining 12.8% had sporadic contact. She also found that very few revisers had had any training in literary revision. The same study was drawn on by Scocchera (2014) to make suggestions for a course in literary revision, and to make a case for the use of specific tools: the Review functions in Word, publishers' house-style guides,

Mossop's (2014a) revision parameters and Berman's (1985) typology of forces that tend to domesticate literary translations. Scocchera (2016) provides her personal reflections on the importance of a collaborative approach to revision, through an anecdote taken from her own experience as a reviser. Finally, still drawing on her survey, Scocchera (2017b) looks at translation revision as rereading and analyses the reviser's strategies and purposes.

Rasmussen and Schjoldager (2011) conducted a survey to find out about procedures, revision parameters and reviser profiles at 22 Danish translation agencies, and then interviewed some of the revisers. She found that 10% of translations are not revised at all, while 90% receive a comparative revision. Few agencies had a revision manual, though most of the revisers are trained translators. Schjoldager et al. (2008) used a survey and interviews to develop a precis-writing, editing and revision module for a course. Hernández-Morin (2009) looked at practices and perceptions of revision in France through a survey with 115 respondents. She found that most freelance translators support the European translation service standard EN 15038, but while they endorse revision, they do not think it is always necessary. Robert (2008) examined the inconsistent terminology of revision through a literature review and then looked at revision procedures using two surveys (48 and 21 respondents). Robert and Remael (2016) conducted a survey (99 respondents) about revision of subtitles. Lafeber (2012) conducted a survey of in-house translators and revisers in order to identify the importance of various types of skill and knowledge, and the extent to which they are lacking in new recruits. The results confirmed that linguistic competence alone is not sufficient. In 2018, she confirmed these first results, explaining that at both the EU and the UN, the skills required also include analytical and research skills as well as procedural and substantive knowledge.

Studies in different environments

Studies in the translator training context are mostly descriptions and analyses of revision courses at the researcher's university. Wolfson (2004, 2005) looks at 10 years of a distance revision course. Hine (2003) relates his experience of teaching revision in a multilingual environment. Brunette and Gagnon (2013) describe how they used translations of Wikipedia entries in their revision course. Pietrzak (2014) describes the operation of group revision within a translation course. Finally, Hagemann (2019) investigates directionality in revision teaching: she taught a course in which the target language was her B language but the students' A language, and she concluded that directionality could be used to promote the instructor's role as facilitator in the translation/revision classroom.

Workplace studies have often been conducted in the translation services of major international organizations. Arthern (1983, 1991) described a revision quality model he developed in order to evaluate the work of revisers in the English division of the Council of the European Communities' translation service. Parra-Galiano (2006, 2007a, 2007b) carried out three case studies (one of them at the

Translation Centre for the Bodies of the European Union, https://cdt.europa.eu/en), on which she bases a proposed methodology for revision that includes principles, parameters and procedures for revision as well as qualifications for revisers. Prioux and Rochard (2007) draw on their experience to describe the cost/benefit approach to revision used at the translation service of the Organization for Economic Cooperation and Development. Yousif (2009) looks at revision in an institutional setting and proposes guidelines involving four tasks, each based on one or two parameters such as the institution's terminology. Allain (2010) considers two-person revision (one speaking the translation aloud, the other reading the source), based on his experience at the Council of Europe. Bertaccini and Di Nisio (2011) describe revision at a private translation agency and at the European Commission's Directorate General for Translation.

Some writers take a look at professional standards. Schopp (2007) looks at the European standard EN 15038 and also at DIN 16511, which deals with proofreading symbols. Biel (2011) analyses EN 15038 from the point of view of its implications for the translation industry and for the training of future translators. Parra-Galiano (2011) looks at various aspects of EN 15038 such as the degree of revision and its parameters. In Parra-Galiano (2017), she looks at the international standard ISO 17100.

Revision of literary translation has rarely been the object of scholarly research. Jones (2006) and Kolb (2013) investigate overall processes and specific, personal procedures adopted by literary translators of poetry and fiction respectively. Buzelin (2007) studies three literary translations "in the making" from a Latourian perspective. Bogic (2010) analyses the translator-publisher relationship during the translation process into English of Simone de Beauvoir's *Le deuxième sexe*. Siponkoski (2013) looks at unpublished editorial commentary on translators' drafts of translations of Shakespeare into Finnish and highlights examples of negotiation between translators and copyeditors. Feinauer and Lourens (2017) report on a case study of revision in literary publishing to determine the loyalties of literary revisers by considering the various agents' discussions with each other about a translation. Ándujar Moreno (2019) draws on the concept of translation universals to look at the way linguistic changes resulting from editorial revision, rather than from translation, can be seen as recurring editing tendencies or patterns at work in any final editing process of a translation. This is done through the analysis and comparison of different stages in the Spanish translation of Charles Bock's *Beautiful Children*, with a particular focus on lexical choice. The study enables the researcher to categorize revisers' activities and to develop a taxonomy of their changes and the reasons behind them. Marin-Lacarta and Vargas-Urpi (2019) study the revision process in literary translation in the context of non-profit digital publishing. Through interviews with translators and revisers, participants' diaries, e-mail correspondence and translation drafts, the researchers expose the complex network of negotiated decisions and interactions between the actors involved, concluding that while revision is greatly appreciated by translators (thus dismantling the common stereotype of the translator-versus-reviser "tug of war"), different revision stages and activities are often blurred.

4. Theoretical publications on post-editing

As in the case of revision, theoretical publications on post-editing include overviews of the use of MT and post-editing in translation workflows. Garcia (2012) presents a historical overview of the use of post-editing and related research based on published research and other sources. Current use has been investigated in surveys by Gaspari et al. (2015) and Porro Rodriquez et al. (2017). Various authors have published accounts of the place of post-editing in the workflows of specific organizations, the post-editing services offered (O'Curran 2014; Silva 2014) and the work of post-editors (Robert 2013). Best practices and guidelines for post-editing have been published for specific organizations and languages and for general use. A comparative overview of various post-editing guidelines can be found in Hu and Cadwell (2016).

As interaction with MT and other technologies is a significant part of post-editing, publications include descriptions of tools for post-editing (Alabau et al. 2013) as well as more general analyses and reflections on tools and their features (Teixeira 2014; Alonso and Vieira 2017). Moorkens and O'Brien (2017) provide an overview of tools used for post-editing as well as a 'wish list' for the design of such tools based on a survey of translators and post-editors.

Theoretical publications also include reflections on post-editing competences. O'Brien (2002) discusses overlaps and differences in the skills needed for translation and for post-editing and argues that post-editing competences are distinct from translation competences, and that specialized training is needed. Other authors since then have addressed specific post-editing competences (Rico and Torrejón 2012; Nitzke et al. 2019).

5. Empirical studies of post-editing

Product-oriented studies

The quality of post-edited texts has been a central question in product-oriented studies about professional contexts (Guerberof Arenas 2017), post-editing by translation students (Ortiz-Boix and Matamala 2017) and non-professional post-editing of user-generated content (Mitchell et al. 2014). Studies have also addressed the correctness and necessity of changes in post-editing and identified unnecessary changes, changes introducing errors and errors missed by professional translators (de Almeida 2013) and by translation students (Koponen et al. 2019).

Research has also addressed questions related to the usability or acceptability of post-edited texts from the perspective of the end user of a translation. Bowker and Buitrago Ciro (2015) present a study of the acceptability of human-translated, machine-translated and post-edited texts and also take into account the time and cost of producing each version. Van Egdom and Pluymaekers (2019) compare various quality aspects and end-user impressions of texts with various levels of post-editing. Screen (2019) uses eyetracking as well as subjective evaluations of readability and comprehensibility to address the end-user perspective. The effect of post-editing on usability has been investigated by having users complete tasks with the help of unedited machine-translated or post-edited instructions combined with measurements of user satisfaction (Castilho and O'Brien 2016).

Product-oriented studies have also investigated the overall patterns of changes made to the MT output during post-editing (Groves and Schmidtke 2009) or choices made by student post-editors (Koponen 2013) as well as terminological and lexical features (Culo and Nitzke 2016; Moorkens and Sasamoto 2017) and textual features such as literality (Carl and Schaeffer 2017) and metaphors (Koglin and Cunha 2019). Čulo et al. (2014) present a study about the influence of post-editing on the strategies of professional translators and translation students and potential interferences from the source language in post-edited products. Drawing on the concept of 'translationese' (wordings that distinguish translated texts from texts originally written in the target language), some research has started to investigate whether specific features of 'post-editese' similarly differentiate post-edited texts from translations and from original texts (Daems et al. 2017a; Toral 2019).

Process-oriented studies

In the translation industry, the rationale for using MT and post-editing relies on the assumption that it requires less effort than translation 'from scratch'. For this reason, the question of effort has received much interest in post-editing research. The influential model of post-editing effort by Krings (2001) distinguishes three aspects: temporal effort (the time needed for post-editing), technical effort to make corrections (for example, keystrokes) and cognitive effort to identify errors and plan corrections. A survey of studies on post-editing effort is given in Koponen (2016).

Technical and temporal effort have been addressed in studies where translators' productivity during post-editing has been compared to translation from scratch (Plitt and Masselot 2010; Läubli et al. 2013) and to translation with the aid of translation memory matches (Guerberof Arenas 2014a, 2014b; Teixeira 2014). Research has also investigated the effects of interactive and adaptive MT (Alabau et al. 2016) and recently the effect of neural MT as compared to earlier technologies (Toral Ruiz et al. 2018; Daems and Macken 2019; Jia et al. 2019; Sánchez-Gijón et al. 2019). Combining product and process, Vieira (2017b) investigates the connections between different measures of post-editing effort and the quality of the post-edited texts.

Cognitive effort is the most difficult of the three aspects to capture and measure, although considerable research interest has been focused on this topic. Some research has investigated the use of think-aloud protocols (O'Brien 2005; Vieira 2017a; Koglin and Cunha 2019). One of the approaches to identifying cognitive effort is based on detecting pauses in keylogging data. It has been suggested that extended pauses are points of increased effort (O'Brien 2005; Screen 2017), as are clusters of short pauses (Lacruz and Shreve 2014). Eyetracking technology has also been applied to investigating cognitive effort, on the assumption that more frequent and longer gaze fixations indicate increased cognitive effort (Moorkens 2018a). Vieira (2017a) investigates and compares different indicators of cognitive effort using eyetracking, think-aloud protocols and subjective ratings. Herbig et al. (2019) experiment with physiological measures such as skin- and heart-based indicators.

Cognitive effort has also been explored in terms of the effort perceived by the person carrying out the post-editing. An annotation scale for collecting sentence-level information about the perceived effort in post-editing was proposed by Specia (2011). Such perceived effort ratings do not, however, always correspond to the technical effort involved in terms of number of changes, as was found by Koponen (2012). Correlations between effort perceived by the post-editor and measures of effort like time and number of keystrokes have also been investigated by others (Herbig et al. 2019).

Specific issues in investigations of temporal, technical or cognitive effort include the impact of source text features (O'Brien 2005; Aziz et al. 2014; Koglin and Cunha 2019), different types of errors in the MT output (Koponen 2012; Koponen et al. 2012; Daems et al. 2017b; Carl and Toledo-Báez 2019) and types of post-editing operations (Popović et al. 2014). Da Silva et al. (2017) investigate the effect of L2 to L1 versus L1 to L2 directionality on the post-editing process. Lacruz (2018) investigates stages of processing in post-editing.

Participant-oriented studies

The adoption and perception of MT post-editing in different settings has been a point of interest for participant-oriented studies. Guerberof Arenas (2013) presents a study based on online questionnaires and "debriefing" interviews with professional translators who participated in a post-editing experiment. Adoption and acceptance of MT and post-editing among translators at the European Commission have been explored in two studies using focus groups (Cadwell et al. 2016) and survey data (Rossi and Chevrot 2019). Bundgaard (2017a, 2017b) investigates translators' resistance to and accommodation of post-editing and "translator-computer interaction" more broadly, through interviews and written answers to questions about expectations and experiences. Sakamoto (2019) also examines resistance to post-editing based on a focus group of translation project managers.

Participant-oriented studies have also examined the profiles, skills and competences of post-editors. Guerberof Arenas (2014b) examines the effect of professional experience on post-editing productivity as well as the quality of the post-edited translations. Alabau et al. (2016) present a longitudinal study of professional translators using an interactive MT system; they examine the effect of post-editing experience, and personal factors such as typing skills, on the post-editing process. Huang (2018) looks at translation students, comparing their profiles and approaches when post-editing, self-revising and other-revising. Daems et al. (2017c) compare the translation and post-editing processes of professional translators and translation students. Aranberri et al. (2014) examine the productivity of professional translators and non-professionals. Temizöz (2016) compares the quality of post-edited texts by professional translators and subject matter experts, and Temizöz (2017) looks into both revision and post-editing by translators and experts.

Studies in different environments

In addition to accounts of individual experiences, post-editing in professional environments has been investigated through surveys, observational workplace studies and focus groups. Porro Rodríguez et al. (2017) present the results of a survey about post-editing among Swiss language service providers. Cadwell et al. (2016) discuss a focus group study of European Commission translators and the degree to which they use MT and post-editing, as well as reasons why it is used or not used. A more recent survey study by Rossi and Chevrot (2019) also examines post-editing by European Commission translators. Bundgaard and Christensen (2019) discuss the ways translators use translation memories and post-edit MT, as well as other resources, drawing on observation and retrospective think-aloud. Bywood et al. (2017) examine the use of MT and post-editing by subtitle translators in the audiovisual context. Post-editing of audiovisual material has also been explored in the case of voice-over (Ortiz-Boix and Matamala 2017) and audio description (Fernández-Torné 2016). Toral Ruiz et al. (2018) report on a case study of post-editing a novel.

Turning to translator training environments, Depraetere (2010) and Flanagan and Christensen (2014) present case studies of the challenges of using post-editing guidelines and advice in training for post-editing; they suggest modifications to guidelines for training purposes. Garcia (2010, 2011) reports on experiments integrating MT post-editing into translator training, and Killman (2016) compares post-editing as a learning activity to more 'traditional' translation approaches. Witczak (2016) discusses post-editing as a part of a language technology course and focuses on the students' attitudes. Yamada (2019) presents an experiment with translation students post-editing neural MT outputs, while an earlier study by Yamada (2015) looks at post-editing carried out by students in language-learning (as opposed to Translation Studies) contexts. Lastly, studies of training environments include descriptions of post-editing courses (O'Brien 2002; Koponen 2015; Guerberof Arenas and Moorkens 2019).

Post-editing has also been researched in contexts where the people performing the post-editing are not professional translators or post-editors. Navarro (2012) discusses cases where MT post-editing is used by journalists for bilingual digital press publications. Mitchell et al. (2014) investigate post-editing of user-generated posts on a technical help forum by other users of the forum identified as subject-matter experts. Schwartz (2014) investigates the feasibility of monolingual post-editing (without source text) by subject-matter experts as a means of identifying the parts of a text needing most attention from a bilingual translator. Aranberri et al. (2014) present a study where university lecturers, who may need to produce materials in more than one language, post-edited a machine-translated text related to their field; the authors compare the lay users' performance to that of professional translators. O'Brien et al. (2018) examine the quality of post-edited texts in a case where academic writers machine-translated and then post-edited their own texts as a support for writing scientific articles.

6. The contributions of this volume

This book is original and relevant in several ways. First, it looks at revision and post-editing together, even within a single chapter (Nitzke and Gros, Chapter 1; Daems and Macken, Chapter 3). This has rarely been done in previous publications, although such a combination of activities might become a common practice in industry in the near future. Under the impulse of new technological developments, it may become the norm for translation, revision and post-editing to be carried out by one and the same person not only during different translation jobs but also during one and the same job.

Second, the book includes both empirical contributions and more theoretical contributions on the conceptual boundaries between translation, revision and post-editing (Carmo and Moorkens, Chapter 2) and the competences related to these activities (Ginovart Cid and Colominas Ventura, Chapter 12). Third, the book covers a wide variety of topics, such as training in revision and post-editing (Konttinen, Salmi and Koponen, Chapter 10; Van Egdom, Chapter 11), post-editing by non-professionals (Parra Escartín and Goulet, Chapter 5), relations between translators and revisers (Valdez and Vandepitte, Chapter 8) and studies of professional practices in three different contexts where revision is carried out: translation agencies (Schnierer, Chapter 6; Korhonen, Chapter 7), translation departments of large institutions (LeBlanc, Chapter 4) and the publishing sector (Feinauer and Lourens, Chapter 9).

Finally, the very extensive list of references at the end of the volume should prove useful to anyone carrying out research on revision and post-editing.

Existing work by TS scholars has brought to light some interesting questions for research, though only some of these are addressed here. First, studies have shown that, whether they are revising their own or someone else's translation, different translators use different methods. Does the method have any effect on speed or on the quality of the output? The answer is still very unclear, and the question also applies to post-editing. Second, existing work has revealed problems: revisers failing to detect errors in translations, introducing errors or wasting time on unnecessary changes. A related problem is the conflict between professional and business concerns: revision seeks to create adequate quality but it takes time, and therefore—unless the time for the drafting phase can be reduced—it increases costs. This situation gives rise to an ethical question: to what and to whom will the reviser be loyal? More generally, little is known about the usefulness of revision: how many problems in translations—especially serious problems—are being corrected (or not corrected) per hour of revision effort in translation services? Again, the same questions apply, at least partially, to post-editing. Since the rationale for using machine output as a raw version to be post-edited rests on the assumption that it increases productivity, the need for changes is a particularly important issue. Studies of revision and post-editing may at some point be able to help here if they shed light on the causes of problems or lead to improved revision and post-editing training. Finally, because revision and post-editing are mostly a reading rather than a writing process (the purpose is to spot problems in the draft translation or raw MT output), the study of revision and post-editing has potential for the development of research focusing on how translators read, whereas most studies in our field today are concerned with how they write.

Notes

1 The term originated by contrast with 'pre-editing' (of MT inputs). It has appeared both hyphenated and unhyphenated since the earliest publications, and both spellings continue to be used. In this volume, we use the hyphenated form, which appears to be more common in the 2010s. The acronyms PEMT, for Post-Editing of Machine Translation, and MTPE, for Machine Translation Post-Editing, are also both in use.
2 Translation genesis is a new area of research inspired by the textual genetics approach in literary criticism. This involves examining the different versions of a work (in this case, a translation) as well as manuscripts and other working documents that may have left traces in the work. See issue 14 (2015) of the Translation Studies journal *LANS* (https://lans-tts. uantwerpen.be/index.php/LANS-TTS/issue/view/16).

PART I

Post-editing versus revision

1

PREFERENTIAL CHANGES IN REVISION AND POST-EDITING

Jean Nitzke and Anne-Kathrin Gros

In this chapter, we will investigate and discuss the phenomenon of preferential changes in revision and post-editing, which we call *over-editing*. Translators over-edit when they revise/post-edit more than is necessary, given certain guidelines. In both tasks, some translators feel the urge to improve all linguistic aspects because they want to achieve perfect quality, even though the guidelines state otherwise. It is very important that revisers and post-editors adhere to guidelines in order to make the process efficient and worthwhile, especially in regard to payment.

Over-editing is a phenomenon that is previously known from research on CAT tools, in particular from work with translation memory (TM) systems. Translators revise the suggested TM match too extensively, when the quality of the match would have been good enough with no edits (for exact matches) or just a few edits (for fuzzy matches), and this is costly in terms of time and consequently money. Mellinger and Shreve (2016) compare the behaviour of nine participants in a study who were asked to each translate seven segments with exact matches, seven segments with fuzzy matches, and seven segments with no matches. The match type was randomly chosen for each segment, and the participants did not know what kind of match they would be confronted with. However, they were instructed not to change a segment if they felt that it did not need to be changed. They were also allowed to delete the entire match if they felt that it would take too much time to edit it. The participants changed 60% of those exact matches which did not require any changes. On the other hand, they changed only 74% of the fuzzy matches, although all of them needed changes. Many of the unnecessary changes were preferential changes on a syntactic or lexical level. The explanation for this phenomenon offered by Mellinger and Shreve is that because the participants do not have to create their own translations when there are fuzzy and exact matches but instead have to compare source and target text, they actively look for mistakes. Further, the participants have their own translations in mind, which results in two competing versions of the target text segment. The participants tend to change the TM match into their own translation.

The same phenomenon can also be observed in PE and revision. Translators might create their own mental concept of the source unit with their own translation ideas and are then confronted with the machine translation or a translation created by another person (see Oster 2017 for information on priming and monitoring). These latter translations are not necessarily defective, but they do not always correspond to the translator's representation. Over-editing was previously examined for PE in De Almeida (2013). In her study, she analysed the edits of 20 participants post-editing IT texts (ten translated into French and ten into Brazilian Portuguese). Her main categories were essential changes, preferential changes, unimplemented essential changes and introduction of errors. 'Preferential changes' are synonymous with what we refer to as over-editing. The participants made 45.16 preferential changes on average in a text with 1008 words; in other words, an unnecessary change was made every 22.32 words.

Specific instructions to avoid over-editing are frequently included in the PE brief. For example, one of the instructions in the study by Aikawa et al. (2012: 7) very explicitly states: "Avoid over-editing: don't try to over-edit if the existing translation(s) . . . are grammatical and readable." As over-editing is a rather abstract concept, the usefulness of such an instruction might be questionable. Participants are reminded that they should keep the editing process to a minimum, but the extent to which the translators adhere to the instructions remains unknown. Further, it might be difficult for translators who are not trained in PE to lower their quality standards and correct only what they are asked to correct. Similarly, it might be difficult to revise only what is necessary and to disregard personal style and habits.

This chapter will focus on the over-editing behaviour of translators in PE and revision scenarios. To that end, datasets from three studies will be analysed, in which the participants were required to perform one of the two tasks. In the following sections, we will first describe the three datasets and present the instructions which were given to the participants. Then we will outline how we identified over-editing instances and report the results for the individual tasks with their similarities and differences, which will be discussed in the last section.

1. The studies

The analysis in this chapter is based on the datasets of three different studies, all of which were conducted with English source texts and German as the target language. There were no strict time restrictions for any of the tasks. They all were conducted in Translog II (Carl 2012), a program used to record keystrokes, mouse activities and gaze data with the help of an eyetracker (either tobii TX300 or SMI mobile). The final product as well as the eyetracking and keylogging data were connected via the alignment tool YAWAT (Germann 2008). All the studies included one or more questionnaires to gather information on the participants and to check how satisfied the participants were with their own work. All sessions[1] of each participant were recorded on the same day, usually one after the other without a break.

Study 1

The first subset of data comes from an experiment in which the participants were asked to perform three different tasks: translate from scratch, full post-edit (FPE) and light post-edit (LPE) texts from either the technical or the medical fields (only the PE sessions will be analysed here). Table 1.1 presents the instructions for the tasks, which were adapted from the TAUS PE guidelines (Massardo et al. 2016). The three technical texts were excerpts from a dishwasher manual, while the three medical texts were taken from documentation included with a vaccine against measles, insulin for the treatment of diabetes patients and a medication for the treatment of cancer. All texts were approximately 150 words long. The MT output was created by Google Translate (at the time, it was still a statistical rather than a neural MT engine).

TABLE 1.1 PE instructions for Study 1 in line with TAUS PE guidelines

Instructions for LPE	*Instructions for FPE*
The output of 'good enough' post-editing (or 'light' post-editing) is comprehensible and accurate, but not stylistically compelling. The text may sound like it was generated by a computer, syntax might be somewhat unusual, grammar may not be perfect, but the message is accurate.	The level of quality is generally defined as being comprehensible, accurate, stylistically fine, though the style may not be as good as achieved by a native-speaker human translator. Syntax is normal, grammar and punctuation are correct.
• Use as much of the raw MT output as possible! • Aim for semantically correct translations. • Ensure that no information has been accidentally added or omitted. • No need to use correct terminology, as long as it is clear what is meant. • Edit any inappropriate or culturally unacceptable content. • Apply rules regarding spelling. • Don't implement corrections that are of a stylistic nature only. • Don't restructure sentences solely to improve the natural flow of the text.	• Aim for grammatically, syntactically and semantically correct translation. • Ensure that no information has been accidentally added or omitted. • Ensure that key terminology is correctly translated and used consistently. • Edit any inappropriate or culturally unacceptable content. • Use as much of the raw MT output as possible. • Apply rules regarding spelling, punctuation and hyphenation. • Ensure that formatting is correct.

TABLE 1.2 Distribution of number of participants by task and text

	Translation from scratch	Light PE	Full PE
Technical text 1	4	4	4
Technical text 2	4	4	4
Technical text 3	4	4	4
Medical text 1	3	3	3
Medical text 2	3	3	3
Medical text 3	3	3	3

The participants consisted of 12 advanced translation students for the technical texts and 9 for the medical texts, all at the University of Mainz, Faculty of Translation Studies, Linguistics and Cultural Studies, Germersheim. They had undergone at least two years of translation training and had passed at least one exam on translating in the relevant field. They were German native speakers who had studied English as a first or second foreign language. Some of them had some PE experience, but only a minority. Each participant had to translate one text from scratch, light post-edit another text and full post-edit a third text. The technical texts were therefore each translated four times, light post-edited four times and full post-edited four times, the medical texts three times (Table 1.2). For further information on the study, see Čulo and Nitzke (2016).

Study 2

This study was also conducted at the University of Mainz, Faculty of Translation Studies, Linguistics and Cultural Studies in Germersheim in 2012, on behalf of the Center for Research and Innovation in Translation and Translation Technology (CRITT), Copenhagen Business School, Denmark. The data[2] are included in the CRITT-TPR database (https://sites.google.com/site/centretranslationinnovation/tpr-db), which collects translation process data for different tasks and in different languages. The source texts consisted of four newspaper articles and two sociology texts with different levels of complexity. The length of the texts varied between 100 and 150 words. The MT output was again created by Google Translate.

In total, 24 participants took part in the study, 12 of them professional translators (with university degrees and some professional work experience) and 12 translation students (students of the university with only a little professional work experience). The participants were asked to translate two texts from scratch, bilingually post-edit two machine-translated texts, i.e. with the source text at hand, and monolingually post-edit two machine-translated texts, i.e. without the source text at hand. Only the bilingual PE task will be considered in the present analysis.

The participants were provided with the following guidelines for the PE task (see also Carl et al. 2014: 153):[3]

- Retain as much raw translation as possible.
- Don't hesitate too long over a problem.
- Don't worry if style is repetitive.
- Don't embark on time-consuming research.
- Make changes only where absolutely necessary, i.e. correct words or phrases that are nonsensical, wrong and, if there's enough time left, ambiguous.

A detailed description of the data subset is available in Nitzke (2019) and of the whole dataset and database in Carl et al. (2016a).

Study 3

In Study 3, we used the results of Study 2 to create a revision task. Of all the translations prepared from scratch in Study 2, we chose six—one translation per source text—independently of the professional status of the participants but based on quality in order to provide natural translations. Each text contained roughly 100 to 150 words and 5 to 11 sentences. The main criterion for choosing a text was that the original translation prepared in Study 2 was flawless regarding errors and style.

After finding suitable texts, we manipulated them by inserting errors that occurred in human translations in other sessions of the experiment, to avoid inserting unnatural errors. A total of three to five errors were added to the texts, but no sentence contained more than one error. The number of inserted mistakes varied from text to text so that the participants would not be able to detect a pattern. However, all mistake categories appeared equally over all the texts. Further, each text contained at least one sentence without errors. We used Mertin's (2006) typology to categorise which error types needed to be included. However, not all categories suggested by Mertin were suitable for our purposes: we could disregard formatting (because the texts were presented and translated in a simple editor environment) and adherence to predefined terms (because there were none). In the end, we applied six error types to our texts: orthography, grammar, sense, omissions, consistency, coherence. Every error type occurred with equal frequency in the texts.

We created two versions of each text (version A and version B) to distribute the errors equally, to have enough material for each error type, and to avoid overloading the texts with errors. The participants saw either version A or version B. Sentences with an error in version A did not have any inserted error in version B. We asked our participants to revise the six translations (either version A or version B), with access to the source text. In total, 38 translators participated in the study (23 professionals, 15 students), each of whom received either text package A or text package B. The following scenario was presented to the participants (originally in German):

> A colleague has translated the following texts from English into German for a renowned German newspaper (print) or for an encyclopaedia and has asked you to now revise the translation before it is published.

Please concentrate on correct content and language and please insert your corrections directly into the texts.

You'll get paid for seven minutes per text.

There is no Internet connection—please revise the text without Internet research.

We did not adhere strictly to the time limit. It was meant only to indicate to the participants that they should not spend too much time on the tasks. However, after about seven to eight minutes, we told them that the initial time was up and that they should slowly come to an end. For more information on the study, see Schaeffer et al. (2019a).

2. Analysis and results

In this section, we describe how we proceeded in analysing the data. First, we will give some general information about the time the participants spent on the tasks and the general editing effort, using some general keylogging measures. Then we will describe how we determined over-editing instances and how we categorised these.

Time and editing effort

In total, our studies comprised 199 revision sessions[4] (Study 3) and 73 PE sessions (Studies 1 and 2). Table 1.3 shows the basic information for the individual studies (task time in minutes and seconds, key logging data in characters). Full and light PE are presented separately for Study 1 as these tasks are quite different, but equally important. All source texts included in the studies consisted of 100 to 150 words.

The FPE task in Study 1 took the most time, which was expected because the guideline demanded the highest quality standards, and more errors needing correction could be found in the machine-translated output. The LPE task in Study 1 and the PE task in Study 2 took on average almost the same time (the texts of Study 2 are slightly shorter but the guidelines are a bit stricter). Finally, the participants of Study 3 took the least time (however, remember that the participants in this study

TABLE 1.3 Mean time, text production and text elimination per session

	Task	Mean time per session (in minutes and seconds)	Mean text production (in characters)	Mean text elimination (in characters)
Study 1	FPE	18 min, 19.9 s (SD: 7 min, 7.5 s)	386 (SD: 156.4)	199.9 (SD: 72.6)
	LPE	12 min, 0.8 s (SD: 3 min, 57.3 s)	224.5 (SD: 150.6)	111.8 (SD: 65.5)
Study 2	PE	12 min, 28.1 s (SD: 3 min, 26 s)	346.8 (SD: 107.7)	323 (SD: 168.9)
Study 3	Revision	6 min, 23 s (SD: 2 min, 20.4 s)	97.2 (SD: 101.2)	91.1 (SD: 97.2)

had loose time constraints). The high standard deviations for all parameters and sessions show that the values vary a lot from one participant to another, which is partly caused by different text lengths, the quality of the MT output for the various tasks and individual working style and experience. Interestingly, the participants in Study 1 inserted more characters than they erased during the PE sessions, while in the other two studies the numbers of inserted and deleted characters are more balanced. Thus, the general editing effort varied a lot between the different tasks and participants.

Quantification of over-editing instances

The first step of the analysis was to determine how many text units were changed (see Table 1.4). As already mentioned, all three studies were recorded with the keylogging software Translog II and aligned on a sentence and word basis. After the alignment, tables could be generated that contained all the keylogging (and eyetracking) information, matched to the words and sentences of the texts. The keylogging information on these tables presents the editing effort of the whole translation process. If a participant changed the target text unit more than once, these changes could still be included in the analysis. For example, in the FPE task, participant P28 inserted the word *Wirksamkeit* [effectiveness] into the MT of "How has Hycamtin been studied?" which the machine had translated as *Wie hat Hycamtin untersucht?* [How has Hycamtin studied?]. The keylogging data show that the translation was created in two steps:

> First edit: *Wur[ru]irkung*
> Second edit: *[gnu]samkeit*
> All edits combined: *Wur[ru]irkung_[gnu]samkeit*

All these changes were mapped to the target text word. Square brackets show the characters that were erased during the translation process in chronological order. Thus, the participant decided to insert *Wirkung*, which they first misspelled but then immediately corrected, erasing first the *r* and then the *u*; they then continued

TABLE 1.4 Overview of editing instances

	Task	Average total editing instances	Average necessary editing instances (of total number)	Average over-editing instances (of total number)
Study 1	FPE	27.81 (SD: 2.92)	19.57 (SD: 3.17)	8.24 (SD: 2.66)
	LPE	23.19 (SD: 4.4)	11.71 (SD: 3.8)	11.48 (SD: 5.0)
Study 2	PE	23.89 (SD: 3.78)	15.75 (SD: 3.02)	8.14 (SD: 3.08)
Study 3	Revision	6.34 (SD: 3.89)	1.95 (SD: 1.15)	4.39 (SD: 3.43)

the writing process. In the second edit, the participant decided that they preferred the word *Wirksamkeit* and therefore erased the suffix *-ung* and inserted *-samkeit*. The final post-edited heading reads *Wie wurde die Wirksamkeit von Hycamtin bisher untersucht?* [How was the effectiveness of Hycamtin so far studied?].

Depending on the type of change, a text unit could consist of at least one word and at most one sentence. Grammatical changes, for example, could be made by changing only one letter in the word (e.g. changing the case of the German definite article: Nominative *der* to Dative *dem*). Reformulating, on the other hand, could take up to an entire sentence and had to be seen as one editing instance, because if every word were counted individually, it would falsify the results.

In the second step of our analysis, we determined which changes were necessary and which could be characterised as over-editing. Finally, we categorised the over-editing instances and quantified them. Nine areas were defined for which over-editing instances could be observed in our dataset:

- lexicon, for example, using synonyms or different terminology;
- syntax, for example, reordering parts of a sentence;
- style, for example, rephrasing a target text unit, formatting issues, register preferences;
- addition, for example, inserting words or information into the target text;
- deletion, for example, deleting words or information from the target text;
- grammar, for example, changing the tense or the definite article in the target text;
- spelling, for example, choosing another spelling variant;
- punctuation, for example, insertion or deletion of commas;
- insecurity, for example, deleting a target text unit and inserting the same unit without any changes.

For these last two steps, we divided the texts between us (we are both German native speakers and trained translators with PE experience), identified the instances of over-editing, under-editing and necessary editing, and categorised the over-editing instances. We then checked each other's assessments. If we did not agree on a category, a third rater was asked to decide which category was correct. An inter-rater agreement was calculated with Cohen's Kappa for two raters. The results were $\kappa = 0.95$, $z = 144$ and $p < 0.0001$, which can be interpreted as an almost perfect agreement.[5]

An overview of editing instances for all the studies can be found in Table 1.4. Study 1 comprised medical and technical texts that were full and light post-edited. In view of the guidelines, the editing effort should have been quite different for these two tasks. However, when the changes were counted, the difference was less striking than we expected: on average, 27.81 changes were made per FPE session (SD: 2.92), while 23.19 changes were made per LPE session (SD: 4.4). However, the difference in total changes between full and light PE is still statistically significant (since the data were not distributed normally, a Mann-Whitney U test was conducted: W = 310.5, p = 0.02349). On the other hand, the differences between necessary changes and over-editing instances were on average much more obvious in FPE than in LPE, where about 70% of the changes could be characterised as necessary (19.57 [SD: 3.17]) and about 30% as over-editing (8.24 [SD: 2.66]), a difference which is statistically significant (W = 440, p < 0.0001). In LPE, the distribution was almost half and half (necessary: 11.71 [SD: 3.8], over-editing: 11.48 [SD: 5.0]) and the difference between necessary changes and over-editing instances is not significant (the datapoints were distributed normally and a t-test was conducted: t = 0.174, p = 0.8629).

In Study 2, only one set of rules for the PE task was given (no differentiation between light and full PE), and on average 23.89 (SD: 3.78) changes were made per session. In total, 15.75 (SD: 3.02) editing instances were characterised as necessary under the guidelines (about 66% of the instances), while 8.14 (SD: 3.08) edits per session were characterised as over-editing (about 37%). The difference is statistically significant (t = 11.698, p < 0.0001). Accordingly, the distribution of necessary and over-editing instances in this study is comparable to the full PE task in Study 1, as the participants made significantly more necessary changes than changes that could be characterised as over-editing.

In Study 3 (the revision study), an average of 1.95 inserted mistakes were corrected by the participants (SD: 1.15), while an average of 1.82 inserted mistakes were not corrected (SD: 1.24). Thus, 3.77 mistakes were hidden in the texts on average. The difference between corrected and uncorrected inserted mistakes is not statistically significant (W = 21310, p = 0.1751), which indicates that as many inserted mistakes were corrected as were not corrected, and this was not expected. Further, an average of 4.39 (SD: 3.43) target text items that were not manipulated (and hence should not have been edited since the original unmanipulated translation was correct) were changed in every session. Accordingly, only about 31% of the changes were necessary, while 69% can be categorised as over-editing. This difference is statistically significant (W = 10748, p < 0.0001). In other words, statistically, more units were edited that did not need editing than units that needed editing. These results show similarities to the results presented in Mellinger and Shreve (2016), where 60% of the exact matches were edited, although they would not necessarily have needed editing, while 26% of the fuzzy matches which would have needed changes in the target segment were not edited.

Looking at the percentages, most of the changes which can be characterised as over-editing were done in the revision study (Study 3), followed by the LPE task in Study 1. This, of course, applies only when we consider the distribution of the changes between necessary changes and over-editing. If we consider total numbers, the picture is reversed: Most changes were implemented in the FPE task in Study 1, followed by Study 2 and the LPE task of Study 1, while by far the fewest changes were made in Study 3. These results indicate that there are many more keystrokes in PE than in revision. This might also be the reason why so many edits were instances of over-editing in Study 3. The participants might have felt the need to edit more instances per text than were actually necessary to deliver good results. They may have expected that we included many more errors in the texts. This may also have been caused by the experimental situation in all three studies. The participants may have felt the need to deliver high quality, because they knew that their translation process was being observed and recorded and they therefore felt pressure to perform exceptionally well, although we, of course, informed all participants that the data would be anonymised.

Classification of over-editing instances

Having reported the overall numbers, we shall now classify the over-editing instances according to the different areas identified earlier. These do not assess whether the editing was correct or incorrect: if a change was categorised as a lexical preference, that does not assess whether the target unit has improved after editing. Rather, the initial target text unit was acceptable according to the given task guidelines for the study but was edited nonetheless by the participant. The distribution of the over-editing instances by area is shown in Table 1.5.

Most often, over-editing is based on lexical or stylistic preferences. This might be caused by the participants' personal preferences and quality standards, although the guidelines specify that only the most necessary changes should be implemented. Especially for the light PE task, this might have been a difficult challenge for the participants, as the guideline specifically states that "syntax might be somewhat unusual, grammar may not be perfect". Still, 8.7% of the over-editing instances were preferential syntactic changes and 4.5% were unnecessary grammatical changes in the revision study. In the PE task of Study 2, only 3.2% and 2.6% respectively were in these over-editing categories, which could be explained amongst other factors by the instructions given for this task, which did not mention syntax and grammar.

TABLE 1.5 Distribution of over-editing instances by area and study

	Study 1 PE (field-specific texts), both PE tasks	Study 2 PE (general texts)	Study 3 Revision
Lexicon	94 (22.5%)	90 (24%)	372 (43.6%)
Syntax	41 (9.8%)	12 (3.2%)	74 (8.7%)
Style	117 (28.1%)	228 (60.8%)	134 (15.7%)
Addition	20 (4.8%)	14 (3.7%)	104 (12.2%)
Deletion	19 (4.6%)	7 (1.9%)	51 (6.0%)
Grammar	51 (12.2%)	10 (2.6%)	38 (4.5%)
Spelling	6 (1.4%)	3 (0.8%)	20 (2.8%)
Punctuation	23 (5.5%)	3 (0.8%)	17 (2.3%)
Insecurity	46 (11.0%)	8 (2.1%)	43 (5.0%)

TABLE 1.6 Distribution of over-editing instances for LPE and FPE in Study 1

	Lex	Syntax	Style	Add	Del	Gram	Spell	Punct	Insec
FPE	41	2	56	13	15	10	4	6	24
LPE	53	39	61	7	4	41	2	17	22

A further reason might be that less obvious mistakes could be found in the revision task, and therefore preferential changes occurred more often. Additions and deletions occurred with similar frequency in all studies, except for additions in the revision task, which made up over 12% of all the over-editing instances in Study 3. Most unnecessary changes in punctuation occurred in Study 1. The reason might be that these domain-specific texts were structured differently from the texts in the other two studies, and therefore punctuation could be handled differently (e.g. commas or semicolons were inserted at the end of each point in an unordered list, or perhaps punctuation marks were avoided). Finally, insecure typing behaviour could also be observed most often in Study 1. This, again, might be caused by the different PE tasks, as the relatively untrained participants could have been uncertain as to when to change a unit and when not.

Finally, let us take a closer look at the differences between light and full PE. As can be seen in Table 1.6, the distribution of over-editing instances is similar for lexicon, style, spelling and insecurities. One reason could be that the guidelines were similar for these characteristics. Additions and deletions occurred twice as much in the FPE task; the total numbers, however, are still quite low in comparison to the other over-editing areas. Still, the difference is not very great. Further, many more syntactic and grammatical flaws were corrected in the LPE task, although they should not have been corrected. A reason for this behaviour might be that it is odd for translators to keep syntactically and grammatically unusual or even incorrect units in the final text, even if the content is still conveyed. The participants probably behaved similarly in the light and full PE task when it came to syntax and grammar. This is judged as over-editing in the LPE task, but not in the FPE task.

3. Conclusion and discussion

Taking into account the number of over-editing instances per task, it seems plausible to state that it is difficult for translators to adhere to guidelines that prescribe quality requirements lower than the translators' own quality standards and stylistic preferences, which they have to suppress. As discussed in Mellinger and Shreve (2016), the translators are actively looking for mistakes in the target text, because there is already a target text proposal which they have to improve. However, in the translator's mind the already-existing MT output and their own potential translation are competing. This might make the translators prefer their own translation, and they then decide to change target text units that do not need any corrections.

Accordingly, both revision and PE tasks require practice (in line with Nitzke et al. 2019 and Robert et al. 2017a); not every translator is necessarily suited to revising translated text or post-editing MT output.

Our results also suggest that revision and PE should be included in university curricula in order to train students for these tasks, which could easily become components of their professional lives. A focus should be placed on adhering to guidelines and predefined quality requirements in training programmes—no matter whether in university courses or training courses for professionals—as this, understandably, seems to be difficult for translators, who are normally used to creating very high-quality final texts. A perfect translation is not always required, especially when machine-translated output is to be post-edited. Usually, other factors like time and money are essential when MT output is created for PE. Further, quality is a subjective matter which people may judge differently, and a PE/revision job may not pay enough to justify very high quality. The final text simply needs to be acceptable under the quality requirements, not perfect. This, however, partly contrasts with Depraetere's (2010) findings. She reports in her study of 10 translation students that her participants did not change the phrasing of the texts as long as the translation was acceptable. The students did not change anything just to improve the natural flow of the translation, even though there may have been a more idiomatic solution. She concludes that it is not necessary, in PE classes, to emphasise that style is not important in post-editing machine-translated output.

We, however, would recommend that one focus of training in revision and post-editing should be on suppressing personal preferences (as was already described in Mossop 2001), especially regarding lexical choices and style. Trainees need to learn to explain how they decided that an edit was or was not necessary. They need to learn how to make reasonable decisions. Further, it seems plausible to train translators to work with what the machine or human has previously produced and improve the text with the least possible effort, so that jobs can become as profitable as possible.[6] Another issue that is quite essential for LPE is to learn to leave grammatical and syntactic errors in the text if requested. This task might be frustrating and even time-consuming at first, but with growing experience it will become easier. Translators who are also trained as post-editors and/or revisers need to be able to rapidly assess which changes are necessary.

Of course, only a few clients would mind additional improvements as long as the costs do not increase, for example, if the job is paid per source or target text word. However, if the job is paid per hour or per implemented change, problems could occur and the post-editor or reviser might have to justify the changes, which is time-consuming and might lead to a less trusting relationship. Further, some colleagues might feel patronised if their translations are revised according to personal preferences during the revision task. Finally, translators lose the most when they put more effort into the task than they are paid for.

This study is only a starting point for further research on editing behaviour in PE and revision tasks. As with the assessment of translation quality, assessing the validity of editing during different tasks and according to different guidelines is subjective, and different raters will come to different conclusions. In future research, more raters and independent ratings would be preferable in order to make the results more objective. It might be a good idea to use less data, perhaps from only one study.

Another research focus could be assessing and categorising data on under-editing. So far, we have identified instances of under-editing only in Study 3, because the texts were manipulated and the introduced errors that remained uncorrected by the participants could be found easily. However, we have not yet analysed these instances of under-editing. Under-editing also needs to be identified and analysed for the PE tasks in Studies 1 and 2, in light of the guidelines for the full and light PE tasks.

It would also be interesting to see whether over-editing instances improved the text, whether errors were sometimes introduced and what influence the translation experience of the participants had on over-editing behaviour, because both possibilities seem plausible: that translators with greater translation experience over-edit more often or that they over-edit less often. Additionally, the influence of experience in revision and PE on over-editing behaviour still needs research. Unfortunately, information about experience was not requested on the questionnaires for the three studies: the PE studies did not ask for revision experience and vice versa. It should be mentioned in passing that it is difficult to find participants who have extensive PE experience as the PE market is still quite young.

It would be useful to include our eyetracking data in the analysis of over-editing instances in order to assess cognitive effort while editing. The eyetracking data have so far been used only in other studies. While Study 2 has been the basis of many studies (for an overview, see Nitzke 2019), only a few publications have been based on Study 1 (e.g. Nitzke and Oster 2016) and Study 3 (e.g. Schaeffer et al. 2019a, 2019b).

Finally, new PE data should be collected using neural MT, where we would expect less editing effort since this type of MT system usually produces more fluent translations from English into German. However, we would hypothesise that more unnecessary, stylistic changes might be introduced on average compared to the probably lower total keystrokes, and this might lead to results similar to those presented for the revision data in the present study. With neural MT, analysing the under-editing instances would be especially interesting because our assumption would be that due to the more natural, fluent MT output—at least in the language combination English–German—it would be more difficult for participants to find content mistakes in the MT output. Such analyses could be supported by eyetracking data.

Quality and efficiency are very important in all translation processes. In PE in particular, the overall quality of the final text might not be as important as the efficiency with which the task is performed. Suppressing personal preferences is also very important for most revision tasks to make them worthwhile. This chapter has presented an initial insight into the editing behaviour of different participants in different PE and revision tasks, and it confirms that over-editing is a phenomenon that is visible in process data. This topic might therefore need to be addressed in PE and revision training.

Notes

1 The concept *session* refers to the recording of the process data for one text.
2 The data also formed part of a multilingual study (the same source texts were translated into six different languages under comparable conditions).
3 The data for the English–German sessions were collected in 2012, and this was one of the earlier process studies including PE data. Accordingly, the instructions presented for this study were rather vague and should have been more precise. Still, we wanted to present the guidelines in order to make the analysis more transparent.
4 Some sessions had to be disregarded because of technical difficulties during or after the recording.
5 Of course, the agreement is so high due to our methodology. If we had conducted an independent rating of all texts by both raters, the inter-rater agreement would probably have been lower. However, due to the amount of data, we decided to split it between us.
6 According to many personal experiences and conversations, the unprofitability of PE seems to be one of the main reasons professional translators are critical of it.

2

DIFFERENTIATING EDITING, POST-EDITING AND REVISION

Félix do Carmo and Joss Moorkens

In her article on the transition from statistical to neural machine translation (NMT), Kenny (2018) argues that NMT is a sustaining rather than disrupting technology, a linear progression along a continuum. Similarly, we believe that for translators whose work processes have evolved alongside translation technology, post-editing (PE) may be just one more step in that progression, with machine-translation (MT) suggestions acting as another contributory input to the translation decision process alongside translation memory (TM) matches, terms and concordances. The aim of this chapter is to draw on the editing task that is present in translation, in revision and in PE to clarify the impact of translators' use of MT. The chapter critically analyses views and narratives about PE from Translation Studies, MT research, and the industry. The alternative view we propose calls for further discussion and study of the technical dimension of translators' work, and it draws on translation process research to recommend a re-understanding of PE as a translation process rather than a revision one. As a consequence of this new understanding, we claim that, for MT content to be used efficiently, specialised users with specialised tools are required.

The first part of the chapter (sections 1 to 3) draws on existing studies of PE, presenting the terms and assumptions upon which the subsequent sections are built, discussing the existing narratives in academia and industry (in section 2), and drawing out implications of these views for professional translators. In section 3, we set out reasons for opposing these narratives and for considering PE to be a form of translation, informed by theoretical considerations and practical analyses of industrial workflows. The second part of the chapter (sections 4 to 6) details the role of editing in our alternative view of PE, analysing the consequences of this view in terms of the need for specialised tools and specialised users of technology. We consider in detail what editing is and its role in the study of PE, supported by translation process research. Two fundamental elements arise from our analysis:

the threshold that separates editing from translating, and the description of editing as four actions. Section 5 applies these elements to the description of tools that specifically support editing, while in section 6, the views that were built up over the chapter converge into our conclusion that, although MT might seem to be a process that replaced translators in the translation process, in fact it requires even more specialisation by translators.

1. Setting the grounding notions

The grammatical metaphor which allows the use of gerunds as nouns in English highlights the connection and differentiation between *words* and *what happens during the processes they refer to* (Halliday and Martin 1993). The use of the form 'post-editing' is preferred to 'post-edition' because this stresses that PE is eminently a *process*. Its analysis should therefore focus more on how it is done rather than on the results. In this chapter, we use gerunds to refer to the tasks and actions that are parts of processes, and nouns when we refer to a whole process from an external point of view.

The term 'translation' is used as a global technological process performed by one person, or by a group of people, each one working on a separate part of the same translation project. The word 'translating' will be used to refer to a specific type of writing task that implies generating and composing a sentence, writing it 'from scratch', as opposed to editing only parts of a translation suggestion.

'Revision' is also used to describe a whole process, performed by a person *different* from the one who created the translation (and thus not 'self-revision'). 'Revising' is used to describe the activities performed while engaged in a revision process.

Translators read the source text and write a translation. If the text they read and the text they create in the target language are clear, the flow of writing is fluid. They only stop when they encounter a problem. Then they read the source text again, along with what they have just written. In this way, translating may be seen mostly as writing with pauses when problems occur. Translation is a process of creation, and it is by writing that the translation is created. Contrary to this, a reviser mostly reads when revising (Mossop 2020: 116). In fact, revisers hope to simply read, check and validate the work done by a good translator. They need only write when they encounter problems.

Writing and reading seem to set the boundary between translation and revision, though this is of course a simplification (translation process research such as Carl et al. [2011] has shown how interconnected these activities are). The difficulty in setting them apart stems from the fact that translating (mostly writing) occurs during revision and revising (mostly reading) occurs during translation.

As will be described in this chapter, the term 'post-editing' entered the industrial world of translation when MT systems started to produce in target languages content that was deemed to be of good enough quality to be edited and improved by translators. So, it is *as if* MT has replaced the translation process, and PE occupies the place of the revision process.

As for the term 'editing', it is used here to describe a type of writing task that is different from translating. In editing, translators act on a segment of text, be it a suggestion already rendered in the target language, or a segment still written in the source language, with either one requiring only a few changes here and there to be ready for validation. The term may be used to describe the actions performed during PE, and it may also be used to describe the actions carried out to update the translation of a fuzzy match from a TM. Editing is a writing action that happens after 'checking', which is a reading task that has the purpose of identifying whether the segment should be validated or edited.

In the film or publishing industries, editing is part of the creation process, but it is only performed once all parts of the intended result have been produced. Editors apply surgical actions to remove bad sections from a sequence, they decide what to fit into a specific place, they move sections to their optimum positions and they try to select the best options for the different parts of a film or a book. Likewise, deleting, inserting, moving and replacing are the four actions that compose 'editing'. These will be referred to as 'editing actions', but one may also talk about 'edits'.

2. Narratives of resistance to post-editing

Descriptions of translation in an industrial environment highlight efficiency and quality as two key requirements (Sager 1993). In this context, any technological advance may be characterised as progress, with any form of resistance inviting criticism. But are the narratives of translators' resistance to PE realistic, or is PE already a common practice, at least for translators working in the localisation industry? We should stress that this industry (consisting of companies that offer translation, language and technology support services to global corporations) is characterised by long workflows and supply chains in which work methods are standardised. Translators who work in these supply chains use tools and follow specifications and instructions that are defined in the upper portion of the chain in response to the technological needs of corporations and global management processes. In the early 1990s, these translators started working with computer-aided translation (CAT) tools because that allowed for more control over the processes and outputs, and they soon became recognised as keen adopters of advanced technologies. The volume of work produced by the localisation industry implies that a large and growing proportion of professional translators currently work with the aid of technology. In this section, we analyse the foundations of the narratives this industry creates and their consequences, and we suggest that these narratives should be based on more realistic descriptions of the production processes.

Many research publications either describe or assume a strong resistance from translators to PE. Allen, for example, says that PE introduced a new challenge to professional translators because of the pressure towards "the acceptance and use of half-finished texts" (2003: 297). Austermühl refers to two major attitudes towards this type of challenge: "satisficers", for whom the correct strategy is not looking for optimal solutions but meeting adequacy criteria, and "optimisers", who commit to "the art of finding the best choice among all choices" and who may face an identity crisis because of industry pressures (2013: 331).

Two examples of studies that have focused on the causes of translators' resistance to PE are Cadwell et al. (2018) and Moorkens and Way (2016). Both studies are based on data from real users and interviews with practising translators. They suggest that use of MT by translators may increase if they feel a greater sense of agency and have greater confidence in the utility of the MT suggestions.

In addition to translators, we can analyse the voice of the industry as expressed in the documents produced to standardise procedures. This is how the ISO 18587 standard explains the reasons for PE adoption:

> The use of machine translation (MT) systems to meet the needs of an increasingly demanding translation and localization industry has been gaining ground. Many translation service providers (TSPs) and clients have come to realize that the use of such systems is a viable solution for translating projects that need to be completed within a very tight time frame and/ or with a reduced budget.
>
> *(ISO 2017: v)*

The justification for such a budget reduction—Lommel (2018) suggests that PE is, on average, paid at 60–65% of the full word rate—is that PE is a form of revision rather than translation (see section 3). The advantages for translators are presented as "to improve productivity", "to reduce turn-around times" and "to remain competitive in an environment where clients show an increasing demand for using MT in translation" (ISO 2017: v). We can easily intuit that these factors add pressure rather than satisfaction. The message to translators is: 'post-edit or perish'. Furthermore, the standard guidelines for post-editing extend further control over translators' work, with the need for results to be comprehensible, readable or indistinguishable from human translation, and the additional requirement that this must be achieved using as much of the MT output as possible (TAUS 2010).

In this context, resistance by translators to the increased pressure from their usual work practice seems quite reasonable. Translators may feel that the limits of job satisfaction are being stretched in professional contexts where translation or textual work is only one of an increasing array of skills and competences that they are expected to embody (European Master's in Translation Network 2017). Unilateral imposition of PE from an unpredictable MT source, paid at a lower word rate, makes PE feasible only if the processes involved are much more efficient than normal translation. Such changes may also bring about the feeling that translators are the sole guardians of quality, the ones with the role of identifying problems of an unknown nature in fleeting details.

There are enough indications, however, that the resistance narrative may not correspond to reality. A close look at the production processes in a typical translation workflow in the localisation industry shows that PE is almost always done using modern CAT tools, designed for optimising work with TM rather than with MT (Moorkens and O'Brien 2017). In these environments, MT suggestions appear intermingled with TM matches as resources for translators to check and edit. In addition, CAT tools show suggestions for terminology, allow for searches of words in context, show predictive writing suggestions and repaired fuzzy matches. The inclusion of suggestions from MT is not a major disruption to the growing complexity of CAT tools, but a natural evolution. When MT becomes an added resource, the distinction between editing TM suggestions and post-editing MT suggestions becomes less obtrusive. This is borne out by the similarities between high-quality TM matches and NMT output, in terms of editing effort and the comparative perceptions of their usefulness, as reported in Sánchez-Gijón et al. (2019).

In translator training, PE has already become a standard practice. Many translation programmes have, in one way or another, incorporated PE into their curricula since at least 2009 (Guerberof and Moorkens 2019), and teaching of PE is now expected for all courses included in the European Master's in Translation Network (2017). Researchers have even presented suggestions for PE to be taught as extensions of translators' skills (Kenny and Doherty 2014). We may thus say that there is a whole generation of graduate translators for whom PE is expected as part of their jobs.

Furthermore, industry statistics reveal that PE is growing steadily, at least since TAUS published their guidelines (2010). Lommel and DePalma (2016) refer to an estimate by 56 enterprise clients that the percentage of PE in the global translation industry could reach 10% in 2019. If we add to these numbers 'unofficial PE' (when translators are given source language text in the target window and they decide to machine-translate it, instead of typing it over with their own translation), the numbers show that, notwithstanding natural variations between local realities, PE is much more widely used than the resistance narratives lead us to think.

There may be good reasons why the discourse on translators' resistance caught on so steadily. In the current state of affairs, any type of empirical research will oppose the narrative of resistance, thus serving as reinforcers of the reasonableness of PE, but in the process it contributes to acceptance with no criticism. In fact, it is easier to argue against unreasonable fears than to answer difficult questions, such as: 'Have the technological advances really helped translators become more efficient and produce better quality, or is the industry simply selecting the satisficers who are happy to quickly select the least bad of all options?' and 'Does the industry want translators to be trained to be satisficers, or is it ideal to train them to be flexible optimisers?' Whether misgivings are reasonable or not, the choice of whether to post-edit should always be consultative, as imposition of any process on the translator will lead them to "feel that the material agent gets precedence and is inevitable, no matter how unfitting it might be for the task at hand" (Cadwell et al. 2018: 17).

We propose that new views of PE should be brought forward, so that questions like these are more frequently studied and debated. In the next sections, we present a few arguments towards the claim that PE needs to be studied in more detail, beyond the acceptance/resistance divide.

3.   Post-editing as a specialised form of translation

Seeing PE as a form of revision assumes that the MT system completed a full translation. This is the prevailing notion behind the views of PE as an undemanding task in terms of language skills, one that can even be performed by monolinguals without access to the source text (Krings 2001; Schwartz 2014).

The arguments in favour of viewing PE as a form of revision are strong. For example, several papers show that most of the time spent on PE is spent on pauses rather than on keyboard actions (Koehn 2009; Ortiz-Martínez et al. 2016). This suggests that PE is, like revision, more associated with reading than with writing. However, we argue that this is not a sufficient reason to classify PE as revision, and that the current context in which PE is performed challenges that view.

The first claim against PE being identified as a type of revision is the argument presented by translators when they are confronted with a translation that needs to be revised but then realise that it has actually been produced by an MT system. Translators, quite properly, refuse the classification of such assignments as revision on the basis that these jobs imply more translation than revision (they involve more writing than reading, or at least the ratio between the two is not consistent with that expected of revision work).

To be a form of revision, the only aim of PE would be to eliminate errors from a finalised translation, the difference being that this finalised translation had been produced by an MT system rather than a human translator. But in a professional translation workflow, this fundamental condition is not met by PE, because MT does not produce a finalised translation. MT text is only an 'output', or a set of 'suggestions' or 'hypotheses' for the translation of a text. Instead, it is the post-editor—the translator—who is responsible for the final translation.

Post-editors must recognise the special status of the suggestions presented by MT systems when accepting a PE job. They need to be aware of their likely error types and unpredictable quality level. In our view, MT processes are what Catford calls 'transference' rather than translation (1965: 43): the output is based solely in source language meaning, without cognisance of how a concept ought to be expressed in the target language. House, for example, comments on how such a strategy is inadequate for translation between German, which requires "informational explicitness", and English, where inference is based on context (2003: 169). If translators fail to consider reader expectations in their target language, they will most likely do a bad job and miss most of the detailed errors that the MT text contains.

A similar situation exists at the end of PE: it is not proven that a PE process produces a revised text. Due to specifications that restrain production time and limit expected quality, post-editors are under pressure not to revise their work before delivery. The perspective of PE as revision considers 'self-revision' of PE a redundant task. This also takes the form of a pressure not to over-correct; the aim is for post-editors to be efficient satisficers, not stalling optimisers. However, in current industrial workflows it is not uncommon for post-edited texts to go through a full revision by a different translator before delivery to clients, because that is the only way to guarantee fitness for purpose. In DARPA's handbook for the Global Autonomous Language Exploitation programme, the description of PE production is of a two-stage process that includes a revision pass by a second translator (Dorr et al. 2010). In a broad study of interactive PE carried out with universities and translation companies in collaboration, the outputs of PE were revised by different translators, not for evaluation purposes, but for quality assurance (Sanchis-Trilles et al. 2014). This revision of PE could not be accepted in commercial contexts, which are so opposed to redundancy, were it not that PE is in fact a form of translation.

The current context in which PE is performed, within CAT tools, also raises questions about classifying PE as revision: does it make sense to say that if translators edit a TM fuzzy match, they are translating, but if they edit an MT suggestion, they are revising? Sánchez-Gijón et al. (2019) found both processes to be quite similar. There are ongoing discussions and tests to identify the threshold at which a suggestion from the MT system is more useful than a fuzzy match from TM, and setting this arbitrarily may harm performance (Moorkens and Way 2016; Zaretskaya 2019). More importantly, this shows how close translating and revising are to each other in PE.

In professional settings, PE is determined by specifications, requirements of style guides, client terminology and consistency, among many other external factors that change from project to project, but which are also updated from assignment to assignment. However, some of the most cited studies on PE productivity exclude most or all of these factors, testing only one of two scenarios: very limited test conditions, employing students who focus on language issues without considering any external factors, or difficult-to-reproduce ideal lab conditions with professional translators who are experienced and work daily in the same conditions used for the tests (Vasconcellos 1987b; Zhechev 2014). One study even suggests that PE does not require as much research as translation or revision (Wagner 1985), a claim which can only be valid in those ideal scenarios in which the expertise of translators makes that research redundant. Moreover, many of these studies are done with simplified interfaces, in which sentences appear in isolated text boxes with no TMs or terminological support (Plitt and Masselot 2010). Often in these studies all segments need to be post-edited, excluding the need for the translator to decide whether to validate, to edit, or to retranslate a segment from scratch because of conflicting support resources, as so often happens in real scenarios. When studies are done in actual production settings, including TMs, termbases and MT content, productivity gains are not as high as other studies claim (Läubli et al. 2013).

Claims about increased productivity have, nevertheless, been generalised to all work environments. This generalisation is particularly problematic when we know that it is impossible to test and measure in the lab all external and internal factors involved in professional PE. To mention just one internal factor, types of errors produced by MT systems are not reproducible if one uses a different system, a different language pair or different training data, or simply changes the test data. This unpredictability of MT output and errors has been especially evident since the advent of neural MT (Castilho et al. 2017; Daems and Macken 2019).

The description of PE, based on these lab tests, is therefore incomplete and of limited validity. Outside of lab conditions, PE may, for example, require more complex reading and writing than revision, or even than translation from scratch. Krings (2001) has shown that reading slows down when MT content is added, particularly when it is medium-quality content, which requires a careful analysis to decide whether it is best deleted or retained to be adequately edited (as was also found with statistical MT by Moorkens and Way in 2016). This also reveals that, although one may consider that any content already in the target language will be a welcome help for translators, even 'satisficers' may not like to have all the segments processed by MT. One needs to accept that the decision to delete and retranslate a whole MT sentence may be the most efficient one, in view of contents that require either extensive reading or extensive writing.

Taking into consideration all that happens at professional translators' workbenches during PE, we propose that it should be considered a type of translation. This is not only because PE represents an evolution of industrial translation processes and because it fulfils the same purpose as translation (to produce a good target text in an efficient and effective way), but also because it requires advanced writing and reading skills in two different languages. In the next section, we focus on one of these skills: editing.

4. What editing looks like

The technical dimension of translation has often been described in terms of editing actions. Nida considers "additions, subtractions, and alterations" to be "techniques of adjustment" (1964: 226). Toury presents "omissions, additions, changes of location and manipulations of segmentation" as indications of what he calls "matricial norms", which govern the presence of target language material reflecting source-language content, the location and distribution in the text of this material and choices in textual segmentation (1995: 95). Pym refers to "actions" being "what we actually observe translators doing (e.g. typing, correcting typographical mistakes, looking up terms in glossaries, etc.)" (2011a: 95), and Angelone classifies the editing activities of "additions, deletions and revisions" as "production-behaviours" (2010: 21). Finally, Alves and colleagues use the term "production segments" as being composed of "revisions, deletions, substitutions, etc." (2010: 125). Consequently, it seems difficult to find a consensual classification of the micro-procedures translators carry out when they are producing their translations, although these lists all incorporate similar action terms.

Krings (2001) mentions that keyboard actions may be good subjects for research because they are easily observed. He analyses linear writing processes and non-linear ones. In linear processes, translators add elements in a sequence with pauses, but without interrupting the sequence. We call this 'translating', because the translation is produced by following a syntactical generation procedure. Non-linear actions are mostly deletions and insertions, with translators primarily engaging in replacement or overwriting operations, especially when making short edits. We call these non-linear actions 'editing', since the translator is reading and intervenes in the text only to delete, insert, move or replace units. Both forms of writing (translating and editing) occur in translation, in revision and in PE.

It is not only in Translation Studies that editing is described in terms of actions. Early studies of edit distance by Damerau (1964) and Levenshtein (1966) estimate the fewest number of operations necessary to transform one segment into a different one. The purpose of those early estimates was to correct spelling errors in typed text or errors in computer code. This approach was later adopted for Translation Edit Rate (TER) (Snover et al. 2006), one of the metrics most used by the MT community for tasks such as automatic PE and quality estimation, or to compare the quality of MT output from different systems. These metrics assume the shortest distance between an unedited and an edited string, but inevitably, translators do not take the shortest possible route from raw MT output to post-edited segment (as described in the later section on complex editing). Consequently, TER is not a fair description of what actually happens during the process, but more a description of translation products (Daems and Macken 2019; do Carmo 2017).

The editing threshold

One of the purposes of quality estimation has been the identification of a threshold to enable the filtering out of MT segments that are of low quality and thus reduce productivity (Specia et al. 2018). This may be called the 'editing threshold', a boundary that sets the point from which a sentence requires much more writing than reading, a point from which editing becomes translating.

Let us say that the threshold is placed at a commonly used lower limit for fuzzy matches in CAT such as 75%, which corresponds to an editing rate of 25% of all words in a sentence. In CAT, sentences with less than 75% matching words in the source language are still considered to require translating (and are thus paid at a full word rate), since it is unpredictable whether the edits in the target language will affect only this proportion of words. But let us concentrate on the level at which the TM does not provide any suggestions: the so-called 'new words' or 'no matches'. This is the band in which MT output is considered to be most valuable. This output may be perfect and require no editing, but it may also include segments that need to be entirely rewritten, giving us an editing range that goes from 0 to 100%. The editing threshold we suggest re-establishes the CAT bands, but now in the context of PE by determining that, above 25% editing, the work should be considered as translating, implying a reading and writing effort that is above what is expected in simple editing.

An argument for the usefulness of the editing threshold is the fact that previous studies have shown particular behaviours and gains in productivity, not close to lower or upper bounds, but in medium quality or editing ranges (Krings 2001; Moorkens and Way 2016). Do Carmo (2017) carried out an experiment with 50 translators all working in the same language pair, using two work modes: one which relied on an auto-complete feature, and another involving an interface which constrained work to the four editing actions. In that experiment, the global average editing was also close to the threshold (26% for the autocomplete mode and 24% for the mode with the four editing actions). The study showed how detailed analyses of results show high variation in editing rates depending on text, user or mode of work.

Further studies of editing could focus on the editing threshold: the effort rates for segments above and below the threshold could be identified in fine-grained studies and the percentage of segments close to upper or lower bounds (with higher or lower quality) could be analysed. Naturally, any threshold will necessarily vary based on different factors, like language pair, TM or MT quality, domain and project specifications. It would also be interesting to try to identify the threshold using typical translation process research methodologies: is it possible to see an effect on effort (be it technical, measured in keystroke frequency, or cognitive, measured by eyetracking) when translators move from segments in which they are below the editing threshold to segments where they need to translate? All this research potential is a strong argument for making the editing threshold an object of study.

Types of editing actions

To study editing, we need to have a clear description of the four actions that compose this task: deletion, insertion, movement and replacement. These four actions may be decomposed into two dimensions: the content of the textual units (words and groups of words) and the positions these units occupy in a segment. This helps to distinguish between primary and secondary actions and to develop better models for describing editing (do Carmo 2017).

The actions can be observed while the translator is editing or afterwards as TER comparisons between, for example, an MT suggestion (created by an MT system) and its edited version (created by the post-editor). Deletion and insertion are primary editing actions. This means that the position of the edited unit is occupied for only one of the elements of comparison: deleted units appear only in the MT suggestion; inserted units appear only in the post-edited version. In each case there is an empty position. These are pure cases of missing words, which makes them easy to identify in an alignment check (edit distance measures like TER start by aligning words and identifying deletions and insertions). Replacement and movement are secondary editing actions. This means that there is no empty position on either side: they represent manipulations of units which exist in both versions, either by replacing content in the same position or by maintaining the same content but moving it into a different position. Replacements are easy to identify, especially in sentences with the same numbers of words, but movements are very hard to identify (Snover et al. 2006).

Secondary actions can be decomposed into primary actions, as sequences of deletions followed by insertions: replacement is the deletion of a unit followed by the insertion of a different unit in the same position, whereas movement is the deletion of a unit in one position and its insertion in a different position. However, further analyses can be made with the four actions. We can, for example, divide the four actions into those that imply writing content (insertion and replacement) and those that do not affect the content but just manipulate position (deletion and movement). Secondary actions are also associated with more efficient methods, like overtyping in the case of replacement, or dragging in the case of movement.

Using the editing actions as a guideline or an instrument of analysis can be very helpful. For example, descriptions of the translation process (usually at the character level, with many recursions and details that do not survive in the final version) could be more interpretable if they followed this model. In addition, since efficiency is a fundamental feature of translation, this simplified view of editing could become an important consideration in translator training (do Carmo 2017).

Complex editing

We should stress that any description of editing consisting merely of a sequence of edits is a simplification of a complex process. When editing and, most relevantly, when translating, translators manipulate segmentation. For example, they select a word but replace it with a phrase or a clause; they make non-linear edits when they apply scattered actions, moving in both directions within a sentence; they make recursive edits, coming back to the same word several times; they replace a word which may be embedded in a larger change within a group of words; and they make partial edits, when only part of a word is replaced, or discontinuous ones, in which, for example, an 's' for plural is added to different words in the same sentence.

Many changes may not be visible in the final result because of backtracks, and only the final edits survive in the translated and revised target text. This complicates the study of editing behaviour, and it is another argument in favour of the editing threshold: we need to partition editing data according to varying degrees of complexity. But even the editing threshold is difficult to measure if we use tools like TER, which estimates the minimum number of edits from the starting text to the final edited text, when the actual number of edits and keystrokes is inevitably greater.

From description to prediction of editing behaviour

In "Towards Statistical Modelling of Translators' Activity Data", Carl and Jakobsen (2009) explain their model for the analysis of typing and reading behaviour, using a method that includes product and process data. On the process side, units of textual data are collected by keystroke logs, essentially composed of deletions and insertions at the character level. They mention that cutting and pasting operations increase the complexity of the analysis, and they add that the smaller the units of analysis, the easier it is to capture the actions. Movement is an operation that affects longer sequences, but it was not recorded during their experiments. They also observe that some of the keyboard activities are not linked to a particular word.

The main conclusion from their data collection is that the difficulties in capturing a description of actions are related to the lack of alignment with source text words and to recursive operations applied to the same units.

In the discussion section of their paper, the authors comment on how best to assist human translation processes with automated tools: "At what moment during the translation would the mechanical help be most welcome? Would a translator be better supported during the 'linear' translation production or during the translation pauses?" (Carl and Jakobsen 2009: 136). They then discuss the distracting impact of typing suggestions and how to integrate these and other aids into translation tools. They advocate that process analysis may help to identify reading patterns and to develop tools even for the reading task.

By 2016, a few signs seemed to indicate that technology and research might have reached the evolutionary state required to pursue the goal of predicting editing actions:

> We are now at a stage in the development where translation research becomes predictive. The records from keylogging software and eye-trackers make it possible to address Holmes' (1972) second main objective, to "explain and predict" translators' behaviour: at present, we have all the necessary tools to address the challenge of building a model of human translation which makes specific, falsifiable predictions regarding the process and the product of translation.
>
> *(Carl et al. 2016b: 4)*

Predicting the editing actions that translators should perform is one of the toughest challenges for the development of tools that specifically support PE. This is the theme of the next section.

5. The need for interactive editing tools

As we have seen, PE has become an accepted task in the industry (albeit one that is cognitively demanding and sometimes contentious on the translator side). Feeding translators MT output is now relatively straightforward, but applying the predictive power of MT to support the work of translators is more challenging.

When translators approach sentences that were produced by a high-quality MT system, they hope to just scan through them, not really reading from beginning to end, but merely looking for the errors to correct. In doing this, they are pressured by opposing forces from externally imposed productivity goals and their learned (and required) focus on small quality details.

Having negotiated this conflict and identified the errors, they decide how to correct them. They click on, or navigate to, scattered words in the text, and apply different techniques to correct errors with surgical precision, based on detailed keyboard and mouse actions applied to the words selected. Alternatively, they simply delete the whole sentence and rewrite it when they consider this the most efficient process, even if it means retyping a few words that were in the original sentence. That was the conclusion of a study which compared two modes of editing: traditional PE (the system presents one full MT suggestion and there is no interaction) and Interactive Machine Translation (IMT), where the translator writes and the system presents the next word (Alabau et al. 2016). In that study, almost all users preferred not to work with such interactive help. This shows that, although the technology is available to model and predict PE work, the question of how to offer the help in a useful and usable way remains open.

There is one very important difference between writing a translation and editing it: if you are writing a translation from start to finish, the whole translation is being generated in your brain even if your tool presents you with suggestions for word or sentence completion. Generating means first creating an abstract notion of the meaning and intention of a sentence, and only then, through syntactic processes, giving it form. When this generation process is confronted with a sequence of ever-changing suggested completions for the sentence, a high cognitive load is created by the dynamics of the process (Alabau et al. 2016).

For editing, the generation process should not be triggered, since the user is looking for mistakes. To actually be 'editable', the sentence presented by the MT system must be good enough for the translator to worry only about certain points that may be corrected through the application of well-directed actions. When that cannot be done, the generation process is triggered. At that moment, the translator decides to delete everything, and this becomes a writing task, which moves us to the level in which editing becomes translating.

Having a good MT suggestion, however, is not enough to support editing. The interface elements—the mechanisms that build the communication between the MT systems and human actions—must also provide the necessary conditions for the editing to proceed in an efficient way. IMT may not be the best model to support editing since it is inspired by translating.

Open challenges for editing tools

Several research projects have delved into the challenges of the interactivity required to reuse MT content in a way that supports translators through consideration of recommendations from fields such as Human-Computer Interaction (O'Brien 2012). Some of these projects explore mobile interfaces (O'Brien et al. 2014), while others consider how to learn from post-edits (Simianer et al. 2016). Interactive forms of PE have been studied within the CasMaCat project (Koehn et al. 2015). Techniques like Online Learning (to learn from user actions and incrementally adapt translation suggestions) and Active Learning (to determine which sentences need to be edited first so as to adapt the translation models most efficiently) have been applied to the task (Ortiz-Martínez et al. 2016). A thorough analysis of the development of interactive systems that apply both MT and TM in complex CAT environments has also been made (Forcada and Sánchez-Martínez 2015). However, this wealth of resources is often associated with an increased cognitive load

(Christensen 2011; Pym 2011b). A more recent study compares statistical MT and NMT interactive systems (Daems and Macken 2019), and another (Coppers et al. 2018) tries to combine several resources in an interface that is intended to be intelligible and practical for users.

Translation throughput is nowadays often limited only by the capacity of the interfaces between humans and technology, as is recognised by analyses of typing speed, mobile input interfaces and voice recognition (Moorkens et al. 2016). Furthermore, technological development must be based on correct models of processes, at the risk of not being useful (in the sense that they solve problems) or usable (in the sense that they improve processes) (Rabadán 2010).

The main conceptual model of how translators produce translations is 'translating': translators write full sentences, typing characters in a linear way. Therefore, auto-completion features have been the basis for the features that support writing in interactive translation systems—as translators start typing, words or full sentences are suggested to them (Green et al. 2014; Hokamp and Liu 2015). However, while auto-completion supports linear writing, editing is scattered and implies other actions, some of which involve only the position of words. These actions cannot be adequately supported by auto-completion systems and would benefit from systems that were able to predict which words may require deletion, or in which positions they should be placed (do Carmo 2017).

An interactive tool that supports editing should present suggestions, depending not only on the words selected but also on a contextual choice from the editing actions available: if there is a learnt model that estimates a high probability that a certain word is to be deleted, the tool may suggest that action beforehand. The interactive tool may use predictive writing functionalities to support the insertion and replacement actions, but it should also incorporate adaptive features to support frequent deletions and movements.

The challenge posed by editing is, as we have seen, not just a technical matter. Having tools that support decisions about which words to delete, or tools that present alternatives to replace words, affects not just the daily life of translators but our own theories and conceptions of the processes involved, as well as our overall perception of the value of tasks performed by professional translators.

6. Conclusions

Throughout this chapter, we have reviewed descriptions and analyses of the editing task (when translators make small changes to text) that enable a clear consideration of the PE process and support our assertion of PE as a translation task. We have discussed how the view of PE as a form of revision may have contributed to devaluing this process, mostly in the professional world, but also affecting pedagogical approaches.

As an argument to counter that view, we propose a threshold that, even if it is based only on a measure of post-editors' technical work, serves to highlight the level of writing and translating that is required during PE. As we have seen, the four editing actions, which are at the centre of our view of editing, appear in very early studies of the translation process such as those by Nida and Toury, but they also appear very early in computer science in the form of edit distance metrics. Although apparently simple, these four actions may be fundamental to supporting descriptions of the complexity of translating, revising and post-editing, and to fostering new methods of studying the details of production behaviours.

Throughout the chapter, there are several indications that PE is a specialised process which should be carried out by specialised translators. We have shown how editing is part of a creation process which has to be efficient and achieve different levels of quality. During PE, translators need to read more content than in normal revision, and they need to write in a more varied way, most frequently editing, but with the ability to quickly decide to delete an MT suggestion and translate the sentence from scratch. Post-editors need to have more strategies than mere transference; they need to know how to avoid replicating the source content in a structure that is inappropriate in the target language. Knowledge and practice of the four editing actions may help translators become more efficient at editing, but this must be done with the awareness that they can move above the threshold, into translating. Finally, the evolution of translation tools, offering more interactivity and support, requires users who are proficient at using these features. That way, the tools and resources at their disposal become instruments that sustain their professional development.

Through the study of editing, we have offered a view in which PE may be a more rewarding process for translators, a process in which optimisers and satisficers alike can identify their role in a demanding professional environment.

3

POST-EDITING HUMAN TRANSLATIONS AND REVISING MACHINE TRANSLATIONS

Impact on efficiency and quality

Joke Daems and Lieve Macken

Revision and post-editing are intuitively comparable: the first is the process of correcting a human-translated text, the second is the process of correcting a machine-translated text. While correcting these texts, revisers and post-editors alike have to be aware of a variety of potential translation solutions, they have to make corrections on different levels (mechanical to conceptual, stylistic to political) and their tasks become even more similar as the degree of expected quality increases (Vasconcellos 1987a).

What is presumed to set them apart, however, is the nature and distribution of the errors, with machine-translation (MT) output containing more errors and more predictable errors compared to human translation (Vasconcellos 1987a). Another presumed difference between revision and post-editing is sociological rather than mechanical: "it is easier to wield the metaphorical red pen on the output of some faceless machine than on one's colleague's hard work, especially if one is slightly predisposed to disparage the machine's capabilities" (Somers 1997). Having to work together with other translators, or 'interpersonal aptitude', is cited as an important component of translation revision competence (Robert et al. 2017a).

The question is whether the assumptions made by Vasconcellos are still valid today. MT systems have evolved enormously since the 1980s, and the output is likely closer to human translation quality than it used to be. In addition, in our increasingly global and digital society, communication often takes place in a virtual manner, which could make sociological issues less relevant, as translation agencies can be asked to revise a translation without knowing the person (or machine) who prepared it. Given that readers and translators are not necessarily capable of distinguishing between human-translated and machine-translated texts (Vasconcellos and Bostad 1992; He et al. 2010), the question is whether a reviser would be.

This chapter is structured as follows. We first discuss relevant research related to differences between post-editing and revision regarding quality and efficiency and introduce our research questions and hypotheses. We then outline our experimental set-up, describing the characteristics of the English source texts (for each of which we used both a human and a machine translation into Dutch) and the data collection process. This is followed by the analysis section, where we describe how we operationalized quality and efficiency and the steps taken in our statistical analysis. In the results section, we present the results of the statistical analysis for each research question and some additional exploration where relevant, without discussion. In the discussion and conclusion section, we discuss the results and link back to our research hypotheses.

1. Related research

Revision is listed as a key way to ensure translation quality in the ISO 17100 standard, and it has been integrated into translator training. According to Allman (2006), it is important for the reliability of a translation to receive special attention during the revision process. He argues that translations by professional translators are more likely to contain transfer errors than language errors. McDonough Dolmaya (2015), on the other hand, found that translations do contain language and style problems in addition to transfer problems. She also found that half of the problems are not detected during the revision process and that most attention goes to the correction of language and style rather than transfer.

This raises the question of whether revision is in fact the most efficient way of obtaining a high-quality translation. Revision can be a time-consuming process, but revisers are often not given the time they need to properly revise a text. According to Parra-Galiano (2016), there must be "a balanced relationship between cost, usefulness and necessity" for revision to be effective, a sentiment that is echoed by Künzli (2007a). Another risk is that the reviser introduces errors. While Robert et al. (2017b) assume that students who have been taught revision would be more tolerant and introduce fewer hyperrevisions (preferential changes), this hypothesis has not been confirmed. Martin (2012) goes so far as to say that revision can do more harm than good and it is often not worth the extra time and effort.

A potentially more efficient solution—at least for some text types—is post-editing of MT. The increased speed of post-editing as compared to human translation has frequently been established, and usually the quality of the final post-edited product is comparable to or even better than that of a human translation (Plitt and Masselot 2010; Koponen 2016; Daems et al. 2017a). McElhaney and Vasconcellos (1988) argue that the errors in MT (which in their case was rule-based MT) are more of a local nature (occurring at word or phrase level) compared to errors made by a human translator, that there are no inadvertent repetitions or skipped passages in MT, and that "while the machine may not always find the correct alternate translation for a word or phrase, neither will it make wild guesses" (p. 141). On the other hand, a possible risk of post-editing lies in the recurrent nature of MT errors and translators' distrust of MT output.

Not only can this cause irritation because translators have to correct the same errors over and over again, but in addition there could be a negative impact on the translators themselves, as they can become so used to the (incorrect) phrasing that they no longer spot the errors (Krings 2001). This fear is countered by de Almeida and O'Brien (2010), who found that more experienced translators made more essential changes as well as preferential changes during post-editing compared to less experienced translators. Interestingly, awareness of the provenance of suggestions may influence the translation process. In a setting where translators worked in a tool without information about the origin of the suggestions, Guerberof Arenas (2008) found that translators processed MT suggestions faster than fuzzy matches from a translation memory and that the quality was better as well. In contrast, Teixeira (2014) found that the presence of origin information in general reduced translation time without a negative effect on the quality. His findings were more nuanced for specific suggestion types: exact matches from a translation memory were processed more slowly and more segments were edited when no metadata was present, whereas for MT suggestions, the presence or absence of metadata had no significant effect on time, editing[1] effort or quality.

Since the publication of these studies, neural machine translation (NMT) has become the mainstream MT technology, mainly due to its ability to produce far better translations than its predecessor, statistical machine translation (SMT). Numerous studies covering many language pairs and translation tasks have demonstrated that NMT outperforms SMT (Bentivogli et al. 2016; Toral and Sánchez-Cartagena 2017). Since NMT systems are able to take into account the context of the entire sentence during translation, they can produce translations that are more fluent. Van Brussel et al. (2018) carried out a detailed error analysis on 665 sentences that were automatically translated from English into Dutch with different translation engines and found that the NMT system produced a higher number of flawless translations. On the other hand, the NMT output contained less transparent errors, such as omissions (for example, the modal marker 'would like to' was deleted in an otherwise faultless Dutch translation); this kind of error might be quite challenging for post-editors.

In this study, we set out to determine differences between revision and post-editing in a modern setting. We compared the interventions made on human-translated and NMT-translated texts in two scenarios: when the instructions matched the origin of the text (translators were asked to revise a human-translated text or post-edit a machine-translated text), and when the instructions did not match the origin of the text (translators were asked to post-edit a human-translated text or revise a machine-translated text). Our research questions were the following:

1   Do participants make more changes in a text when they assume they are post-editing, or when they assume they are revising?
2   Is the revision of higher quality when participants assume they are post-editing, or when they assume they are revising?

3   Are the most optimal translations produced when participants assume they are post-editing, or when they assume they are revising?
(See section 3 for definitions of 'revision quality' and 'optimality'.)

The corresponding hypotheses based on findings from previous studies are:

1   Participants will make more changes during post-editing than during revision, regardless of the actual origin of a text, as translators are generally more critical of MT output and could find it harder to criticize the work of a fellow translator (Somers 1997).
2   Revision quality will be highest for post-editing, as post-edited quality can be even better than that of human translation (Koponen 2016).
3   (Assumed) post-editing will be more optimal than (assumed) revision as post-editors are generally trained to avoid changes related to fluency or style and to focus only on actual errors that need to be corrected to improve the MT output, whereas revisers are often trained to detect issues of fluency and style as well. Additionally, in the case where people believe they are post-editing MT while in reality the text is a human translation, they might be more critical and therefore notice more errors than they would if they believed the text was translated by a person.

2.   Experimental set-up

Text selection

We selected articles from the Dutch Parallel Corpus (Macken et al. 2011) that were originally published in the English newspaper *The Independent* and in the Dutch newspaper *De Morgen*, which can be considered a high-quality newspaper. The selection was made on the basis of text length (minimum 500 words), number of sentences, topic (including some items that would have to be researched, but no specialist content) and relative timelessness (not obviously discussing a specific historical moment). Texts fulfilling these criteria were translated with the free online NMT systems DeepL[2] and Google Translate[3] in December 2018. The quality of the translations was evaluated by the authors and by two language experts with respectively more than 5 and more than 20 years of experience in translation technology and translation quality evaluation. The two source texts for which the MT quality was best, that is, the machine translation had the lowest number of errors and the lowest number of critical errors (for example, contradictions or unintelligible passages), were chosen for the experiment. A few source text sentences that had no corresponding translation in the target text were deleted to allow for a fair comparison between human translation and MT. The final source texts were 603 words (38 sentences) and 595 words (37 sentences) long, their corresponding human translations 609 and 634 words respectively. DeepL was chosen for the final MT version, as its quality was slightly better than that of Google Translate for these texts. The MT versions were 641 and 625 words long respectively.

Identification of problems

To be able to distinguish between necessary and unnecessary changes, all problems in the human and machine-translated versions of both texts were first identified. The approach of Daems et al. (2013) was adopted, with manual annotation of problems using a categorization scheme[4] that is based on the dichotomy between adequacy and acceptability. Annotations were performed by the authors, who have more than five years of experience working with this annotation scheme as well as high inter-annotator agreement (see Daems et al. 2013 for a discussion). Cases where the annotators disagreed were discussed before settling on a final annotation.

Apart from annotating the problems, we also assigned a severity weight of 0 to 3 to each problem. A severity weight of 3 was used for critical problems that have a major impact on the accuracy and/or intelligibility of the translation; for example, word sense problems such as the English word *drug*, used in the sense of *medicine*, being translated in Dutch as *drug* (the Dutch translation for the illegal substance) instead of *geneesmiddel* (the Dutch translation for medicine) or unintelligible translations in the target text such as *maakt een veel urgenter geval* as a word-for-word translation of *makes a far more urgent case*. A severity weight of 2 was assigned to problems that cause a shift in meaning between the source text and the translation or that affect the intelligibility of the translation; for example, deletion of modality markers (the words *potentially* or *practically* are omitted in the translation), a change in modality (no distinction between *could* and *can*) or the use of hypernyms (*petrochemical* being translated as *chemical*). A severity weight of 1 was used for minor problems, where the text can still be understood without effort and the information contained in the translation is equal to that of the source text, but there is a small error (for example, a spelling mistake such as the wrong plural form *enzymes* instead of *enzymen*) or the intelligibility is affected a little (the name of an organization is not translated or explained). A severity weight of 0 was reserved for differences that are not actual problems; for example, explicitations or omission of non-essential information. An overview of the different error types found in each of the texts can be seen in Figure 3.1.

For both texts, the MT output contains more errors than the human translation, especially adequacy errors (not counting additions and deletions), and more errors with severity weight 3. Deletions are far more common in human translation than in MT output. Additions appear only in the human translation of text 2. Note that additions and deletions were counted as errors only when they removed information crucial for the reader or when they added information that could not be derived from the source text and was therefore incorrect. Cases of deletion that did not alter the meaning and cases of explicitation necessary for a target reader were not counted as errors. Grammatical errors are found only in the MT output of text 1. Style and lexicon issues are more common in MT than in human translation.

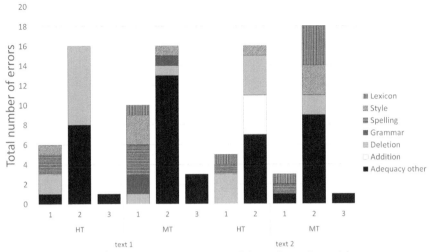

Distribution of error types per text, text origin, and severity weight

FIGURE 3.1 Total number of errors in each category by text, text origin (HT = human translation, MT = machine translation) and severity weight

This supports Allman's (2006) claim that the most important thing to check during revision of human translations is reliability.

Participants

To ensure the ecological validity of the experiment, we worked with actual translation agencies. We selected eight different translation agencies in Belgium that offered revision and/or post-editing as a service on their website and contacted them by e-mail. They were asked to have two translators perform the same task independently. Other instructions were minimal: the agencies were asked to ensure that the final text would be of publishable quality for a general Dutch-speaking audience (in Belgium and the Netherlands) and they were asked to submit a Word document with 'Track Changes' enabled. The agencies were not aware that they were participating in a research project.

Four of the agencies were told that the texts were human translations and were asked to perform revision; the other four agencies were told the texts were machine-translated texts and were asked to perform post-editing.

In reality, the texts could occur in one of four sets: (1) both text 1 and text 2 were human translations, (2) both text 1 and text 2 were machine translations, (3) text 1 was human translation and text 2 was MT, (4) text 1 was MT and text 2 was human translation. Since two of the agencies had only one translator available, we reached out to two additional agencies to ensure a balanced design, with each set and each condition (instruction to revise/instruction to post-edit) occurring an equal number of times.

TABLE 3.1 Experimental design. HT = human translation, MT = machine translation

Participant	Text 1	Text 2	Instruction
1A	HT	HT	revise
2A	MT	MT	revise
3A	HT	MT	revise
4A	MT	HT	revise
1B	HT	HT	revise
2B	MT	MT	revise
3B	HT	MT	revise
4B	MT	HT	revise
5A	HT	HT	post-edit
6A	MT	MT	post-edit
7A	HT	MT	post-edit
8A	MT	HT	post-edit
9A	HT	HT	post-edit
10A	MT	MT	post-edit
7B	HT	MT	post-edit
8B	MT	HT	post-edit

The distribution of tasks, eliminating potential task or task order effects, can be seen in Table 3.1. The number in the participant code indicates the translation agency, the letter the participant; for example, participants 1A and 1B both worked for the same translation agency.

Prices charged by the translation agencies were somewhat higher for revision than for post-editing. We calculated the price per text per participant (including VAT). Prices ranged from 36.24 euros to 75.2 euros for post-editing (with a mean of 53.85 euros and a median of 56.87 euros) and from 49.16 euros to 72.6 euros for revision (with a mean of 62.58 euros and a median of 64.28 euros).

3. Analysis

As explained in section 2, we obtained 32 Dutch translations in total: 16 different versions for each of the two source texts, of which 8 were based on the human-translated text, and 8 on the translation generated by DeepL. Half of the human translations and machine translations were revised; the other half were post-edited. To analyse the changes made to the original translations by the revisers/post-editors, we combined automatic metrics with manual annotations.

An automatic metric that is often used in the field of MT is (H)TER (Snover et al. 2006), henceforth referred to as TER (Translation Error Rate), which quantifies the amount of editing (insertions, deletions and substitutions of single words as well as shifts of word sequences) applied to the translation suggestion to create the final translation. We used TERCOM[5] to obtain TER scores at segment and text level for each text, using either the human translation or the MT as the translation suggestion and the revised or post-edited versions as the final translation. To be able to calculate the TER scores, we first manually aligned all translations at sentence level, taking the source texts as base files, and tokenized all texts using the Moses tokenizer.[6]

The resulting TER scores quantify how different the final translation is from the original human translation or machine-translated text (higher TER scores indicate that more editing took place), but the automatic scores cannot distinguish between necessary and unnecessary changes and might therefore be hard to interpret. To solve this problem, we created baseline translations in which we corrected only the problems with severity weights of 1 to 3, on the basis of which we calculated baseline TER scores. A baseline TER score of 8, for example, indicates that around 8% of the text has to be edited to correct all errors with severity weights of 1 to 3. We could then use this baseline TER to identify cases of hyperrevision (preferential and unnecessary changes). Someone who corrects all errors but has a TER score of 40, for example, has likely introduced many preferential changes (they edited around 40% of the text as opposed to the necessary 8%) and is therefore not very efficient. This is an important measure to take into account, considering the issues surrounding the efficiency of revision (Martin 2012).

In addition to the baseline TER score, we determined the baseline error score for each sentence and each text for each text origin (human translation or MT) by taking the total of all errors in that sentence or text, multiplied by their respective severity weights. The baselines can be seen in Table 3.2.

TABLE 3.2 Baseline TER and error scores for each text and origin, on text and sentence level. μ = mean (sum of all values divided by the number of items), M = median (for an uneven number of items, the middle value when sorting all items in ascending order; for an even number of items, the average of the two middle values)

Text	Text origin	TER baseline text level	TER baseline sentence level	Error score baseline text level	Error score baseline sentence level
1	HT	7.479	max = 42.105, min = 0, μ = 8.037, M = 3.176	41	max = 4, min = 0, μ = 1.08, M = 1
1	MT	9.643	max = 62.5, min = 0, μ = 9.42, M = 6.67	51	max = 5, min = 0, μ = 1.34, M = 1
2	HT	7.682	max = 100, min = 0, μ = 9.88, M = 0	35	max = 4, min = 0, μ = 1, M = 0
2	MT	6.787	max = 41.1, min = 0, μ = 5.829, M = 2.22	42	max = 4, min = 0, μ = 1.14, M = 1

For the manual annotations, we looked at the revision interventions made by participants for each of the errors identified in section 2. The types of intervention were based on Robert et al. (2017b): 'necessary' for changes that corrected the error, 'underrevision' for errors that had not been corrected, and 'overrevision' for changes that introduced an error. We focused only on the interventions related to errors (either present in the original Dutch translation or introduced in the revision or post-editing process), as all other changes could be considered preferential. Comparing the TER baseline to participants' actual TER values yields an approximation of the preferential changes without having to manually annotate every intervention made by the participants.

Intervention optimality, revision quality and edit efficiency

We could now compare the participants' data with the baseline scores to determine which of the conditions (post-editing or revision) worked best. This is dependent on two factors: the quantity of text that was edited (as expressed by TER) and the quality of the interventions made by a participant. The best scenario is when a participant solves as many problems as possible with as few changes as possible. It is important that a reviser or post-editor works efficiently because lack of efficiency is likely an indication of a greater time investment, which, given the often limited budget available, is less cost-effective. Still, a 2016 SDL Translation Technology Insights research study on quality in the translation industry (over 2700 respondents in 115 countries) indicated that quality was 2.5 times more important than speed.

To ensure this importance is reflected in our analyses, we combined edit efficiency and revision quality in a formula for intervention optimality that attaches greater importance to quality.

Intervention optimality is calculated as follows:

$$intervention\ optimality = \left(1 + \beta^2\right) * \frac{revision\ quality * edit\ efficiency}{revision\ quality + \left(\beta^2 * edit\ efficiency\right)}$$

with:

$$revision\ quality = \frac{\left(necessary\ changes * severity\ weight\right) - \left(overrevisions * severity\ weight\right)}{total\ number\ of\ errors * severity\ weight}$$

and:

$$edit\ efficiency = \frac{MAX\left(100 - actual\ TER, 1\right)}{MAX\left(100 - baseline\ TER, 1\right)}$$

Intervention optimality is the weighted harmonic mean of revision quality and edit efficiency, weighting revision quality higher than edit efficiency[7] with $\beta = 2.5$, as quality was deemed to be 2.5 times as important in the SDL study.

The revision quality formula is adapted from the second formula suggested by Robert (2012): taking the number of necessary changes, subtracting the number of overrevisions, and dividing the result by the total number of errors. In our adaptation, the errors are weighted according to their corresponding severity. If the total number of errors equalled zero, revision quality was automatically set either to 1 (high), if the participant did not introduce any errors of their own, or to 0 (low), if the participant introduced errors of their own, in order to avoid division by zero. If the outcome of the revision quality formula was negative, for example, when the number of errors introduced by the participant was greater than the number of errors solved, revision quality was also set to 0.

Edit efficiency compares the actual TER value with the baseline TER value. It is possible that either or both of these values will equal zero. To avoid division by zero, we reversed the values by subtracting them from 100 (a proxy for max TER). As such, they become measures of how much of the original text was expected to be retained (100—baseline TER) and how much of the text was actually retained by a participant (100—actual TER). In cases where this value was less than or equal to zero (for example, if TER was exactly 100 or greater than 100), it was automatically set to 1 (indicating that almost everything was edited). Edit efficiency was then calculated by dividing the reversed actual TER score by the reversed baseline TER score. For example, if a sentence had a baseline TER of 30, and an actual TER of 80, their reversed values would be 70 and 20 respectively. By dividing the reversed actual TER by the reversed baseline TER, we get an edit efficiency of 0.29, indicating that a participant retained only 29% of the text they were supposed to retain according to the baseline.

Mixed effects models

The scores by participant and text were analysed with linear mixed effects regression models in R using the lme4 package (Bates et al. 2015), with lmerTest (Kuznetsova et al. 2017) to obtain significance scores and sjPlot (Lüdecke 2018) to plot the models. Mixed effects models can contain random effects in addition to fixed effects (independent variables). For all models discussed here, we included intercepts for participants as random effects. Random slopes could not be included as these made the model unidentifiable. The main analysis was performed on a text level, as text was the unit of interest; that is, we asked translation companies to ensure that the revised or post-edited texts were of publishable quality. To verify our text-level findings, we repeated the analysis with the sentence as the unit of observation. While performing the analysis on a sentence level yields more data points and allows for the sentence itself to be added as a random effect, the nature of the data complicates such an analysis. Sentence-level data contain many zero values, and differences on a sentence level easily lead to more extreme values. For example, a sentence that did not need to be edited but was changed completely would lead to an extreme edit efficiency value, whereas on a text level this would not influence the data much.

We started from a null model including only the dependent variable and random effects and compared this with models including independent variables, to verify whether the assumed predictors—condition (revision versus post-editing) and text origin (MT versus human translation)—had any predictive effects on the dependent variable. To compare and select models, we calculated Akaike's Information Criterion (AIC) value (Akaike 1974) and selected the model with the lowest AIC value, and we used the step function from the lmerTest package in R to perform backwards elimination of non-significant effects.

We built different models to test our research questions. The predictor variables (text origin and condition) were always tested independently as well as with interaction effects, as we expected the dependent variables to be influenced differently by different combinations of predictor variables (revision for human translation, revision for MT, post-editing for human translation, post-editing for MT). We also included text as a fixed effect, as it had only two levels (text 1 and text 2) and could therefore not be included as a random effect. Including interaction effects for text with either condition or text origin did not improve the model.

Returning to the three research questions we asked in section 1:

1   Do participants make more changes in a text when they assume they are post-editing, or when they assume they are revising a text? To model this, actual TER was used as the dependent variable, with condition (revision/post-editing), text origin (MT/human translation) and text as predictors.
2   Is the revision of higher quality when participants assume they are post-editing, or when they assume they are revising a text? To model this, revision quality was used as the dependent variable, with condition, text origin and text as predictors.
3   Are the most optimal translations produced when participants assume they are post-editing, or when they assume they are revising a text? To model this, intervention optimality was used as the dependent variable, with condition, text origin and text as predictors.

For the sentence-level analysis, the models that were tested always consisted of the dependent variable (TER, quality or intervention optimality), with condition and text origin plus interaction as potential predictors. We included intercepts for participants and sentences as random effects, as well as by-sentence random slopes for the effect of text origin. A by-participant random slope for the effect of text origin was included in the TER model only, as it led to a singular fit for the other models.

We supplemented the statistical analysis with a more detailed exploration of our data where relevant, using exploratory graphs in Excel, to try to gain a better understanding of our findings.

4.   Results

TER

Linear mixed effects analysis showed a significant interaction effect between text origin and condition on actual TER scores (effect size: 13.08, standard error: 4.4, $p < 0.01$), indicating that while actual TER scores were comparable for human translation in both conditions (revision and post-editing), the score was significantly higher when revising MT output than when post-editing MT output. There was also a significant effect of text, with more edits taking place in text 2 than in text 1 (effect size = 5.86, standard error: 1.75, p < 0.01). There was no significant main effect of either condition or text origin. The predicted values for the interaction effect can be seen on the plot in Figure 3.2.

The effect plot in Figure 3.2 shows the predicted TER score values depending on text origin and condition. We can see that the predicted mean TER score for HT in both conditions and MT in the post-editing condition is close to 12, with the lines indicating the 95% confidence interval (there is a 95% chance that this interval contains the true mean). The less overlap between confidence interval lines, the more likely that the difference in mean is statistically significant. The significant interaction effect of 13.08 can be seen on the plot as the difference between the predicted TER value for HT in the post-editing condition (used as a baseline) and the predicted TER value for MT in the revision condition.

Figure 3.3 indicates that there is some individual variation across participants regarding TER scores, with participant 4B editing the most and participant 2A editing the least. The lmerTest step function did indeed show a significant contribution of this random factor to the model (p = 0.01).

If the intercept for a participant is close to zero, this indicates that their mean TER score is close to the baseline of 12 shown in Figure 3.2. The more to the right, the higher this individual participant's TER scores generally are; the more to the left, the lower. Here as well, the lines indicate confidence intervals with a 95%

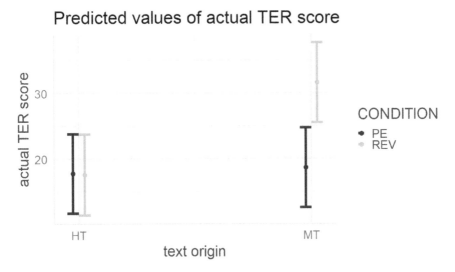

FIGURE 3.2 Interaction effect plot for the impact of text origin (HT = human translation, MT = machine translation) and condition (PE = post-editing, REV = revision) on actual TER scores

Random effects of participants

FIGURE 3.3 Random effects of participants for TER scores

Maar op een schaal van een miljoenste van een millimeter kunnen materialen ongewone en onvoorspelbare eigenschappen krijgen. Daarom wordt gevreesd voor gezondheids- en milieurisico's. Sommige ~~specialisten deskundigen~~ roepen op tot een tijdelijk verbod op nanotechnologie omdat ~~volgens hen~~ de ultrafijne deeltjes die gebruikt worden in cosmetica, de industrie en de ~~spits~~technologie volgens hen dodelijk zouden kunnen zijn.	Maar op een schaal van een miljoenste van een millimeter kunnen materialen ongewone en onvoorspelbare eigenschappen krijgen. Daarom wordt gevreesd voor gezondheids- en milieurisico's. Sommige specialisten roepen op tot een tijdelijk verbod op nanotechnologie omdat volgens hen ultrafijne deeltjes die gebruikt worden in cosmetica, de industrie en de technologie dodelijk zouden kunnen zijn.
De organisatie Friends of the Earth ~~schat~~ zegt dat in Australië ~~mogelijk~~ ~~naar schatting~~ 300.000 mensen in de raffinage- en ~~lassector~~ ~~assemblage~~blootgesteld worden aan nanodeeltjes. Verder zouden 33.000 mensen blootgesteld worden bij ~~de verwerking van~~ het werken met poeders, vooral in de farmaceutische en cosmetische industrie. Friends of the Earth pleit ook voor een ~~moratorium~~ ~~verbod~~ op het onderzoek, de ontwikkeling en de productie van synthetische nanodeeltjes tot er een ~~regelgeving~~ ~~wetgeving~~ is ontwikkeld: "~~Daarmee~~Dat zou een enorme menselijke en financiële kost ~~vermeden worden, en~~ alsook schadeclaims van ~~mensen die aangetast zijn~~ slachtoffers, ~~net~~ zoals het geval was met asbest, vermijden."	De organisatie Friends of the Earth zegt dat in Australië naar schatting 300.000 mensen in de raffinage en assemblage blootgesteld worden aan nanodeeltjes. Verder zouden 33.000 mensen blootgesteld worden bij de verwerking van poeders, vooral in de farmaceutische en cosmetische industrie. Friends of the Earth pleit ook voor een verbod op onderzoek, ontwikkeling en productie van synthetische nanodeeltjes tot er een wetgeving is ontwikkeld: "Daarmee zouden een enorme menselijke en financiële kosten als ook veel schadeclaims van mensen die aangetast zijn, zoals het geval was net als met asbest."
In Amerika gaan soortgelijke stemmen op. In oktober verklaarde Mihail Rocco, vicevoorzitter van de Nationale Wetenschaps- en Technologieraad, ~~Tijden~~stijdens een ~~workshop~~ nanotechnologie~~workshop~~ van het Milieubeschermingsagentschap ~~verklaarde Mihail Rocco, vicevoorzitter van de Nationale Wetenschaps- en Technologieraad,~~ dat "federale agentschappen niet ~~beschikken~~ over methodes ~~beschikken~~ om de uitstoot van nanodeeltjes te controleren. Toch kunnen ze in de hersenen terechtkomen en ~~mogelijk~~ schade aanrichten."	In Amerika gaan soortgelijke stemmen op. Tijdens een workshop nanotechnologie van het Milieubeschermingsagentschap verklaarde Mihail Rocco, vicevoorzitter van de Nationale Wetenschaps- en Technologieraad, dat "federale agentschappen niet beschikken over methodes om de uitstoot van nanodeeltjes te controleren. Toch kunnen ze in de hersenen terechtkomen en schade aanrichten."

FIGURE 3.4 Revision of human translation for text 1, performed by two different participants

chance of capturing the true mean. To better understand these findings, we looked at our data in more detail. The degree of individual variation is clearly visible in Figure 3.4, showing a screenshot of the revision of the human translation for text 1, performed by two different participants from different translation agencies.

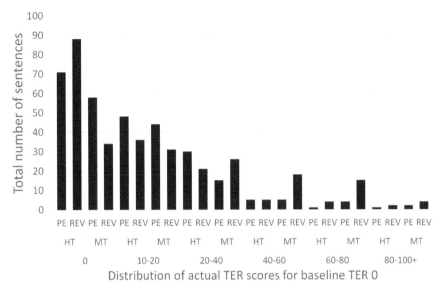

FIGURE 3.5 Distribution of actual TER scores for sentences with baseline TER 0 by text origin (HT = human translation, MT = machine translation) and condition (PE = post-editing, REV = revision)

We further found that more than half of the sentences requiring no editing (baseline TER score of 0) were nevertheless edited (actual TER scores of 1–100+) and that, especially for human translation, around half of the sentences requiring some editing (baseline TER of 20–60) received no editing (actual TER scores of 0). In particular, the sentences where we expected no editing (baseline TER score of 0) showed interesting patterns (see Figure 3.5): a higher number of sentences were lightly edited (TER scores of 10–20) in the post-editing condition than in the revision condition, regardless of text origin. This changed with a higher degree of editing (20+), where we found more sentences in the revision condition, but only for MT origin.

Revision quality

Revision quality was best predicted by the mixed effects model including text origin, condition and text as predictors, with interaction effect for text origin and condition. There were no main effects of either condition or origin on quality, but a significant interaction effect ($p = 0.01$) with effect size 0.27 (standard error: 0.098), as can be seen on the effect plot in Figure 3.6: the quality is lower when revising human translation as opposed to post-editing human translation, and higher when revising MT as opposed to post-editing MT. There was also a significant effect of text, with text 2 being of better quality (effect size = 0.15, standard error: 0.04, $p < 0.01$).

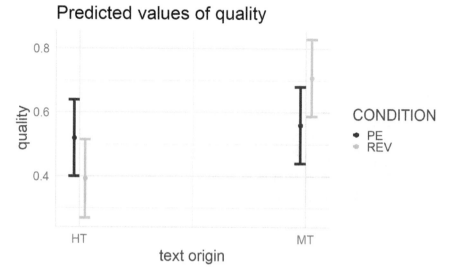

FIGURE 3.6 Interaction effect plot for the impact of text origin (HT = human translation, MT = machine translation) and condition (PE = post-editing, REV = revision) on revision quality

Random effects showed some variation across participants, as can be seen in Figure 3.7, with participants 6A, 5A and 3A obtaining the highest revision quality and 8B and 2A the lowest. While the lmerTest step function did retain the random factor in the model, its contribution only approaches significance (p = 0.08), indicating that the variation in quality is influenced less by individual variation across participants.

As the highest level of editing was found for MT in the revision condition (see Figure 3.2), where we also find the highest level of quality (see Figure 3.6), we built a further model in which we added TER as a predictor of quality. This model performed better than the previous one (AIC reduction of 9 points, p < 0.001). Interestingly, in this model, only TER (effect size: 0.01, standard error: 0.003, p < 0.01) and text (effect size: 0.09, standard error: 0.04, p < 0.05) significantly helped predict the variation in quality. The interaction effect between text origin and condition was no longer significant (p = 0.18), and the main effect of condition was approaching significance (p = 0.08), with revision negatively impacting quality (effect size: −0.13, standard error: 0.07). This seems to indicate that more editing generally leads to higher quality, regardless of condition or text origin, and that the higher quality found in the revision condition for MT is mostly due to the higher level of editing taking place.

To better understand these findings, we again took a closer look at our data to explore interesting differences. Figure 3.8 gives an overview of the percentage of all

Random effects of participants

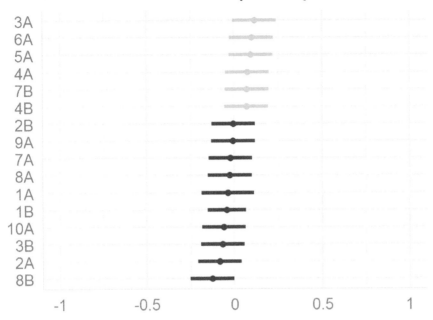

FIGURE 3.7 Random effects of participants for revision quality

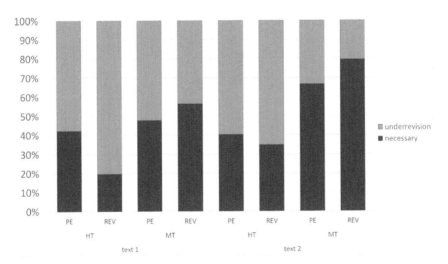

FIGURE 3.8 Percentage of errors that were revised (= necessary) and not revised (= underrevision) by text, text origin (HT = human translation, MT = machine translation) and condition (PE = post-editing, REV = revision)

errors that were corrected (= necessary interventions) and those that should have been but were not (= underrevision). It is striking that, overall, less than half of the error items were corrected. More errors were corrected in the MT output, regardless of condition. Interestingly, fewer necessary changes were made when the text origin matched the instructions (post-editing a machine-translated text or revising a human-translated text) than when they did not (post-editing a human-translated text or revising a machine-translated text).

If we compare the number of necessary revisions and underrevisions across conditions and text origins for different error categories (Figure 3.9), there seem to be only minor differences between error categories. Errors in adequacy, the most common error category, were corrected somewhat more often during post-editing than during revision when the text was a human translation, and somewhat more often during revision than during post-editing when the text was MT. Lexical issues in MT were solved more often during revision than during post-editing.

In addition to the error items in the original texts, we also looked at the number of overrevisions (that is, errors introduced by a participant)[8] and found that they mostly occurred with MT, regardless of condition: there were five instances of overrevision for text 1 in the revision condition, and nine instances of overrevision in each of text 1 in the post-editing condition, text 2 in the revision condition and text 2 in the post-editing condition. With human translation, there were two instances of overrevision in text 1 in the post-editing condition, and one instance of overrevision in each of text 1 in the revision condition, text 2 in the revision condition and text 2 in the post-editing condition. This indicates that, while more

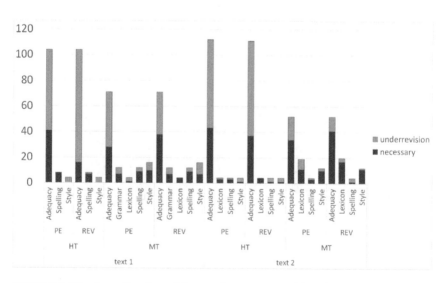

FIGURE 3.9 Number of underrevisions and necessary revisions by error category for each text, text origin (HT = human translation, MT = machine translation) and condition (PE = post-editing, REV = revision)

errors are corrected in the MT output than in the human translations, participants also introduced more errors of their own while editing MT output.

Intervention optimality

Intervention optimality was best predicted by the model including condition and text origin with interaction effect as predictors and text as predictor. There was no significant effect of either condition or text origin, but a significant interaction effect, with revision being more optimal when the origin of the text was MT (effect size = 0.27, standard error: 0.096, p = 0.01). There was also a significant effect of text, with intervention optimality being higher for text 2 (effect size = 0.15, standard error: 0.04, p < 0.01). The interaction effect can be seen in Figure 3.10.

Sentence-level models

The final models, that is, the models with the best fit according to AIC values, are presented in Table 3.3, with significant effects marked in bold.

Analysis at sentence level generally confirms the text-level findings: the interaction effect between origin and condition on TER is comparable and the interaction effect between origin and condition on quality is somewhat smaller but still significant. Though the sentence-level model for intervention optimality shows the

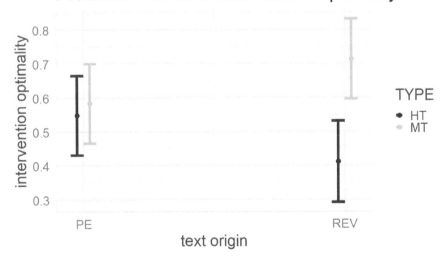

FIGURE 3.10 Interaction effect for the impact of text origin (HT = human translation, MT = machine translation) and condition (PE = post-editing, REV = revision) on intervention optimality

TABLE 3.3 Summary of sentence-level model effects

Dependent variable	Random effects	Fixed effect	Effect size (+ standard error)	p-value
TER	text origin | participant id + text origin | sentence id	text origin MT	−0.47 (3.6)	0.9
		condition REV	−0.19 (4.8)	0.97
		text origin MT: condition REV	**14.24 (4.6)**	**0.01**
quality	participant id + text origin | sentence id	text origin MT	−0.02 (0.05)	0.65
		condition REV	−0.07 (0.04)	0.1
		text origin MT: condition REV	**0.12 (0.045)**	**< 0.01**
intervention optimality	participant id + text origin | sentence id	text origin MT	−0.02 (0.05)	0.7
		condition REV	−0.07 (0.04)	0.08
		text origin MT: condition REV	0.07 (0.04)	0.09

same trends as those of the text-level model, none of the predictors was found to significantly influence intervention optimality. Here, the random effects at the sentence and participant levels explain more of the variance than the main effects.

5. Discussion and conclusion

In this chapter, we sought to discover whether there are any differences between revision and post-editing practice by letting professional translators revise or post-edit texts that were MT or human translations, without the translators knowing the real provenance of a text. Our hypothesis was that participants would make more changes when they believed they were post-editing than when they believed they were revising, regardless of the actual provenance of the text. This was based on two assumptions: that translators generally disparage MT output and expect it to be of lower quality, as evidenced by the fact that translators often believe MT suggestions to be TM matches if they are not told about the actual provenance of a suggestion (He et al. 2010), and that there may be a sociological influence when translators have to criticize the work of a peer as opposed to the work of a machine. We expected participants to be less critical while revising, and therefore assumed that fewer errors would be detected in the revision condition, and that there would be more overrevisions in the post-editing condition, regardless of the provenance of the text. Regarding optimality, we expected that post-editing would be more optimal than revision, regardless of provenance.

We could not confirm our first hypothesis, as we found significantly more changes taking place with MT in the revision condition. In general, we found that a lot of preferential changes were made in all conditions. Earlier studies also found that professional translators made many preferential changes (de Almeida and O'Brien 2010; Robert 2012). Thus the question arises: how can we adapt revision training to reduce the number of preferential changes (Robert et al. 2017b) in order to increase efficiency?

In addition to the edit rate, we looked at revision quality. For human translation, the quality of post-editing was found to be higher than that of revision, whereas for MT, the quality of revision was found to be higher than that of post-editing. This increase in quality was found to be mainly due to the increased number of changes. For human translation, this is in line with our second hypothesis: when they believe they are post-editing, people dare to suggest more changes than when they believe they are revising a text. A possible explanation for MT could be that participants pay more attention to adequacy issues when they believe they are revising than when they believe they are post-editing, and since adequacy issues often carry the greatest severity weight, this has a direct impact on overall quality. A further factor is that we worked with translation agencies that offered post-editing as a service, which means that they presumably have some experience with post-editing. As a post-editor is usually taught not to introduce too many changes, this could explain the lower editing score and quality score for MT in the post-editing condition compared to the revision condition. An additional factor could be the quality of the text. The MT output contained more problematic errors than the human translation, so that when a participant revised the MT text thinking it was a human translation, they may have become more critical because of the higher number of errors. There is some evidence in writing research suggesting that people become more critical of certain errors if a text contains more of them (Broekkamp et al. 1996). In general, over half of the errors went uncorrected in both conditions, in line with findings by Robert (2012) and McDonough Dolmaya (2015), although more errors were corrected in MT.

With respect to our third hypothesis, the analysis for intervention optimality indicated that, while post-editing was more optimal for human translation, this was not the case for MT, where revision was found to be more optimal. The main conclusion is that participants performed better when they had the wrong assumption about the provenance of a text (post-editing human translations and revising MT), which indicates that assumptions about the nature of a text are likely to influence the optimality of the revision or post-editing process. This raises questions about the differences between revision and post-editing. Is it necessary to maintain the distinction, or would it be better to offer translators texts to review without giving them any idea about the provenance of the texts? This question is up for debate, especially given the contradictory evidence about providing provenance information (Guerberof Arenas 2008; Teixeira 2014). As translation itself is becoming an increasingly integrated process with the advent of interactive, adaptive systems (where the distinction between translation memory and MT suggestions is not always clear-cut), the distinction between revision and post-editing might become less relevant as well.

The main strength of this study is at the same time its main limitation: working with actual translation agencies greatly increases the ecological validity of our findings, but the associated costs lead to a relatively small number of observations (four per text for each text origin and each condition). Conducting the same experiment on a larger scale could further improve the predictive power of the models presented. A limitation of using TER as a measure of editing effort is that it measures the difference between a reference and a final text, but it does not reflect actual effort, as keystroke logging can. We did not use keystroke logging because we wanted to ensure the ecological validity, but it is likely that a comparable study employing keystroke logging could generate additional interesting insights.

Acknowledgements

This study is part of the ArisToCAT project (Assessing The Comprehensibility of Automatic Translations), a four-year research project (2017–2020) funded by the Research Foundation—Flanders (FWO)—grant number G.0064.17N.

We would like to thank the anonymous reviewers for their suggestions, which greatly helped improve the quality of this chapter. In particular the suggestions related to the statistical analyses were helpful. We would further like to thank our department's statistician, Koen Plevoets, for helping us determine how to best implement the reviewers' suggestions.

Notes

1 Throughout this chapter, 'editing' is used to refer to changes, regardless of whether participants thought they were revising or post-editing. Whenever 'post-editing' is meant, the term 'post-editing' is used in full.
2 www.deepl.com/translator
3 https://translate.google.com/
4 http://users.ugent.be/~jvdaems/TQA_guidelines_2.0.html
5 www.cs.umd.edu/~snover/tercom/
6 https://github.com/moses-smt/mosesdecoder/blob/master/scripts/tokenizer/tokenizer.perl
7 This calculation is inspired by the F2-measure, which is the harmonic mean of precision and recall, weighing recall higher than precision. In information retrieval, precision is a measure of result relevancy, while recall is a measure of how many truly relevant results are returned.
8 Preferential changes were not counted as errors; only changes introduced by the participants that caused errors were counted. For example, the word 'science' correctly translated as 'wetenschap' (science) was changed into 'theologie' (theology), or sentences that contained modality ('could', 'might') were translated as facts, changing the original meaning.

PART II

Non-professional revision and post-editing

4

NON-PROFESSIONAL EDITING IN THE WORKPLACE

Examples from the Canadian context

Matthieu LeBlanc

Unlike non-professional interpreting and translation (NPIT) (see Antonini et al. 2017), the practice of non-professional revision or editing does not seem to have garnered much attention from Translation Studies scholars, given the limited number of publications on the subject. Yet this practice, which may be commonplace in specific settings, should be of interest to researchers, and it raises multiple questions related not only to the specific needs of the end users of translations but also to the process of translation, the relationship between translators and commissioners of translation, and professional norms of practice.

In this chapter, I will present the partial results of a study carried out in the offices of a government department in the Canadian province of New Brunswick. While the study's main goal was to focus on the language of work of civil servants in a bilingual (English-French) setting, data were also collected on the practice of professional translation within the public service and, more particularly, on the practice of non-professional editing of translations within the department in question. The study as a whole was especially concerned with language ideologies, understood as "beliefs, feelings, and conceptions about language that are socially shared and relate language and society in a dialectical fashion" (Piller 2015: 4). As Piller adds, "Language ideologies undergird language use, which in turn shapes language ideologies; and together, they serve social ends, in other words, the purpose of language ideologies is not really linguistic but social" (Piller 2015: 4).

In the first part of the chapter, I will provide essential details about the sociolinguistic setting as well as the language and translation policies of the government of New Brunswick. In the second part, I will provide information on the workplace and the methods used for collecting data. In the third and main part of the chapter, I will look at the editing of French translations by non-professionals. Using excerpts from interviews with civil servants who occasionally edit professional translations, as well as interviews with professional translators, I will try to better understand *why* civil servants feel the need to edit French translations that they deem—paradoxically—to be of excellent quality. I will also look at how my observations compare to those of Dubois, who conducted a larger-scale study of translation practices within the government of New Brunswick (Dubois 1999). I will conclude by outlining the reasons why non-professional revision and editing are worthy of investigation.

1. The sociolinguistic setting

New Brunswick is one of ten Canadian provinces and three territories. It is located on the Atlantic seaboard, to the east of the French-speaking province of Québec, and shares a border with the American state of Maine. It is the only province in Canada to have declared English and French as its official languages. The *Official Languages Act of New Brunswick* was enacted in 1969, the same year the federal *Official Languages Act* was adopted.

As of 2016, according to Statistics Canada, New Brunswick had a total population of 739,000 inhabitants, 64.8% of whom have English as mother tongue, while 31.5% have French. Members of these two linguistic groups are commonly referred to as "Anglophones" and "Francophones". Speakers of non-official languages represent less than 2.4% of the population. New Brunswick's French-speaking population is dispersed throughout the province, with major concentrations in the north and east. The rates of English-French bilingualism are quite asymmetrical, as is often the case in linguistic minority settings: while 68% of Francophones are bilingual, only 16% of Anglophones can claim the same.

In the Greater Moncton area, where the study was conducted, the proportion of Anglophones and Francophones is roughly the same as it is for the whole of New Brunswick; that is, two-thirds of the 2016 population of 144,000 have English as their mother tongue, while one-third have French. However, the rates of bilingualism are somewhat different: close to 88% of Francophones in Greater Moncton are bilingual while 24% of Anglophones have a knowledge of both official languages (Statistics Canada).

During the 1960s and 1970s, New Brunswick was the scene of conflict and dissension between the two main linguistic groups. After English and French were declared official languages in 1969, Francophones, who had lagged behind economically, made tremendous progress on many fronts: educationally, socially and economically. The gap between the dominant group and the minority has shrunk considerably, and the Francophone minority is now much stronger than it was in the 1960s and 1970s; it has its own institutions, most notably a French-language university. Since the 1980s and 1990s, the provincial government has been fostering harmonious relations between the two linguistic groups, and in an interesting reversal of fortunes, governments and businesses started capitalizing on what they referred to as the "bilingual capacity" of its population, notably its Francophones. Many prominent figures touted the added value and economic advantages offered by bilingualism, which quickly became a selling feature to multinational firms and businesses. This led to the creation of many customer call centres, which made use of the region's bilingual workforce. In other words, bilingualism had in some ways become a valued resource that was to be marketed and capitalized on. This brings us to our study of the New Brunswick public service.

When one examines New Brunswick's official Language Policy, most recently updated in 2015, it becomes clear that the provisions with respect to the language of work are not at all binding. This can be explained by the fact that, under the *Official Languages Act of New Brunswick*, "language of work" is not mentioned. The policy on language of work states:

> The Government of New Brunswick recognizes the often-superior con-
> tribution made by employees when they are able to work in their official
> language of choice.
>
> It is the policy of the Government of New Brunswick to promote the use
> of both official languages within the New Brunswick Public Service and to
> encourage and enable employees to work in their official language of choice.
> *(Province of New Brunswick 2015a)*

The fact that that this policy merely *encourages* members of both official lan-
guages to work in the language of their choice without actually giving them the *right* to do so sets it apart from the federal language policy, whereby federal civil servants have the right to work in English or French in designated regions of the country.

As an officially bilingual province, New Brunswick has defined obligations under the *Official Languages Act*. More specifically, the Language of Service Policy and Guidelines state that:

> The Government of New Brunswick recognizes its obligations under the
> *Official Languages Act*. Government is committed to actively offering and pro-
> viding quality services to the public in the public's official language of choice.
>
> It is the policy of the government of New Brunswick to actively offer and
> provide services of equal quality in both official languages.
>
> Members of the public or organizations who wish to communicate with
> any department, agency, Crown corporation or institution of the Provincial
> Government can do so in the official language of their choice and they can
> expect to be offered and receive the available service in the official language
> of their choice, wherever the government service is provided.
> *(Province of New Brunswick 2015b)*

In order to meet its obligations under the *Act*, the provincial government must make use of translation and interpretation services. The New Brunswick Transla-
tion Bureau assists the government in fulfilling its obligations to provide bilingual services as outlined in the *Act*. The Bureau provides services such as written translation (from English into French and from French into English), simultane-
ous interpretation for conferences, seminars and other gatherings, consecutive

interpretation for court proceedings and administrative tribunal hearings, and other linguistic services. Services are provided to the various government departments as well as to the Legislative Assembly.

Services provided by the Translation Bureau are governed by a policy (AD-1502 *Translation and Interpretation Services*). The objective of this policy is "to establish the principles for a working relationship between Departments and the Translation Bureau, in order that public expectations and legal requirements regarding the availability and quality of communication in the official languages are expediently met". More precisely, the policy states:

> The Translation Bureau will provide quality translation, interpretation and terminology services as required by government departments as well as for the Legislative Assembly and its committees.
>
> Whenever possible, Departments will use their own staff to deal with the public on a day-to-day basis in both official languages. Departments should develop the ability to handle routine matters such as correspondence, interviews with clientele and work of a short and minor nature in the official language preferred by the client. Where departmental staff do not have sufficient capability to handle such matters in either official language, the services of the Translation Bureau should be used.
>
> *(Province of New Brunswick 2013: 18)*

As the main provider of translation services, the Translation Bureau translates an average of 12 million words per year (Province of New Brunswick 2013: 20). The vast majority of translated texts—88%—are from English into French. This is another indication of the dominance of English as the language of work within the public service: "[t]he Commissioner believes that these percentages could indicate a disproportionate usage of the English language in the preparation of written materials in the provincial public service, which he finds worrisome" (Province of New Brunswick 2013: 20).

2. Work environment and methodology

The main objective of the study I conducted in the New Brunswick public service was to analyse the implementation of the recently modified language policy. I was seeking to better understand the underpinnings of the government's language policy and to compare the results with those of a previous study I had conducted in the federal public service more than ten years previously.

My particular interest was the language practices of government employees who work within the various government departments. What languages are used, by whom, when and in what instances? What is the language *of* work (language(s) used for drafting, during meetings, etc.) and what is the language *at* work (language(s) used informally among colleagues)? Is language choice the source of tension and/or conflict? Most importantly, what are the language ideologies that underpin language choices? And what role does the sociolin-guistic setting play?

For the purposes of my study, I chose to focus on the Moncton offices of a large government department. The department was chosen because it was located in a bilingual region of the province and it employed a fairly significant number of civil servants, 240 to be precise. Of these, 63 are Anglophones while 177 are Franco-phones. The proportion of Francophones (74%) is extremely high, given that they represent only a third of the Greater Moncton population. However, this can be easily explained: since many of the positions are designated as "bilingual" (meaning that they require a knowledge of both English and French), Francophones are more likely to be hired, given their higher rate of bilingualism. Most positions require at least a two-year college diploma or a four-year bachelor's degree. Furthermore, the work environment requires employees to make use of their language skills on a daily basis. These are professionals who are called upon to draft a variety of docu-ments, such as e-mails, letters, minutes, website/social media content and reports. They meet very frequently, are required to make presentations and must commu-nicate with civil servants within and outside the department, as well as with the department's "clients"[1] and the general public. In other words, language use is at the core of their work.

Semi-structured interviews

For the purpose of my study, I focused on three subsections of the Moncton office, as it was not possible to gain access to all the subsections. The department's work is very sensitive; it has a social mandate, and most of its clientele receive social assis-tance. Given the confidential nature of the work, I was not granted permission to take part in meetings or training sessions, or to shadow employees at work. I was, however, able to conduct 21 semi-structured interviews, which provided the bulk of the information gathered, and to carry out non-participant observation.

Of the 21 interviewees, 19 were Francophones. These 19 individuals were interviewed in French, the 2 Anglophones in English. I have translated into Eng-lish the excerpts from the French interviews cited in this chapter. The interviews lasted between 40 and 65 minutes, and all participants were required to sign an informed consent form.

Participants were recruited using various methods. The department's general manager was instrumental in helping me identify the subsections of the office and the employees that would best suit my needs. In a memo sent by the gen-eral manager to all employees, information was provided on the research and the researcher, and employees were invited to contact the researcher if they wished to be interviewed formally or to discuss the topic informally. I was also allowed to approach employees directly in their offices (face-to-face interactions) and to ask interviewees to recommend other participants.

Finally, the questions for the semi-structured interviews dealt with several mat-ters: the linguistic background of the civil servants, their language practices at home, the government's language policy and the languages used at work (for drafting, during meetings, while interacting with co-workers, etc.). Since the interviews were semi-structured, many other topics were broached, including translation, minority language rights and language varieties. The topic of translation came up in almost every interview.

3. Findings and analysis

Language choice in the workplace: English as the language of work internally

A preliminary analysis of the data reveals that both French and English are widely heard and spoken in this particular workplace. Over the last 20 years, the department's office in Moncton has expanded considerably, and so has the number of Francophone employees. Given the large number of Francophones in the subsections in question, it would be only logical to assume that French is used as a language of work, at least to some extent. But exactly what role does French play at work? When exactly is it used? To answer these questions, it is useful to examine the place of English in the three subsections observed.

First, English remains in large part the "language *of* work". The reasons cited by participants for the predominance of English are numerous and revolve mostly around efficiency, that is, the practical nature of working in one language, the presence of a certain number of Anglophones with limited or no knowledge of French, the fact that work is carried out with employees from outside the area, the minority group members' fluency in English and in some cases their higher comfort level in English when it comes to work-related tasks, the time-consuming and sometimes costly nature of translation, and the fact that English is, according to some, "the language of business" or even "the language of work".

For these reasons, English remains the main language for conducting meetings in this department. Some Francophones will occasionally use French, but for the most part discussions take place in English. In addition, very few Francophones use French for writing documents or e-mails. In informal conversations, Francophones will often switch to English if an Anglophone colleague joins the group. Conversations among Anglophones and Francophones usually take place in English, but there are, of course, exceptions. The Francophones admit that they have a strong and almost instinctual tendency to switch to English in those situations. Overall, the practices observed in the workplace among Anglophones and Francophones are no different from those observed in Moncton and other situations of diglossia. (See LeBlanc 2014 for the results of a similar study in the Canadian public service.)

French as a language of work with clients

Given the nature of the service provided by the department, many of its employees work closely with the public. This is the case with most of the department's social workers, who are called upon to work with a particular "clientele" (internal term used within the department). The social workers are the ones who are directly responsible for child welfare, child protection, children and youth under the care of the department as well as programs for young offenders and youth at risk and for public housing, to name a few.

The role of translation in the New Brunswick public service

The literacy skills of the department's clientele vary greatly, a reality social workers are used to in their daily contacts with their clients. While dealings with clients are sometimes limited to oral interaction, in most cases clients are handed written material, whether forms to be filled out, specific instructions related to benefits or programs, notices of changes to benefits or programs, questionnaires, general literature related to services or consent forms.

As the vast majority of written material is drafted in English, translation into French is the norm (Province of New Brunswick 2013). As explained previously, translations are done by trained professionals and revised by professional revisers[2] who work for New Brunswick's Translation Bureau. Translation services are centralized in one location in the province's capital city, which means that there are no on-site translators working directly within the various provincial departments. Translators are thus often far removed from their own clients—that is, the civil servants—and the end users of the translations. While translators are most often assigned to specific departments and are thus familiar with many of the terms used within those departments, they do work under very tight deadlines and must comply with specified productivity requirements. In their translation requests sent to the Translation Bureau, government departments very rarely, if ever, include specific guidelines with respect to the intended audience. In other words, translators are most often unaware of the end users' specific needs or literacy skills. While translators are trained to adapt texts to specific audiences and possess cultural competence, that is, knowledge of the locale, translation request forms provide no room for such details. As a result, translators sometimes have no idea of the *specific* audience for whom they are translating. This means that translations are produced in standard Canadian French as per the doctrine of "idiomatic translation" whereby the target text reproduces the structure of the target language and sounds natural while communicating the exact message of the source text. Idiomatic translation is more specifically a

> translation strategy that produces a target text that conforms to the conventions established in the target language and the spontaneous form of expression commonly used by native speakers. The concept of idiomatic translation, which is closely associated with conventions, rules and social context, takes into account the constraints of the target text and of current usage as well as the rules and conventions observed by the majority of speakers.
>
> *(Delisle et al. 1999: 144)*

This is consistent with what Mossop observed for the Canadian Public Service:

> [t]he federal government's approach has been inspired by the role of English-to-French translation. It has been pointed out (for example in Juhel 1982, p. 55ff) that English is overwhelmingly the translat*ed* language in Canada, and French the translat*ing* language. Translation in Canada is a form of communication that goes mainly in one direction only. Given that Quebeckers read so much translation as opposed to original French writing, it is argued that if the translations are not idiomatic, then the French language will cease to be an instrument of cultural identity and ultimately political survival.
>
> *(Mossop 1990: 347)*

The same arguments are made for Francophone minorities outside of Quebec. Since French is almost exclusively the translat*ing* language, translations are expected to be idiomatic.

Editing of French translations by non-professionals

As mentioned, the topic of translation into French came up naturally in almost every conversation with Francophone civil servants about their use of official languages at work. They regularly send documents to the Translation Bureau for translation, whether it be their own texts produced in English or those of their colleagues. When asked about the prevalent role played by translation and translators, they were unanimous in saying that translation services are of the utmost necessity given the province's obligation to provide all services to its citizens in both official languages. They pointed to the professional nature of the services provided by the Translation Bureau and the overall good quality of the translations produced by translators. References to "good French" and "proper" or "standard French" came up regularly in conversations. It was implied that translators, given their authoritative command of French, were linguistic models when it came to all language matters.

That being said, of the 19 Francophone civil servants interviewed, more than 10 admitted to editing the French translations produced by professional translators. The general consensus among these non-professional editors was that French translations, regardless of having been produced in perfectly "good" French (*bon français*) and thus deemed to be of the highest professional quality, were not always suited to the target audience. They referred to those instances where texts were destined for Francophone end users with limited knowledge of standard administrative French. As mentioned previously, many of the texts sent to translation by social workers are destined for recipients of social assistance whose literacy skills in French may vary greatly from one individual to another. The prevailing comments made by interviewees about the French translations in question revolved around the *stylistic and lexical choices* made by the translators.

This stance is typified in an excerpt from one interview (M: interviewer; C: civil servant):

M: And the translations into French?

C3: Well they're always perfect, really. Perfect in that they're done in proper French but . . .

M: But you . . .

C3: I sometimes, well it depends on the texts. Sometimes I have to edit, change some of the wording. Not that it's bad or anything.

M: What do you mean exactly by wording?

C3: Well, take this form right here, it's a good example.

M: Ok.

C3: If you read it, if I read it, it's fine, it's clear, there are no problems.

M: Absolutely.

C3: But most of my clients [end users of the translations] would not understand the wording of some of those sentences. It's just the way it is. First of all, it's too formal, for one. The English sounds right, but the French is too, I don't know, just too formal.

M: In that no one really writes like that, you mean?

C3: Yes. Maybe for something that's going to be sent internally, for us to read. But not for our clients on social assistance. Some of them have not even finished grade school, let alone high school.

M: Ok, I see where you're going.

C3: I'll show you. This sentence here. It's in a brochure for some of the services we offer. The English says "referrals for services". In French, they [the translators] wrote *les aiguillages vers des services*. Why not say something like *fournir de l'information sur les services* [provide information on services]?

M: That would be more clear, that's what you're saying?

C3: Yes, clearly. When I see things like that, I change them. I think it's my job to do that.

In this excerpt, it is clear that no judgement is being made on the translator's ability to translate into idiomatic administrative French. The fact that the interviewee states "They're always perfect" and the reference to "proper French" are a testament to this. That being said, the interviewee thinks that parts of the translation are not suitable for its intended audience and that it must be edited to better fulfil its function.

In another interview, the discussion focused on the use of the French word *abus* in French translations. While the interviewee knew that the preferred term in French for translating "abuse" was not always *abus*, she questioned the choices made by translators in this respect. In the case of "sexual abuse", for example, translators often use *agression sexuelle*, *violence sexuelle* or *atteinte sexuelle* in the French translations.

C13:   In those cases, cases like "abuse", you have to be so clear. You want people to understand. That's the first thing.

M: Of course.

C13:   I regularly change it to *abus*, for example in *abus sexuel*. My clients don't say *violence sexuelle à l'égard des enfants* [sexual violence against children]. They don't understand that.

M: Ok, because you . . .

C13:   Well, because *abus sexuel* is what everybody says, at least in Canada. Apparently someone somewhere must have decided that it's not quite right or that it sounds too close to English, I'm not sure.

M: Ok.

C13:   Strangely enough, it's [*abus sexuel*] in the dictionary, so I don't see what the real problem is. Even the government's database [*TERMIUM*] says it's ok, so . . .

M: Right, right.

C13:   But translators are afraid to use it I guess [laughter].

M: Maybe because they've been told not to use it or something?

C13:   No doubt. But that's sort of irrelevant, isn't it? When you want someone to understand the message, I don't know. This is an important matter, as you know.

M: Absolutely.

The question in this last excerpt is not to determine whether the use of *abus sexuel* in French is right or wrong. (To be clear, the use of *abus* and the expression *abus sexuel* have been criticized by language specialists, but their use is so widespread that they are now considered "correct" by several dictionaries and other resources.) The real question is to know why questions related to language norms—or correct usage—seem to take precedence over transparency and communication. The use of "irrelevant" by the interviewee can be interpreted as an indication of frustration. According to her, the logical thing would be for the translator to choose words or expressions that speak to the end users of the translation, regardless of their contested status among language experts.

In a third interview, a civil servant reflects on the conditions under which the translations are produced and the sometimes difficult position that translators find themselves in:

C7:   We sometimes complain about the [French] translations. I am guilty of that. [Laughter.] Yes, yes.

M: And what exactly is it about the translations? What is it that doesn't sit well with you?

C7:   It's just that sometimes, not always, they're not, how would you say, adapted to our clients, to their needs, to their way of speaking.

M: Ok, ok.

C7:   But then again, you can't really blame the translators.

M: No?

C7:   Well they're in a difficult position; they're in their offices 200 kilometres away. They translate I don't know how many things a day for all kinds of departments. They don't really know what exactly our clients need. And we don't really specify our needs, either. We just send things to translation and hope to get it back before the deadline.

M: So are you saying that translators are sort of in the dark, because of the way the whole thing is structured?

C7:   Yes.

M: So in some ways they're not close enough to the people working in the departments, you for example, so they're not aware of your specific needs?

C7:   Yes, that's the problem. Half the time they probably don't even know who they're translating for, so it's not their fault.

M: Ok, I see what you mean.

C7:   The government is a big bureaucracy. There is not always time to personalize things, if you know what I mean.

This last comment clearly speaks to the distance that separates the translators—in fact, all of the translational activity—from the civil servants in the departments and thus from the end users.

In a previous study carried out in three translation services and agencies in New Brunswick (see LeBlanc 2013), translators were unanimous in saying that increased automation and use of computer-assisted translation tools meant that they were now further removed from their departmental clients (civil servants) and the end users of the translations. What is more, many translators had reflected on their inability to take into account the specific needs of the end users given the increased productivity requirements over the previous 15 years and the streamlining of the translation process. In all three agencies and services, translators had very little contact, or none at all, with the clients requesting the translation. In that 2012 study, one translator-reviser commented on the fact that her translations were sometimes edited by the client:

M: So you are aware of that? That your client sometimes modifies your translations?

T21:   Yes, of course. I'm not saying that it happens a lot, but in specific cases it does. I kind of discovered it by accident. Once the client even sent us the modified text.

M: Very interesting. So how does that make you feel?

T21:   You mean that the client edits my translation?

M: Yes.

T21:   I'm not sure. I feel ambivalent about that. It's tricky for us, you know.

M: Ok.

T21:   Take for example a text that's for a specific type of reader, someone who is for example less educated or someone who doesn't understand technical terms or long, complex sentences [laughter].

M: Ok, ok.

T21: Well, the clients [civil servants] are not always in the wrong when they change some of the words we use or the wording of the text.

M: How so?

T21: Because there is usually no way for us to know who the reader is, except in really obvious cases, of course. The client, though, knows this. And if the end goal is to clearly communicate the message, well then, the client might be doing the right thing by editing our translations. By making them more, I don't know, appropriate.

M: For the reader.

T21: Yes. But what's tricky, as I was saying, is that if I as a professional translator were to use some of the wording or words used by the civil servant when he edits my translations, I'd be reprimanded by my reviser [laughter].

M: You would, you would.

T21: That's the paradox in some ways, isn't it? There's very little latitude, at least on our end [translators and revisers], when it comes to conventions. It's as if we always have to stick to what is safe, what is not contentious, you know, to what's prescribed by language authorities and what not. I can see why we do that, because translators are in some ways the guardians of French. But when you think of it, we don't always remember that our first goal is to communicate. We sometimes do a disservice to the reader by not adapting our translations.

M: Very interesting, very interesting.

T21: Yes it is.

This is, in essence, a situation wherein the needs of the end users of the translations are not being fully met and where the civil servants who commissioned the translations are required to edit some of the wordings. They reported this being the case with translations destined for a specific audience, namely beneficiaries of social assistance, for reasons they made very clear. The main concern for social workers is that the French texts are sometimes too formal or too standard in their wording or that the terms used are too technical or unknown to the end user.

This raises many questions regarding not only the process of translation *per se*, but also the ideological underpinnings of translation into French in the Canadian context. First, as the New Brunswick Translation Bureau is a centralized entity and its translators are far removed from the civil servants working in the departments as well as the end users, there is very little contact between the translators and their clients. There is also no practical way for these clients to make it known to translators during the translation process that end users have specific needs in terms of linguistic adaptation. Finally, the translators have a vested interest in not using terms that are objectionable or wordings that are considered stylistically unacceptable, even if these terms and wordings might speak more to the end user. In translation school, in translations services and agencies and for certification exams, translators are judged on their knowledge of standard French and are often times penalized if they deviate from the norm or established order. As one translator from my 2012 study pointed out, this would be a "risky endeavour", a subversive act in some regards.

Civil servants in the departments, however, are not under pressure to "perform" linguistically, to use the correct, sanctioned terms or wordings, and are thus in a safer position to adapt the translations to their intended audience without any consequences. They are the ones "ordering" the translations and are thus free to do what they want with them. If they modify the translations, then these translations become the "official" translations. They are also the ones who are the most aware of the end users' needs in the cases considered here.

Parallels with Dubois (1999)

This study has interesting parallels with Dubois's (1999) study of the New Brunswick Translation Bureau. Working directly with Francophone translators and Francophone civil servants in the New Brunswick civil service, Dubois looked into the tensions between members of the two groups. She observed that on the whole, translators shared similar attitudes with regard to translation strategies and language norms, notably with respect to French. Translators were unanimous in stating that official documents translated from English into French needed to be translated into standard French. They were convinced that the Translation Bureau played an important role in promoting the French language in New Brunswick and in upholding linguistic standards. According to them, translation played an important role in disseminating French in New Brunswick, and translations should therefore be of irreproachable quality. More specifically, in their view, translations into French should serve as linguistic models for Francophone New Brunswickers, especially since English is the dominant language within and outside the civil service. Translations should thus contain no grammatical or stylistic errors and show no trace of their English origin. Translators see themselves as playing a sociolinguistic role, one that directly contributes to the survival of French in New Brunswick.

Dubois further observed that Francophone civil servants were not always of the same opinion. While some did agree with the translators, others felt that translations into French did at times need some editing, and in fact they edited French translations in order to adapt them to internal usage within their respective departments. Changes were mostly lexical in nature and considered minor by these civil servants. However for some, the reasons given for editing translations were more complex. They were of the opinion that it was necessary for them to "lower the bar" and make French translations less complicated and thus more in tune with the linguistic realities of Francophone New Brunswickers. A few commented on the use of the French vernacular and insisted that Acadian French (the French spoken in the provinces east of Quebec) was different from Quebec French and Continental French. Hence the need for editing. These latter opinions, however, were not widespread.

What is different in my study is the realization that Francophone civil servants are editing French translations not so much because of the sociolinguistic differences between the varieties of French (Acadia, Quebec, France), but more because of the specific needs of the intended audience, most of whom have lower levels of formal education and literacy. Since education levels of end users come into play, questions of style and register are brought to the fore.

4. Concluding remarks: the link with non-professional interpreting and translation

While more and more research is being conducted in the emerging field of "non-professional interpreting and translation" (NPIT), the same cannot be said for the practice of editing by non-professionals. As Antonini et al. (2017) point out, there has been a significant increase in "the number of academic studies that have attempted to shed light on a variety of largely invisible, yet widespread, NPIT practices" (2017: 1). Just as it is worthwhile to look into the practice of NPIT, non-professional editing of professionally produced translation is also worth exploring. According to Pérez-González and Susam-Saraeva (2012),

> [t]ranslation studies finds itself today at a stage where its traditional focus on translator and interpreter training and on the advancement of the status of translators and interpreters as professionals is no longer sufficient to address the complexity of real-life situations of translating and interpreting. As increasing numbers of non-professionals translate and interpret in a wider range of contexts and in more diversified forms, their work emerges not only as an alternative to established professional practice, but also as a distinctive phenomenon, which the discipline has yet to recognize as a noteworthy area of study.
>
> *(2012: 149)*

The same can be said for "revision" or "editing". Most of the focus has been on the work of professional revisers, as is the case with translators and interpreters. But as my study shows—and as Dubois's study highlights—the practice of non-professional editing is most likely common as well, including within public institutions. It should for this reason be of interest to Translation Studies scholars.

The questions raised in the case study I presented here are numerous and serve to show that non-professional editing should not be considered as a marginal activity. Firstly, we have gained a better understanding of what compels civil servants to edit translations produced by professional translators. This sheds light on the process of translation itself and shows that, in this specific instance, professional translators are not informed or aware of the specific requirements of the intended audience of the texts they are called upon to translate, to the point that we are left to wonder if the process of translation—from commission through production to delivery—is so decentralized that translators and commissioners no longer communicate directly with one another. Does the fact that translators are more than ever translating *parts* of texts, sometimes even stand-alone *sentences*, have an effect on the end product (LeBlanc 2013)?

Secondly, this situation causes us to reflect on the professional norms to which translators adhere, and on the expectations around translation in Canadian public institutions. As Francophone translators are evaluated on their adherence to strict linguistic norms and constrained by very specific conventions, they are compelled to not deviate, even slightly, from established practices for fear of negative performance evaluations, even when deviation means simplifying translations in order to better reach the intended audience. As translators resist—for obvious reasons—using terms or expressions condemned by language authorities in their translations, it is the commissioners of the translations—that is, the civil servants—who end up editing the final product. That is why it is important to explore in greater depth the language ideologies held by professional translators and editors in the Canadian context.

Ultimately, it may be worth exploring the question of what, precisely, we can learn from the practice of non-professional editing in these specific circumstances. It certainly raises the question of translation/language expertise and professionalism. As Neather (2012) has suggested in his study of translation in the Hong Kong/Macau/Guangzhou museum community, this could be a setting "in which no one community [professional translators or non-translation experts in my case] possesses the complete set of competences required to produce a fully competent piece of translation" (Neather 2012: 266). Neather showed that "providers in the translation community may be stronger in the [target language], but weaker in regard to the more technically-oriented and genre-specific aspects of the discursive competence in the target language" (2012: 266). There are interesting parallels to be made with regard to the knowledge possessed by civil servants, that is, by non-professional translators who seem to possess a better "technical discursive" competence because they are more in tune with the communicative needs of the target audience. They may also be "more prepared to 'innovate', play around with the material in hand, retell it in a way that is likely to be more . . . intelligible for the audience" (Pérez-González and Susam-Saraeva 2012: 158).

This state of affairs could serve to highlight the need for translators to work more closely with the commissioners of the translation, although there are challenges in light of the centralization of translation activities and the increased automation of processes. That is why

> [t]ranslation and interpreting studies would do well to learn from the interlingual activities of non-professionals, instead of trying to control these activities, or focus exclusively on the quality of output and/or perceived loss of status by translators and interpreters vis-à-vis non-professionals translating and interpreting. Otherwise, translation scholars will lose valuable opportunities for enhancing their scholarly knowledge, and translators and interpreters will miss valuable opportunities for professional growth.
>
> *(Pérez-González and Susam-Saraeva 2012: 158)*

The same can be said for the editing of professional translations by non-professionals. What can we, as researchers in the field of translation and revision, learn from the work performed by non-professionals? And what of the professional norms to which translators and revisers adhere and the conventional ways of translating in certain contexts? While these are only a few of the questions raised by this case study, they are a testament to the importance of the study of non-professional revision and editing, and proof that they are worthy of investigation.

Notes

1 The word *client* is used in this chapter in two ways. First, *client* is used by civil servants to refer to the actual individuals they serve, in this case the beneficiaries of social assistance. Second, translators and the government translation service use the word *client* to refer to either the civil servants who commission the translations or the government departments. To avoid confusion, whenever possible I will use *civil servants* to refer to those who commission translation services and *end users* to refer to the individuals to whom the translations are destined, that is, the actual readers of the translations.

2 In this context, a "professional reviser" is a trained professional whose primary responsibility is to revise translations produced by professional translators. Professional revisers are in most cases experienced translators who, later in their career, are promoted to the rank of reviser (or sometimes senior translator/reviser).

5

WHEN THE POST-EDITOR IS NOT A TRANSLATOR

Can machine translation be post-edited by academics to prepare their publications in English?

Carla Parra Escartín and Marie-Josée Goulet

Nowadays, any individual with Internet access can avail themselves of one of the multiple machine-translation (MT) services available online either for free (e.g. Google Translate, Bing Translator, DeepL, Reverso)[1] or for a fee (e.g. Lilt, DeepL Pro)[2]. In fact, MT is currently used for personal and professional purposes by a myriad of users, from professional translators to individuals that resort to it as an aid in drafting documents in languages that they do not master or as a means of communication, be it to interact with others or to understand texts written in a foreign language.

Despite the increasing popularity and quality of MT, it is a well-known fact that MT output still requires post-editing. In this chapter, we focus on a specific type of MT user, namely non-native speakers of English who wish to publish their research in English but draft their research papers in their first language (L1). Given that English is the undisputed *lingua franca* in academia (Bennett 2013, 2014a, 2015) but that there seems to be a stronger ability to think by writing in the first language (Breuer 2015), we carried out an experiment aimed at determining whether Spanish-speaking physicians would be able to publish their research in English by first drafting a paper in their L1 (Spanish), and then post-editing a machine-translated version of that paper in their L2 (English). We term this process self-post-editing, as the authors themselves are the ones doing the post-editing of their own texts.

The experiment was designed as a follow-up of a similar one that was carried out in an exploratory phase of our project and was reported elsewhere (O'Brien et al. 2018; Goulet et al. 2017). Here, we focus on the different types of edits performed by five Spanish physicians when carrying out self-post-editing tasks, and we compare them with the subsequent edits made by a professional proofreader who was hired to proofread the self-post-edited texts and had no access to the original Spanish documents. The comparison is made in an attempt to determine the types of edits that non-native speakers of English are able to identify and the types they cannot identify.

We first look at the research related to our work that inspired our experiments (section 1), and at the main motivation for the analysis presented in this chapter (section 2). In section 3, we summarise our research methodology and experimental set-up. Section 4 discusses the results of the experiment, while section 5 summarises our work and hints at new avenues of research for future work.

1.   Related research

English is undoubtedly the dominant language of scholarly publications (Flowerdew 2001; Graham et al. 2011; Bennett 2013, 2014a, 2014b, 2015; Breuer 2015). According to Bennett (2013, 2014a, 2014b), non-native-English speakers are discriminated against by editors and referees of international journals. Flowerdew (2001) suggests that this disadvantage goes against natural justice and is likely to impoverish the creation of knowledge. For an author, the decision to publish an article in English as a Foreign Language (EFL) rather than in their L1 might be influenced by various factors, such as the desire to disseminate their results internationally (Burgess et al. 2014; Martín et al. 2014) or to be recognised by their peers (López-Navarro et al. 2015). For example, in a survey of 1,717 Spanish researchers across different fields, a strong association was found between publication in English and the desire to be recognised and rewarded (López-Navarro et al. 2015). The researcher's discipline would also be a determining factor in this decision (Fernández Polo and Cal Varela 2009; Burgess et al. 2014). For example, a study conducted in 2009 at the University of Santiago de Compostela showed that researchers from the experimental and health sciences were more likely to publish in EFL than researchers from the humanities and social sciences (Fernández Polo and Cal Varela 2009).

Scientific writing in EFL is challenging. Hanauer and Englander (2011) addressed this issue by attempting to quantify the "burden" of writing in EFL. They showed that writing in EFL was associated with greater anxiety and less satisfaction once the article was completed, compared to writing in L1. Studies of second language writing among university students are also relevant. For example, Van Waes and Leijten (2015) found that students were less productive when writing in a second language (English, German, Spanish or French) compared to their mother tongue (Dutch). For her part, Breuer (2015) reported that the freewriting technique had a less exhilarating effect in the second language (English) than in the mother tongue (German), which could indicate a weaker ability to think when writing in a second language, compared to writing in the mother tongue.

Non-native speakers who want to publish in English sometimes have to resort to the services of professional revisers or translators to make their articles suitable for publication in international journals. In a survey for one medical journal, Benfield and Feak (2006) showed that the acceptance rate was the same for authors who were not native speakers of English, but that many more revisions were required for the articles submitted by these contributors. However, professional revisers or translators may not possess adequate domain knowledge and may have to enter into discussion with the author in order to clarify certain issues (Willey and Tanimoto 2015). Resorting to literacy brokers, then, costs time and money. Considering these previous studies, it is clear that the use of MT could provide some advantages in the context of scientific writing in EFL.

We carried out an exploratory study on this subject, engaging nine participants from different scientific disciplines and with different L1s. The experiment consisted of drafting abstracts both in the L1 (+MT) and directly in English. The initial findings, described in O'Brien et al. (2018), showed that the differences in terms of quality were not significant. Nor were there significant differences in the median times needed for drafting the abstract in L1 (+MT and self-post-editing) vs. in EFL. This initial data was further analysed in Goulet et al. (2017), where we compared the edits implemented by the proofreader under each condition (self-post-editing or EFL writing). Our findings suggested that there were no substantial differences in the number of edits performed (5% and 6% of the total number of words in EFL and MT respectively). This more in-depth analysis allowed us to hypothesise that MT does not have a negative impact on the quality of the texts.

2. Motivation

The results of our preliminary study encouraged us to do a follow-up study focusing on the self-post-editing process, one specific field, and a single language pair. This would allow us to carry out a more in-depth analysis of the suitability of MT as an academic writing aid. Bearing in mind that the quality of MT systems between Spanish and English is relatively high and that Spanish L1 writers usually struggle to write in English, we chose to focus on this language pair. The domain of medicine was chosen due to anecdotal evidence that Spanish physicians seek to publish in English, which was confirmed by the study carried out by Fernández Polo and Cal Varela (2009).

The work reported in this chapter builds on the work done in Parra Escartín et al. (2017), where we report on an initial analysis of the edits performed by the participants and the proofreader, focusing on whether the edits were of an essential or preferential nature, but not entering into further linguistic analysis. *Essential edits* are those that are required in order to ensure that the sentence (or part of it) is grammatically correct and/or accurate in comparison to the source text (c.f. Parra Escartín et al. 2017). *Preferential edits* are those that are performed but the unedited machine-translated sentence would still be grammatically correct, intelligible and accurate, in relation to the source text, even if the edit was not implemented (c.f. Parra Escartín et al. 2017).

Our aim was simply to determine whether the physician-participants would be in a position to submit research papers for publication using a general machine-translation engine followed by post-editing. Our analysis revealed that both the physicians and the proofreader performed essential as well as preferential edits. The fact that essential edits were also performed by the proofreader indicates that the physicians would still benefit from hiring a linguistic broker before submitting their texts for publication. In other words, the level of quality achieved during the post-editing task by the authors alone would not have been sufficient for publishing their papers in English. Similar findings were observed by Temizöz (2016), who compared professional translators to subject-matter experts performing post-editing tasks and found out that the professional translators made fewer errors.

We also noticed that the proofreader seemed to have taken the role of an editor, not only proofreading the text but also making more preferential edits than essential edits (9.02% vs. 7.75%). Mellinger and Shreve (2016) and Bundgaard (2017a) observed a similar phenomenon in professional translation workflows, suggesting that despite the small number of participants in our study, the results seem to be in line with what happens in the translation industry.

To gain further insights into the type of MT errors the physicians were able to identify, we decided to carry out a more detailed analysis of all the edits. In doing so, we also expected to be able to identify the type of edits that an automated post-processing system should be capable of identifying and correcting. The main research questions we seek to answer in this chapter are:

1   *Without any training in MT or post-editing, what types of errors are non-native speakers capable of identifying in a machine-translated text?*
     This question seeks to identify the types of linguistic units (e.g. nouns, verbs, phrases, and so on) and dimensions (e.g. semantics, syntax, style) involved in the edits made by the physicians.
2   *What types of edits are still required after post-editing to yield a grammatically correct document?*
     This question seeks to identify the types of linguistic units and dimensions affected by the edits performed by the professional proofreader we subsequently hired.

3.   Methodology and experimental set-up

Several research tools and tasks were combined to carry out our experiments: questionnaires (pre- and post-task), writing and post-editing, proofreading, and annotation of the edits made under each condition (self-post-editing and professional proofreading).

Participant recruitment and profiles

Before our experiments, we conducted a general survey to determine whether Spanish-speaking physicians already use MT as a personal writing support. The link to our questionnaire was sent to various medical associations and unions, faculties of medicine in Spanish universities and other research institutes in Spain. In Parra Escartín et al. (2017), we offer a summary of the 50 responses collected. Despite the limited response rate, the responses confirmed that in order to write articles in English, some Spanish physicians do feel the need to rely on additional supports (other colleagues with a better level of English, native speakers, professional translators and proofreaders), provided they have access to them and/or the budget to pay for professional services. The questionnaire also confirmed that, in some cases, MT is already being used as a writing aid, although its usage is limited to short passages of text or individual words, rather than full documents.

At the very end of the questionnaire, respondents were invited to participate in an experiment using MT as a writing aid. Although initially 31 respondents showed interest in our experiment, only 5 (3 men and 2 women) were available for the experiment and completed it. Our participants belong to different medical specialties: neurosurgery (1), internal medicine (1), gynaecology (2) and immunology (1). Four of them were between 20 and 30 years old and were engaged in their residencies (that is, they are at an early stage of their careers). The fifth participant works as a researcher in a university or research centre and is between 30 and 40 years of age. They are all native speakers of Spanish (a requirement to participate), and besides English speak other languages (Catalan, French, German, Italian and/ or Portuguese). We asked them to report their self-perceived level of English and subsequently to take an online English test at the Cambridge English website[3] and report back to us the grade obtained. As can be observed in Table 5.1, except for one of them (P03), the participants' test result was the same or better than their self-perception of English level. All of them had at least a B1 level of English, which means they can produce simple connected text on topics which are familiar or of personal interest, among other abilities (CEFR 2019).

Not surprisingly, the participant who works in a university or research institution (P05) had the most experience publishing research papers. In fact, P05 reported publishing 15 papers, 5 of which had been written in English. The other participants (except P01, who had not published any papers previously) had published papers, although not as many as P05. P03 reported publishing a paper in English. When asked about their strategies for writing texts in English, all of them reported the same one: they write in EFL and then carry out a self-revision. P02 was the only one who reported having used Google Translate as a support tool, but just to confirm the translation of individual words or sentences.

TABLE 5.1 Participants' level of English

Participant	Self-assessment (CEFR, writing)	English level test
P01	B2	C1–C2
P02	B1	B1
P03	C1	B2
P04	B2	B2–C1
P05	B1	B1–B2

Experimental set-up

Our experiment consisted of three distinct phases: (1) publication drafting in Spanish, (2) MT and self-post-editing, and (3) professional proofreading.

After they had completed the pre-task questionnaire and the English placement test, we asked the five participants to provide us with drafts of a future publication in Spanish. Where a full text was not possible, we asked them to provide us with a section of a publication of at least 750 words, preferably the discussion section or a section similar to it. All participants complied, with some sharing a draft version of their papers (P01, P03). Our reasoning for choosing the discussion section was that it is usually more discursive than other sections (Skelton and Edwards 2000), and we therefore thought it could be one of the most challenging sections to write for EFL writers, and a good test set for our experiment. The only instruction we gave the participants was to try to avoid writing sentences longer than 20 words (or approximately 1.5 lines in Microsoft Word), whenever possible.

Bearing in mind that our participants are not experts in MT, and with the aim of mimicking a real scenario where they resort to the tools they know, we chose to use Google Translate.[4] We sent the English translations to the physicians and asked them to post-edit the translations as well as they could using the Track Changes functionality of Microsoft Word. As the experiment was carried out remotely, the Track Changes functionality was used as a way of allowing us to study their edits without requiring them to install any software and figure out how to send us the additional files with the meta information. No training in post-editing was done: our participants were asked to correct the English text they had received without any further intervention on our side. Once they had sent us the post-edited files, we asked them to fill in a post-task questionnaire about their experience.

We then hired a professional medical translator as a proofreader, to edit the texts and correct any remaining mistakes. The proofreader was provided only with the English texts post-edited by our participants, with all the changes introduced by them confirmed. We did not explain to her the origin of the texts, and she did not have access to the original Spanish. As our goal was to measure the extent to which extent physicians with a limited knowledge of English are capable of correcting MT output, we also instructed her to focus on the surface level and avoid over-editing. These were our instructions:

> The texts are written in English and we are looking for a surface revision, that is, pay attention to grammar, orthography, punctuation, syntax, and major stylistic problems. We would like the texts to read well enough to be submitted to a scientific conference, for example. The texts belong to the medical domain and are all parts of scientific papers written by doctors.

As with our participants, we asked the proofreader to use the Track Changes functionality in MS Word to allow us to analyse her edits. Table 5.2 illustrates how the original text written in Spanish underwent modifications at each stage of the experiment prior to annotation.

TABLE 5.2 Sample sentence written by P05 and all transformations undergone during the experiment

Step 1: Drafting in L1 (Spanish)	El factor subyacente que parecía explicar dicha asociación era el impacto del tabaco como factor independiente tanto en la ulcerogénesis como en el desarrollo de EPOC.
Step 2: Machine Translation (English)	The underlying factor that seemed to explain this association was the impact of smoking as an independent factor in both ulcerogenesis and COPD development.
Step 3: Self-Post-Editing (English) with access to the original source text in Spanish	The underlying ~~factor~~ *element/aspect* that seemed to explain this association was the impact of smoking as an independent factor in both ulcerogenesis and COPD development.
Step 4: Monolingual proofreading (English)	The underlying element/~~aspect~~ that seemed to explain this association was the impact of smoking as an independent factor in both ulcerogenesis and *the development of* COPD ~~development~~.

Edit annotation

As previously mentioned, we first did a round of annotation focusing only on whether the edits made by the physicians and the proofreader were essential or preferential (Parra Escartín et al. 2017). In order to answer our new research questions (see section 2), we required a more fine-grained taxonomy that would allow us to determine the type of edits performed and the type of linguistic units affected. Before going forward with the annotations, we revisited the edit and error typologies developed for different purposes that might be applicable for our study. Among the ones we considered, there were typologies for the annotation of errors made by second language learners (Breuer 2015; Niño 2008), as well as for the annotation of human- or machine-translation errors (Costa et al. 2015; Yamada 2015; Mitchell et al. 2014; Daems et al. 2013; de Almeida 2013; Bojar 2011; Temnikova 2010; Mossop 2007b; Vilar et al. 2006; Llitjós et al. 2005). We finally decided to use Laflamme (2009), as we had done in our preliminary study involving participants with different mother tongues and from different disciplines (O'Brien et al. 2018; Goulet et al. 2017), because it was the only typology that would allow us to annotate the types of edits made in both contexts: the text post-edited by the physicians and the text proofread by the proofreader.

The typology proposed by Laflamme (2009) had proven to be useful in a similar experiment, and it would also allow comparisons across experiments. To ensure annotation quality, we created a decision tree (see the Appendix at the end of this chapter). Forty edits were annotated by the two authors of this chapter to verify the annotation quality. We observed that the main sources of discrepancies came from the linguistic dimension, namely in the different "style" categories and in cases where it was not clear if the edit was of a more semantic nature. Moreover, we also flagged most of the cases of disagreement as "to be discussed" in a post-annotation meeting to reach an agreement, or else we kept the original annotation by the author who subsequently annotated the rest of the data. The verification proved that the decision tree was effective, and thus that a single annotation with discussion of potential doubts was possible. One of the authors then annotated all 1126 edits (307 made by the participants and 819 made by the proofreader) and consulted the other author for 31 difficult cases (2.7% of all annotated edits).[5]

Laflamme's typology (Laflamme 2009) allowed us to annotate the modifications according to three aspects: the type of operation, the type of unit and the linguistic dimension (see Figure 5.1). However, we had to make some minor changes to this typology. First, since it focuses only on lexical changes, that is, those that affect words, we added the "punctuation" dimension, which includes punctuation marks, and also an "unknown dimension" category to account for all those cases where the linguistic dimension is not clear. We also decided to distinguish between stylistic changes due to a preferential choice and those required to elevate the register of a text. In addition, when an edit affected more than one word, we considered the sequence of words as a unit, rather than annotating each word. We used the category "phrase" for these word sequences and additionally included clauses and full sentences as an option. The final typology is presented in Figure 5.1, and some examples of annotated phrases follow.

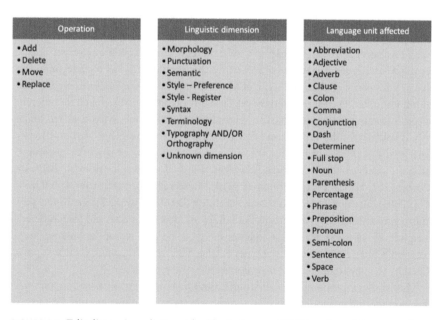

Operation	Linguistic dimension	Language unit affected
• Add	• Morphology	• Abbreviation
• Delete	• Punctuation	• Adjective
• Move	• Semantic	• Adverb
• Replace	• Style – Preference	• Clause
	• Style - Register	• Colon
	• Syntax	• Comma
	• Terminology	• Conjunction
	• Typography AND/OR Orthography	• Dash
	• Unknown dimension	• Determiner
		• Full stop
		• Noun
		• Parenthesis
		• Percentage
		• Phrase
		• Preposition
		• Pronoun
		• Semi-colon
		• Sentence
		• Space
		• Verb

FIGURE 5.1 Edit dimensions distinguished by Laflamme (2009) and possible annotations in our data

- "Obstruction at the level of *the* Magendie foramen is a rare cause of obstructive hydrocephalus . . ." (P01, self-PE text)

  Add—Syntax—Determiner

- "We present a case ~~report~~ *history* of a 15-year-old woman surgically treated the previous year . . ." (P01, proofread text)

  Replace—Terminology—Noun

- "Some of the complications ~~were~~ developed simultaneously in the same patient." (P05, proofread text)

  Delete—Syntax—Verb

4. Data analysis

Once all data had been annotated as explained in Section 3, we compared the results across participants. Although we asked our participants to send us a text of at least 750 words, the overall word count per participant varied, ranging from the 686 words provided by P05 to the 1413 words provided by P01. Additionally, as shown in Table 5.3, the number of words differed after each phase of our experiment.

General edit statistics

In order to allow for comparisons, we estimated the overall edit rate per participant as well as the proofreader's rate. Overall, our participants performed fewer edits than the proofreader (307 against 819 in total). As shown in Figure 5.2, P03 and

TABLE 5.3 Word counts by experimental condition

Participant	P01	P02	P03	P04	P05
Number of words in Spanish text	1413	759	1058	908	686
Number of words MT (EN)	1340	685	959	865	639
Number of words MT+Self-PE (EN)	1364	677	945	857	646
Number of words MT+Self-PE+PROOF (EN)	1389	685	934	859	611

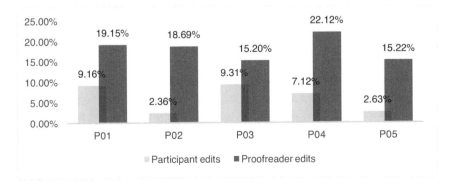

FIGURE 5.2 Edit rates of proofreader vs. participants

P01 were the participants with the highest edit rates, followed by P04. Participants P02 and P05, for their part, performed very few edits in the self-post-editing stage.[6] A potential explanation is that the English level of P02 and P05 was lower than that of P01, P03 and P04. However, given the small number of participants, we can only hypothesise that the English level has a certain impact on their ability to post-edit a machine-translated text. This hypothesis is partially confirmed by P02's comment on the post-task questionnaire that the MT output was better than her own level of English.

If we now compare the participants' edit rates with the proofreader's, the edit rate increases for all participants: the proofreader's interventions range from 15.20% (P03 and P05) to 22.12% (P04). It also seems that a higher English level does not necessarily imply a better ability to post-edit, as the two participants with the highest level of English (P01 and P04) are also the ones with the highest edit rate by the proofreader, followed closely by P02, who was one of the participants with the lowest level of English. As mentioned, however, a previous analysis of the edits revealed that the proofreader had also introduced a significant number of stylistic edits, despite having been instructed not to: between 6.26% and 11.09% of the edits performed by the proofreader were of a stylistic nature (Parra Escartín et al. 2017). This will be further discussed when we present the detailed analysis of the edits.

Let us recall that the overall objective of our annotations was to answer our two research questions: (1) *Without any training in MT or post-editing, what types of errors are non-native speakers capable of identifying in a machine-translated text?* and (2) *What types of edits are still required after post-editing to yield a grammatically correct document?* To this end, we will now describe the types of edits made by all participants and compare them to the edits made by the proofreader. Where necessary, we will differentiate between participants.

During the annotation process, we discovered that some edits were not of a linguistic nature. The participants tended to go beyond the post-editing task and add additional content directly in English, content that had not been included in the Spanish text (16% of the edits). In fact, P01, the participant who added the most content, inserted a completely new paragraph. The proofreader also added content occasionally (3% of the edits), although in her case it was usually to explain a technique or procedure better because it was not clear enough from the English text she had been given. The benefits of engaging a proofreader specialised in the medical field were also apparent, as she added justifying comments in this regard when she felt that new content had to be added.

One of the challenges of annotating the edits was that some edits were obviously linked to others, but it was not possible to determine which edit had provoked the other. In those cases, we annotated only one edit, as we had done on previous occasions. To account for these cases, we included a specific question in our decision tree (see the Appendix). The following example from one of the proofread texts illustrates this. As shown in bold, a number of elements in the sentence were replaced by others and strike-through is used to indicate that the words were deleted.

A. Hence, as a future objective, ~~it~~ would *therefore* be ~~necessary~~ to ~~carry out~~ *conduct* well-designed studies, with ~~a~~ larger sample size~~s~~ and with greater uniformity.

(P05, proofread text)

Overall, 7% of the edits made by the participants were prompted by or linked to other edits, as compared to 17% in the proofread version of the texts.

During our annotation work, we learned that the linguistic elements undergoing an edit vary from a single element (for instance, a noun or determiner) to groups of elements (a phrase or even a sentence). To account for this, we again included a question in our decision tree. Figure 5.3 shows that 59% of the edits made by the participants dealt with an individual element. In the case of the proofreader, the figure was as high as 71%. This seems to indicate that our participants tended to edit chunks of text, whereas the proofreader tried to reuse the existing text as much as possible and hence focused on individual words. Finally, we also encountered some cases in which there was an edit, but its cause could have been explained only if we had engaged in a retrospective interview with the participants or the proofreader. Due to the experimental set-up, this was not possible, and we therefore categorised the edits in a way that would identify the percentage of edits requiring further information from the participants. These cases were annotated as "unknown non-linguistic reason". This happened more often in the self-post-editing condition (15% of all edits) than in the case of the proofreader (1%), which is not surprising considering that the original writer of the text might be prompted to change the content when carrying out the self-post-editing task. Figure 5.3 summarises the general statistics.

Edit distribution

As explained earlier, the edit typology proposed by Laflamme (2009) distinguishes three main aspects: (1) the type of operation, (2) the type of linguistic unit affected and (3) the linguistic dimension affected by the edit. The types of operation carried

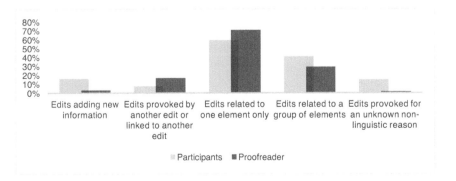

FIGURE 5.3 General edit statistics

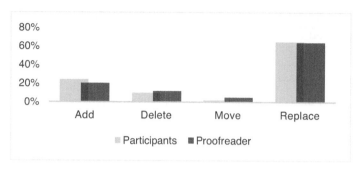

FIGURE 5.4 Edit distribution by type of operation (participants vs. proofreader)

out by our participants and by the proofreader were very similar. As shown in Figure 5.4, replacements account in both cases for approximately 64% of the edits. Next come addition (24% for the participants and 20% for the proofreader) and deletion (10% and 12% respectively), while movement is by far the least used operation (2% and 5% respectively).

These results are in line with those obtained in another study with different participants, although in that case we analysed only the edits made by the proofreader. In Goulet et al. (2017), the distribution was 56% for replacements, 23% for additions, 13% for deletions and 7% for movements. Taking into account that the previous study involved nine participants from different disciplines and language pairs, we can conclude that there seems to be a tendency to have twice as many replacements as additions.

If we now take a closer look at the individual results, the relative frequency of additions and deletions was the same in all cases except the proofread text of P03, where there were more deletions (25%) than additions (18%) (see Figure 5.6). This could indicate that, although there seems to be a general trend, differences may be observed depending on the text being proofread. It is not possible to determine at this stage whether this difference observed for P03 in the second most frequent type of operation is correlated with the participant's level of English. P03 had a B2 level of English, which could be considered similar to the level of P04 (B2–C1) and P05 (B1–B2), who both followed the general tendency of the group. Furthermore, the distribution varies slightly across participants (see Figure 5.5), while it seems to be more consistent in the case of the proofreader (see Figure 5.6).

Figure 5.7 shows the distribution of the overall number of edits by linguistic unit. Unsurprisingly, the largest number of edits involves a phrase (37% in the case of the participant edits, and 28% in the case of the proofreader edits). Next by order of frequency are nouns (10% and 19% respectively), verbs (9.4% and 8.9%), determiners (11% and 7%), adjectives (5.5% and 4.5%) and prepositions (4% and 6%). These results differ from the ones in our first study, where these same linguistic units were the ones most often affected, although their relative frequencies differed. In Goulet

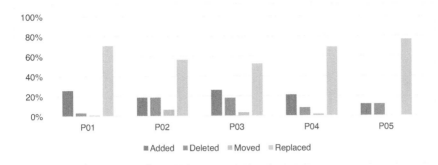

FIGURE 5.5 Participants' edit distribution by type of operation

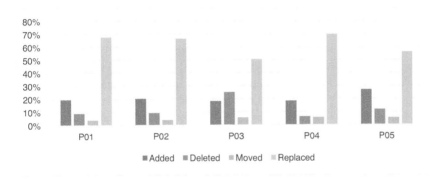

FIGURE 5.6 Proofreader's edit distribution by type of operation

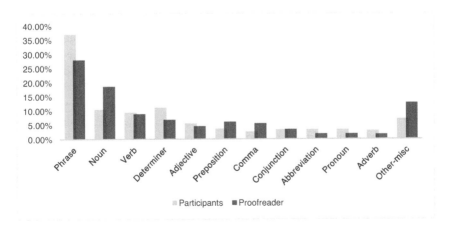

FIGURE 5.7 Edit distribution by type of linguistic unit (participants vs. proofreader)

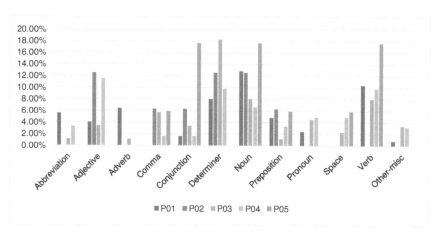

FIGURE 5.8 Edit rates by type of linguistic unit per participant

et al. (2017), nouns were the largest group undergoing edits (27%), followed by determiners (16%), phrases (13%), prepositions (13%) and verbs (11%).

If we look more closely at the individual participants (see Figure 5.8), it is surprising to see that P05 had an equal edit rate (17.6%) for conjunctions, nouns and verbs, followed by an equal edit rate (5.9%) for commas, prepositions and spaces. P02 focused on adjectives, determiners and nouns (12.5% of the edits in each case), followed by commas, conjunctions and prepositions (6.3%). The remainder of the participants had a more balanced rate of edits across linguistic units. P01 focused primarily on nouns (12.8%), followed by verbs (10.4%), determiners (8%), adverbs (6.4%) and abbreviations (5.6%). P03, on the other hand, focused on determiners (18.2%), nouns (8%), verbs (8%), commas (5.7%) and pronouns (4.5%). Finally, P04 focused on adjectives (11.5%), determiners (9.8%), verbs (9.8%), nouns (6.6%) and pronouns (4.9%). While the largest number of edits were performed on nouns, followed by determiners, verbs, adjectives and prepositions, the only frequently edited unit across all participants was nouns. Four of the five participants also had high numbers of edits for determiners (P01, P02, P03 and P04) and verbs (P01, P03, P04 and P05), while adjectives were ranked high only for P02 and P04. Prepositions were also highly ranked for only two participants (P02 and P05), who, interestingly, were the two with the lowest English proficiency. This seems to indicate that individual participants focus on different language units and with an uneven distribution. In order to be able to confirm whether a correlation exists between the linguistic units affected and the English proficiency level, further data would need to be gathered.

Let us now look at the linguistic dimensions affected by the annotated edits. As seen in Figure 5.9, the linguistic dimension most affected by the participants' edits is clearly stylistic changes, although the edit rate for stylistic edits introduced by the proofreader is significantly higher (34% as opposed to the 21% for the participants).

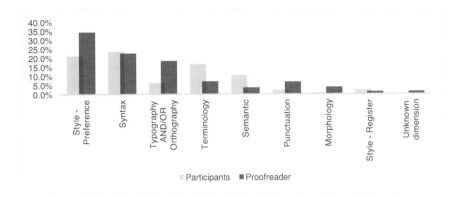

FIGURE 5.9 Edit distribution by affected linguistic dimension (participants vs. proofreader)

In second place comes the edit rate for the syntactic dimension: 23.5% for the participants and 22.6% for the proofreader. The third largest group varies. In the case of the physicians, 16.6% of edits are related to terminology, while only 7.1% of the proofreader edits belong to this category. We hypothesise that this could be due to the fact that the physicians, being as they are specialists in their field, know the terminology of their field in English and hence were able to correct the MT output in that regard, while failing to correct other MT issues that were more related to their overall English competence (e.g. fluency issues). In the case of the proofreader, the third most common type of edit was related to typographic and ortho-typographic errors, which seems to indicate that a proper use of tools such as the grammar and spellchecker available in Microsoft Word could have reduced the need for those edits. Finally, 10.4% of the edits performed by the physicians were semantic edits (10.4%), whereas only 3.5% of the proofreader edits were semantic edits. This could again be due to the fact that the physicians are specialists in their fields and decided, upon reading the English machine-translated text, that a semantic change was required to properly express what they wanted to say. Temizöz (2016) reports similar results, although her dataset was also rather reduced (a 482-word document machine-translated from English into Turkish and post-edited by 10 subject-matter experts and 10 professional translators). Her subject-matter experts performed best when correcting terminology and performed like professional translators when fixing mistranslations and accuracy and consistency issues. In her study, professional translators performed better than subject-matter experts only in the language fluency category.

5. Conclusion and future work

In this chapter, we have analysed the post-edits performed by five Spanish physicians who engaged in an experiment aimed at determining whether they would be able to use machine translation effectively as a writing aid. To evaluate the quality of their post-editing, we hired a professional proofreader specialised in the medical field and annotated the edits she introduced to correct the English texts post-edited by the physicians. Our results suggest that, without any training in MT or post-editing, Spanish physicians were able to identify a certain quantity of MT errors. More precisely, they were able to correct issues related to syntax and terminology, and additionally they performed a significant number of stylistic edits. We also found that, when carrying out the post-editing task, they also made semantic changes and even added new content to the text. This outcome could be due to the self-post-editing scenario used in our experiment. It seems that the authors not only engaged at a linguistic level with the text, but also aimed at polishing the text they would afterwards submit as a paper. Also, most of the terminological issues not correctly solved by the machine-translation system were corrected by the physicians, as only 7.1% of the proofreader edits were related to this matter.

Even though these findings show that the physicians were capable of carrying out a post-editing task to a certain extent, we also discovered that the post-edited text would not be of a good enough quality to be published. Up to 22.6% of the proofreader's edits were related to syntactic issues. She also introduced a significant number of stylistic edits (34.4%), contrary to our request not to over-edit.

We were able to successfully annotate most of the edits in order to answer our two research questions. However, in future work, triangulating our data with cued retrospective recall would probably help to understand the motivation for edits. This would reduce, if not eliminate, the relatively high number of edits for which a straightforward annotation was not possible (15% of the participants' edits were for an unknown reason).

Finally, while our results indicate that the intervention of a linguistic broker would still be necessary at this stage, this conclusion should be taken with caution due to the small number of participants in our experiment. During our analysis we also identified a number of issues related to the quality of the original Spanish text (misspellings, overly long sentences) that could have been fixed before machine-translating it. In future work, we will use the edit analysis described here to plan the development of an automatic post-processing module that could be used to correct major errors before the self-post-editing phase. We also plan on testing whether the self-post-editing process can be enhanced by using grammar correction tools.

Acknowledgements

This research was carried out while Carla Parra Escartín was working at the ADAPT Centre in Dublin City University. Her contribution was supported by the European Union's Horizon 2020 research and innovation programme under Marie Skłodowska-Curie grant agreement No 713567, and by Science Foundation Ireland at the ADAPT Centre (Grant 13/RC/2106) (www.adaptcentre.ie).

APPENDIX

The annotation decision tree

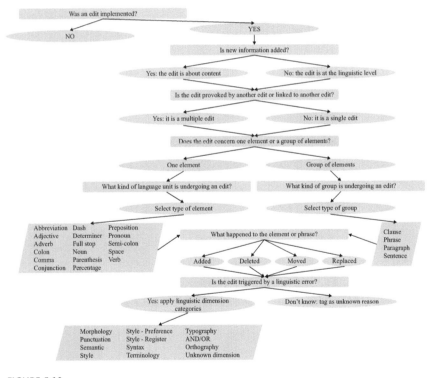

FIGURE 5.10

Notes

1 https://translate.google.com; www.bing.com/translator; www.deepl.com/translator; www.reverso.net/text_translation.aspx?lang=EN.

2 https://lilt.com; www.deepl.com/pro.html.
3 In order to cross-check their self-assessment with their actual English level, participants were asked to complete an English-level test of 25 questions and to let us know their final results. The test can be found here: www.cambridgeenglish.org/test-your-english/general-english/
4 The experiments were run in the first half of 2017, when the shift to neural MT had already occurred.
5 In this chapter we focus on the analysis of the edits performed. In our previous work, we also referred to essential edits not implemented. On average, each participant missed between 0.6% and 1.32% of those necessary edits (Parra Escartín et al. 2017).
6 The percentages reported here, although similar, differ slightly from the ones reported in Parra Escartín et al. (2017). This is due to the new annotation process we used, where some edits previously not accounted for have been taken into account to allow a more detailed analysis.

PART III

Professional revision in various contexts

6

REVISION AND QUALITY STANDARDS

Do translation service providers follow recommendations in practice?

Madeleine Schnierer

The quality of human translations is regularly discussed in Translation Studies. One issue addressed is the objective evaluation of quality. What is high-quality translation? What objective criteria can be used? Accordingly, scholars have produced matrices (e.g. Mertin 2006; Hansen 2008) and formulas (e.g. Arthern 1991; Robert 2012) in order to be able to objectively measure the quality of translation.

One potential means of ensuring quality is the use of quality standards. Initially developed in the context of the industrialisation and internationalisation of production and trade, these subsequently found their way into the service sector. Translation services are now subject to a range of standards at the national, European and international levels, which help to structure processes and measure translation products against criteria. The foreword to ISO 17100 states: "This International Standard specifies requirements for all aspects of the translation process directly affecting the quality and delivery of translation services" (ISO 2015a: vi). Special attention should be paid to the fact that, according to ISO 17100, the parameters, the preparation, the translation process itself and the follow-up work directly affect the quality of the translation. This is discussed by a number of scholars; for example, in their descriptively titled book *Alles hängt mit allem zusammen* [everything is connected to everything], Ende et al. (2013) present discussions of interdependencies among all the factors involved in a translation project. Although there are no empirical studies, professional translators also appear to believe that the concept of quality assurance addresses not just the quality of the TSP's process but also the quality of the product of translation.

Amongst those who have addressed the question of how other-revision is carried out and to what extent quality standards have an impact on the organisation of other-revision are Rasmussen and Schjoldager (2011), who investigated these matters in the Danish context, as did Morin-Hernández (2009) in the French context. Kurz (2016) discussed the two standards EN 15038 and ISO 17100 and their impact on translation projects. Robert (2012) and Ipsen and Dam (2016) looked at translation revision and the correlation between revision procedure and error detection.

This chapter seeks to address this area of research by, firstly, describing the awareness of quality among the TSPs who participated in a survey and, secondly, investigating whether TSPs follow the recommendations of EN 15038/ISO 17100 in practice. According to EN 15038/ISO 17100, one central quality assurance measure is the obligatory step of translation revision, which also is supposed to lead to a more objective evaluation of the translation due to the fact that this step is carried out by someone other than the translator (cf. ISO 2015a: 10–11). If one wishes to work in line with the standards, this step must be carried out for every translation project. Given that EN 15038 was the first standard to define translation revision as an obligatory step in the translation process, it is quoted several times in this chapter. The empirical investigations supporting this present chapter were also largely based on questions related to EN 15038 because it was still in force when the survey was carried out. ISO 17100, the subsequent standard, primarily differs from its predecessor in the following ways, as set out in May 2016 in the foreword to the German edition of DIN EN ISO 17100 (my translation):

The following changes have been undertaken vis-à-vis DIN EN 15038:2006–08:

a   The structure of ISO 17100 differs from that of EN 15038; this new structure reflects the general workflow of a translation project in that it presents the individual steps of the process in a chronological sequence: preparatory processes and activities, production processes and follow-up processes.
b   Special attention has been paid to the expansion of the defined terminology so that the areas of services, technology, language and content, involved parties and processes are presented in a thematically separated way.
c   The skills required by a translator now also include their specialist expertise.
d   A translator can now also prove his or her translation qualification in the form of an official certificate.
f   The skills required by project leaders (e.g. project managers) are defined.
g   The use of translation technology and translation tools is explicitly discussed.
h   The issue of "requirements for the project management of translation services" is more strongly focused.
i   The requirement for the targeted processing of client feedback has been included in the standard.

(ISO 2015b: 2)

As one can see, ISO 17100 may well have been restructured and, in certain areas, expanded, but the key requirements have remained the same. These include the requirement for translation revision, and therefore the survey underlying this chapter and its results can be considered as valid for ISO 17100 as well.

In addition, ISO 17100 includes detailed lists of those linguistic and content-related aspects which should be considered during the translation and revision process, and which can therefore be seen as revision parameters. The extent to which these aspects are actually used in practice will be one of the main subjects of this chapter.

The chapter will begin by listing the standards relevant to TSPs and describing certification processes (sections 1 and 2) and the possibility of registration (section 3). Section 4 will deal with translation revision as it is understood by EN 15038 and ISO 17100. Finally, the results of our investigation of TSPs in Austria will be presented in section 5.

1. Standards governing the translation sector—an overview

Tables 6.1 and 6.2 summarise the standards relevant to translation services. They include national (Austrian and German) standards because, firstly, everyone is free to apply these to their services or products, regardless of where they are based, and, secondly, these often serve as the basis for new national or international standards.

TABLE 6.1 Standards for TSPs

No.	Standard: Year of publication	Subtitle/Area of application
1	**DIN 16511: 1966**	Correction marks
2	**ISO 2384: 1977**	Documentation—Presentation of translations
3	**ISO 12616: 2002**	Translation-oriented terminography Efficient establishment and updating of terminology databases and creation of simple accessibility for the translation process
4	**ÖNORM D 1210: 2004**	Requirements for technical communication and documentation services
5	**ÖNORM D 1201: 2009**	Translation services—Translation contracts
6	**DIN 2340: 2009**	Short forms for terms and names
7	**ISO 704: 2009**	Terminology work—Principles and methods
8	**DIN 2342: 2011**	Vocabulary of terminology
9	**ISO/TS 11669: 2012**	Translation projects—General guidance (this 2012 standard is currently being revised)
10	**DIN 2330: 2013**	Concepts and terms—General principles
11	**ISO 3166–1: 2013**	Codes for the names of countries and their subdivisions—
	ISO 3166–2: 2013 **ISO 3166–3: 2013**	Part 1: Country codes Part 2: Country subdivision code Part 3: Code for formerly used names of countries
12	**ISO 4217: 2015**	Codes for the presentation of currencies

(*Continued*)

TABLE 6.1 *(Continued)*

No.	*Standard: Year of publication*	*Subtitle/Area of application*
13	**ISO 17100: 2015**	Translation services—Requirements for translation services
	ISO 17100: 2015/AMD 1: 2017	Translation services—Requirements for translation services—Amendment 1
14	**ISO 26162: 2016**	System for the management of terminology, knowledge and content—Design, organisation and support of terminology management systems (ISO 26162:2012)
15	**DIN 2335: 2016**	German names for Alpha 2 code in line with ISO 639–1 (see No. 19)
16	**ISO 18587: 2017**	Translation services—Post-editing of machine-translation output—Requirements
17	**ISO 1087: 2019**	Terminology work—Vocabulary
18	**ISO 20539: 2019**	Translation, interpreting and related technology—Vocabulary
19	**ISO 639**	ISO 639 is composed of five different parts
		Part 1 (ISO 639–1: 2002) provides a two-letter code that has been designed to represent most of the major languages of the world. Part 2 (ISO 639–2: 1998) provides a three-letter code, which gives more possible combinations, so ISO 639–2:1998 can cover more languages. Part 3 (ISO 639–3: 2007) provides a three-letter code and aims to give as complete a listing of languages as possible, including living, extinct and ancient languages. Part 4 (ISO 639–4: 2010) gives the general principles of language coding and lays down guidelines for the use of ISO 639. Part 5 (ISO 639–5: 2008) provides a three-letter code for language families and groups (living and extinct).

Lists of standards with varying degrees of detail can be found in publications such as Arevalillo (2005), Budin (2007), Thelen (2013), Ottmann (2017), Schmitz (2017) and ISO (2020). Table 6.1 contains standards that could be relevant to TSPs, and Table 6.2 lists standards for quality management systems, which TSPs are also using with increasing frequency to certify their services. Where necessary, the subtitles have been translated from German into English.

TABLE 6.2 General quality management standards (ASI 2019)

No.	Standard	Name/Area of application
1	**ISO 9000**	Definition of the principles and terms for quality management systems. An explanation of quality management systems and the terms used in the series of standards ISO 9000.
2	**ISO 9001**	Model description of the entire quality management system. Basis for a comprehensive quality management system.
3	**ISO 9004**	Guidelines regarding both the effectiveness and efficiency of the quality management system. Contains instructions for organising a company along the lines of Total Quality Management (TQM).

Table 6.1 consists of 19 standards that make qualitative recommendations regarding both the process (the project workflow) and the end product (the translation). The standards will not be described in detail because that would go beyond the scope of this study. However, the precise name of each standard, and the short description of its area of application, do provide information about its subject matter. Many different issues can be regulated with the help of these standards, which can thus provide helpful reference material and guidance to TSPs.

TSP revisers can also benefit from referring to such generally applicable standards as those for quality management listed in Table 6.2.

ISO 9001 is used for certification purposes by companies from a wide range of sectors, including increasing numbers of TSPs around the globe. There are already a number of translation agencies that have been certified in line with both ISO 17100 and ISO 9001. The following section considers the advantages and disadvantages of such certification and of the certification process.

2. Certification

Standards are not laws but rather non-binding recommendations. According to Austria's standardisation body ASI (Austrian Standards International), a standard is a qualified recommendation that, although publicly accessible, is not free of charge and is drawn up by consensus according to an internationally recognised process. It should offer maximum benefits to everyone and is accepted for general and recurring use by a recognised standardisation organisation (Austrian Standards 2014). An example of a more detailed description of the design and scope of application of standards can be found in Schnierer (2019).

By undergoing certification, one is also making a commitment to meet the requirements of a standard. According to Austrian Standards (2019), the potential advantages of certification (in terms of increased competitiveness) can be summed up in three ways:

- Certification creates trust and confirms the quality of products and services. An independent body confirms that a product, service, management system or set of employees meets the requirements of the relevant standard and that compliance is continuously reviewed. This distinguishes the company from its competitors.
- Certification can also bring a competitive advantage, in particular because it is often a requirement in tender processes.
- Certification opens up new markets. Certification can help in winning new clients and creating alternative sales and marketing channels. In an age of globalisation, the introduction of standards and certification under them are creating global reference values.

Opinions differ regarding the importance of certification to TSPs. Translation journals and websites often publish first-hand reports on this question, such as the example of two translators in Germany who, while personally concluding that certification is definitely worthwhile, gave the following more measured assessment of the situation in Germany:

> Since 2015, freelance translators and translation companies have been able to obtain ISO 17100 certification. Response from freelancers has been limited. This is partly due to the fact that many colleagues remain unaware of the possibility of getting certified, are discouraged by the associated costs or believe that certification fails to bring measurable benefits. . . . To date, clients have rarely required ISO 17100 certification.
>
> *(Maier and Schwagereit 2016)*

This scepticism about the ability of standard-based certification to lead to the professionalisation of the sector can be ascribed to both the cost of certification and the sometimes extremely complex certification process. Following is a description and comparison of the certification processes carried out by a German and an Austrian certification body.

Certification process of the LRQA (Lloyd's Register Quality Assurance)

Here is a summary of the stages of an LRQA certification process (LRQA 2016):

- Initial audit part 1—System check and initial requirements

  Auditors investigate such aspects as the structure of the management system, the process landscape, the sequence of and interaction between the processes and the strengths and weaknesses of the company's organisation. The TSP being certified then has the opportunity to remove any weaknesses before the next stage of the audit.

- Initial audit part 2—Practical implementation

  The implementation of the requirements placed upon the management system is audited. The team of auditors is formed according to the scope of the audit. This initial audit concludes with a comprehensive audit report that offers a simple overview of possible strengths and weaknesses and indicates potential for improvement.

- Certificate

  If the requirements of the relevant standard are all fulfilled, an internationally recognised certificate is issued, which is valid for three years. If shortcomings are identified, these must be adequately addressed so that the certificate can be issued after a follow-up audit.

- Surveillance audit—Continuation of the certification

  Selected aspects of the management system are audited between 6 and 12 months after the completion of the initial audit. This surveillance audit is principally designed to benefit the company.

- Focus audit—Planning for the future

  The results of the final audit before recertification (focus audit) are summarised and considered in the planning of future auditing. These are used as the basis of a new three-year certification cycle (recertification).

Certification process of the LICS (Language Industry Certification System)

Here is a description of a certification process carried out according to ISO 17100 (Austrian Standards 2015):

- Application

  The application is accompanied by documentation from the applicant that includes general information, descriptions of the company profile, specialisations and processes (related to ISO 17100) and the average number of employees working in the relevant locations (over the past 12 months) and of translators (employed and freelance, over the past 12 months).

- Initial and recertification audit

  The initial and recertification audit looks at all requirements specified in ISO 17100. The audit comprises interviews with the CEO/head of the service provider, translators/freelancers/vendors and project managers, and other staff responsible for tasks relevant to the certification criteria (e.g. accounting/invoicing, human resources, quality management). The conclusions of the audit are presented and further steps defined.

- Audit findings

  In case of deviations from the requirements of the standard, appropriate corrective actions are specified by the lead auditor. The auditor may also make recommendations regarding issues of quality and opportunities for improvement related to the operations of the service provider. Such recommendations are documented in the audit report without affecting the issuing of the certificate.

- Audit report for certification

  The information provided by the lead auditor to the body responsible for the certification decision includes the audit report, comments on deviations and the corrective actions taken by the client and a recommendation of whether or not to grant certification.

- Issuing the certificate

  The certification body decides whether to issue the certificate, which is valid for six years.

- Surveillance activities

  Surveillance audits are carried out on a two-year cycle to ensure that the certified service provider continues to meet the requirements of ISO 17100 between recertification audits.

- Recertification

  A recertification audit is carried out in order to extend the validity of the certificate.

A striking feature of the LRQA process is the fact that most contacts between auditors and the company take place at the management level. The LICS process, on the other hand, gives employees at every level the opportunity to speak during the audit phase. A further difference between the two processes relates to the period of validity of the two certificates. An LRQA certificate is valid for three years, with surveillance audits beginning after a maximum of 12 months. In the case of the LICS, the certificate is valid for six years, and surveillance audits are carried out every two years. The certification processes of both institutions are clearly structured but appear very complex to applicants. One should also consider the costs of these processes, about which neither institution provides any information on its website.

3. Registration

Registration is not an entirely uncontroversial means of circumventing certification. It is simply an independent declaration in the form of a fee-based registration that is made public and can be used for marketing purposes. Such registration is offered by DIN CERTCO GmbH, which belongs to TÜV Rheinland, although this company has not only been warned about its practice of making statements that could lead to confusion between the terms *registration* and *certification* but also obliged, in the form of a final judgement, to refrain from doing so (Schneider 2012).

At the time of this present research (January 2019), the situation appeared unchanged because the section *Certificates and Registrations* on the DIN CERTCO website continued to list 280 companies that have *registration numbers* and are described as *certificate holders* according to ISO 17100. At first glance no clear distinction is made between *registration* and *certification*, although the list of companies consists exclusively of registered companies who claim to comply with ISO 17100 without confirmation by an independent or recognised body. This is made clear by the fact that, in the *valid until* column, the expiry date of these so-called *certificates* is given as *unlimited*, which would never occur in the case of a proper certification. At least each entry ends with the following *Note* (DIN CERTCO 2019):

> This is a DIN Registration, i.e. a statement of conformity to the requirements of the international standard issued by the translator on his own responsibility. This is not a certification by an independent third party.

Of the companies registered in this way, 219 are based in Germany, 54 are active in other European countries, and 7 are outside Europe, as shown by the list on the corporate website of TÜV Rheinland in January 2019.

The advantages of registration are obvious: it is a simpler and cheaper process that involves neither an audit nor ongoing control. Once registration has been obtained, it has no time limit and generates no further costs.

4. Translation revision in EN 15038 and ISO 17100

Section 5.4.1 of EN 15038, entitled 'Translation', included the following recommendation (CEN 2006a: 11):

> Throughout this process, the translator shall pay attention to the following:
>
> a) Terminology: compliance with specific domain and client terminology, or any other terminology provided, as well as terminology consistency throughout the whole translation.
> b) Grammar: syntax, spelling, punctuation, orthotypography, diacritical marks.
> c) Lexis: lexical cohesion and phraseology.
> d) Style: compliance with the proprietary or client style guide, including register and language variants.
> e) Locale: local conventions and regional standards.
> f) Formatting (see Annex D).
> g) Target group and purpose of the translation.

If the restriction mentioned next had not been made, one could have seen these quality criteria as parameters for revision.

Regarding revision methods, EN 15038 (CEN 2006a: 11) made the following recommendation:

> The TSP shall ensure that the translation is revised. The reviser . . . shall be a person other than the translator and have the appropriate competence in the source and target languages. The reviser shall examine the translation for its suitability for purpose. This shall include, as required by the project, comparison of the source and target texts for terminology consistency.

The restriction "as required by the project" led to confusion—and was much criticised by such writers as Mossop (2007a), Robert (2008, 2012) and Parra-Galiano (2016)—because it apparently offered the option of not revising every translation or at least avoiding the systematic comparison of the source and target texts.

The recommendations of ISO 17100 are no longer qualified in this way (ISO 2015a: 10):

> The TSP shall ensure that the target language content is revised.
>
> The reviser, who shall be a person other than the translator, shall have the competences mentioned in 3.1.5 in the source and target languages. The reviser shall examine the target language content against the source language content for any errors and other issues, and its suitability for purpose.

In the section entitled 'Revision' (ISO 2015a: 10), the international standard details several key aspects of the revision process:

> This shall include comparison of the source and target language content for the aspects listed in 5.3.1. As agreed upon with the project manager, the reviser shall either correct any errors found in the target language content or recommend the corrections to be implemented by the translator.
>
> NOTE Corrections can include retranslation.
>
> Any errors or other issues affecting target language content quality should be corrected and the process repeated until the reviser and TSP are satisfied. The reviser shall also inform the TSP of any corrective action he/she has taken.

Section 5.3.1 mentions the following aspects (ISO 2015a: 10):

a) compliance with specific domain and client terminology and/or any other reference material provided and ensuring terminological consistency during translation;

b) semantic accuracy of the target language content;

c) appropriate syntax, spelling, punctuation, diacritical marks, and other orthographical conventions of the target language;

d) lexical cohesion and phraseology;

e) compliance with any proprietary and/or client style guide (including domain, language register, and language variants);

f) locale and any applicable standards;

g) formatting;

h) target audience and purpose of the target language content.

The translator shall raise any uncertainty as a query with the project manager.

These recommendations are presented as detailed requirements in ISO 17100 and thus as concrete parameters that can be applied when revising a translation. The extent to which these are used in practice will be presented and discussed in the next section, together with findings regarding other aspects of translation and revision.

5. Reception and use by Austrian companies of the former EN 15038 and current ISO 17100

The findings presented in this section are drawn primarily from a comparison between certified companies and those that, while uncertified, follow the recommendations of EN 15038 and ISO 17100. Empirical studies were conducted in 2015 and 2016 in order to discover more about revision practices at TSPs in Austria. The detailed results are presented in Schnierer (2019). Here, selected findings will be presented, leading to discussion and conclusions about the reception and application of the EN 15038 and ISO 17100 standards.

The first study was carried out with the help of an online questionnaire in early 2015—just as EN 15038 was being replaced by ISO 17100. The basis for the survey was the database of the Austrian Economic Chambers (WKO) which, at the time, listed 1,240 companies/individuals in the area of translation services. The first selection criterion for the shortlist was that a TSP must have an internet presence that offered enough information about its areas of activity to allow one to conclude that it was a suitable candidate for participation in the survey. This reduced the number of companies to 111, all of whom were asked by telephone if they would be interested in participating. Those companies who agreed received a link to the online questionnaire. This link was accessible for six weeks (cf. Schnierer 2019).

Naturally, the participants in the survey could be questioned only about their experiences with EN 15038. Conversely, participants in the subsequent interview-based study that took place in spring and summer 2016 were asked about their experiences with ISO 17100. A total of 31 people participated in the online survey, while 5 people (of the 11 who made personal contact on their own initiative after sending the answers) said that they were prepared to answer further questions and were invited to participate in a follow-up interview study, which took place via Skype and telephone. The results were analysed with the help of the SPSS software package and then fed into Excel because it has better presentational options.

The questionnaire and interview setting followed the recommendations of Giroux and Tremblay (2002, 2009) concerning their structure: The online questionnaire consisted of 10 subject areas with a total of 48 open and closed questions. The follow-up interviews were structured in line with the 10 subject areas of the online questionnaire, and almost every area included more detailed, follow-up questions. The interviews were recorded and subsequently transcribed. The data analysis was carried out in line with the recommendations of Dörnyei (2007) concerning the method of labelling the interview answers, and the recommendations of Field (2013) in that we used simple statistical tools and rejected the application of inferential statistics since we had only 31 participants.

Firstly, some overall results—the answers from all 31 participants—will be presented (Figures 6.1 to 6.3). Then comparisons will be drawn between the answers from those 19 participants who are the focus of this study because they are either certified or, according to their own information, are not certified but work in line with the standards (Figures 6.4 to 6.8 and Tables 6.4 and 6.5).

Company profile

The profile of each company was established from answers to questions about its annual project volume and the number of translators with whom it works (see Figure 6.1). The survey participants operate with networks of translators (working directly or as subcontractors) that range in size from 2 to 500 people. More than half work with small networks of up to 10 translators and handle a total of 2950 projects per year. Moving clockwise on the pie chart, seven of the companies have a medium-sized network of 20–30 translators and carry out a total of 2750 projects, three have large networks of 40–90 translators and deal with 5400 projects per year while five

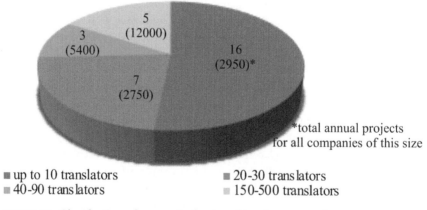

FIGURE 6.1 Classification of companies by size of translator network

companies with very large networks of 150–500 translators handle an annual total of 12,000 projects. The sample is thus broad—from tiny to huge companies.

Quality standards in practice

The survey paid great attention to the issue of quality standards in the translation sector. It sought to gather information about the reception of EN 15038 and ISO 17100 and to measure attitudes to certification carried out in line with the standard (cf. Schnierer 2019).

The first subject to be addressed was registration. Participants were asked whether their companies had registered with, for example, DIN CERTCO in Germany.

As Figure 6.2 clearly shows, the practice of circumventing certification through registration was not usual amongst the TSPs questioned in 2015 and 2016. The interviews similarly revealed that this possibility is completely unknown. It was in fact impossible to find a body in Austria that offered registration in line with EN 15038 or ISO 17100. In January 2019, however, it was clear that there are Austrian companies that take advantage of this opportunity, even if it is not recommended by the standards institutions: The list of companies that have been registered in line with ISO 17100 by DIN CERTCO (see section 3) includes six Austrian companies (TÜV Rheinland DIN CERTCO 2019).

Regarding the level of awareness of EN 15038, it was striking that in 2015—nine years after its introduction—awareness of the standard was still well below 100%, with only around two-thirds of those surveyed (n = 22) stating that they were aware of EN 15038 (see Figure 6.3). The response to the question about the relevance of the standard was similar: Once again, some two-thirds (n = 21) believe that standards make sense for the translation sector.

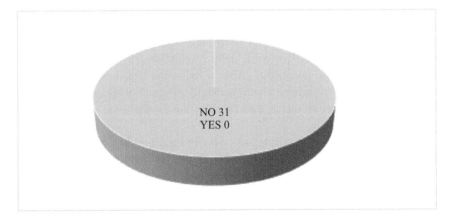

FIGURE 6.2 Registration in line with EN 15038

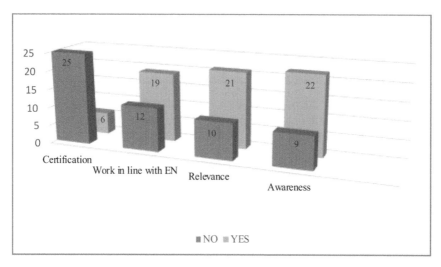

FIGURE 6.3 Reception of EN 15038

Size of certified companies

Table 6.3 gives the size of the six certified companies shown in Figure 6.3. A comparison between the results in the two categories "Work in line with EN" and "Certification" in Figure 6.3 reveals a discrepancy between the acceptance of standards as a basis for working and the desire for or possibility of certification. The greatest apparent difference here was between companies with larger and smaller networks. Five of the six certified companies work in large networks of 150 to 500 translators. Only one company working with a small network of just 10 translators was certified.

Why would so many forego certification despite working in line with EN 15038? As already made clear in section 2 on certification, the process requires considerable resources. This is also confirmed by the answers of the 13 participants who claim that they work in line with EN 15038. Three of these participants answered this optional question by stating that their companies are too small and that certification would generate too much work. As they do not have significant labour resources, they probably see themselves as unable to commission certification.

Given that ISO 17100 had only just come into force at the time of the survey, it was possible to seek similar information about this standard only during the interviews. Even though the interviews were conducted almost a year later, it was apparently still too early to look for answers because only two of the five interviewees admitted to being acquainted with ISO 17100. Most were aware of the change and of the new version but knew nothing in detail about the differences between the international standard and the European standard.

TABLE 6.3 Size of certified companies

Company	Translators	Projects/year
1	10	200
2	150	2000
3	200	4000
4	300	1500
5	350	1500
6	500	3000

Compliance with recommendations of the standards in practice

Let us now consider the extent to which the participants who work with and without EN 15038 certification meet the requirements of the standard in practice (see Figure 6.4). The participants were questioned about whether they work in line with the recommendations of EN 15038.

As already shown in Table 6.3, at the time of the survey, 6 of the 31 respondents were certified in line with EN 15038. A further 13 (around 40% of the respondents) indicated that, although uncertified, they complied with the guidelines of EN 15038. This is twice the number of certified companies. Thus a total of 19 companies work in line with EN 15038. None of the five interviewees was certified, but three stated that they worked in line with the principles of EN 15038 or ISO 17100. Let us look at the profile of these companies in more detail (Table 6.4).

Table 6.4 lists the companies according to the number of languages they offer (in increasing order). Certified companies are marked dark grey, and uncertified companies that work in line with EN 15038 light grey. Further distinguishing features are the annual volume of translations and the size of the network of translators and revisers working directly or as subcontractors for the company. Two factors are particularly interesting. Firstly, all companies (with the exception of #13) with an annual volume of translations of 1500 or more are certified. Secondly, two companies (3 and 8) claim to work in line with EN 15038 yet also claim to work without revisers, despite the fact that, according to the standard, these are essential to the revision of a translation. One possible explanation is that it could be a question of terminology. Third-party revising is done by translators, who are not necessarily called revisers. Apart from this, the discrepancy between the number of languages offered and the size of the network of translators and revisers is remarkably high, as exemplified by companies 15 and 16, who manage with just two and five revisers respectively, despite large annual project volumes. This could also be explained by the fact that not all languages that are translated are fully revised (as opposed to being merely proofread in order to check superficial elements).

FIGURE 6.4 Compliance with the guidelines of EN 15038

TABLE 6.4 Profiles of certified companies and uncertified companies declaring that they work in line with EN 15038

Company	Languages offered	Translations per year	Translators	Revisers
1	2	500	5	1
2	2	200	10	10
3	3	400	0	0
4	3	170	4	5
5	4	150	4	3
6	5	50	10	5
7	5	500	1	3
8	10	50	20	0
9	15	500	25	25
10	15	800	25	5
11	20	150	20	20
12	30	4000	200	200
13	30	3000	50	6
14	30	2000	150	10
15	36	1400	90	2
16	40	1000	40	5
17	40	1500	350	70
18	50	1500	300	15
19	50	3000	500	500

Two certified companies and one uncertified company that works in line with EN 15038 report changes in their workflow. These changes are described as follows: "Unlike earlier in the company's history, revision has become a standard"; "we work in a more structured way", and "using the standard as a basis has enabled us to meet demands for transparency". As could be expected, workflows are affected in only a few of the certified companies and uncertified companies that work in line with the standard, according to respondents. This is unsurprising because the workflows recommended in the standards come from practice or, put another way, the standards recommend the best practices, which these companies are likely to apply already.

Revision without exception

As already mentioned, one of the key demands of both standards is the revision of all translations, without exception. The participants were asked if they would subject every translation to a revision. The behaviour of the investigated companies in this regard is shown in Figure 6.5.

This result is somewhat surprising because a third of the certified companies (two out of six) admit to not upholding this part of the standard. Almost a third of the companies stating that, although uncertified, they meet the requirements of EN 15038 (4 out of 13) also fail to uphold the standard regarding revision without exception. This can be explained by the restrictive formulation of EN 15038: "as required by the project" (CEN 2006a: 11). This, as already mentioned, can also be interpreted as stating that revision is a project-specific requirement and that there are therefore projects for which it is unnecessary. It seems important to investigate

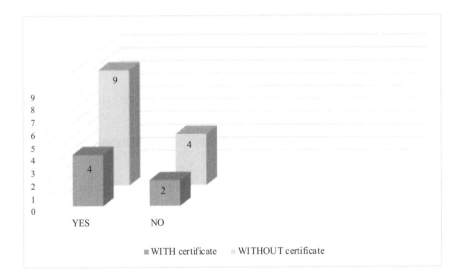

FIGURE 6.5 Revision without exception

this question again against the background of ISO 17100, where there is no doubt that every translation has to be revised. If translation agencies do not always carry out revisions and therefore cannot meet the requirements of ISO 17100 (and, formerly, EN 15038), the translation profession will not gain credibility. However, the small size of our sample means that such generalisations cannot be made.

Revision methods

Figures 6.6 and 6.7 show how revision is carried out by the 19 questioned companies that responded to the non-compulsory question about methods. They were asked to choose among the revision methods considered as most common by Robert (2008, 2012) as well as Robert and Van Waes (2014): (1) monolingual revision of the final translation, (2) bilingual revision (comparison between translation and source text), (3) monolingual revision followed by bilingual revision and (4) bilingual revision followed by monolingual revision. The question was asked in such a way that, for each revision method, participants could choose between *always, mostly, rarely* und *never*.

Figure 6.6 shows the choices of certified companies. Most of them (five out of six) practice the simple bilingual revision method. The answers show that, without exception, the certified companies always carry out at least a bilingual revision. One even always carries out the double-method (bilingual followed by monolingual revision). On the other hand, the answers show that certified companies rarely (two out of six) or never (four out of six) use the monolingual revision method. It is thus reasonable to assert that certified companies uphold the core requirement of EN 15038/ISO 17100.

As Figure 6.7 shows, the situation among uncertified companies that work in line with EN 15038 is somewhat less clear. More than two-thirds of them (9 out

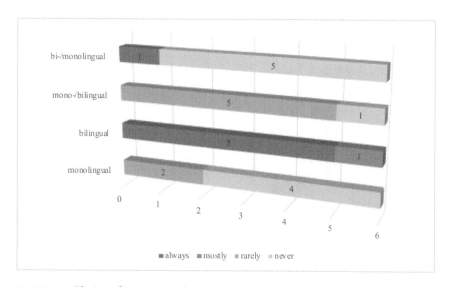

FIGURE 6.6 Choice of revision method—certified companies

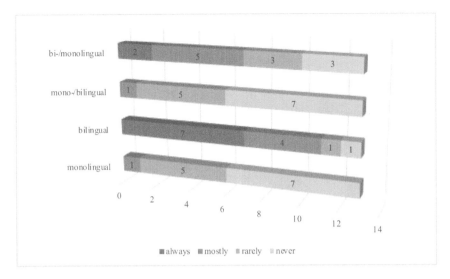

FIGURE 6.7 Choice of revision method—uncertified companies that work in line with EN 15038

of 13) claim that they either *always* carry out at least a simple bilingual revision (7 out of 13) or—in the case of two companies—the double-method of bilingual followed by monolingual revision. Only one company states that it *mostly* uses the monolingual method, which does not meet the requirements of the standards.

It can thus generally be asserted that all the certified companies uphold the requirement of "comparison of the source and target texts" (CEN 2006a: 11) and that most of the uncertified companies working in line with EN 15038 meet the requirement as well. This assertion also applies to ISO 17100, given that it has the same requirement: "examine the target language content against the source language content" (ISO 2015a: 10–11) and that certifications carried out in line with EN 15038 were carried over to ISO 17100.

Quality criteria and revision parameters

Despite the fact that detailed aspects of revision were first specified in ISO 17100 and that participants in the online survey could be questioned only about EN 15038, the questionnaire did separately ask about their use of clearly defined parameters as they now appear in ISO 17100 section 5.3.1 and are to be considered during revision according to section 5.3.3: "comparison . . . for the aspects listed in 5.3.1" (ISO 2015a: 11).

As seen in Figure 6.8, the use of revision parameters is evidently more common among certified than among uncertified companies: 5 out of 6 certified companies use revision parameters as opposed to just 6 out of 13 uncertified companies. Given that certified companies are periodically subject to certification processes

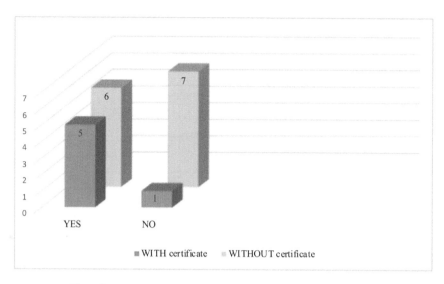

FIGURE 6.8 Use of revision parameters

TABLE 6.5 Quality criteria

Ranking	Quality criteria	Frequency
1	—linguistic correctness	13
2	—correct reproduction of the content	8
3	—meeting client needs	7
4	—completeness	5
	—good style	5
5	—use of the correct specialist terms	3
6	—no additions	1
	—acceptable linguistic register	1
	—correct formulation	1

and thus have to adhere to the quality criteria listed in 5.4.1 of EN 15038 and 5.3.1 of ISO 17100, it is clear that they also adhere to these quality criteria during the revision process, using them as revision parameters. As mentioned in ISO 17100, these criteria are also concretely recommended for revision. Furthermore, revision parameters are an excellent tool for the objective treatment of mistakes (they receive a label as a result of which they can be classified). Also, when used regularly, they can be seen to be very time-efficient—it is no longer necessary to individually comment on each intervention. Table 6.5 lists the quality criteria that were named by the respondents in answer to an open question.

If one compares these criteria with those set out in EN 15038 and ISO 17100, one can see that the criteria 'completeness' and 'correct reproduction of the content' do not appear in the standard but were mentioned by a considerable number of those questioned (13 out of 31). Special attention should also be paid to the criterion 'meeting client needs'. This criterion is not addressed in the standards but should not be neglected by TSPs (and it was, indeed, mentioned by almost a quarter of those questioned).

6. Summary and conclusion

This chapter has primarily sought to shed light on the reception of standards for translation services ten years after EN 15038 was published and to demonstrate the extent to which, firstly, certification was an issue and, secondly, the recommendations of standards were used in day-to-day practice (according to the companies themselves). Standards relevant to translation services were listed with the aim of providing an overview and stating the extent to which these could advantageously influence professional practice. This was followed by an investigation of the question of certification and the presentation of two certification processes used in Germany and Austria. The issue of registration and the related problems were also discussed.

An analysis of the results of an investigation carried out in 2015 and 2016 was then presented, with a particular focus on respondents who are either certified or are uncertified yet work, according to their own information, in line with EN 15038. The certified companies, except for one, are all among the largest companies, with networks of up to 500 translators. The uncertified companies that claim to work in line with EN 15038 are found in companies of all sizes, ranging from single-person companies to large service providers. Regarding compliance with the requirement of EN 15038 for revision without exception, the proportion of companies that comply is, astonishingly, higher amongst uncertified companies. Four out of six—or two-thirds—of the certified companies revise every translation whereas the figure for uncertified companies that claim to work in line with EN 15038 is 9 out of 13, or almost three-quarters of those companies. The revision method suggested by the standard is the bilingual method, in which the translation is compared with the source text. This is also the method that is most commonly used by both the certified companies and the uncertified companies that work in line with the standard. While EN 15038 contains no explicit suggestions for revision parameters, these have since appeared in ISO 17100. A large majority (five out of six) of the certified companies work with revision parameters, whereas just under half of the uncertified companies work in line with the standard use of the parameters.

The minimum number of participants for quantitative analysis (according to Dörnyei 2007) is 30. With 31 participants, the results reported here cannot really be seen as representative for the whole translation market in Austria, but tendencies can nevertheless be seen. Furthermore, it would have been interesting to ask more detailed questions about awareness of standards and their application in order to discover whether standards other than EN 15038 and ISO 17100 are relevant to professional practice. A further drawback of the investigation concerns the company profiles. It would also have been useful to distinguish clearly between freelancers and agencies to show similarities and differences in their revision practices and opinions concerning standards. In any further investigation it would therefore be of interest to discover, firstly, which other standards are relevant to the translation service sector and, secondly, the current situation regarding certification in line with ISO 17100. How has the number of certified companies developed since the standard was introduced in 2015, and which factors have influenced this development? Last but not least, post-editing should be examined as well, given that more and more TSPs offer this service.

7

FROM LANGUAGE CHECK TO CREATIVE EDITING

Exploring variation in the revision stage of the LSP workflow

Annamari Korhonen

According to Arnt Lykke Jakobsen (2019: 64), "translation and revision are more in transition than ever before". Jakobsen is referring to the transition that is brought about by new technologies, above all machine translation. This chapter, however, discusses another way in which revision could take on a bigger role in the translation industry's workflows: different kinds of revision tasks could be used in the design of new services when language service providers (LSPs) expand from translation into a wider selection of multilingual communication services. In such production environments, revision takes on a purpose beyond translation quality assurance.

Jakobsen (2019: 69), like many others, groups translators together with writers. Dam-Jensen and Heine (2013: 90–1; see also Risku et al. 2016) discuss writing, translation and adaptation as three types of text production and consider similarities and differences between these three tasks. This chapter builds on that line of thought, seeing translation first and foremost as text production, as creating communications for many different purposes, and it looks at the potential of revision not only in correcting translators' errors, but also in editing texts further. To help understand the flexibility, complexity and vast potential of revision, the concept of revision continuum is introduced.

The ideas presented here are based on the different ways in which LSPs that operate in Finland, and that mainly serve corporate and public sector clients, use translation revision in real-life business contexts. These different ways have been investigated by means of an online survey of LSP representatives. Specific focus is firstly on revision task specifications in terms of revision parameters (see Mossop 2014a) and the allowed degree of creativity, secondly on various circumstances that may require revision to be carried out in a specific manner and thirdly on who decides the scope of revision. The role of revision in the production workflow of different creative translation services will also be discussed based on the survey. The survey results, as well as the idea of the revision continuum, is expected to be of interest to various stakeholders including LSPs, translator educators and researchers.

The survey was sent to LSPs in May 2018 with the aim of increasing the so far rather meagre body of empirical studies of revision policies (see Rasmussen and Schjoldager 2011; Uotila 2017; Ko 2011). The questionnaire was largely based on Brian Mossop's (2014a) comprehensive discussion of revision policies and procedures. When presenting and discussing the results of the survey later in this chapter, I will also draw on the experience accumulated in my 20 years as a translator working at LSPs.

Before moving on to the results of the survey, I will briefly discuss the importance of studying the LSP workflow and, more specifically, the revision task. I will also introduce the idea of a revision continuum, and take a look at some previous research on revision policies. The survey design will then be introduced, and the findings from the survey presented with the help of diagrams. Before the final conclusions, I will return to the concept of revision continuum and how it could help us chart revision policies in all their inherent flexibility.

1.   Revision as part of the translation workflow

In this chapter, the focus is on revision as a separate step in the workflow performed after translation, and by someone other than the translator. Self-revision as well as other types of revision, such as the kind a translator does when producing a translation based on translation memory matches, remain outside the scope of this chapter. This means that revision is primarily defined in terms of its position in the workflow and role in producing a service for clients.

In Translation Studies, process research traditionally refers to investigating the translator's (or sometimes the reviser's) thought processes (see Englund Dimitrova 2010). However, translations are hardly ever produced in isolation. In reality, translators work in production networks (see, for example, Abdallah 2012; Solum 2018) with many different people taking on various roles. These roles and the workflow that consists of the tasks they perform have a great impact on how translators work, and Drugan (2013: 40) quite appropriately calls attention to the need for investigating the production processes and models of translation industry operators. Lauscher (2000: 161) even states that the lack of knowledge of translation production processes—the workflow—results in a lack of real-life foundation for all scholarly models of translation quality. In their discussion of contextual factors that influence the production of translations, Dam-Jensen and Heine (2013: 91, 94) list the physical environment, technical tools and collaborative networks—but the networks are referred to only in terms of social interaction, ignoring the role of the workflow. More empirical research is therefore needed to lay down a proper theoretical foundation that will help understand the implications of different workflows.

LSPs usually follow a more or less standardised production workflow that consists of various tasks from planning and file preparation to translating, revising and generating target files (see, for example, Drugan 2013: 105–6; Dunne 2011: 169–70; Gouadec 2007). Although descriptions of workflow differ in some specifics, they generally agree that revision is a well-established and necessary part of the workflow. The translation industry standards EN 15038 (European Committee for Standardization 2006a) and ISO 17100:2015 also require revision of the target texts as part of the translation workflow.

Bisiada (2018: 290–1) presents a workflow description that is of particular interest in that it foregrounds the text modification phases. His model includes a translation stage (Orientation—Drafting—Revising), which takes place within a translation company, and an editing[1] stage (Stylistic editing—Copyediting—Structural editing—Content editing), which takes place outside the translation company (within a publishing company in the case of Bisiada's data). However, such a straightforward division may not apply in the context of translation services offered to corporate clients. When an industrial client outsources the translation of its corporate communications to an LSP, they usually expect to receive finalised products that are ready for publication online or in printed form. While in most cases they review the materials before actually publishing them, this review may not constitute an actual editing process. From the point of view of efficiency and financial viability, it makes sense to include the editing stage in the translation stage or, more specifically, in the revision task that is considered part of the translation stage in Bisiada's workflow model and takes place within the LSP.

2. The revision continuum introduced

The revision continuum is a visual representation of the hypothesis that the scope of revision can be, and in fact frequently is, adjusted to meet different objectives in a manner that also secures the financial viability of LSPs' operations. According to Martin (2007: 60), "fit-for-purpose translation, when applied systemically to a varied workflow, is a viable way of using translation and revision resources intelligently". This is precisely what the revision continuum aims at—providing a systematic model for the intelligent and flexible use of revision resources to produce fit-for-purpose translations. The continuum will help pin down the various revision practices that LSPs apply when processing many different text types from technical manuals to marketing materials and blogs.

The survey presented in this chapter provides information on some of the variables that together define the revision task, and reveals some factors that LSPs consider when making decisions about the scope of the task. The survey is a step towards placing different kinds of revision tasks on a continuum ranging from simple linguistic review—or just a quick proofreading—to creative stylistic editing and tailoring for a specific readership (see Figure 7.1). Between these two extremes, any number of revision levels with different task definitions may exist, all of them used for a specific purpose.

LINGUISTIC REVIEW	CREATIVE EDITING

FIGURE 7.1 The revision continuum

The revision continuum could be used in two different ways: firstly, as a theoretical model that would help us imagine all the possible ways in which revision could be carried out, and secondly, as a practical tool that describes the different revision levels applied by an individual LSP. Building such a theoretical model and creating such a practical tool are not simple tasks, and are in fact well beyond the scope of a single survey. In-depth interviews and analysis and classification of revised materials would probably be necessary. I will return to the potential uses and benefits of the revision continuum after the analysis of the survey data.

3. Previous studies of revision policies

Much of the academic study on revision focuses on revisers' working procedures and mental processes. Important studies in this area have been carried out by Künzli (for example, 2007b); for an account of other interesting studies, see Mossop (2007a). The practical viability and benefits of certain procedures have also been investigated (see, for example, Robert and Van Waes 2014). Less attention has been paid to LSPs' policies and workflows, and only a few systematic surveys of them have been published. Perhaps the most important of these is the research project of Rasmussen and Schjoldager (2011) on Danish LSPs. They used a questionnaire and interviews to find out whether unilingual or comparative revision was preferred, which revision parameters were included and who the revisers were. They found, among other things, that problems in financial viability and tight schedules often prevent thorough revision.

Uotila (2017) repeated Rasmussen and Schjoldager's questionnaire, but not the interviews, in Finland for her master's thesis. Most of Uotila's findings regarding revision policies agree with those of the Danish study, but she found that fewer Finnish than Danish LSPs have specific guidelines for revision. Neither Uotila nor Rasmussen and Schjoldager consider the advantages of designing the revision task to suit different purposes or text types; they only look at whether texts are subjected to revision or not, and why. From the point of view of the present study, however, Uotila's survey provides valuable additional insight into the revision policies of Finnish LSPs.

Ko (2011) considers revision in the Chinese translation market through some personal experiences but discusses revision as well as the review carried out by clients under the single concept of translation checking. The analysis is based on case studies. Ko's approach brings out the client's role in the translation production process more clearly than the surveys carried out by Rasmussen and Schjoldager or Uotila. Ko (2011: 133) also states that as translation jobs have different purposes and requirements, general guidelines applied to all revision or review jobs would be impractical. Instead, any guidelines for revision or review should be tailor-made. The need to tailor the task description for different purposes of course resonates well with the idea of a revision continuum.

All these studies discuss revision as quality assurance. Variation in the scope of revision is not a particular area of focus in any of them, nor are the creative aspects of revision tasks considered. The present study aims to fill this gap and take revision research in a new direction to uncover the full potential of this important part of the workflow.

4. Research design

The survey to be discussed here looked at workflow processes from the LSPs' viewpoint, examining how they have designed their production workflow and the related revision policies. The participants were therefore representatives of Finnish LSPs that identify primarily as translation agencies. Based on publicly available sales information, LSPs that were at least medium-sized as translation businesses, although not very large from the point of view of Finnish businesses generally, were selected as recipients of the online questionnaire. To allow the inclusion of an adequate number of companies, no definite sales limit was established; instead, sales figures from several years were examined to identify companies with steady annual sales of several hundred thousand euros or more.

In order to obtain some preliminary quantitative data on the kinds of revision policies and practices that might be prevalent among LSPs, the link to the questionnaire was sent to a single representative of each company. They were informed that their responses would be used for research purposes and published. To ensure protection of business secrets, the survey recipients cannot be described in greater detail here.

In the cover letter, it was emphasised that the respondent should be familiar with the company's revision processes and services. The respondents were thus expected to provide answers based on the companies' established ways of working instead of the respondents' own preferences. However, it was not possible to control who actually responded to the survey. The respondents were not required to enter their own or the company's name, because it was assumed that they would then be more reluctant to respond. This means that the respondent may have been someone with incomplete or outdated knowledge. Similarly, it cannot be confirmed that an actual company policy or practice exists regarding all the details addressed by the survey; some of the matters discussed here may not have been considered by some LSPs at all. In these cases, the responses would in fact reflect the respondents' individual preferences.

A link to the online questionnaire was sent by e-mail to 26 Finnish LSPs. Reminders were sent, and some of the large companies were contacted via personal connections to ensure a response. A total of 11 LSPs responded to the survey (response rate 42.3%); these represent a major portion of the Finnish translation

industry in terms of combined sales. The most prominent LSPs were well represented among the respondents.

The questionnaire had 29 questions, some with two parts. The questions were posed
in Finnish and divided into four sections: (1) basic background information about the
company, (2) the company's service range, (3) the revision procedure and (4) creative
translation and editing services offered. Both open and closed questions were used.

Not all the data yielded by the questionnaire are analysed in this chapter; here,
the focus is on the section dealing with the revision procedure, with particular
attention to the scope of revision, its allowed level of creativity and who has the
authority to make decisions about these matters. To learn more about the role of
revision in the workflows for creative translation and editing services, some of the
questions in the fourth part of the questionnaire were also examined. The following questions are discussed here:

1   Does the typical translation workflow include a revision task carried out by
    someone other than the person who translated the text?
2   Which text features is the reviser expected to pay attention to?
3   What types of stylistic editing is the reviser expected to carry out?
4   In what situations may the reviser make or propose changes to deviate from
    source text content?
5   Has the company defined different revision levels, or may the reviser decide
    the scope of revision?
6   Is the reviser provided with a description of the scope and objectives of each
    revision task?

Basic information about all these matters was obtained from closed questions,
and the responses to them are presented in section 5. However, some of the open-
ended questions provided a more nuanced picture by revealing contextual factors
behind the practices. Information from these questions has therefore also been
included in the present analysis.

In analysing the responses, the companies were divided into major (five respondents)
and minor operators (six respondents) based on their number of employees, countries
of operation, service range and selection of language pairs. The responses to the background information section of the survey showed that all the major operators offered
translations in all language pairs, had operations in several countries, and had an extensive
service range including creative translation services. The division into major and minor
operators will be used in the presentation of the survey results in the next section.

5.   Results of the survey: revision policies of LSPs operating in Finland

In this section, I will go through the responses to the six questions listed in the
previous section and briefly discuss the possible implications of the responses. With
the exception of the first question, the results will be presented in a graphical

format. As the data were limited, it must be kept in mind that any conclusions are only preliminary, hypotheses for further study at best. Since it is difficult to obtain a larger sample among Finnish LSPs, any further study will have to rely on in-depth methods such as interviews.

The status of revision in the typical workflow

To begin charting the LSPs' revision policies, they were asked whether the typical translation workflow included other-revision, that is, a revision task carried out by someone other than the person who translated the text. The question was worded to ask about a *typical* translation process, because based on Rasmussen and Schjoldager's (2011) as well as Uotila's (2017) findings, it was expected that most LSPs allow some flexibility in their processes and do not revise each and every translation. Rather surprisingly, only 7 of the 11 respondents stated that their typical translation workflow includes revision. Among large operators, only 2 of the 5 companies did, which was even more surprising as large companies could certainly be assumed to have adequate resources for revision. When asked to give an account of the entire workflow, however, most of those who did not indicate revision as part of the typical workflow still mentioned it as a possible step; only one did not mention revision at all.

In Uotila's (2017) survey of Finnish LSPs, the respondents were not asked whether a typical workflow included revision. Instead, they were asked to estimate what percentage of their translations are revised. Of Uotila's nine respondents, four claimed that they revise all translations, and nearly all revised more than half of the translations. The texts were chosen for revision based on criteria such as the language pair, the client's requirements, knowledge of the translator's skill, and whether the translation had been subcontracted to another service provider that has its own quality assurance process (Uotila 2017: 48–50).

Uotila's findings as well as the present survey indicate a strong emphasis on flexibility in LSPs' workflows. It would be interesting to find out more about why so many LSPs, even the large ones, do not include revision into their typical translation process despite the fact that revision is strongly recommended in the literature on translation workflow and even required by the translation industry standards EN 15038 and ISO 17100. One of the possible reasons is that they have a very reliable translator base. Perhaps they translate high volumes of non-critical text types where low pricing does not allow revision, or subcontract a large proportion of translations to other service providers that have their own QA procedures. Further research is needed to achieve any degree of certainty about why some companies do not consider revision so important as to make it a standard part of the workflow.

Revision parameters

Figure 7.2 lists 14 revision parameters from four groups (A–D) and shows the number of respondent companies that included each parameter in the scope of typical

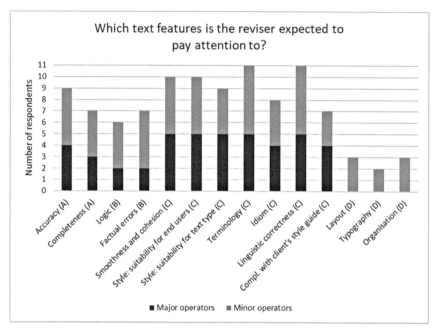

FIGURE 7.2 Parameters to be checked

revision. The respondents were able to select several options—which was also the case for most of the other questions presented in this chapter.

The options used in the questionnaire roughly follow the revision parameters identified by Mossop (2014a: 134–5). Some modifications were made to use wordings that were more likely to be familiar to the respondents;[2] this was somewhat challenging as the jargon used at LSPs varies considerably from one company to the next (see Uotila 2017: 45). Two of Mossop's parameters were divided further so that more detailed information of the task content could be obtained: the parameter 'sub-language' was divided into 'stylistic suitability for the text type' and 'terminology', while 'mechanics' was divided into 'linguistic (grammatical) correctness' and 'compliance with client's style guide'. It is true that client-specific style guides often include instructions on appropriate grammar. Still, general grammatical correctness and compliance with a style guide constitute two different things to check, which made it logical to separate them in this context. Similarly, style and terminology, while both aspects of sub-language, are different from each other in that style can be understood as a feature of all texts, while terminology is more important in some texts than in others. The differences in how many respondents selected each of these options proved the divisions justified.

The only two parameters that all respondents marked as part of the typical revision procedure were 'linguistic correctness' and 'terminology'; the same two parameters were considered most important by Uotila's (2017: 54) respondents.

Most of the parameters related to language and style—Mossop's (2014a: 134) parameter group C—were, in fact, routinely included in revision by nearly all respondents. 'Idiom' and 'compliance with a client's style guide' were selected slightly less frequently than the other parameters in this group.

The first two parameters, which deal with meaning transfer (Mossop's group A), were also included by the majority of respondents, although 'completeness' was selected less often than 'accuracy'. As accuracy can be verified only if a comparative revision is carried out, it can be concluded that this revision method seems to be the norm. Uotila's (2017: 51) findings support this conclusion: seven of her nine respondents used a comparative procedure for all their revisions. In their survey of Danish LSPs, Rasmussen and Schjoldager (2011: 104–5) also found that comparative revision was the prevalent practice, although it was not always carried out for the entire text.

Perhaps most striking about Figure 7.2 is how marginal the visual aspects of the text are (parameter group D). This group includes the parameters 'layout', 'typography' and 'organisation', which refers to the use of headings and footnotes. Each of these parameters was selected by only two or three respondents, and by none of the major operators. One respondent explained that the working file formats used in the translation environment prevent a layout check, even though reference material with the original layout is often available. Layout may be separately checked at a later stage, but the check is not part of the revision task and is offered to clients as an additional service by this particular LSP.

The parameters related to content ('logic' and 'factual errors', group B) are an interesting category. More than half of the respondents included them in the normal revision procedure, but the difference from the language and style parameters was clear. While it is generally agreed that obvious source mistakes such as dates that do not match should be corrected—and the client notified—many apparently consider the content parameters to fall under the client's and not the LSP's responsibility.

Variation in the level of creativity

When the logic of the text or factual errors are corrected during translation or revision, the resulting target text will naturally differ at some points from the source text. The question of whether the logical and factual errors should be corrected in a translation thus takes us towards a bigger question: are actual changes to the content of the text allowed during translation and revision? Two of the survey questions addressed this issue. The first of these concerned the degree of creativity allowed in stylistic modifications, and the second dealt with the specific situations in which the reviser was allowed to make changes to the content of the text. The options and responses are presented in Figures 7.3 and 7.4.

Nearly all respondents expected the reviser to correct the style of the text in accordance with text type-specific target language conventions, to make the text flow better through improved word choices and constructions, and to sharpen the text by small changes. However, many drew the line at actual content editing.

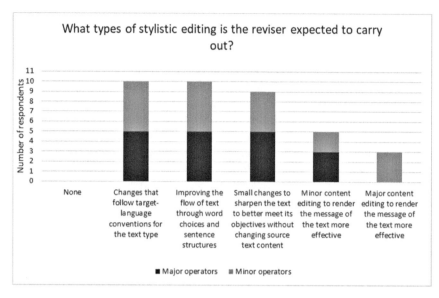

FIGURE 7.3 Types of stylistic editing

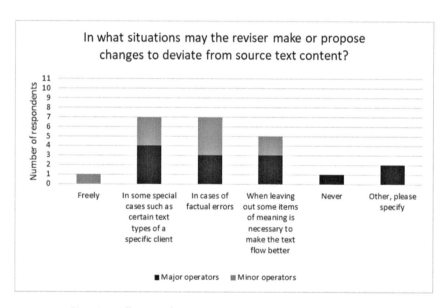

FIGURE 7.4 Situations allowing changes in source text content

None of the large operators expected the reviser to engage in major content editing. It is rather interesting that three minor operators did, but we can only speculate whether these companies specialise in creative translation and communication services, or whether the respondents perhaps just had a different definition of major content editing in mind.

Figure 7.4 lists some situations in which LSPs may allow content editing during revision. Only one respondent indicated that they allow revisers to freely deviate from source content; on the other hand, one respondent allowed no deviations at all. It seems to be a fairly common practice that changes to content are allowed with certain text types of specific clients. In my own experience, which is supported by the responses to some of the open-ended questions in the survey, this is usually based on an agreement between the LSP and the client to the effect that some text types are given a special treatment. Two respondents selected the 'Other, please specify' option: both described cases where the client has specifically ordered a creative translation or wanted the text to be edited further. It must be noted that both of these respondents also selected other options; these were therefore not the only situations where they allowed deviation from source text content.

The responses to some of the open-ended questions in this survey indicate that the client's requests and what had been agreed with the client are the most important factors in deciding what kinds of changes are allowed during the revision task. The respondents repeatedly mentioned the wishes of the client and the fact that service specifications must be mutually agreed upon. In some other translation contexts, the client's wishes may not need to be automatically observed, and Mossop (2014a: 123) indeed does not recommend doing so. When producing a commercial service in an extremely competitive operating environment, however, listening to the client is clearly of crucial importance. Dunne (2011: 176) stresses that a translation can be adequate or inadequate only in relation to the communicative function that it should fulfil (see Nord 1997: 34–7), which is "not a quality inherent in a target text, but rather is a quality assigned to the target text by an evaluator from his or her particular point of view"—and that point of view, in the context of a business-to-business translation service, can only be the client's.

Other factors that respondents mentioned as having an impact on the scope of revision include the text type, the target audience and the intended use: the text must be revised so that it works as intended in the target context. However, the target audience, or the end user, was mentioned far less frequently than the client, which clearly implies that in all considerations, the client comes first. Other factors to be considered include local legislation, which may require changes to the text, and layout, which may require omission of some content so that the text can fit into the designated space. With some text types, strict limits on the number of characters are imposed.

One respondent foregrounded a further factor that can be best described as a precondition for all the other revision policy choices: the pricing of the job must allow enough time to produce the necessary quality level. As creative editing is a time-consuming activity, it can be carried out only if the price of the project has been negotiated to allow the use of adequate time. According to the respondent who raised the price issue, translations of marketing texts must be sold to clients under service labels that justify the higher price. The label makes it easier for the client to accept that creative quality takes time to produce. This is a crucial matter for LSPs, because in the commercial reality within which they now operate, translation prices are often pushed down to the limits of profitability (see European Commission 2018a), and it is simply not possible to spend enough time on all translations to hone them to perfection.

Distribution of decision-making power

Who then decides what the scope of revision will be and what the reviser can or cannot do? Do revisers receive instructions, or a brief, for each task? In this area, the respondents seemed to give somewhat contradictory answers to two slightly overlapping questions (Figures 7.5 and 7.6). The first question is whether the LSPs have defined revision levels that are given to revisers as instructions, and the second explores different situations in which instructions may be provided.

For the question presented in Figure 7.5, the respondents were allowed to select only one option. It seems that large operators favour providing instructions, while smaller ones more often rely on the reviser's judgement. It remains unclear whether the respondents who always apply the same revision level communicate their revision principles to revisers. These responses also provide proof that most LSPs recognise that variation exists between revision tasks: the responses represented by the first and the third columns are based on the assumption that the scope of revision needs to be decided at some point. The respondents who selected the first or the third option differ only on whether the decision is made by the LSP or whether the reviser may decide the scope independently.

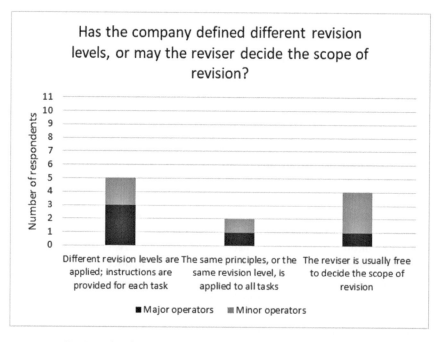

FIGURE 7.5 Revision levels and decision–making power

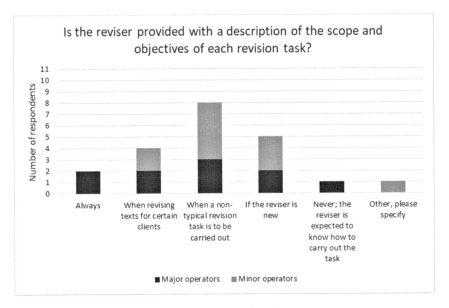

FIGURE 7.6 Availability of scope and objectives of revision

The responses presented in Figure 7.5 seem straightforward enough—until Figure 7.6 is examined. The respondents were now again allowed to select several options. While five respondents had previously indicated that the company applies different revision levels and that revisers receive instructions for each task, now only two stated that revisers always receive a description of the scope and objectives of the task. This can be understood only by assuming that in the previous question, the respondents did not mean that instructions would be provided for each and every task; instead, they meant that instructions for different revision levels existed and would be provided when necessary. Furthermore, eight respondents now state that a description is provided when a non-typical revision task is to be carried out, although only five had previously said that such descriptions exist. This must mean that a task description can be provided on an ad hoc basis for each case even when definitions of revision levels have not been established in advance.

One respondent did not find an appropriate option among those provided and explained that the procedure was well established and no actual instructions were usually required, but when they were, even detailed instructions could be provided by the project manager, the translator or the account manager. This seems to be a good summary of all the responses to this question: the procedure is very flexible for most LSPs, and is based on only providing instructions when they are needed. In other cases, instructions would only waste the reviser's time. On the other hand, if the procedure is indeed well established and revisers are normally expected to know the routine, this could mean that there is little variation in how revision is carried out, and that the service that is being provided is usually the same. There may therefore be a lot of untapped potential in how the workflow's revision phase could be used to produce different services for clients.

Some of the responses to the fourth section of the questionnaire, which charted the creative translation and editing services of the LSPs, provided proof that revision is already being used in that manner by some LSPs. Respondents from companies that offer both a transcreation[3] service and a separate creative editing service were asked to explain how these two differ in terms of the workflow or the practical execution of the task. Two respondents answered this question; both stated clearly that the workflows used when producing these two services are similar. One of the two also explained that both services are based on a regular translation workflow to which a more extensive editing phase is added.

Although this shows that dividing the work into phases is clearly considered a useful practice, using the same production process for different services could also indicate a need for further service development. Such a need was in fact identified by several respondents: when asked whether they have established definitions for their creative translation and editing services, only one respondent stated confidently that service descriptions exist for all services. All the others were more or less unhappy with their current service definitions or admitted that service design had not yet been completed. Five of the eleven respondents did say that their companies had increased their service range in recent years, most of them in the area of marketing and content production services. With the development of new services, service design is probably an ongoing effort for many LSPs.

6. Role and benefits of a revision continuum

Section 2 of this chapter introduced the concept of a revision continuum that ranges from simple proofreading to extensive creative editing of a translation. As we have seen, editing can indeed be used to produce creative translation services. Furthermore, Figures 7.4, 7.5 and 7.6 showed that variation exists in the revision tasks carried out at LSPs. All in all, the survey yielded important information about how different situations influence revision practices and seem to require specific procedures. This information helps us understand the flexibility inherent in LSP policies. To turn this flexibility into efficient workflows, systematic definition of specific revision types that meet different needs will be required.

As was mentioned in section 2, the revision continuum could be used as a theoretical model, providing insight into all the different ways in which revision could be carried out, or it could be a valuable practical tool used as a basis of daily operations at LSPs. At least two practical uses can be identified: firstly, as a service design tool when defining the scope of a revision task that is part of a specific service, and secondly, as a way to help ensure the financial viability of LSPs' operations.

When using the revision continuum as a service design tool, the first step is to consider which variables will be involved in the different types of revision that would be useful to LSPs. Choosing which revision parameters to apply is an obvious starting point. Going by the results shown on Figure 7.2, some revision parameters are considered more essential than others. This makes it fairly easy to define a budget revision service that includes only the most important parameters (linguistic correctness and terminology being the most obvious candidates based on both the present study and Uotila's 2017 findings), as well as a full service that would encompass all or most of the revision parameters. The level of creativity to be allowed—which was discussed earlier as deviation from the source text content but could also be understood as creative use of language—is another powerful way of making a difference between types of revision. Further variables would include choosing between a spot check and complete revision, and between unilingual and comparative revision, or including both in the workflow as separate steps.

Next, let's look at how the revision continuum could help LSPs avoid wasting resources. LSPs often engage in fierce competitive bidding in which price is the most important factor. The company that has the best production process, resulting in adequate quality at the lowest price, wins. Adequate (or fit-for-purpose) revision can be considered as key to adequate quality. In practice, this means that LSPs must consider when to apply extensive revision and when a less thorough check will do, and the depth of revision must be reflected in the price.

The need to make the task description and the price meet has not previously been fully recognised in revision research. Martin (2007: 58), for example, takes it for granted that revision needs to be kept "within sensible and affordable limits". The underlying assumption appears to be that the price the client pays for revision is always the same, and the cost to the LSP of revision must be affordable with respect to that price, which of course often limits revision to a minimum level. This results in problems that could be solved by increased variation in the price of revision. The survey results presented here have shown that LSPs already use the revision step in the workflow to produce services that are sold under various labels for which a higher price is charged, for example creative editing or transcreation. This proves that revision is an important part of the workflow, with potential to make a difference between regular translation and a high-quality creative communication service; charging different prices for different types of revision is thus justified. From the clients' point of view, it also makes sense that they receive texts with the quality level and style that they need in each case, and pay only for the level that they need.

It could of course be argued that in the case of extensive editing of a translation, we are no longer talking about revision in the sense usually ascribed to the term in Translation Studies. Creative editing could be seen as falling outside the realm of translation revision, and ample justification for that approach can certainly be provided. One such justification can be found within this very survey: it seemed to be a fairly common practice that when the translation workflow includes creative editing, it also includes another revision step such as language review or proofreading. However, I believe creative editing should be discussed under the overall concept of revision when it is carried out within the LSP directly after the translation phase in the workflow, by the same people who also do other revision work.

The revision continuum is presented here as a hypothesis only, and its further development and practical application is left to future work. The factors that determine the placing of tasks on the continuum must be elaborated based on more thorough empirical research on LSP practices. Different revision tasks can then be identified and defined in order to create a representation of how revision is currently being used. On that basis, new, efficient ways to make use of revision in service production could be revealed. The very shape of the visual representation could change as a result of more detailed research: a simple continuum between two extreme task types might not be adequate for dealing with all the different factors involved. The roles of different actors or agents, such as the project manager as the one who decides what to include in the workflow (see Stoeller 2011: 296), as well as the client as an agent that influences all decision-making, are also worth examining.

7. Conclusion

The survey results presented here make it clear that although LSPs are often seen as a fairly unified entity, a closer look at their service workflows reveals many differences between them and in how they serve their clients. It is logical that differences should exist: LSPs are free enterprises that compete against each other and work hard to find the best practices that will allow them to get a larger share of the available business. It is unlikely that clients, whose knowledge of translation is usually limited, are aware of all the differences in how the services are produced. Clear definitions of services, referring to workflow and task content, and using terminology that can also be understood by people who are not experts in translation, would be useful to clients and would allow them to make informed purchase decisions.

It must be noted that when revision is expanded to include creative editing, it no longer equals quality assurance. Revision and quality assurance have always been strongly linked by both researchers and practitioners. When Drugan (2013: 37) asked her interviewees how they manage translation quality, they responded by explaining their revision procedures—forgetting at first all the quality management measures that take place at other stages of the process. However, if we look at revision as a task that goes beyond checking and reaches into the production of creative translation services, we must also accept that quality assurance is only one possible purpose of revision. A shift in how revision is seen and defined is therefore necessary: instead of merely checking for errors, it needs to be seen as part of the text production effort.

As mentioned earlier in this chapter, the translation industry standards EN 15038 and ISO 17100 both take a strict view on revision, requiring that all target language content be revised. Considering the flexibility of practices generally adopted by LSPs, and the need to ensure profitable operations by not wasting resources, it seems that any widespread adoption of the standards may not take place unless these requirements are reconsidered. As has been repeatedly found in empirical studies, for example Rasmussen and Schjoldager (2011: 101) and Schnierer in Chapter 6 of this volume, revision is sometimes not possible for practical reasons. Adoption of the standard would, therefore, mean having to follow requirements that are not financially and practically viable in the translation industry.

Research into LSP workflows challenges the way a translator's work is traditionally seen—as an individual, isolated effort where a translation is created as a result of one person's thought processes. Any up-to-date theory of translation must account for how translations are created in real production contexts. In the ongoing effort to bridge the gap between translation theory and practical work (see Chesterman and Wagner 2014), a move towards recognising the impact of teamwork in everyday working environments would be a welcome development. Research in areas such as the sociology of translation has already resulted in great advances in our understanding of such environments in recent years; more detailed investigations of translation workflows would contribute to this same goal.

Notes

1 While Mossop (2014a) uses the term 'editing' primarily when discussing non-translations, Bisiada (2018: 290) explicitly states that he uses the term for both translations and non-translations. There is really no reason why the various editing tasks could not be performed for a text that has been previously translated; the text is then no longer treated as a translation. This process is also recognised by Mossop and is in fact included in his glossary definition of the term 'editing' (Mossop 2014a: 224).
2 A good example of the terminological variation is that Finnish LSPs generally do not use the concept of revision (or the direct Finnish correspondent of the word) when referring to checking translations (Uotila 2017: 44–5), and that for Danish LSPs, it is only one of several terms that are used (Rasmussen and Schjoldager 2011: 100).
3 Risku et al. (2017: 54) cite Rike's (2013: 72f) definition of transcreation as "a concept in which the advertising text and message are completely rewritten and redesigned in order to produce a creative and effective target text". The term is used here in this sense, referring to a commercial service that meets this definition.

8

EXPLORING A TWO-WAY STREET

Revisers' and translators' attitudes and expectations about each other in biomedical translation

Susana Valdez and Sonia Vandepitte

What motivates revisers' and translators' decision-making and, hence, their options is a common interest among researchers within process-oriented DTS and translator training.[1] Revisers' and translators' attitudes and expectations are particularly relevant if we wish to describe, understand and explain the motivations of these professionals. Their attitudes and expectations have been the subject of some investigations, in particular those concerned with how professionals do and should perform various translation activities in different domains.[2] However, although much progress has been made in researching translation revision (for example, Mossop 2007a, 2014a; Robert 2014a; Robert et al. 2017a, 2018), to the best of our knowledge, there is no research concerning attitudes and expectations about revision practices in medical or biomedical translation. It is not known what attitudes and expectations revisers have about professional translators and translation in biomedical settings. How translators think they should translate and what they think revisers expect from them are also not fully understood.

At the intersection of Descriptive Translation Studies and social sciences, our interdisciplinary, empirical and descriptive study addresses the question of whether revisers' attitudes and expectations about competences and working practices are similar to or different from those of translators. To do so, we shall look at the results from a questionnaire circulated among professional revisers and translators from June 2017 to April 2018. The questionnaire was originally part of a larger descriptive study about the beliefs, translation behaviours and translation options of 60 agents[3] with different roles and levels of experience, namely novice translators, experienced translators, revisers and health professionals. Different types of beliefs were elicited and then compared with translators' behaviour and with revisers' and health professionals' preferences regarding translation options in biomedical translation (Valdez 2019). The analysis showed that translators and revisers not only expressed beliefs associated with source and target orientation (which was the focus of the study), but also beliefs about competences and working practices. Consequently, a follow-up study was conducted with a larger group of participants (n = 71), to whom the same questionnaire was administered. The findings discussed here concern the attitudes and expectations expressed about competences and working practices in revision and translation.

The next section provides a brief overview of the main guiding concepts of our research, that is, 'attitudes' and 'expectations' and their connection to translation norms. Then we contextualize biomedical translation within medical translation and define what is meant by these terms. The chapter then goes on to describe and discuss the methods used in our study. In the final sections, the results are described and discussed, together with the implications and our conclusions.

1.   Attitudes, expectations and norms

Attitudes and expectations have been a prolific subject of research in the social sciences, where they are sometimes described as "the primary building stone in the edifice of social psychology" (Allport 1954: 45). One of the main reasons why attitudes, in particular, take centre stage in the study of behaviour is that they are considered "precursors of behavior" (Cohen 1964: 137–8).

Before discussing attitudes and expectations in connection with revision and translation norms, we must first clarify the concepts of 'attitudes' and 'expectations'. To do so, Bicchieri's theoretical framework is adopted and adapted to revision and translation, as it proves to be particularly useful for a distinctive account of social norms as "a behavior-guiding force" (Bicchieri 2000: 153). Her philosophical approach based on game theory and social norms critically includes the role of agents' beliefs (as a more general and encompassing term), and attitudes and expectations as conditions on agents' behaviour.

Against this background, Bicchieri's typology of self-beliefs and beliefs about other agents was adapted to this study (mainly Bicchieri 2006, 2017a, 2017b; Bicchieri et al. 2018). In her view, three main types of beliefs should be considered, namely (1) the beliefs the agent has about her/himself, (2) the beliefs the agent has about other agents' actions, and (3) the beliefs the agent has about other agents' beliefs. The beliefs can be further characterized as empirical or normative.[4]

The study elicited revisers' and translators' belief statements about all these beliefs. This chapter, however, will be limited to normative attitudes, empirical expectations and normative expectations about other agents, because the participating revisers and translators expressed these only when referring to competences and working practices (grey cells in Table 8.1).

TABLE 8.1 Overview of beliefs about other agents

What the agent believes about→ *Type of belief↓*	**Beliefs about other agents' actions**	**Beliefs about other agents' beliefs**
EMPIRICAL	*what other agents do* = **empirical expectations**	*what others believe s/he does* = second-order empirical expectations
NORMATIVE	*what other agents should do* = **normative attitudes**	*what others believe s/he should do* = **normative expectations**

Source: Adapted from Bicchieri 2017a: Kindle location 1153.

More concretely, the beliefs that translators and revisers expressed about competences and working practices were:

- the agent's beliefs about what 'other agents should do' in a situation, henceforth *normative attitudes* (for example, how revisers think translators should translate, and how translators think revisers should revise);
- the agent's beliefs about what other agents 'do' in a particular context, which will be referred to as *empirical expectations* (for example, how revisers think translators translate, and how translators think revisers revise);
- the agent's beliefs about what 'others believe s/he should do', called *normative expectations* (for example, what revisers believe translators think revisers should do, and vice versa).

The distinctions between different types of beliefs are often overlooked within social sciences in general and Translation Studies in particular. Within the former, Bicchieri clarifies that "important distinctions . . . are often missed in surveys, because questions about attitudes are often too vague to capture these distinctions" (2017a: Kindle location 346).

In addition, research has suggested that even though the attitude-behaviour relationship has motivated a considerable body of literature in the social sciences, the relationship between attitudes and behaviour is at least arguable. In his much-cited literature review, Wicker concluded that there is "little evidence to support the postulated existence of stable, underlying attitudes within the individual which influence both his verbal expressions and his actions" (Wicker 1969: 75), and he added that "it is considerably more likely that attitudes will be unrelated or only slightly related to overt behaviors than that attitudes will be closely related to actions" (Wicker 1969: 65), a view that the authors of this chapter share.

In other words, what people say they 'believe' may or may not coincide with what they actually 'do'. In translation, too, "there may . . . be gaps, even contradictions", Toury (2012: 88) explains, "between explicit arguments and demands, on the one hand, and actual behaviour, on the other". This lack of convergence between what people say they believe and what they do may have multiple causes: they may lack awareness of their own behaviour, their statements may be deliberately or unintentionally misleading and they may model their behaviour on what they believe others expect of them, because people are "social animals embedded in thick networks of relations" (Bicchieri 2017a: Kindle location 311).

What agents believe they should do in a particular situation is largely based on the shared beliefs, attitudes and expectations within a particular group about what is considered appropriate and inappropriate behaviour in a specific situation within a certain target culture, language and system (Valdez 2019: 46). That is precisely the topic of this study.

Within this perspective, behaviour is conditioned by the belief that most agents in one's network conform to the norm and believe they ought to conform to the norm. These beliefs are assumed to inform the conditional preference to act in a certain way in a specific situation.

An agent's interpretation of what should be done, given their community's shared beliefs about appropriate and inappropriate courses of action, is actually already present in Toury's definition of translation norms "as the translation of general values or ideas shared by a community—as to what is right and wrong, adequate and inadequate—into performance instructions appropriate for and applicable to particular situations" (Toury 2012: 63). Here revision and translation norms can be interpreted as non-binding *orientations* of behaviour: revisers and translators always have a choice. It is their expectations of what they consider appropriate and what they think the community expects of them that tends to constrain their options and hence their decision-making.

Revisers' and translators' behaviour is not only influenced by what they believe most other agents believe they *should* do, but also by what they (revisers and translators) think most agents in their community *actually* do. It is all these beliefs that inform an agent's preference to act in a certain way in a specific situation and what the agent believes others should do. As Hermans (1999: 74) formulates it, translators' decisions result from "certain demands which they [translators] derive from their reading of the source text, and certain preferences and expectations which they know exist in the audience they are addressing". In this study, it is assumed that this also applies to revisers.

Since individual choices depend on what agents believe others in their community do and what they believe is appropriate and inappropriate behaviour (Bicchieri 2017a: Kindle location 232), revision and translation can be considered interdependent actions. In other words, it is not sufficient only to elicit what revisers and translators think they should do, since what they believe should be done in a specific situation may be constrained by what they believe others expect of them and what they believe others do.

Revisers' and translators' statements about attitudes and expectations can thus be seen as extratextual data and an essential source for the "reconstruction" of translation norms referred to in the literature as "semi-theoretical or critical formulations, such as . . . statements made by translators, editors, publishers and other persons involved in or connected with the activity" (Toury 1995: 65). Such statements also respond to Chesterman's (2016: 83) call for more evidence of norm-governed behaviour:

> We also need text-external indicators of normative force, such as belief state-ments by the translator ("I think I should do this"), criticism of breaches of the assumed norm, perhaps even norm statements by relevant authorities ("Translators of such texts must do this").

The present study of attitudes and expectations about biomedical translation answers Chesterman's call for more evidence of norm-governed behaviour.

2.   Biomedical translation

Medical translation is generally considered a type of scientific-technical transla-tion concerning medicine and a range of subject areas related not only to health (including pharmacology, surgery, psychology) but also to other fields (such as law) (Karwacka 2015: 271; Montalt 2011: para. 4). The importance of medical trans-lation in the dissemination of knowledge and new discoveries is unquestionable (Karwacka 2015: 271). The facilitation of specialized and non-specialized com-munication (expert-to-expert, and different combinations and variations of expert to layperson and layperson to expert) through medical interpreting has also been attracting the attention of translation scholars (for example, Lesch and Saulse 2014; Li et al. 2017; Major and Napier 2012).

Within the healthcare environment, the medical devices industry has been playing an increasingly important role in the European economy (European Com-mission 2018b, under "The importance of the medical devices sector"). On the one hand, "medical devices are crucial in diagnosing, preventing, monitoring and treating illness, and overcoming disabilities" (European Commission 2019b). Med-ical devices are even considered by the World Health Organization as "ever more indispensable" in healthcare provision (World Health Organization 2018). The medical devices industry also represents a growing sector of 27,000 companies and 675,000 employees in the European Union and hence "an influencer of expendi-ture" (European Commission 2018b).

Biomedical translation is defined here as the translation of content from bio-medicine, the science and profession responsible for medical devices, from "innovation, research and development, design, selection, management [to their] safe use" (World Health Organization 2017: 20). It includes mainly texts related to medical devices. A medical device is considered "any product intended by its manufacturer to be used specifically for diagnostic and/or therapeutic purposes and necessary for its proper application, intended by the manufacturer to be used for human beings" (European Parliament 2007: 23–4). In accordance with European legislation (Council of the European Union 1993: 30), each medical device is accompanied by an instructional text. These texts are written or commissioned by the manufacturer and are thus written by experts to be read by experts (health professionals) or laypeople. The aim is to instruct the health professional or layperson on how to correctly and safely use the device.

3.   Methodology

Within the field of biomedical translation, this chapter describes how revisers think translators translate, how translators think other translators translate and how revisers revise (empirical expectations); how revisers think translators 'should' translate and how translators think revisers 'should' revise (normative attitudes); and what revisers believe are the essential characteristics of a good translation, what translators think about other translators' expectations of their work and what translators think about revisers' expectations of translators' work (normative expectations) (Table 8.1).

Questionnaires were the method selected for data collection since they are seen as the optimal instrument to elicit beliefs not only in social sciences (for example, Bicchieri 2017a: Kindle location 1134) but also in Translation Studies (Kuo 2014: 106; Robert and Remael 2016: 586). The well-documented problems associated with the elicitation of beliefs in general and the use of questionnaires in particular were taken into account in the data collection and the design of the questionnaires (for example, see Callegaro 2008 on social desirability bias). This was done mainly by (1) adopting a self-administered method of data collection, (2) assuring participants that their personal information would be treated confidentially, (3) pilot testing the questionnaires, and (4) acknowledging that the respondents' answers may not be truthful (Gile 2006).

Data collection

The links of the online questionnaires[5] were sent by e-mail, together with the informed consent form, to the pre-contacted participants recruited (1) from a call for participants posted on dedicated Facebook pages for Portuguese translators and associations; (2) on the basis of a pre-selection of profiles of translators and revisers who self-identify as specialized in medical or biomedical translation on Proz.com and on the websites of Portuguese translation associations (APTRAD and APT); (3) through a request sent to Portuguese universities with the intent of recruiting novice translators that might fit the profile; and (4) from personal acquaintances. Each participant received a questionnaire tailored to their experience and/or profession, namely reviser, novice translator or experienced translator. No financial compensation was offered to the participants.

Questionnaire design and data analysis

The questionnaires were in English and included both open questions and closed questions (multiple choice, check-all-that-apply, rating scale (Likert scale and star scale) and yes/no). Each of the three questionnaires had 21 questions divided into different sections. The revisers' questionnaire was divided into five sections: (1) professional profile (five questions), (2) assessment of the quality of a translation (two multiple choice questions), (3) reviser's beliefs about revisers (self-beliefs and beliefs about others) (three open questions and two Likert scale questions), (4) reviser's beliefs about translators (two open questions and two Likert scale questions), and (5) reviser's beliefs about the readers of the translation (three open questions and two Likert scale questions). The translators' questionnaire was divided into four sections: (1) professional profile (five questions), (2) translator's beliefs about translators (self-beliefs and beliefs about others) (two open questions, two Likert scale questions, one star scale question and one yes/no question), (3) translator's beliefs about revisers (three open questions and two Likert scale questions), (4) translator's beliefs about the readers of the translation (three open questions, two Likert scale questions and one star scale question).

Normative attitudes about competences and working practices were elicited by asking revisers the open question "In general, how do you think translators 'should' translate?" and novice and experienced translators the open question "In general, what criteria do you think reviewers 'should' use to judge the quality of a translation?" In order to elicit empirical expectations, revisers were asked the open question "In general, how do you think translators 'actually' translate?" while translators (both novice and experienced) were asked "How do other translators with the same experience as you translate?" and "In general, how do you think reviewers assess a translation?" Finally, to elicit normative expectations, revisers were asked the open question "In general, which are the essential characteristics of a good translation?" while translators (both novice and experienced) were asked "In general, how do other translators with the same experience as you think you 'should' translate?" and "In general, what expectations do you think reviewers[6] 'have' of your work?"

The questionnaires were designed using the online SurveyMonkey tool,[7] which allows for the collection of responses and their export for external codification and analysis in the NVivo quality analysis software. NVivo 12 Mac allows for the processing of qualitative unstructured data resulting from the open questions to which a participant "gives the response in his or her own words" (Ballou 2008: 547), which is especially useful when conducting an exploratory study regarding an unexplored topic like attitudes and expectations in biomedical translation. The rich raw data provided by the participants were systematically coded and organized by emergent themes (following Saldanha and O'Brien 2013: iBook location 564). Thematic analysis has been defined as "the process of working with raw data to identify and interpret key ideas or themes" (Matthews and Ross 2010: 373).

Participants

In total 71 participants answered the questionnaires, all native speakers of European Portuguese, with experience in biomedical translation and/or revision. There were 23 revisers, 32 novice translators and 16 experienced translators. The different levels of experience (novice vs. experienced translators) and the distinct professions of the participants (translators vs. revisers) allowed for a comparison and contrast of their belief statements.

4. Results

Revisers' profiles

The 23 revisers (7 men) had experience in the revision of biomedical translation ranging from 1 to 20 years (average of 7 years). All revisers had a degree in translation at the BA or post-graduate level and/or a degree in medical sciences. All revisers worked with the language pair English to European Portuguese (95.65%), with the exception of one that revised Spanish–Portuguese translations. Some of the revisers worked in several language pairs besides the main English–Portuguese pair and also revised from Spanish (43.48%), French (26.09%) and German (8.70%).

Revisers were asked to select, from a list of text types in the (bio)medical domain, all the types they had worked with.[8] From that list, the most frequently revised were patient information leaflets (56.52%), user manuals for devices (56.52%) and software (43.48%), summaries of product characteristics (52.17%), (material) safety data sheets (47.83%) and training material (47.83%).

Novice translators' profiles

The 32 novice translators (8 men), with up to two years of full-time experience, held a higher education degree from a Portuguese university, and the majority (all but 2) had completed at least the first year of a master's programme in translation. All translators worked from English to Portuguese, but some also worked from other languages, such as from French (18.75%), Spanish (12.50%), German (6.25%), Russian (3.13%), Italian (3.13%) and Chinese (3.13%).

The most frequently reported text types among the novice translators were: patient information leaflets (46.88%), user manuals for medical devices (21.88%), patient consent forms (28.13%), clinical guidelines (18.75%), case reports (18.75%) and news releases (18.75%).

Experienced translators' profiles

The 16 experienced translators (3 men), with experience in translation ranging from 10 to 29 years, including experience in (bio)medical translation, translated from English to Portuguese (as in the case of the novice translators), and also from French (37.50%), German (31.25%), Spanish (25%), Italian (6.25%) and Dutch (6.25%).

The most frequently reported text types among the experienced translators were: patient information leaflets (53.33%), fact sheets for patients (33.33%), user manuals for medical devices (26.67%) and software (20.00%), training material (26.67%) and labels (20.00%).

Revisers' attitudes and expectations

As mentioned in section 3, in order to elicit normative attitudes, revisers were asked "In general, how do you think translators 'should' translate?" while in order to elicit empirical expectations, revisers were asked "In general, how do you think translators 'actually' translate?" and finally, to elicit normative expectations, revisers were asked "In general, which are the essential characteristics of a good translation?"

Two broad themes emerged from the analysis of the answers in NVivo: revisers directly or indirectly referred to quality parameters, and they referred to the process itself.

Regarding the quality parameters, revisers reported that they mainly expected a translation to follow 'terminological norms' (31 mentions), 'accuracy' (18 mentions), and 'language norms' (17 mentions) (Figure 8.1). In other words, what was considered important for biomedical translation by the majority of revisers was the use of industry terminology—the target language terminology used by medical experts. Next, revisers expected the translation to be accurate, which was described by some as "Check[ing] if the target text is faithful to the source's message" and by others as "Check[ing] if the translation conveys the meaning of the original text". Finally, revisers expected translations to follow the language norms of the target language, including grammar, spelling and syntax.

To a lesser extent, revisers referred to the need to adapt the text to the target audience (11 mentions), readability, natural sounding text and fluency (5 times each), detail-orientation and consistency (3 times each), conciseness and reduction of source text nuances in the target text (1 time each).

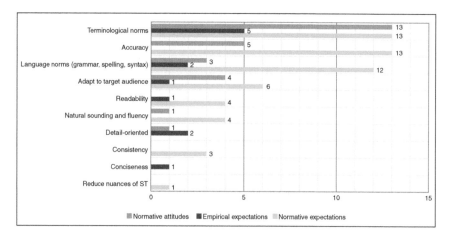

FIGURE 8.1 Revisers' normative attitudes, empirical expectations and normative expectations about translators and translations

Regarding the process, revisers described their expectations about translators and their beliefs about the way in which translators actually did translate (normative attitudes and empirical expectations).[9] As far as normative attitudes are concerned, two revisers explained that, first and foremost, the translator needed to understand the source text and only then translate. During that first reading, one of the revisers commented, the translator should identify the translation problems and "specific terminology which needs research". The first translation should be a draft, two revisers mentioned, one of them suggesting that the translator should "mentally formulate and develop a tentative target sentence with the same information". The next step according to this reviser was to "rewrite from scratch in the target language, for the target language reader—as if it had not been translated at all" and only then should a comparative self-revision be performed in order to assess "if information is correctly conveyed and matches target language's specificities". Another reviser expressed a similar idea: "Revise the target text against the source to identify possible inaccuracies." The next and final step for these revisers was a unilingual self-revision. Establishing realistic deadlines in order to avoid mistakes that arise from rushed translations, and communicating with the client to clarify questions, also emerged as common and important aspects of the process.

When asked how translators actually translated, that is, their empirical expectations, revisers mainly expressed negative expectations, agreeing that most translators translated on "automatic pilot", as one reviser put it. Other revisers called this strategy "direct correspondence" between segments, "too close to the original" or "literal translation". On literal translation, a reviser took the opportunity to explain:

> A lot of the times, we get literal translations that immediately give away it is a translation and not the original text. This makes it hard to read and means that, most of the time, we need to read the text several times to understand. As well as this, it provides leeway for errors (false friends, etc.).

Revisers also referred to potential causes of this "automatic pilot" translation procedure, namely lack of self-revision and tight deadlines. Self-revision, identified as a must for translators, was also identified as a root cause of lack of quality, which together with the "automatic pilot" procedure is attributed by some revisers to lack of time. As explained by some revisers, "[s]ometimes 'shortcuts' are taken in order to comply with deadlines, perhaps, resulting in translations of inferior quality" and "[t]hey actually work for the deadline, which is extremely short and sometimes non-realistic. Considering the demands of the client in quality and sometimes the load and complexity of instructions and workflows, this has consequences for the translation quality."

Translators' attitudes and expectations

In order to elicit normative attitudes, both novice and experienced translators were asked "In general, what criteria do you think reviewers 'should' use to judge the quality of a translation?"; to elicit empirical expectations, translators were asked

"How do other translators with the same experience as you translate?" and "In general, how do you think reviewers assess a translation?"; and to elicit normative expectations, translators were asked "In general, how do other translators with the same experience as you think you 'should' translate?" and "In general, what expectations do you think reviewers 'have' of your work?".

In their responses to these open questions, the majority of novice and experienced translators referred to the high expectations held by other professionals and, more concretely, by revisers (that is, normative expectations). Some novice and experienced translators believed that revisers expected perfection. Two of the novice translators, for instance, clearly stated that they believed revisers did not accept any types of error. "In a professional environment", one of the novice translators wrote, "all jobs are expected to be perfect in terms of achieving the goals companies give you. If you work on your own, then you should be hard on yourself." However, the majority expressed the belief that revisers expected and accepted a translation that shows some small or minor "slips". Two of the experienced translators believed revisers expect them to deliver a good translation "that will not take too long to revise", as one translator noted, and three other translators believed that revisers held high expectations: "I think their expectations are high", "I strive to deliver excellent quality translations", "they expect high-quality work".

Other novice and experienced translators believed that revisers expected a less-than-perfect product: "that it is good, even if it is not perfect", as one wrote, and "if I have translated a text related to a field I do not usually work with, the reviser might need to check/change some of my terminological choices", another clarified.

Two more broad themes emerged from the answers of the biomedical translators: they directly or indirectly referred to translators' competences and, like the revisers, they referred to the translation process itself.

Regarding the competences, novice and experienced translators alike reported normative expectations and attitudes. They are expected by other translators and revisers, and they expected other translators and revisers, to be proficient in 'information mining'. They referred specifically to the documentation and terminological process (52 mentions), followed by 'planning and management', mainly time management (16 mentions) and 'language' competence (11 mentions)—professionals are expected to know and comply with writing and linguistic norms (including grammar, spelling and punctuation) (Figure 8.2). Less frequently, translators also referred to detail orientation (five times), which is described by the translators as "being thorough" and "with attention to detail". Surprisingly, subject-matter and technological competences were mentioned only three times each, suggesting that these translators believed that they are expected to prioritize 'information mining' and 'planning and management' over their knowledge of the subject and the effective use of software. From an industry perspective, the fact that 'information mining' outweighs 'subject-matter knowledge' may suggest that knowing how to conduct research and documentation is more desirable than knowledge of a specialist field. Finally, among the least mentioned themes were 'defining and

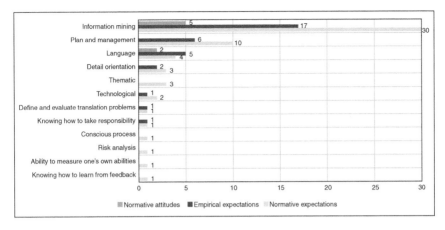

FIGURE 8.2 Translators' normative attitudes, empirical expectations and normative expectations about other translators and revisers

evaluating translation problems' and 'knowing how to take responsibility' as well as knowing how and when to perform a 'risk analysis' and prioritize tasks, 'measure one's own abilities' and 'learn from feedback'.

When asked about the expectations of revisers and how they thought revisers assessed a translation, novice and experienced translators reported clear expectations about biomedical revisers (that is, normative expectations). The majority of translators expected revisers to perform a unilingual revision and not a comparative one, mainly based on checking the correct use of the linguistic norms of the target language (grammar, spelling and syntax). One of the experienced translators, in a critical tone, commented that revisers "just read the target text and consider the translation to be good if it sounds good".

A large majority of the experienced translators in fact expressed a more negative view of revisers' work. They claimed that revisers are not objective and "mark errors that are not errors at all", as one translator wrote. Revisers are "too focused on assessment", wrote another. Another commented: "Some revisers assess a translation negatively . . . because they feel their obligation is to amend the translation". And,

> I think revisers should not act as judges, but as part of the value chain. So, their purpose should be to create a better product than what they get from the previous stage. If the product has the adequate level of quality, the reviser should not change the product received.

When translators were asked about how revisers should assess a translation (that is, their normative attitudes), experienced translators indicated that they should focus on objective criteria such as grammar and style, which "in fact correct and improve a text and not criteria of 'changing just for the sake of changing,' only to justify their own revisers' salary and, sometimes, even to humiliate the translator". Another experienced translator commented:

> more often than not I find myself refuting marked errors that are not errors at all. Either the error severity is not correct, or there's no error at all. I believe revisers work in good faith, but sometimes I begin to wonder.

5.   Discussion and conclusion

This chapter has offered an overview of the attitudes and expectations of bio-medical revisers and translators (novice and experienced) regarding each other and regarding best practices in the translation and revision of biomedical content in the Portuguese context.

Given that statements of beliefs can be consciously or unconsciously biased, the findings should be interpreted "conservatively" (Gile 2006). Nevertheless, when compared to other studies, the number of participants can be considered significant since they all come from a single specialized subdomain and work into one target language and in one relatively small language market (EU Portuguese).

The following five aspects are worth some discussion: source language, text type, norms and competences, self-revision and deadlines, and subjective preferential changes. With regard to the most common source language among the participants, the predominance of English comes as no surprise when the target language is European Portuguese, given that English is widely accepted as the most common source language in the European Union (House 2013). The findings suggest that this is also true for biomedical translation.

User manuals for medical devices and software, patient information leaflets, training material and summaries of product characteristics are the most common text types handled by the 71 participants. The figures suggest that user manuals are the most translated text type, at least for the surveyed participants. However, very little research has been done about this text type within medical translation.[10] More research is therefore needed. Both the World Health Organization (2018) and the European Commission (2018b) recognize the key role of medical devices in healthcare provision.

As far as norms and competences are concerned, both groups of profession-als agreed that 'terminology' is key in the translation and revision of biomedical content.[11] A qualitative examination of the ways in which revisers and translators communicated their most common beliefs about each other and about translation showed that they described 'terminological norms' and 'information mining' com-petence as encompassing:

- documentary and terminological research in reliable sources (mention was made of online glossaries and medical documents originally written in the target language by medical experts);
- network-building, so that reliable experts can be consulted;

- terminology management (the use of terminology management software to process the terminological information that was highlighted);
- compliance with the client's reference materials (mention was made of the importance of following guidelines, glossaries and any reference material provided by the client).

These expectations are not surprising, as the ISO 17100: 2015 standard makes reference to "competence in research, information acquisition, and processing" as one of the professional competences of translators, and also indicates that during the translation process the translator is expected to comply with industry terminology (both the terminology specific to the domain and to the client) and with the reference material provided (including style guides) (ISO 2015a: 6; 10). Even though compliance with reference material was one of the aspects most referred to by both revisers and translators, one of the experienced translators clarified that, in his experience, "we normally don't have access to reference material nor contact with specialists on the client side". This is an important point for revisers to consider when checking and assessing a translation.

Although reliance on a network of translators and domain experts is not included in ISO 17100: 2015, it was frequently mentioned by novice and experienced translators as part of their needed competences. For instance, one of the novice translators welcomed the opportunity to focus on the increasing importance of collaborative work:

> Though translating is, in some ways, a solitary task, particularly for freelancers, at the same time, teamwork is important as it ensures the quality of the provided translation services and allows for additional viewpoints of a single item or topic. Sharing knowledge means gaining knowledge and expanding experience. Translators are not infallible machines. Therefore, seeking help and advice from fellow translators should be encouraged as a means of growth.

Regarding self-revision, it is remarkable that it was only seldom referred to by the biomedical translators surveyed (11 mentions). Furthermore, none of the translators explained how one should go about self-revising, as if the procedure is so well known among translators that there is no need for further explanation or detail. The relatively low percentage of references to self-revision could thus be interpreted as a sign that the procedure is so common that there is no need to make reference to it. However, when expressing their beliefs about how other translators should translate, two experienced translators pointed out that "several translators do not perform self-revision" or that "revision is very superficial". These beliefs were also shared by revisers. Lack of comparative self-revision together with lack of time due to tight deadlines contribute to quality problems, revisers reported. Even though ISO 17100: 2015 considers self-revision as part of the translation process, the data suggest that translators may not consider it so important, at least in comparison to revisers' expectations.

Most striking about the data was translators' strong negative attitudes towards revisers' preferential changes. Subjective preferential changes refer to those corrections made by a reviser that are based not on objective parameters of quality but rather on subjective ones. These changes, also referred to in the literature by the terms 'hyper-revision' and 'over-revision' (Mossop 1992: 85), are considered "suggestions for improvement" rather than errors since "nothing is technically wrong" (Densmer 2014). More often than not, these changes create problems in the quality control process and particularly in the relationship between the reviser and the translator. That is probably why the surveyed experienced translators expressed clear opinions about preferential changes. For them, the work of revisers is subjective, and it generates a sense of injustice. Their changes introduce insecurity and doubt about the revision process, such that one of the experienced translators wrote, "I already know that the reviser is going to change the text a lot, which is rather unpleasant from an emotional point of view, but tough luck."

Belief statements such as this suggest a power struggle between revisers and translators with potential consequences for the translation process. The frictions between these two groups of professionals indicate that the authorship of the translation is being put into question. Even though scientific-technical translation is increasingly seen (and accepted) as the product of a collaborative endeavour, as was expressed by some of the participants, the translators' belief statements may signal the challenging of the role of the reviser and translators' diminishing decision-making power over the last version of their translations.

To conclude, the potential lack of communication and trust between revisers and translators can hinder the quality of the translation and ultimately damage the image of the translator. The findings suggest that translators are questioning what is expected of them. If translators do not understand the reasons motivating revisers' corrections, they are not able to follow revisers' feedback and their competence can be put into question, as expressed in the revisers' belief statements. This may lead to the perception that the quality of translators' work is below the expected standard. As a consequence, translators receive negative feedback from revisers, which jeopardizes their professional reputation. Thus, working relationships between revisers and translators can be contentious even though both groups agree on the quality parameters that should govern biomedical translation, in line with ISO 17100: 2015.

Though exploratory in nature, our study has aimed to lay the foundations for further research. Future lines of research should include studies of scientific-technical translation, which increasingly seems to be considered a collaborative effort demanding that revisers and translators work together. This raises the question of how the industry will cope with these challenging power relations. For instance, even if the Codes of Ethics of Portuguese translators' associations do not yet contemplate potential limits to revisers' work, the codes should be monitored in order to assess how the industry is dealing with these challenges. Likewise, given that university training is based mainly on developing individuals' competences in translation/revision, starting with an assessment of individual student performance, there is a pressing need to inquire into how training can adapt to the increasing need for collaborative translation processes. It would therefore be interesting to consider how to develop interpersonal communication in translation/revision trainees, focusing on potential problems of communication between translators and revisers and on any preconceived ideas the two types of professionals may have, including lack of trust with regard to the nature of revisers' changes.

Acknowledgements

Special thanks are due to Alexandra Assis Rosa for her comments on an earlier version of the chapter, as well as to the anonymous peer reviewers and Isabelle S. Robert for insightful feedback.

Notes

1 For example, Schwieter and Ferreira (2017); Ehrensberger-Dow et al. (2015).
2 For example, Sosoni (2017) reported on translators' attitudes about translation crowd-sourcing; Corrius et al. (2016) examined students' and professionals' attitudes to gender in advertising translation; Feinauer and Lesch (2013) discussed the "idealistic" expectations of healthcare professionals about interpreters.
3 While a variety of definitions of the term "agent" has been put forward, this chapter adopts the definition suggested by Simeoni, who saw it as a sociological concept for "the 'subject,' but *socialized*. To speak of a translating agent, therefore, suggests that the reference is a 'voice,' . . . inextricably linked to networks of other social agents" (1995: 452). For an overview on agents and agency in TS, see Buzelin (2011).
4 Concerning the nomenclature of attitudes and expectations, attitudes can be defined as a relatively stable system of beliefs concerning an object or person which results in the evaluation of that object or person (Lawson and Garrod 2001: iBook location 91; Marshall 2003: Kindle location 1156; Abercrombie et al. 2006: 21; Bruce and Yearley 2006: 13; Darity 2008: 200; Fleck 2015: 175). Normative attitudes can be expressed by statements like "I believe that others should/shouldn't do X" and should not be confused with preferences (Bicchieri 2017a: Kindle location 293–5). In turn, expectations are defined, according to Bicchieri (2017b), as "just beliefs" that can be empirical or normative about what happens or should happen in a given situation. Empirical expectations are typically expressed in sentences such as "I believe that most people do X", "I have seen that most people do X" and "I am told by a trusted source that most people do X" (Bicchieri 2017b). Normative expectations are expressed by statements such as "I believe that most people think we ought to do X", "I believe that most people think the right thing to do is X", "I think that others think I should X" (Bicchieri 2017b).
5 For the questionnaire aimed at revisers, visit www.surveymonkey.com/r/95VVFGJ; for novice translators, visit www.surveymonkey.com/r/9BJDXBR; for experienced translators, visit www.surveymonkey.com/r/9PZMNDS.
6 On the questionnaires, the term 'reviewer' was used instead of 'reviser' to refer to the same professional, since, according to our research, this was the most common term in biomedical revision.
7 For more information on this tool, visit www.surveymonkey.com.
8 Since these answers respond to an 'all that apply question', a translator could choose more than one text type and, therefore, the percentages do not add up to 100%. The same applies to the questions aimed at novice translators and revisers.
9 Concerning the translation and self-revision *process of translators*, revisers' normative expectations are not applicable because revisers' normative expectations would refer to the *revisers' own process*, that is, revisers' beliefs about what others believe the reviser should

do in the course of their work. In this section we are concerned with revisers' beliefs about the process of translators.

10 A systematic search conducted in September 2018 in the Translation Studies Bibliography by keyword and abstract was not able to identify studies of user manuals for medical devices and software within medical translation.

11 It should be noted that 'accuracy' and 'plan and management' also emerged as common themes in the topic analysis, but given that they were not expressed when eliciting all three types of beliefs, they are not considered, for the purposes of this study, to be beliefs as strong as 'terminology' and 'language'.

9

ANOTHER LOOK AT REVISION IN LITERARY TRANSLATION

Ilse Feinauer and Amanda Lourens

In the literature on revision-related activities, the term 'revision' is used to refer to the process of checking human translations. Two types of revision are often discerned, as pointed out by Mossop (2014a), namely 'self-revision' for a translator's check of his/her own work and 'other-revision' for a check by a second translator. It is often believed that these two types of revision are employed in a coordinated way in real-life projects—meaning that self-revision by the translator will be followed by other-revision by a second translator before the manuscript is submitted for publication.

Feinauer and Lourens (2017) undertook a study of the loyalties of literary revisers during revision-related activities performed on a draft translation in preparation for publication.[1] That study aimed to shed some light on the focus of loyalty of literary revisers—whether their loyalty during the revision of the draft lies with the source text author, with the source text, with the target text or with the target text reader. No clear preference for the needs of the target text readers was displayed in any one phase of any of the revision processes, but the single most important conclusion drawn from the study (Feinauer and Lourens 2017: 116) was that the processes of revision do not seem to be coordinated. The researchers therefore suggested that the concepts of self- and other-revision need to be examined closely, in order to address the question of whether it is indeed the case that they point towards two discretely demarcated processes following each other in a linear way. Another suggestion was to revisit the terminology related to revision and editing, since these two terms are often used interchangeably or in a haphazard way during actual revision processes. In fact, it might even be necessary to ask whether a distinction between revision and editing is necessary at all (Feinauer and Lourens 2017: 117).

The present study suggests that the binary projection of the act of revision as self-revision on the one hand, and other-revision on the other, can be contested. Furthermore, the term 'revision', with self- and other-revision as its sub-categories, is brought under scrutiny, and the relationship between these activities is reconsidered. (The distinction between revision and editing is not under consideration here, and we use the term 'editor' or 'proofreader' as assigned by the project managers to describe the revision-related activities.)[2]

The 2017 study as well as the present study involve professional revisions performed on three works of fiction translated from Afrikaans into English[3] for one of the larger book production companies in South Africa that employs freelance translators, revisers and editors. For both studies an empirical analysis of the documented relationships between the agents involved in three different literary translation projects was conducted.

Scocchera (2013: 144–5) points out that revision seems to be identified through the *comparative* aspect, as can be seen in the following definitions. Delisle, Lee-Janke and Cormier (in Scocchera 2013: 144) describe revision as

> a detailed *comparative* examination of the translated 'text' with the respective 'source text' in order to verify that the 'sense' is the same in both texts and to improve the quality of the 'target text'.
>
> *(our emphasis)*

Palumbo (in Scocchera 2013: 146) adds to this:

> the term revision refers to a *comparative* check carried out on the TT and its respective ST in order to identify problems and errors and introduce the necessary corrections or amendments. In the context of professional translation, revision indicates one particular stage in the chain of production of translated documents and can be defined as the process aimed at identifying features of a draft translation *that fall short* of the required quality standards and at introducing the necessary *amendments* and *corrections*.
>
> *(our emphasis)*

For Robert et al. (2017a: 4), revision is the reading of a *draft translation* by a person *other than the translator* to detect features of the draft translation that *fall short* (we would say *may* fall short) of what is acceptable (according to the translation and revision brief) and to make appropriate *corrections* and *improvements* before the translation is delivered to the client. However, Mossop (2014a) states that revision is performed not only by a person other than the translator, but also by the translator. He draws a clear distinction between two main types of revision, depending on the agent doing the work.

Scocchera (2013: 143) sheds new light on the concept of revision by introducing an etymological perspective: Revision has as its root *revisere*, meaning "to look again". This points towards revision as an *additional* examination of the text, when the translator or reviser takes a fresh approach and sees "with new eyes" as if seeing it for the first time. Even though Scocchera (2013: 143) is of the opinion that this etymological definition does not tell us much about the actual nature and scope of the actions performed by revisers, we believe that this etymological perspective might prove to be extremely useful when reconsidering the current definitions of 'revision' and 'editing'.

Scocchera (2013: 144–5) goes further, stating that a 'comparative examination' is a typical and critical trait of revision, with the implication that revision takes place only when a cross-check between the source text and target text is performed. However, she remarks that the extent of the cross-check will vary in different situations, and allows that revision might at times be a unilingual activity:

> The need for 'comparative examination' is perceived in very different ways in translation practice, whatever the textual genre and professional field. Different attitudes and approaches range from a full reading of both ST and TT followed by a line-by-line examination, to a 'sample comparative examination'—where the ST is referred to only when the translation sounds lame, thus indicating likely translation problems, shortcomings or actual mistakes,—and finally to a revision based on TT reading only, without any direct reference to ST.
>
> *(Scocchera 2013: 145)*

This, we believe, might translate into a cluster of possibilities for different instances of self- and other-revision, ranging from a full reading of both source and target texts to a revision based on a target text reading only, without consulting the source text.

The latter type of revision undermines the premise that a revision always relies on a *comparative* reading. Following this thread of thought, we argue that such a conceptualization of degrees of revision implies that unilingual editing of a translation would also be seen as 'revision'. The problem, then, would be: How can editing be distinguished from revision, given that the comparative aspect might be absent from a specific revision-related activity? We further want to problematize the definition of revision as fundamentally based on the comparative aspect, and ask: Does revision necessarily always involve a comparative check?

Mossop (2014a: 18) uses the metaphors of gatekeeping and language therapy to describe the various tasks performed during editing and revising. Gatekeeping refers to the function of correcting a text in order to bring it in line with existing rules, while language therapy refers to activities ensuring that the reader's interaction with the text is optimal in order to facilitate the transmission of the message. Mossop's revision parameters include language therapy as well as gatekeeping in revision: see his Parameter 6, Tailoring, which addresses a major aspect of language therapy: "Is the language suited to the users of the translation and the use they will make of it?" Parameter 9, on the other hand, addresses typical gatekeeping concerns: "Have the rules of grammar, spelling, punctuation, house style and correct usage been observed?"[4] (Mossop 2014a: 134).

1.   Hypothesis and research questions

The terms 'self-revision' and 'other-revision' are traditionally presented as one-dimensional and linear, and we aim to contest and repackage the current definitions. We hypothesize, based on our 2017 study, that in literary translation practice there are different combinations of involvement by the translator and the reviser, as well as other agents such as the author, editor and proofreader. These combinations entail that the translator at first engages only in self-revision, but at a later stage the translator and reviser are simultaneously involved in both a self- and other-revision process, with both parties suggesting changes and justifying choices. This leads us to formulate the following research questions:

- Is the binary projection of self- and other-revision as two opposites reflected by actual processes?
- Is it not possible that translators perform a self-revision, but that this also happens on the basis of feedback from others, for example the author?
- Will translators not be doing other-revision when they work through the author's revised version of the translation, although with an element of self-revision when they again revise their own translation?
- Is it not also possible that revisers might do other-revision based on the author's feedback on the translator's work?
- Might revisers not be engaging in self-revision of their own revision product after the other agents have given their feedback?

The rationale behind this research was to investigate whether the theoretical underpinnings of the revision process are enacted by the various real-life agents in our case study. In other words, we wanted to know whether theory speaks to practice as far as literary revision is concerned. If this is not the case, could the theoretical base be enriched by a description of the real-life events taking place during a literary translation production process?

2.   Scope and methodology

Our study involved the revision processes for three Afrikaans works of fiction[5] that were translated by the same award-winning translator (Elsa Silke), namely *Niggie* by Ingrid Winterbach (2002), translated into English as *To hell with Cronjé* (2007, 2010); *Vaselinetjie* (2004) by Anoeschka von Meck, translated as *My name is Vaselinetjie* (2009) and *In bushveld and desert: A game ranger's life* (2008), a selection from a novel and three volumes of short stories (*Die lang pad van Stoffel Mathysen* [2004], *Stoffel by die afdraaipad* [2004], *Stoffel in die wildernis* [2006] and *Stoffel se veldnotas* [2007]) by Christiaan Bakkes.

The award-winning *Niggie/To hell with Cronjé* is set against the backdrop of the South African War and deals with the traumatic and sometimes bizarre experiences of two scientists towards the end of the war. The source text was awarded the prestigious Hertzog Prize for Afrikaans literature in 2004, and it occupies a prominent position as a serious literary text in the Afrikaans literary polysystem (Spies 2013: 191–2).

The award-winning youth novel *Vaselinetjie/My name is Vaselinetjie* tells the coming-of-age story of an abandoned white baby girl who was raised by a couple of colour and, in a heart-breaking turn of events, was taken away by child welfare services and sent to a state orphanage at the age of 11. *Vaselinetjie* was awarded the prestigious MER Prize for Afrikaans youth literature as well as the Jan Rabie/Rapport Prize in 2005. The source text is canonized as a youth novel that has been prescribed at high school level but is also seen as a 'crossover' book that both teenagers and adults can relate to (Spies 2013: 193–4).

For the volume of short stories published in English as *In bushveld and desert: A game ranger's life*, a number of stories by Christiaan Bakkes, who is well known as a seasoned traveller and game ranger in Africa, were selected by the publisher to be translated. Bakkes, not having won any literary prizes, does not enjoy the same status in the Afrikaans literary system as, for example, Winterbach. The target readers of *In bushveld and desert* are people who enjoy well-written stories about Africa and nature, and especially international tourists in Southern Africa (Spies 2013: 195–6).

We undertook an investigation of the various revision activities—comparative as well as unilingual—performed during the revision of the three aforementioned manuscript translations. 'Revision' is used to refer to all the activities pertaining to the checking of the draft translation until the manuscript is ready for publication. This choice is motivated by the haphazard use of the terms revision, editing and proofreading in the archival documents. Only one of the cases, for example, mentions a reviser, while the other two cases refer only to editors and/or proofreaders. In the case of *In bushveld and desert: a game ranger's life*, the agent doing the revision refers to herself as an 'editor'. Although we do not agree with these naming practices, we refer to the various agents in the terms used by the publishing house: namely *author, translator, reviser, editor, compiler*[6] and *proofreader*. The various revision activities were mapped as different discernible stages, structured via the flow of the e-mail correspondence.[7] In the production process of *To hell with Cronjé*, for example, five stages could be identified (see section 3). The only constant factor across these processes is the translator, who was responsible for all three translations.

Following the approach adopted by Munday (2012) in his case study of three literary translation and/or revision processes, this study utilized archival material in order to study three different sets of agents involved in the translation process. According to Munday (2012: 104), archival documents have been underutilized in Translation Studies, even though they hold the possibility of providing detailed retrospective insight into the decision-making processes involved in translation and revision. Since then, this kind of study, in which manuscripts, drafts and other working documents such as e-mail correspondence are investigated, has emerged as a discipline known as genetic Translation Studies. According to Cordingley and Montini (2015: 1), this field aims to reveal "the complexity of the creative processes engaged in [the production of modern literary works]". Our study can therefore be classified as a genetic translation study: the productions investigated here are three literary translations, and we investigated all stages of revision the manuscripts went through before publication. See also the genetic study by Scocchera (2015), where her focus was on the active roles of both translators and revisers in the genesis of literary translations in Italy. Her object of study was the interplay between translators and revisers in the form of text changes, suggestions and comments on the various manuscript versions.

Our working documents consisted of all e-mail correspondence among the agents involved in the translation and revision of three Afrikaans works of fiction. These three sets of correspondence were substantial[8] and include all discussions between the agents working on the various drafts. The e-mail discussions were the various agents' only mode of dealing with translation challenges, including terminological queries and grammar as well as content issues. Our analysis included the agents who were involved, as well as how the production played out through the different stages of the process that was shaped by their actions and interactions. The actual draft manuscripts were not analysed; rather, we performed a discourse analysis on the correspondence in order to describe the revision processes, including the sometimes intricate interplay between acts of self- and other-revision. We compiled an inventory of the various acts performed by the agents, as reflected in their documented discourse, and summarized these as the main activities performed in separate stages.

3. Findings

Niggie/To hell with Cronjé

Five successive stages in the revision process were identified:

- the translator's initial revision process;
- the author's revision of the translator's work;
- revision by a reviser;
- revision by the translator;
- the editor's intervention.

The translator makes translation notes on her own translation, which can be interpreted as the footprint of her self-revision of her work. However, these notes are aimed at an audience (the commissioning editor and the author), so that she does not perform the action of self-revision in isolation before the draft enters a phase of other-revision. She rather positions herself within a network of agents on whom she relies for help, but to whom she also provides the justification for some of her translation choices. For instance, she relies strongly on the author to answer certain questions, especially those dealing with factual issues. In this phase she shows an adherence to gatekeeping activities and specifically tries to ensure that an accurate translation is rendered. It is definitely a comparative activity, as indicated by her references to the source text:

> [p 89 of the original text. *Klassifikasie van stollingsgesteentes hang af van oorsprong*. I have translated this (*oorsprong*) with 'origin', but maybe this is not correct. Does this perhaps mean it depends on where the rock is found? Would the author please have a look and correct?] (our translation; word in parentheses added as explicitation).[9]
>
> p 89 van die oorspronklike teks. *Klassifikasie van stollingsgesteentes hang af van oorsprong*. Ek het dit vertaal met 'origin', maar dink dis dalk nie reg nie. *Beteken dit dalk dit hang af waar die klip gevind word? Sal die skrywer asb kyk* en regstel?

Next, the author engages in other-revision when she revises the draft translation, but once again this does not happen with the author as the only agent at work in this phase. Instead, she enters into a dialogue with the translator, providing answers but also asking her own questions. The dialogic nature of her revision is emphasized by the fact that she asks for advice from the translator, even when she disagrees with the translator's choices:

> In the Afrikaans text I use *hy sê* virtually with no variation. I have often changed words like he declares, remarks, muses, etc back to he says, as this is characteristic of my style. But it is a difficult one. Please advise.

The network of agents is further expanded when the author's notes to the translator are also sent to the reviser, who in the third stage of revision busies herself with an other-revision, during which she often refers to the source text:

> p 41 (Niggie). The word 'furious' in 'furious swirling' is too strong, I think. The Afrikaans is *hewige gekolk*. Perhaps just leave out 'furious'—'the swirling and the pitching of the stars' works nicely.

In the fourth stage, the translator performs a revision of the already twice-revised version (excluding her initial self-revision). In this stage, she is seen doing a self-revision once again (the draft being her product), but she is simultaneously performing an other-revision of both the author's and editor's suggestions:

> ['in what way the appalling nature of the day had been affected'—I am afraid it does not make sense to me. Would you please reformulate?]
>
> 'in what way the appalling nature of the day had been affected'—ek is bevrees dit maak nie vir my sin nie. Sal jy asb maar herformuleer?

She positions herself predominantly as a gatekeeper, and focuses on both the accuracy of the translation and the target language usage:

Accuracy of the translation:

> [It seems to me the recognised translation for *hardedopsprinkaan* is 'stout bodied'. I googled and have found this.]
>
> Dit lyk vir my asof die erkende vertaling vir *hardedopsprinkaan* 'stout bodied' is. Ek het gegoogle en kry dit so.

Target language usage:

> [I don't think one can use 'accursed' in this way—usually as adjective. I have simply removed it.]
>
> Ek dink nie mens kan 'accursed' so gebruik nie—gewoonlik as adjektief. Ek het dit sommer net uitgehaal.

Shifting roles are apparent during this stage: The author becomes a reviser during the second stage, but her product is revised in this fourth stage by the translator, who is now in the role of (other-)reviser.

During the fifth stage, the editor is seen performing an other-revision of the draft, but with the focus on gatekeeping activities, especially pertaining to the target language. However, this is not a unilingual check since the source text is consulted and used as a basis for the editing decisions in this last stage.

> p 34 rank as a billy goat: The Groot Woordeboek does translate *geil* as rank, fertile, sensual, so strictly speaking rank would be correct here. But rank in English implies foul smelling, and while we know that Oompie does smell, I get the impression that what is being suggested here is his sexual appetite—the next sentence is a reference to his many wives. So wouldn't randy as a billy goat be a better description?

Vaselinetjie/My name is Vaseline

Six stages in the revision process could be identified, namely:

- the translator's initial revision process;
- the editor's revision of the translator's work;
- the author's revision of the draft translation after the editor's revision;
- the editor's revision of the author's changes to the draft translation;
- the author's responses to the editor's comments;
- the translator's revision after the author's changes.

As with the first translation, the translator writes accompanying notes to justify or to explain her translation choices, and to ask questions. Once again, her activities during this stage reveal networking actions rather than a solitary process of self-revision:

[The *huistannies*—or simply the *tannies*. They are also called *huismoeders*. I browsed websites of children's homes and have seen *huismoeders* are indeed called house mothers on various websites. Sometimes I have used this, but I feel one cannot use this all over before it turns irritating. I have also steered away from *Auntie*—used this sporadically only. As in the case of *Auntie S'laki* as well as *Tannie Hilde* and in some instances *Auntie Meredith*. When 'die tannies' is mentioned, I have frequently used 'matrons'. It works for me. Please see whether you agree. I myself was in a school hostel and we always referred to the matrons.]

Die huistannies—of net die tannies. Hulle word ook huismoeders genoem. Ek het op die webwerwe van kinderhuise rondgekyk en gesien dat die huismoeders wel op verskillende webwerwe house mothers genoem word. Ek het dit by tye so gebruik, maar dit voel nie vir my mens kan dit oral gebruik sonder dat dit hinderlik word nie. Ek het ook weggeskram van Auntie—dit net hier en daar gebruik. Wel in die geval van Auntie S'laki en ook Tannie Hilde en hier en daar Auntie Meredith. Wanneer daar dus van 'die tannies' gepraat word, het ek dit dikwels 'matrons' gemaak. Dit werk vir my. Kyk gerus of julle saamstem. Ek was self in 'n skoolkoshuis en ons het altyd van die matrones gepraat.

In a second stage, the editor revises the translation but refers back to the source text, and points out that a problem that has been spotted during the translation can actually be traced to a problem in the source text (the editor was involved in the production of the source text as well):

[Yes, this was one of the problems in the Afrikaans not addressed then. There was a lot of work needed for the manuscript, and one of the strange things is that one would reach saturation point and just leave things as they are since there were numerous more urgent issues screaming to be resolved. I have told myself this is probably how it would have worked in real life— the term [Peppie] shows a type of "floating" meaning, depending on the circumstances where it is used. I have indeed now solved the issue of Hefner who wanted to get rid of Peppie as head boy. He now wants to get rid of "*that particular Peppie*"]

Ja, dit was een van die probleme in die Afrikaans wat destyds nie aangespreek is nie. Daar was ongelooflik baie werk aan die manuskrip, en een van die vreemde dinge is hoe mens naderhand 'n versadigingspunt bereik en dinge maar los soos hulle is as daar talle dringender kwessies is wat roep om opgelos te word. Ek het vir myself gesê dit is waarskynlik hoe dit in die werklike lewe sou gewerk het—dat die term [Peppie] 'n soort van 'n "swewende" betekenis het, afhangende van die omstandighede waarin dit gebruik word. Ek het wel nou die kwessie opgelos van Hefner wat van 'n Peppie as hoofseun ontslae wou raak. Hy wil nou van "that particular Peppie" ontslae raak.

The editor mostly approves the translator's choices, although she sometimes indicates that she has changed the translator's text:

[I have felt there could be a misunderstanding when one now reads about house mothers and then about matrons. (As if there is a number of house mothers with one matron at the head of all of them.) Therefore I have made all matrons. I have kept the Aunties and Tannies unchanged.]

Ek het gevoel daar is ruimte vir misverstand as mens nou van house mothers lees en dan van matrons. (Asof daar dalk 'n klomp house mothers kan wees met een matron aan die hoof van hulle almal.) Ek het dit dus deurgaans matrons gemaak. Die Aunties en die Tannies het ek onveranderd gelaat.

In a third stage, the draft translation is other-revised by the author. She goes beyond being dissatisfied with the translator's and editor's changes:

[EXPLETIVES: in my first attempt I mostly kept the English and Afrikaans expletives added by Elsa as is, but now and then I have added something else. (cunt, clit) The word "motherf. . . ." however continued to bother me, and I have realised I could not make peace with it. The children do not know that word and I HATE that word. Even "bitch" is bad to me, since in English expletives tend to lose the humour present in Afrikaans and Coloured-Afrikaans.

My decision: I have decided I want the expletives mostly as they stand in the original Vaselinetjie.]

VLOEKWOORDE: in my eerste probeerslag het ek die Engelse en Afrikaanse vloekwoorde wat Elsa ingesit het, meestal net so gelos maar hier en daar iets anders gaan byvoeg. (cunt, clit) Die woord "motherf. . . ." het my egter bly pla en ek het net besef ek kan nie daarmee saamleef in vrede nie. Die kinders ken nie daai woord nie en ek HAAT daardie woord. Selfs "bitch" is vir my erg, want in Engels verloor vloekwoorde vir my die humoristiese neiging wat daar is in Afrikaans en Hotnos-Afrikaans?

My besluit: Ek het besluit dat ek die vloekwoorde oorwegend wil he soos hulle in die oorspronklike Vaselinetjie staan . . .

However, the author also expresses her dissatisfaction with some of her own choices in the Afrikaans source text and indicates that she has engaged in some rewriting of the original during the revision process:

[GANGSTER TALK: There are hidden benefits to rewrite one's book in a rehab centre for drug-addicts . . . I could learn my new drug vocabulary from

real addicts to keep it as REAL and CURRENT as possible. Hope you like
it? I think it puts *Vaselinetjie* once again in the NOW and not in the past any
longer (I have also added mobile phones, Mxit and iPods.)

Beers and cigarettes were upgraded to marijuana, meth and crack.

Gatte refers to the police.]

GANGSTER TALK: Daar is versteekte voordele om in 'n rehab sentrum
vir dwelmverslaafdes jou boek te sit en oorskryf . . . so het ek dus by egte
druggies gaan kers opsteek vir my nuwe dwelm woordeskat om dit so EG en
HEDENDAAGS as moontlik te maak! Hoop julle hou daarvan? Ek dink dit
plaas *Vaselinetjie* weereens in die NOU en nie meer in die verlede nie. (Ek
het ook selfone, Mxit en iPods ingebring.)

Biere en sigarette is ge-upgrade na dagga, tik en crack.

Gatte verwys na polisie.

If we were to use Mossop's terminology, we could view this rewriting by the
author as self-revision of her Afrikaans source text. This would suggest that the
author is also a revising agent in the production network, as opposed to Mossop's
perception of only translators and revisers being involved in the revision process
and dealing with a static source text. We could therefore argue that Mossop's terminology does not take into account that the source text could undergo adaptation
by its author.

In a fourth stage, the editor performs an other-revision of the author's changes—
a revision of an already revised but now altered text. During this process, the editor
frequently refers back to the source text and explicitly states her loyalty to the
original source text, as in the following example:

[Regarding A's changes: Many are good and a distinct improvement, but
sometimes it seems to me as if A was in a totally different "mode" to what she
had been while writing the original *Vaselinetjie*. Therefore I could not keep
all her changes as is in the text, since some would have harmed the book.
And since after all these years I am still CRAZY about *Vaselinetjie*, I would
not like to see anything being done to the book that will spoil it.]

Wat A se veranderinge betref: Baie daarvan is goed en 'n besliste verbeter-
ing, maar soms is dit vir my asof A in 'n heel ander "modus" is as wat sy was
toe sy die oorspronklike Vaselinetjie geskryf het. Ek kon haar veranderinge
dus nie slaafs in die teks aanbring nie omdat party daarvan die boek skade sou
aangedoen het. En omdat ek ná al die jare nog steeds MAL is oor Vaselinetjie,
sou ek nie graag wil sien dat daar enigiets aan die boek gedoen moet word
wat dit bederf nie.

In a fifth stage the author again self-revises her adapted text. Now she bases her
revision activities on the editor's comments which she addresses one by one—a
self-revision that is shaped by an agent other than the self. Self-revision occurs
when she insists on certain decisions to rewrite. A form of other-revision occurs

in the same comment when she revises the editor's suggestions, as in this example where she agrees with the editor:

[Editor: Some of the scenarios and expletives are just too crude—it will sink the book totally when it comes to considering it for use in the classroom.

Author: Another snag. I agree. Whereas *werfetter*, *poester*, and *jou nageboorte* could be quite humorous in Afrikaans, "motherfucker" and "clit" and "cunt" are simply just terrible. To me even "bitch" is worse than "teef?" I struggled here. "Motherfucker" and "clit" have been removed. I've kept one "cunt", but that's negotiable. I've made a few Afrikaans additions and INSIST THAT THEY STAY THERE. ("Untie that naai,". . ., *tanggeboortes*, etc.) it is almost impossible to find a child in the poorer community who speaks pure Afrikaans or English. In that sense it saves our attempt in telling *Vas* in English. English *Vaselinetjie* has a chance to be the MOST GENUINE CAPE SOUTH AFRICAN BOOK up til now!]

Editor: Party van die scenarios en vloekwoorde is net te kru—dit sal die boek heeltemal kelder wanneer dit kom by gebruik in die klaskamer.

Author: Nog 'n tamelêtjie. Ek stem saam. Waar *werfetter*, *poester*, en jou *nageboorte* in Afrikaans nogal humoristies kan wees, is "motherfucker" en "clit" en "cunt" plainweg net aaklig. Selfs "bitch" is vir my erger as "teef?" Hier het ek gesukkel. "Motherfucker" en "clit" is verwyder. Ek het een "cunt" oorgehou, maar dis onderhandelbaar. Ek het 'n paar Afrikaanse toevoegings gemaak en DRING AAN DAT DIT INBLY. ("Untie that naai,". . ., tanggeboortes, ens.) Daar is amper nie meer iets soos 'n kind wat 'n suiwer Afrikaans of Engels praat in jou armer gemeenskap nie. In daai sin, red dit ons poging om Vas in Engels te vertel. Engelse Vaselinetjie staan dus die kans om die MEES EG KAAPSE SUID-AFRIKAANSE BOEK tot op hede te wees!

Lastly, the translator revises the draft, thereby engaging in self-revision once again, but she also engages in other-revision. She tries to persuade the other agents in the network to retain more of the style and tone of the original source text, instead of accepting all of the author's changes and rewrites:

[The whole part about the mobile phones seems inserted. I would omit it. This does not belong here.

I do not agree with all the Americanisms littered throughout the text. I don't think it rings true in the South African context—regardless of how deep the influence is of television, etc. See e.g. outta—p. 123; cussing (p. 57)—I've never heard someone use the word except for in a cowboy movie/book. I also do not like bootie at all and shall really prefer it to not be used. Can we please replace this with something else? Dissed (p. 100)—I can maybe go along with that, but would prefer that it is not used so often. (See also pp. 79; 115; 194.) And oh, I also do not like homie at all. (pp. 115, 131.) It's so American gangster!]

Die hele gedeelte oor die cellphones klink aangelas. Ek sou dit weglaat. Dit hoort nie hier nie. Ek stem nie saam met die Amerikanismes waarmee die teks nou besaai is nie. I don't think it rings true in the South African context—al is die jonges ook hoe onder die invloed van televisie, ens. Sien bv. outta—p. 123; cussing (p. 57)—ek het nog nooit gehoor dat iemand die woord gebruik behalwe in 'n cowboy-fliek/boek nie. Ek hou ook absoluut niks van bootie nie en sal regtig verkies dat dit nie gebruik word nie. Kan ons dit met iets anders vervang, asb? Dissed (p. 100)—ek sal nog daarmee saamgaan, maar sou verkies dat dit nie so baie gebruik word nie. (Sien ook pp. 79; 115; 194.) En, ai, ek hou ook niks van homie nie (pp. 115, 131.) Dis so American gangster!

In bushveld and desert: a game ranger's life

Six stages could be identified for the revision process of this compilation, namely:

- the translator's initial revision process, including notes on an additional translation that was requested after the initial translation;
- the author's revision of the draft translation;
- the translator's revision after the compiler's edit;
- the translator's revision after the editor's edit;
- the proofreader's revision;
- the author's last revision.

In the first stage, the translator once again engages in self-revision but relies strongly on the establishment of a dialogue with the author. The translator is acutely aware of her own lack of knowledge regarding the outdoors and asks for the author's help with the meaning and uses of certain words and phrases:

[The leopard: I truly cannot find a translation anywhere for *muisneuse*. And the only Afrikaans *vingerhoede* I know are 'foxgloves'—and they are not indigenous, therefore this must be a different type of *vingerhoed*. C, please help.]

The leopard: Ek kry sowaar nêrens 'n vertaling vir *muisneuse* nie. En die enigste Afrikaanse vingerhoede wat ek ken, is 'foxgloves'—en hulle is nie inheems nie, dus moet dit 'n ander soort vingerhoed wees hierdie. C, help asb.

Apart from just revising her own translation, the translator frequently comments on aspects such as content which lead to some translation problems:

[I have no idea what *speklap* is. Could also not find it anywhere. I have stuck to 'a roll of cloth'. Help will be appreciated. Someone has asked in the meantime whether this is not perhaps 'shammy' (chamois) in other words *seemsleer*]

Ek het geen idee wat *speklap* is nie. Kon dit ook nêrens kry nie. Ek het maar volstaan met 'a roll of cloth'. Hulp sal waardeer word. Iemand het intussen vir my gevra of dit nie dalk 'shammy' (chamois) is nie, maw seemsleer.

When the author revises the draft translation in the second stage, he engages in an other-revision, but specifically via a process of answering the translator's questions—once again a dialogue instead of a solitary activity:

> [Translator: I also do not know so well what 'boomeilande' are. I have said 'wooded islands'. But is it an island in the river with trees on, or is it something such as 'a clump of trees', C?
>
> Author: Also see the story Fed up. *Boomeilande*—tree islands—wooden islands—these are clumps of trees on an elevated area in the floodplains that usually are grassplains. Floodplains are usually dry, only during floods they are under knee-deep or deeper water. Then the tree islands are true islands.]
>
> Translator: Ek weet ook nie lekker wat 'boomeilande' is nie. Ek het gesê 'wooded islands'. Maar is dit 'n eiland in die rivier met bome op, of is dit iets soos 'a clump of trees', C?
>
> Author: Sien ook die storie Fed up. Boomeilande—tree islands-wooden islands—hierdie is groepies bome op verhewe grond in die vloedvlaktes wat oor die algemeen gras vlaktes is. Vloedvlaktes is die meeste van die tyd droog, net tydens vloede is dit onder kniediep of dieper water. Dan is die boomeilande ware eilande.

The translator performs an other-revision in the third stage, but her activities are informed by a strong loyalty to the source text and the author, as is evident from the following example where she criticizes the editor's changes to her version (which stays loyal to the source text):

> [In the first paragraph I (and C) said "Next to the Land Rover . . . Horace McAllistair cleared his throat softly." S has removed the man's surname, to only read
>
> ". . . Horace cleared his throat . . ." C has a tendency to call certain people by their names and surnames. It's a type of 'signature' thing. I think of this man as Horace McAllistair—not as Horace.]
>
> In die eerste paragraaf het ek (en C) gesê "Next to the Land Rover . . . Horace McAllistair cleared his throat softly." S het die man se van uitgehaal, sodat dit slegs lees ". . . Horace cleared his throat . . ." C het nogal 'n neiging om deurgaans sekere mense op hulle naam en van te noem. Dis weer 'n soort 'signature' ding. Ek dink aan hierdie man as Horace McAllistair—nie as Horace nie.

In the fourth stage, the translator's other-revision takes the form of an edit of the editor's edit—this time without referring back to the source text, but with a strong adherence to the author's suggestions. In this stage, the focus is on gatekeeping activities in the sense that the target language receives emphasis, although personal opinion seems to dictate a substantial number of her changes:

['In the setting late afternoon sun . . .' now sounds terrible to me. Can we not only use 'In the setting sun'?]

'In the setting late afternoon sun . . .' klink darem nou vir my aaklig. Kan mens nie volstaan met 'In the setting sun' nie?

In the fifth stage, the proofreader performs other-revision as a light edit without any reference to the source text and focuses on the correct and authentic form of the target language:

This may be nitpicking, and the sense is clear, but 'Two metres of brute force was Fighting'—as it stands, the subject is 'two metres', not 'force', so strictly speaking it should be 'were fighting'. Perhaps it could be changed to 'Two meter's worth of brute force'.

'Larder' is a very English[10] word—I don't think I have ever heard the word referring to a South African one—we would call it a pantry.

Lastly, the author engages in other-revision but uses the source text as the norm for his final decisions. An example is:

[Hauptmann Von Estorff NOT Von Estdorff]
Hauptmann Von Estorff NIE Von Estdorff

4. Discussion and interpretation of findings

A possible framework for the interpretation of our findings is offered by Buzelin (2005: 197), through Latour's notion of actor-networks. These networks:

differ from technical networks because, unlike the latter, they are *not necessarily stable*; they 'may have no compulsory paths, no strategically positioned nodes'. In other words, whereas technical networks (e.g., electronic, rail, etc.) appear as a given structure that can be extended—hence as something that can be mapped—actor-networks can only *reveal themselves when activated*. By highlighting creativity and unpredictability, both concepts, that of actor-network and that of translation, point to the difficulty of reifying the process by which (scientific) facts and artefacts are produced, hence the need to analyze this process *from the inside*, to observe how actors make their decisions and interact while still unsure of the outcome.

(our emphasis)

By viewing the revision processes from the inside and by observing the actors' decisions and interactions, we were able to see that there is no clear-cut line between self- and other-revision. Our main findings can be summarized as follows: It does happen that a translator performs an initial self-revision, but this process may involve a dialogue with other agents in order to solve certain problems encountered by the translator, or to justify and/or explain certain decisions. The translator will engage in self-revision but may be engaged in other-revision when working through the author's revised version of the translation or the author's suggestions; the author may also engage in other-revision, but sets up a dialogue with the translator; the author may also engage in self-revision based on comments from other agents. Along the same lines, the editor may engage in other-revision with reference to the source text after the first phase of revision, or during the final edit, while the translator may engage in an edit of the editor's edit. The proofreader may also engage in a light edit.

Regarding the research questions, we conclude that the binary projection of self- and other-revision as two discrete actions should be contested, at least in literary production processes. Translators may engage in self-revision based on feedback from other agents, suggesting that self-revision is not a solitary process that needs to be completed before the draft can be sent off to another agent for other-revision. Translators will then engage in an other-revision when working through the author's revised version, but with an element of self-revision contained in the process, since their own translation remains the basis of the revision. Revisers may then engage in other-revision based on the author's feedback about the translator's work. Revisers may be engaging in self-revision of their own revision product after the other agents have given their feedback.

5.   Revision: a proposed framework

Our hypothesis projected revision as a cluster of possible combinations of self- and other-revision. The findings suggest that revising and editing (as they are defined in the literature) are not clearly delineated, and that various combinations exist. The findings also suggest that the processes are even less structured than simple combinations of self- and other-revision actions. Instead of being a linear process or a mere matter of the agents switching roles between self- and other-revision, the empirical analysis suggests a complex loop of revision actions that seem to be dictated by the sociology at work in a particular translation process. This means that an agent's activities are the product of that agent's position in the social network and his/her relationships with the other agents, together with the particular workflow needed to produce the final target text. This state of affairs could only be revealed by studying the process from the *inside*, as suggested by Latour.

We therefore propose a repackaging and possible recoining of the terms for the processes used to rework manuscripts—either original or translated. One possibility would be to use *revision* as the *encompassing term* for *all activities* which involve a "looking again" (currently referred to as revision, editing and proofreading) as suggested by *revisere*. This would imply that the current distinction between editing and revision would fall away. Such a terminological approach may be able to describe the real-life action performed by the various agents in a more logical and simple manner.

Further distinctions could then be drawn, based on (1) the presence or absence of comparison with the source text and (2) the agent at work. A division could then be made depending on whether comparative activities are involved, so that two main types of revision are discerned: (1) *unilingual revision* and (2) *source text-informed revision*.

Unilingual revision could include the rewriting of a text in plain language, or the final reading of a translated manuscript. Source-text informed revision could include any type of comparative reading, whether you compare the whole translation to the source or refer to the source text only when a passage in the translation is questionable. An editor could also be contracted to do a unilingual check of a text for publication but may stumble across an unintelligible passage, for which the solution may lie in finding the source of the text (in another language) in order to clarify the meaning.

These two main types of revision could then be refined into *agent-driven tasks*, so that unilingual revision would include *unilingual editor-revision* as well as *proofreader-revision*. Unilingual editor-revision could, for example, be the more encompassing type of editing as typically performed by the commissioning editor or compiler (where content issues may be addressed). It could also be a combination of stylistic editing (thus prioritizing the needs of the readers) and copy-editing in the sense of a focus on adherence to linguistic rules, depending on the specific task. Proofreader-revision could then be conceptualized as a solely gatekeeping activity depending on the task at hand—a last mechanical check for errors in typing, punctuation and typography, or even a last thorough copy-edit to ensure that no language errors slip through. In all of these instances, the project manager could brief the agents that a comparative check is not needed, but include in the brief the ratio of gatekeeping and language therapy tasks to be performed.

Source-text informed revision may be conceptualized as *translator-revision*, *author-revision*, *reviser-revision* (by a second translator) or *source-text-informed editor-revision* (editing with reference to the source text). Once again, the project manager can assign tasks as required by the project. If the author is willing to be involved in the translation and revision process, author-revision may be more or less emphasized depending on the author's envisioned role. There might even be some rewriting by the author—a process that could be called transcreation, although this should be carefully overseen by the project manager, so as not to jeopardize the entire translation process. Translator-revision may refer to the first translator's initial check of his or her own translation, but it may also refer to this translator's revision of the author's inputs. Furthermore, it can be seen as an interactive process involving questions, clarification and justification. Reviser-revision would be congruent with the traditional notion of other-revision, meaning that another translator checks the work of the first translator against the source text. Editor-revision happens when a non-translator revises the manuscript with the main focus on gatekeeping activities, especially those pertaining to the target language. This may also include the editor consulting the source text in order to solve some remaining issues.

For all these activities, the specific styles and applications will vary from project to project and also from agent to agent, depending on the nature of the text and on individual working styles and personalities. It is therefore of vital importance that the project manager take all these factors into account in order to ensure that the production process runs smoothly. We therefore want to emphasize that our proposed repackaging of terminology is not a universal model, but rather a framework that can be adapted for individual projects. This framework is a data-based one, drawing on patterns that emerged from the analysis of real-life data.

With this contribution of a repackaged sociologically driven, empirically based terminology for literary revision, we hope to have added to the theoretical basis of language practices.

6. Concluding remarks

A similar investigation should be undertaken for non-literary translation projects, both for publication and non-publication purposes as well as for other literary translation projects where, for example, not all agents have command of both source and target languages. This would make it possible to see whether our findings have wider application than this case study and whether other revision roles could be ascribed if additional agents were to be involved. This might be of particular significance for translation where English is paired with a South African indigenous language other than Afrikaans. It might also be worthwhile to investigate non-human translation processes to see whether a terminological distinction between revision, editing and post-editing is still necessary, or whether the term 'revision' is sufficient to cover these revision activities as well. The lumping of these activities under the sole term 'revision' may also make it easier to follow a more sociological approach in researching real-life translation projects as "agent-grounded researches . . . from the viewpoint of those who engage in it, in particular (social, cultural or professional) settings" (Buzelin 2011 in Scocchera 2016b).

Notes

1 The archived e-mail correspondence between the agents about their processes (the same material used for the current study) was analysed in a qualitative way. We suggest that this chapter be read in conjunction with Feinauer and Lourens (2017).

2 We found that the terms 'revision' and 'editing' were used in an apparently haphazard way in the archival material. In our view, these terms are used in practice without all the agents having agreed on the precise content of a task labelled 'revision' or 'editing' by project managers.

3 It is important to note that in South Africa, all agents (including the source text author) working with Afrikaans and English as a language pair are fully bilingual. This implies that a comparative reading for accuracy, readability and target language literary style could be done by all agents involved.

4 Mossop lists 12 revision parameters, categorized into four groups. Tailoring as well as grammar, spelling, punctuation, house style and correct usage fall into Group C, which deals with problems of language and style. The other groups deal with content, transfer and presentation (Mossop 2014a: 134).

5 The authors would like to express their gratitude to Carla-Marié Spies for the use of the dataset collected by her and published as appendices to her PhD dissertation (Spies 2013).
6 *In Bushveld and desert* is a compilation from four volumes of Afrikaans short stories, selected and arranged chronologically by a specific agent (the compiler) tasked by the project manager.
7 The full set of e-mail correspondence can be requested from the authors.
8 Nearly 30,000 words in total (66 pages, 1.5 line spacing).
9 Our English translation of the original communication between the agents will be given first, followed by the original Afrikaans as copied from the e-mail correspondence. In cases where the correspondence took place in English, only the English will be given. Quoted excerpts from the source texts are italicized.
10 The proofreader means British English.

PART IV

Training

10

REVISION AND POST-EDITING COMPETENCES IN TRANSLATOR EDUCATION

Kalle Konttinen, Leena Salmi and Maarit Koponen

The translation industry and institutional translation services obey two competing principles: maximisation of productivity and quality. For long-term success, a translating organisation needs to balance productivity with adequate quality assurance measures. The two primary ways to safeguard the quality of translation are revision and, when machine translation (MT) is part of the workflow, post-editing. Even with ongoing automation in many aspects of translation service, revision and post-editing rely on human skill and expertise. Revision and post-editing in digital translation environments are part of the same workflow as translation and depend on similar skill sets. Graduates of translator education programmes are thus well placed to perform these tasks. Consequently, revising and post-editing belong to the core objectives of translator education, as reflected, for example, in the inclusion of both skills in the EMT Competence Framework (European Master's in Translation Network 2017).

Revision is typically carried out in "translate-edit-proofread" workflows (Kockaert and Makoushina 2008) that rely on translation service standards like ISO 17100 (2015) and reflect "traditional hierarchical approaches to managing professional translation" (Drugan 2013: 125). Alternatives to such top-down quality assurance scenarios exist in crowdsourcing (see Jiménez-Crespo 2018), where it is to some extent possible to remedy any shortcomings in professional expertise or attitudes among the contributors through alternative quality control mechanisms and workflow practices that replace traditional revision (Zaidan and Callison-Burch 2011). However, standardised translation workflows still prevail as the dominant form of translation service.

Integration of MT has shown promise for improving productivity in translation workflows, but post-editing by humans is still indispensable as the only practical means to ensure targeted quality levels. Technological developments and changing practices in translation production are leading to increased integration of human translation with MT. Through this "reconfiguration of the translation space" (Pym 2013: 492), revision and post-editing come closer to each other both conceptually and in practice. The partial confluence of translation, revision and post-editing tasks in a digital translation environment, together with the need to find efficient and pedagogically effective curricular solutions for teaching these tasks, present translator education with the challenge of identifying both shared features and differences in the relevant competences.

In this chapter, we look at the commonalities and differences in revision and post-editing competences in order to identify a basis for an efficient and pedagogically effective model for teaching revision and post-editing in translator education programmes. Utilising the commonalities of revision and post-editing, while taking into account their differences, we present objectives, learning content and teaching methods for revision and post-editing training in the translator education programme at the University of Turku. Section 1 discusses previous work on teaching revision and post-editing. Section 2 presents an analysis of the overlap and the differences between post-editing and revision competences. Section 3 describes a translator education curriculum where the initial training in revision takes place in translation courses and the initial training in post-editing in translation technology courses, while integration of the two activities into the translation workflow takes place in project-based translation courses. Section 4 summarises the key ideas for pedagogical planning.

1.   Teaching revision and post-editing: previous work

As pointed out in the introduction to this book, most studies that address the teaching of revision are descriptions of revision courses given by or at the institution of the author(s) of the study. The country with the highest number of publications related to revision is Canada, where revision has long been taught in most university translation programmes.

Brunette and Gagnon (2013: 100–1) describe a revision course taught at a late stage of university studies after the students have learned to translate. As the most critical objectives, they list learning to separate revising from translating, learning to evaluate the quality of a translation and to make corrections while distinguishing corrections from suggestions, and learning to create a cooperative rather than a hierarchical relationship with the translator whose text is being revised (Brunette and Gagnon 2013: 100–2). As an example, they describe an experiment where students revised translated Wikipedia entries, chosen to give the students authentic revision tasks, including an opportunity to justify their modifications to the translators.

Schjoldager et al. (2008) describe a module on précis-writing, revision and editing, based on a survey of translation professionals from international organisations and the private sector and planned as cross-university collaboration. One of the expressed training needs was that of "'real-situation' practice (for instance, working with poor texts, under time constraints), which can teach students/trainees to be more pragmatic about the task" (Schjoldager et al. 2008: 804). The module itself consisted of an intensive week with lectures, workshops and introduction to the tools used, distance-learning assignments, and a final exam that included revision from B-language to A-language (Schjoldager et al. 2008: 808–9).

Another example of advanced training in revision is discussed by Way (2009), who describes a course that integrates professional practices, including revision, in the final year of translator education. The course includes an introduction to the mechanics of the revision and editing process through suggested reading as well as an introduction to using spell checkers. After examining real examples of a revising and editing process at a translation agency, practical revision tasks are carried out, first as other-revision and then as self-revision, using an evaluation sheet as an aid (Way 2009). Revision taught as part of a translation course is also described by Pietrzak (2014), who uses a method she calls "group feedback", where students revise each other's translations of the most problematic passages in the source text, compiled and anonymised by the teacher. According to Pietrzak, this way the students learn to concentrate on the text under revision without feeling that their errors are exposed, and also gain experience in quality management. Scocchera (2019) reports on an experimental revision module within a translation course, where students were asked to revise the same translated text at four stages, first without and then with the source text, and subsequently write comments to the imagined translator, before and after theoretical training on revising.

Revision is generally taught into the students' A-language. Robert et al. (2018: 7) state that revision into the foreign language may not be considered the best practice; however, "it is common in countries with languages of lesser diffusion". Revision into the B-language may be more problematic than in the A-language, as Mossop (2007a: 19), citing Lorenzo (2002), points out: "the more time the students spent revising, and the more changes they made, the worse the output". Lorenzo (2002) also found that students were better at revising others' translations than their own. Way (2009) also considers self-revision to be more demanding than other-revision and advocates starting with other-revision in training. In contrast, Mossop (2020) suggests that other-revision may differ psychologically from self-revision and finds no basis in current translation pedagogy research for deciding when to introduce self-revision and other-revision.

Training in post-editing has been integrated into translator education curricula either as specific courses or as part of translation courses. An early proposal for post-editing course content was made by O'Brien (2002), who argues that post-editing involves particular skills separate from translation, and therefore, specific training is needed. Doherty and Kenny (2014) describe a course design covering hands-on development and implementation of a (statistical) MT system as well as post-editing through both theoretical lectures and practical labs. Flanagan and Christensen (2014) describe a course where translation students were first introduced to the basics of MT as well as post-editing guidelines and then completed two independent post-editing tasks, one following the guidelines for "good enough" quality and the second for "publishable" quality as defined by TAUS (2010). Koponen

(2015) provides an outline of a post-editing course that includes the basics of MT and quality evaluation as well as post-editing assignments covering "light" and "full" post-editing and monolingual post-editing. In the MT course described by Rossi (2017), students both compared their own translations (created without MT) to statistical MT outputs and carried out post-editing assignments.

In addition to post-editing training as a separate course, post-editing tasks have been included in translation courses. An assignment described by Shuttleworth (2002) involves the use of both translation memories (TM) and MT in a large project. He considers combining TM and MT post-editing vital because it enables students to learn about the complementarity of these technologies in translation projects. In fact, this is how many TM systems already currently work: they provide the functionality to integrate an MT tool. Torrejón and Rico (2002) focus on controlled language situations, such as when translating technical documentation, and they describe an assignment where post-editing is combined with error analysis of a machine-translated text and pre-editing of the source text to improve MT quality prior to post-editing. Post-editing tasks have been implemented into both the students' A-language (for example, Torrejón and Rico 2002; Koponen 2015) and B-language (for example, Flanagan and Christensen 2014). Garcia (2011) also describes post-editing tasks into both the students' A-language and B-language as part of translator education but notes that the students received no specific training in post-editing (Garcia 2011: 218).

Introducing translation students to the basics of MT is generally included as an essential part of such courses, although the level of detail varies. Building and training an MT system is central to the syllabus of Doherty and Kenny (2014), while Flanagan and Christensen (2014), Koponen (2015) and Rossi (2017) employ freely available online systems or the translation system provided by the European Commission. Until recently, most courses have focused on statistical MT, possibly covering also rule-based approaches, but the emergence of neural MT naturally makes it necessary for current and future courses to address features particular to those systems and their effect on post-editing.

2. Revision and post-editing competences

Revising a (human) translation and post-editing MT output both require specific skills and competences, but are those competences the same, different or overlapping, or is one perhaps a subset of the other? In this section, we discuss the commonalities and differences between revision and post-editing competences based on existing competence models. Competence, as defined in the Recommendation of the European Parliament and of the Council on the establishment of the European Qualifications Framework for lifelong learning (European Communities 2008: 11), is understood as "the proven ability to use knowledge, skills and personal, social and/or methodological abilities, in work or study situations and in professional and personal development". Skills are defined as "the ability to apply knowledge and use know-how to complete tasks and solve problems". Thus both 'competence' and 'skills' are defined by 'ability', and various authors use them interchangeably. For the purposes of this chapter, we follow the terminology used by each author cited in the following.

Some translation competence models, such as the European Master's in Translation (EMT) Competence Framework, revised in 2017 (European Master's in Translation Network 2017), list revision and post-editing among the skills related to translation, and MT skills among those related to technology. Overall, the role of MT in the framework has changed from the previous EMT competence document, which emphasised "knowing the possibilities and limits of MT" (EMT Expert Group 2009: 7), to the current document, in which "the ability to interact with machine translation in the translation process is now an integral part of professional translation competence" (European Master's in Translation Network 2017: 7). In the "Translation Competence" section, the revised EMT framework lists the ability to "check, review and/or revise [the student's] own work and that of others according to standard or work-specific quality objectives", the ability to "apply post-editing to MT output using the appropriate post-editing levels and techniques according to the quality and productivity objectives", as well as the ability to pre-edit the source text "for the purpose of potentially improving MT output quality" (European Master's in Translation Network 2017: 7). Post-editing and revision skills are thus considered part of translation competence. The specific MT skills listed under the section "Technology" involve the ability to "master the basics of MT and its impact on the translation process" and to "assess the relevance of MT systems in a translation workflow and implement the appropriate MT system where relevant" (European Master's in Translation Network 2017: 9).

For a more detailed view of revision and post-editing competences, we next examine models related explicitly to revision and post-editing. These models include the revision competence model presented by Robert et al. (2017a), the revision competence model by Scocchera (2017a, 2019), the skills or competences needed in revision described by Künzli (2006b) and Mossop (2020), as well as the competences needed for post-editing listed by Rico and Torrejón (2012), and Pym's (2013) list of 10 skills needed in the "Machine Translation age", which combines MT and TM skills.

The revision competence model of Robert et al. (2017a) is a multicompetence model which borrows translation-related parts from two competence models. From the PACTE model (see, for example, Hurtado Albir 2017), it borrows the Bilingual and Extralinguistic subcompetences as well as the Knowledge-about-Translation subcompetence; from Göpferich's (2009) TransComp model, it borrows the Translation routine activation subcompetence and the Tools and Research subcompetence. To these, Robert et al. add subcompetences specific to revision: the Strategic subcompetence, which forms the centre of the model, the Knowledge about Revision, Revision Routine Activation and Interpersonal subcompetences, as well as psycho-physiological components addressing, for example, a "revising frame of mind as opposed to retranslating" (Robert et al. 2017a: 14). The Strategic subcompetence is the most essential, as it involves planning and carrying out the revision task ("selecting the most adequate procedure in view of the task definition, reading for evaluation, applying a detection strategy [and] applying an immediate solution or problem-solving strategy, making only the necessary changes") and evaluating the result (Robert et al. 2017a: 14). Scocchera (2017a, 2019) presents a multicompetence model of revision that comprises a partly similar set of components: analytical-critical competence, operational competence, metalinguistic-descriptive competence, interpersonal competence, instrumental competence, and psycho-physiological competence.

Künzli (2006b) identifies a set of three competence categories to consider in syllabus design for revision: strategic competence, professional and instrumental competence, and interpersonal competence. Strategic competence involves revision-specific elements of defining the task at hand, applying relevant evaluation criteria, and deciding how to address a problem (Künzli 2006b: 11), while professional competence refers to "knowledge related to professional translation practice" and instrumental competence to knowledge of the tools and information sources (Künzli 2006b: 15). Interpersonal competence is the "ability to collaborate with the different actors involved in a translation project: translators, revisers, translation companies, commissioners and/or source-text authors" (Künzli 2006b: 13–14).

A specific and practice-oriented list of abilities necessary for revisers is presented by Mossop (2020: 118–19) as part of his description of the work of a reviser. According to Mossop, these abilities include detecting problems in a translation, quickly deciding on revisions, and making small changes instead of retranslating, which also requires an understanding of different revision procedures (unilingual reading of the translation only, reading only part of the translation, reading with a focus on only specific features), and applying them where appropriate. Some of the abilities listed by Mossop are interpersonal, such as being able to explain the necessary changes to the translator and the more trainer-oriented ability to identify weaknesses and strengths and provide feedback. According to Mossop, the reviser should also be able to "appreciate other people's approaches" and not judge translations simply for being different from their own. Finally, Mossop lists what he calls personal qualities: diplomacy in conflict situations, leadership in group projects, and cautiousness to avoid making the translation worse.

Many parallels to these revision competence models can be seen in various discussions of post-editing competences. Rico and Torrejón (2012) present three categories of post-editing competences: linguistic skills, core competences, and instrumental competences. They divide core competences into attitudinal or psycho-physiological competence (the ability to cope with specifications and client expectations for text quality and the ability to overcome uncertainty) and the strategic competence required to arrive at informed decisions when choosing among alternatives (Rico and Torrejón 2012: 170). Instrumental competences, on the other hand, include knowledge of MT systems and their capabilities, skills related to terminology, MT dictionary maintenance skills, skills in assessing corpus quality, controlled language pre-editing skills and some programming skills, while linguistic skills cover language and textual skills as well as cultural knowledge (Rico and

Torrejón 2012: 170). Like the revision models of Künzli (2006b) and Robert et al. (2017a), some of these competences can be seen to overlap with translation.

The skills presented by Pym (2013) are grouped under three headings: "learning to learn", "learning to trust and mistrust data" and "learning to revise". Learning to revise comprises the detection and correction of errors, substantial stylistic revising, and the ability to revise and review in teams (Pym 2013: 496). According to Pym (2013: 493), the translator's skill set is undergoing "a very simple and quite profound shift" from identifying and generating translation solutions to selecting a solution from those automatically proposed by TM and MT systems integrated in the translator's computer-assisted translation (CAT) tool, and adapting the solution to the context. Robert (2018: 130, 145) presents a similar integrative view, noting that the use of TM matches is, in fact, a form of other-revision just like the revision of human translations. A parallel can thus be drawn between other-revision, modifying TM suggestions and post-editing MT output, particularly as these activities are increasingly integrated in the same software tools.

All the revision and post-editing models discussed thus far include subcompetences they share with translation. Leaving these aside, the subcompetences specifically related to revision and post-editing can be grouped into three larger categories for purposes of identifying commonalities and differences: (1) strategic subcompetences related to the revision or post-editing process, (2) interpersonal, psycho-physiological or attitudinal subcompetences, and (3) instrumental or tools subcompetences related to the use of translation technology. Table 10.1 presents the three groups of subcompetences, divided into those common to revision and post-editing and those specific to each. For revision, operationalisations for a largely similar set of constructs can be found in Rigouts Terryn et al. (2017), Robert et al. (2017b), Robert et al. (2018) and Scocchera (2017a, 2019). In contrast to the models in Robert et al. (2017a), Künzli (2006b) and Rico and Torrejón (2012), the category of strategic subcompetences also encompasses declarative knowledge about revision, post-editing and MT. In syllabus design and pedagogical practice, a strategy and the domain where it is applied are intrinsically linked. Thus, learning how to "arrive at informed decisions when choosing among alternatives" (Rico and Torrejón 2012: 170) relies on "knowledge related to professional translation practice" (Künzli 2006b: 15) and on knowledge about typical errors that need to be attended to when revising or post-editing. Metalinguistic knowledge, a part of metalinguistic-descriptive competence in Scocchera's model, falls here under the category of strategic subcompetences, although it is also an important prerequisite for interpersonal subcompetence when communicating with the translator.

In the first group in Table 10.1, strategic subcompetences, the differences between revision and post-editing are mainly due to the origins of the texts: human translation versus MT. For revision, the defining characteristics involve the professional roles of the translator and the reviser, as well as the typical features of translations produced by human agents. For post-editing, the distinguishing trait is the fact that the "agent" producing the translation is an algorithmic machine,

TABLE 10.1 Breakdown of revision and post-editing competences or skills

	Common to revision and post-editing	Specific to revision	Specific to post-editing
Strategic subcompetences	Detecting, identifying and evaluating errors; information-seeking	Knowledge about revision and aspects of the profession Knowledge of typical (human) translation errors	Knowledge about MT systems and their capabilities Knowledge of typical MT errors
Interpersonal, attitudinal or psycho-physiological subcompetences	Revising frame of mind as opposed to retranslating	Communication with the translator: justifying corrections, feedback	Applying required post-editing level
Instrumental subcompetences	Use of the appropriate (CAT) tools	Use of revision-specific tools	Use of MT- and PE-specific tools Tools management and maintenance Controlled language pre-editing skills Programming skills

and this origin of the translation is likely to be reflected in the features of the MT output, including typical errors.

In the second group, interpersonal, psycho-physiological or attitudinal sub-competences, an important characteristic feature of revision is communication. While revision often involves communication between human agents, post-editing is usually conceptualised as a process that involves the post-editor and the text, and possibly some form of interactive use of the MT system. Thus, the main characteristic feature of post-editing in this group of subcompetences seems to be the ability to apply a set of principles or rules in choosing a post-editing level that suits the intended purpose. In terms of communication, the use of MT may also involve communication with developers of the MT system in a workflow where the translator identifies and analyses MT errors and reports them to the developer to improve the quality of the output.

As for the third group, 'instrumental subcompetences', post-editing requires some knowledge of MT, and in some cases it may even involve technical tasks. Revision is less dependent on knowledge of technology, even when carried out in a technological environment. However, user interfaces specifically designed for revising, and the improved functionalities of corpus tools and grammar-checking and spell-checking tools, are becoming increasingly important technical aspects of revising.

It is interesting to note that in previous studies, revision is often seen as a demanding task more suited to later stages of translator education and for more experienced translators (for example, Way 2009; Mossop 2020), whereas post-editing is sometimes envisioned as a task for beginning translators or even non-translators familiar with the subject matter. For example, Guerberof Arenas (2014b) found no significant differences in the post-editing competences of experienced translators and translation students, and some studies (for example, Zaidan and Callison-Burch 2011; Mitchell 2015) have shown potential for non-translators as post-editors in specific situations. On the other hand, Yamada (2015) found that foreign language students (as opposed to translation students) did not reach overall post-editing quality comparable to professional translators, and others too have argued for post-editing as a specialised task suitable for translators (see O'Brien 2002). The different perceptions of reviser versus post-editor backgrounds may reflect cases where MT post-editing is associated with "fit-for-purpose" or "good enough" quality, emphasising the correctness of information content over fluent language (see TAUS 2010; ISO 1858: 7). As the adoption of neural MT approaches has been seen to improve particularly the fluency of MT output, the competences for evaluating translation solutions and identifying potential errors in meaning are arguably becoming even more important, supporting the need for translation-related competences in the post-editing workflow.

3. Placing revision and post-editing training in the translation curriculum

Due to the dual nature of translator education as academic study and practical training, instruction in revision and post-editing should enable translation students to develop a comprehensive understanding of revision and post-editing as quality assurance activities, while at the same time they learn to perform the tasks at the level required of a novice reviser or post-editor in preparation for working life. We propose distributing revision and post-editing content among several courses in a translator education curriculum, in order to allow for a reasonable amount of practical training. This holistic view is in line with Mellinger's (2017) suggestion to embed MT and post-editing in multiple courses. To promote the students' conceptual understanding of revision and post-editing, we also consider it beneficial to include both processes in a collaborative project-based translation course, as quality assurance activities in the workflow of a translating organisation.

In many examples of revision and post-editing training cited in the literature, revision training takes place in a separate course (see, for example, Brunette and Gagnon 2013; Schjoldager et al. 2008), and post-editing training is also placed in a separate course of its own (see, for example, O'Brien 2002; Flanagan and Christensen 2014; Koponen 2015). One reason for this may be that post-editing has been, until recently, considered a relatively new and perhaps more peripheral skill, which has therefore been taught in a separate, optional course. While building a course around one principal activity comes with the benefit of allocating ample teaching resources and student time for creating an understanding of the specific character of the task and for learning to perform it well, a downside of this approach is that it may lead the students to perceive that task as isolated from other related activities. Furthermore, separate courses for revision and post-editing may not be the optimal solution if there is a need to economise teaching resources and the students' time due to the constraints of a master's programme that lasts only one or two years. In our view, the similarities and differences in the subcompetences required for revision, post-editing and translation provide a solid basis for distributing the learning content over the curriculum, with a view to achieving both efficiency and effectiveness.

Our proposal for the first rough division in the learning content utilises the differences between revision and post-editing in the categories of instrumental subcompetence and interpersonal, attitudinal or psycho-physiological subcompetence (see Table 10.1). Much of the introductory content for revision in the category of interpersonal, attitudinal or psycho-physiological subcompetence is non-technological and focused on communication between the agents of translation production. Such content fits well into translation courses, where communication with the translator, justifying corrections and giving feedback can be practised along with learning to translate. On the other hand, much of the preliminary content associated with post-editing is technical and focused on interaction with algorithmic machines. Such content can be adequately dealt with in translation technology courses, where the connections between post-editing and translation technology are in focus.

The full picture is more complicated, of course, as many of the text modification skills in the category of strategic subcompetences are shared by revision and post-editing, and some of the skills associated with revision are technological. For most students, translation technology is likely to be an unfamiliar domain, while improving texts is a skill that may be familiar from previous studies, albeit mostly as monolingual editing of one's own texts or those of peers. It is mainly due to the expected unfamiliarity of the students with MT as a translator's tool that we find it useful to emphasise the close connection between technology and post-editing by placing post-editing in the translation technology course and not in regular translation courses.

The second part of our proposal puts the revision and post-editing knowledge and skills acquired in the introductory courses to the test in real-life-like situational constraints. One suitable approach takes the form of collaborative project-based translation courses that simulate the business processes of a translating organisation (for a more detailed description, see Konttinen et al. 2017). There, translation, revision and post-editing can be integrated into the technology-supported translation service workflow. Besides opportunities to practise the skills, the collaborative workflows in such courses provide a setting where students gain a comprehensive overview of the various aspects of revision and post-editing as quality assurance activities.

To illustrate the application of such combinations of distributed and integrated curricular solutions, we shall now look at the revision and post-editing training given in the two-year master's-level Multilingual Translation Studies Degree Programme at the University of Turku (120 ECTS credits). The programme offers studies in five language pairs: English–Finnish, French–Finnish, German–Finnish, Italian–Finnish, and Spanish–Finnish. The students enter the programme after a three-year BA with one of these five foreign languages as their major and usually one (or more) of the other languages as their minor(s). The number of students in individual courses ranges from five in language-pair-focused courses to 30 in multilingual and language-independent courses. The expected level of language proficiency upon entering the programme is B1 to C1 in the Common European Framework of Reference (Council of Europe 2001).

Table 10.2 shows an outline of the curriculum, with the recommended order in which the courses should be taken over two years;[1] how students advance is not controlled on a yearly basis. Of the total 120 ECTS, 90 are for compulsory courses, while the remaining 30 are for optional courses. These can be translation courses offered by the programme (for example, translation in specialised fields such as technical or audiovisual translation), other courses offered by the programme (such as terminology or the history of translation) or courses offered by other programmes (such as languages not taught in the programme, or business studies). Compulsory courses are marked with regular font; optional courses are *in italics*. Courses that include revision are marked with light grey, and courses that include post-editing with dark grey. The number of ECTS credits is given in parentheses.

TABLE 10.2 Outline of the Multilingual Translation Studies Degree Programme[2] at the University of Turku

	Autumn semester	*Spring semester*
Year 1	Translation A-to-B-language (5)	Translation Studies Research Methodology (5)
	Translation B-to-A-language (5)	Multilingual Translation Workshop I (10)
	Language Technology and Translation Tools (5)	*optional courses* (5 each)
	Translation Studies (5)	
	Career Opportunities in the Translation Industry (5)	
	Norms of the Finnish Language for Translators, Revisers and Editors (5)	
Year 2	Multilingual Translation Workshop II (10)	*Language Technology and Translation Tools: Advanced Course* (5)
	optional courses (5 each)	*optional courses* (5 each)
	Master's Thesis Seminar and work on Master's Thesis (5 + 30)	

Revision training in translation courses

Revision is introduced in the compulsory translation courses, Translation A-to-B-language and Translation B-to-A-language, which are taught in the first semester of the MA curriculum. As revision in the B-language is likely to be more demanding than in the A-language, training in the B-language consists primarily of self-revision, while other-revision practice takes place when translating into the A-language. Self-revision is a required workflow step in the ISO 17100, labelled as 'checking', and it is an indispensable part of translation work. Thus, it has a place in revision training for both directions.

The compulsory translation courses present an overview of revision and introduce its core competences. This is done by presenting the concept of revision and its underlying principles; for example, revision procedures, degrees and parameters (Mossop 2020), along with the role of the reviser in translation service workflows as defined in ISO 17100. Practice consists of having all students translate the same text at home and discussing it in class, as well as having students translate different parts of a longer text and then revising each other's translations. With five language pairs and several teachers of translation in the Multilingual Translation Studies Degree Programme, the methods used by individual teachers to achieve learning outcomes related to revision may vary, but one method that has proved to be useful for discussing the translations in class is to present the translations of two or three students to all participants and then compare and improve them as a collaborative effort. This can also be done in small groups or pairs. The teachers have also agreed on a model for error categorisation in the assessment of translations, based on the translation quality metrics framework MQM (see Lommel et al. 2014).

The learning outcomes of the compulsory translation courses, as stated in the study guide, include the ability to justify translation solutions and to give, receive and use feedback, and the ability to understand how language guides and linguistic norms can be applied in translation. The compulsory translation courses aim to develop the students' interpersonal, attitudinal and psycho-physiological subcompetence, in terms of keeping a revising frame of mind (as opposed to retranslating), justifying corrections, and giving feedback through discussion of translation problems, errors and solutions in class, small groups or pairs. In developing the strategic subcompetence of detecting, identifying and evaluating errors, use of the error categorisation model helps the students to structure peer feedback and other-revision. The instrumental subcompetence of using appropriate tools is only touched upon, for example, by presenting the review functionalities of word-processing software.

Various optional translation courses, which can be taken after the two compulsory translation courses, build on the learning outcomes of the compulsory courses and offer specialisations in the various subfields of translation, for example, technical translation, translation in the EU context, audiovisual translation or the production of legally valid translations. The specialist translation courses address revision training flexibly in small groups and respond to individual learning needs. With increased specialisation, revision is practised on progressively more challenging texts and in multiple settings, first as revision in class, then in pairs, and later in team projects. Also, the role of the teacher changes gradually from an instructor to a collegial mentor and reviser of the students' translations.

Since each of the five language pairs may offer as many as five optional specialist translation courses, we are presenting their learning outcomes regarding revision in summarised form. The students are expected to learn to function independently in the role of a reviser; identify, categorise, indicate and correct errors and deficiencies in texts; apply style guides and other authoritative sources; prioritise various needs for corrections; and balance the severity of deficiencies against project specifications, client expectations and the prospective readership. Finally, the students are supposed to have learned to accommodate situational constraints (for example, time, cost and efficiency) and to communicate and justify any corrections and amendments made. In some of the translation courses, students learn the use of a few computer aids and the functionalities of word processing software useful for revision, such as spelling, grammar and style checkers, displaying changes, inserting comments and comparing documents, but the more challenging aspects of technology are left for the translation technology courses.

Post-editing training in translation technology courses

Post-editing is first introduced in the compulsory introductory course Language Technology and Translation Tools (5 ECTS), which is taught in the first semester of the MA curriculum. Further post-editing practice is integrated into the optional course Language Technology and Translation Tools: Advanced Course (5 ECTS), which students generally take during the second semester of the MA curriculum. These two courses lay the foundation for developing instrumental competence in the use of translator's tools, including translation memories, termbases, corpora and concordance tools, subtitling software, speech recognition and translation project management tools, in addition to machine translation. The courses approach MT and other tools from the user point of view, utilising available systems rather than having the students build their own. The tools include domain-specific MT such as the eTranslation platform offered by the European Commission, and systems for technical domains (for example, information technology) made available by industrial partners of the MA programme, in addition to free online systems like Google Translate. A central goal for both these courses is to develop a positive attitude toward MT, and translation technology more generally, but also a realistic understanding of the both the potential and the limitations of technology (see O'Brien 2002; Pym 2013).

The compulsory course Language Technology and Translation Tools presents the basics of various translator's tools and their use. The learning outcomes given in the study guide state that after the course, the student knows the most important language and translation technology tools in the translation field, has practised basic use of translator's tools, including machine translation, and is familiar with workflows involving the use of language technology, such as MT post-editing. To achieve these learning goals, the course covers the basics of MT (rule-based, statistical and neural) and post-editing in lectures and practical post-editing tasks. The course introduces uses of post-editing in the translation industry as well as post-editing guidelines and quality levels (TAUS 2010; ISO 1858: 7). This provides a conceptual framework and contextualises post-editing in the translation workflow, thereby supporting the learning outcome of familiarising the students with post-editing workflows. Practice consists of light post-editing of a short machine-translated text and writing a reflective commentary about the task. This develops the students' strategic subcompetences by familiarising them with MT technology and typical errors, and it also develops their competence in post-editing to a specified level. Light post-editing is used because it has been found to be difficult for students (see Flanagan and Christensen 2014; Koponen 2015), and because focusing on that level of post-editing prompts the students to consider the question of necessary versus unnecessary changes. Post-editing practice is mostly conducted into the students' A-language, as MT errors in the B-language may be more difficult to detect. To provide a more realistic view of how the tools are used in translation workflows and how they complement each other (see Shuttleworth 2002; Pym 2013), MT output is also used in combination with TM in an integrated interface.

The optional Language Technology and Translation Tools: Advanced Course aims to develop more in-depth insight into working with MT and to provide further practice in post-editing, pre-editing and controlled language. The learning outcomes given in the study guide state that after the course the student is able to apply various language and translation technology tools in translation assignments, has practised more advanced functionalities of these tools and is able to apply various computer-assisted translation workflows, such as MT post-editing, appropriately in translation assignments. This optional course involves more technical aspects of MT and more demanding post-editing assignments, which are carried out in an environment that integrates TM matches and MT suggestions. Assignments also include post-editing under time constraints, which further develops the strategic subcompetences of evaluating post-editing alternatives and making only necessary changes as well as subcompetences involved in dealing with post-editing specifications and client expectations, and the ability to post-edit to a specified quality level. The course also addresses MT quality assessment and error analysis, which develops the strategic subcompetences of learning to detect MT errors and to discard suggestions requiring too many changes. Additionally, the course utilises process-oriented methods involving the use of keystroke logging and screen recording and retrospection. The rationale for including this approach is to make the processes "visible" (see Hansen 2006; Massey 2017), helping students gain insight into their own approaches. For this purpose, the students first post-edit a short text using keylogging and screen-recording software such as Translog-II (Carl 2012). They then view a replay and analyse their own process, observing and reflecting on their overall approaches like the order of corrections and pauses. Based on the process data and their observations, the students then write a brief retrospective reflection on their post-editing process, and general observations are discussed in the class.

Revision and post-editing training in project-based translation courses

The revision skills developed in previous courses are placed in the context of a translation workflow in the courses Multilingual Translation Workshop I and II (Konttinen et al. 2017), a two-semester-long project-based translation course (10 + 10 ECTS); post-editing skills are included in Multilingual Translation Workshop II. The students carry out 12 demanding translation-related assignments as a simulated translation company, in addition to other tasks like setting up the company and planning its translation service workflow in compliance with the quality assurance steps required by ISO 17100. The standard provides a framework for the course: the student companies organise their workflows according to the standard and undergo a mock audit.

As the ISO 17100 workflow model requires the students to act as revisers of each other's work, it places revision conceptually in the context of translation workflow and thus helps the students to develop advanced aspects of revision competence. The course syllabus also includes an individual revision assignment (see also Künzli 2006b). The assignment consists of a relatively long text (10–15 pages) in the A-language, and part of the assignment is writing a letter with an evaluation of the text and justification for the changes. The exercise develops the strategic subcompetences of revision and simultaneously allows the students to practise the interpersonal aspect of revision. Interpersonal, attitudinal and psycho-physiological subcompetences also develop in face-to-face communication that takes place in the quality assurance activities of the simulated translation company. The strategic subcompetence of evaluating translation product quality is practised in a translation assessment task using a quality framework (for example, MQM; see Lommel et al. 2014). Simulating the workflows of a translating organisation develops necessary professional and interpersonal subcompetences like the ability to collaborate, the ability to estimate workloads, negotiate and keep deadlines, and justify and accept corrections. As students in the course integrate revision as a step in a realistic translation workflow and in a business process that needs to be economically sound, they learn to view revision from the point of view of quality, efficiency and profitability.

Post-editing is integrated in the Multilingual Translation Workshop II in the form of an in-class assignment where a simulated client commissions an assignment specifying the use of post-editing. The translation brief specifies that the texts are needed to facilitate discussions in a meeting held the same day, and that due to the tight time frame and the use that will be made of the translation, light post-editing (as described in ISO 1858: 7) to fit-for-purpose quality is desired. The assignment develops the students' ability to adapt to client specifications and quality levels, and to work under time restrictions. Furthermore, the assignment encourages the students to consider post-editing as a service and to discuss and decide in their simulated translation companies on adequate compensation for a commission involving post-editing.

4. Conclusion

The translation, revision and post-editing competences are fundamental building-blocks in a translator's skill set. Continuing advances in MT technology and improvements in the user interfaces of digital translation environments have already brought, and will continue to bring, the three activities ever closer together in actual textual operations. TM systems mix human and machine-originated text, as some of their contents are entirely translated by a human translator, some are machine-translated and post-edited, and some may be raw MT output. The information on the origin of a text segment may not always be visible, thereby blurring the boundaries between human and machine output. Given this trend, we advocate a holistic and integrative approach to teaching the strategic subcompetences for all kinds of textual operations, as described in this chapter.

What is likely to remain unchanged in the face of technological development is the need to make corrections and improvements in translated texts, whether the text is a human translation, a machine translation or a fuzzy match from a translation memory. There will always be dyadic relationships between the agents who carry out the textual operations, and thus a need for interaction, whether the agents are a human translator and a reviser, or an algorithmic machine and a post-editor. For curriculum planning, a crucial difference between training in revision and training in post-editing lies in how to teach the students to communicate any requirements and suggestions for changes in human translations, on the one hand, and in MT and TM output, on the other. While communication between human agents is best learned in translation courses, human-machine interaction can be more effectively practised in technology-oriented courses.

A further consideration for curriculum planning is the need to integrate the subcompetences learned in translation courses and translation technology courses into the translation service workflow. For this, we suggest using learning environments that are as close to the real-life challenges of the translation market as possible but without all the risks of real-life translation. In our view, translation company simulations like the Multilingual Translation Workshops offer a promising way to achieve this goal.

Notes

1 The structure of the Degree Programme in Multilingual Translation Studies at the University of Turku is presented online in the study guide at https://opas.peppi.utu.fi/en/degree-programme/3220. The learning outcomes cited in the text are translations of course descriptions that are available in Finnish.
2 Specific course titles may be subject to change. Titles given in the table are in accordance with the curriculum for the academic year 2019–2020.

11

IMPROVING REVISION QUALITY IN TRANSLATOR TRAINING WITH translationQ

Gys-Walt van Egdom

As evidenced in the introduction to this volume, recent decades have seen a surge of interest in revision. The growth in the number of publications on revision is, for the most part, due to the gradual understanding of revision as an expert subtask of translation ("self-revision") and as a task in its own right ("other-revision") (see Englund Dimitrova 2005; Shih 2006; Allman 2007; Parra-Galiano 2016). Revision is considered an activity that requires a specific set of competences, all of which are to be strategically deployed to obtain a successful outcome (see Robert et al. 2017a, 2017b, 2018; Scocchera 2019). Debate about revision competence is interwoven with debate about translation quality, which has also been quite lively in recent years (see Huertas-Barros and Vine 2019; Huertas-Barros et al. 2018; Moorkens et al. 2018). There are two reasons why revision competence is bound up with quality: (1) thorough revision seems to be a sine qua non for high-quality translation (ISO 17100 2015a; see section 1); (2) a competent reviser is a person who is "good" at his job, who displays expert behaviour (see also Kim 2009).

Further impetus is given to the debate on revision by the ongoing technologization of translation services. One of the consequences of the susceptibility of translation to technologization and automation is that Language Service Providers (LSPs) are probably spending more time on revision and revision-related activities such as post-editing (see Mossop 2007a; Martin 2007; for a discussion of the role of revision skills in post-editing and of the differences between revision and post-editing, see O'Brien 2010).

Due to the gradual recognition of revision as an activity requiring specific competences and the perceived prominence of revision-related practices in the translation workflow, revision also seems to be high on the agenda of translator trainers. In the revised EMT competence framework, it is stated that, upon graduation, students must be able to "check, review and/or revise their own work and that of others according to standard or work-specific quality objectives" (European

Master's in Translation Network 2017: 8). In recent decades, scholars have tried to find ways to cultivate revision skills within academic and vocational translation programs. For example, Mossop (1992) spearheaded research into revision competence in the early 1990s by setting out the learning objectives of a revision course. Around the turn of the century, extensive empirical investigation of revision processes had become possible with the development of keystroke logging software (such as Translog). Around that time, scholars like Jakobsen (2002) started to compare the revision processes of experts and novices (trainee translators). In part, such profiling of revision behaviour along a cline of expertise has been done with a view to providing measures that can distinguish non-expert from expert behaviour, distilling good practices and thereby creating ways to speed up competence acquisition during training, and ultimately improving revision quality.

The person who must ensure that students' revision skills are honed—the translator trainer—has been largely relegated to the fringes of revision research, however. Generally speaking, the trainer receives attention in studies in which the impact of teaching strategies on learning processes is measured (Nakanishi 2007; Pietrzak 2014; Vandepitte and Hanson 2018).

In this chapter, trainer-to-trainee revision will be observed from the translator trainer's (and to a lesser extent from the trainee's) perspective. More specifically, a closer look will be taken at technological solutions in trainer-to-trainee revision practices. Tools are scarce in translator training. Still, it seems that trainers and trainees might benefit greatly from systems that are geared to everyday practices such as trainer-to-trainee revision. Trainer-to-trainee revision is usually a repetitive task that consists of detecting and correcting similar and identical errors time and again, which is not only tedious for trainers but also tricky, because errors should be labelled, weighted and corrected in a consistent manner. One can easily understand how trainers (and trainees) might reap the benefits of a tool that does away with repetitiveness.

With translationQ (TELEVIC/KU Leuven), a tool has been introduced that is designed to help translator trainers speed up their revision work. An assessment will be made of the extent to which translationQ is likely to contribute to quality in trainer-to-trainee revision. The assessment is undertaken not because translationQ is hailed by its developers as a "game-changing" tool that increases "consistency and objectivity" in revision and evaluation, but mainly because it promises to make lighter work of revision practices.[1] This claim seems to mesh well with the recent expansion of the notion of "quality" in Translation Studies, an expansion which includes the virtual and non-virtual working environment and working conditions (D'Hulst and Gambier 2019: 408; Angelelli 2019; Pym 2019b). Given this shift in the understanding of overall quality in Translation Studies, we will critically examine the tool's functionalities and assess whether they can help improve the quality of feedback in trainer-to-trainee revision as well as the ergonomic quality of revision in a didactic setting.

Before looking at the tool through the lenses of revision standards and ergonomic principles, a brief introduction to revision quality will be provided along with an introduction to ergonomics (section 1). Section 2 will bring translationQ to the fore. The main functionalities will be discussed, in order to allow the reader to understand why the tool is said to meet requirements not only for high-quality revision, but also for sustainable revision practices. Then revision standards and ergonomic principles will be brought to bear on translationQ in a critical examination (section 3).

1. The construct of "quality": revision standards and ergonomic principles

The conceptual construct of "quality" that is adopted in this chapter includes the quality requirements for good revision practices and the quality requirements for efficient and sustainable technology-driven revision practices. In this section, both approaches to quality will be introduced and placed in a didactic setting.

Revision quality in translator training

The topic of revision quality has prompted a lively debate. One of the reasons why quality seems to have demanded reinvigorated attention in recent years is that the concept remains ill-defined (Van Egdom et al. 2018b; Angelelli 2019). In the context of revision, it has proven difficult to formulate clear quality criteria for revision, because revision is not always clearly distinguished from other activities such as editing, evaluating, reviewing and proofreading (see also Mossop 2020: 116–18; Van Egdom and Segers 2019). In the second part of the international translation services standard ISO 17100 ("Terms and definitions"), a distinction is made between revision and revision-related activities. The definition of revision reads as follows: "The bilingual examination of target language content against source language content for its suitability for the agreed purpose" (ISO 17100 2015a: 2). In other words, in revision, close attention is to be paid not only to the target text but also to the source material, and revision ought to be carried out with one eye on the translation brief. However helpful this concise definition might be, it still leaves room for interpretation. Fortunately, the process description in part 5.3.3. ("Revision", pp. 10–11) sums up the tasks of the reviser (who is described as "a person other than the translator"):

* carry out a detailed inspection of the target language content, bearing in mind the source content and the purpose of the target content;
* correct errors in the target language content and/or recommend the implementation of corrections;
* inform the LSP of corrective actions;
* repeat the revision process until reviser and LSP are satisfied with the product.

However, the task description in the ISO standard does not eliminate all the vagueness, not even when the relevant "aspects" of the comparative examination are taken into account (accuracy, syntax, spelling and so on; p. 10). As observed by Rasmussen and Schjoldager (2011) and Mossop (2020), little heed is paid to concrete procedures in revision standards. Empirical research findings suggest that when it comes to error detection or output quality, no procedure is more successful than other procedures (Robert and Waes 2014). The only revision procedure that leads to poorer performance is a "monolingual examination" of target language content. Strictly speaking, such monolingual examination cannot be aptly described as "revision" under the ISO standard. However, in a recent empirical study, Ipsen and Dam (2016) have shown that revision quality is better when the translation serves as the focal point rather than the source text.

What is often seen in research on procedural quality is that the revised translation is ultimately the yardstick for quality. But which procedure yields the best results? In a professional revision setting, it is only logical that this question of results should be central: when looking at a revised translation or even a revision process, focus is on the successful detection and correction of errors. In translator training, however, feedback about errors ought to be given more weight as it gives students an opportunity for learning; trainer-to-trainee feedback serves a formative purpose. Ideally, reviser feedback is tailored to students' need for transparency and completeness of information (Van Egdom and Segers 2019: 64).

Omer and Abdulahrim (2017) have put forward a general theory of constructive feedback and they list the following criteria for high-quality feedback:

- immediate;
- specific;
- helpful;
- non-judgemental;
- accurate;
- relevant;
- tailored;
- solicited;
- frequent;
- balanced;
- confidential;
- understandable;
- based on first-hand data;
- conducive to better results (i.e. "[feedback] suggests plans for improvement").

These quality criteria have been applied to the context of trainer-to-trainee revision by Van Egdom and Segers. To make these criteria more tangible, the authors provide an example of constructive revision practices (2019: 64):

> When a student has committed an error in his translation, the teacher can *indicate* that an error has been made (by underlining [the error]), *provide information* about the nature of the error and the severity of the error (by

categorizing the error, weighting it and/or providing the student with extra information) and *suggest plans for improving the text*.

For instance, when a student uses 'Mr.' as an abbreviation of 'mister' in a Dutch translation of an English source text, the teacher can underline the error, mention that the error is the result of interference, that it is a minor error, and that 'Mr.' and 'mr.' are false friends, and indicate that the solutions 'meneer' or 'de heer' would be more suitable. Further feedback can be given in the form of a reference to an authoritative source that discusses the error [in this case: www.taaltelefoon.be/dhr-m-mr].

(our translation; emphasis added)

A quality criterion that is of great importance, but also very elusive, is "quality". The importance of the notion of "quality" in translator training cannot be overstated. In trainer-to-trainee revision in the classroom, the reviser usually performs bilingual assessments of several translations that have been derived from the same source text. The "face validity" of trainer-to-trainee revision is at stake when feedback is not consistent throughout a single student's translation or across the translations of all the students. Low face validity is generally a direct consequence of low inter-reviser or intra-reviser reliability. Inter-reviser reliability refers to the degree of agreement between revisers. The translation of the abbreviation 'Mr.' can serve to illustrate this notion. The website 'Taaltelefoon' states that, despite the fact that use of the abbreviation is not recommended, 'mr.' *is* sometimes used in Dutch as an abbreviation of 'meneer' and 'mijnheer'. As this authoritative source leaves room for flexibility, it is not unthinkable that one reviser will underline 'mr.' as an error while another reviser will leave the abbreviation as is. When this happens, inter-reviser reliability is low.

Intra-reviser reliability can be defined as the degree of agreement among multiple revisions of the same translation performed by a single reviser. Again, the translation of 'Mr.' is an excellent case in point. When three students commit the same error (e.g. 'Mr.' as an abbreviation of 'meneer'), each error (each instance of 'Mr.') ought to be treated equally. When the instructor-reviser fails to revise identical errors in the same way, intra-reviser reliability is low. Low reviser reliability can have serious consequences: students tend to discuss grades and feedback amongst themselves, and they sometimes become aware of inconsistencies and start questioning the "objectivity" of revision feedback, the fair-mindedness of the instructor, and, ultimately, the competence of the instructor (see ISO 17100 2015a: 6; Bowker 2000, 2001; Van Egdom et al. 2018a, 2018b).

To sum up, mistakes that can give rise to low reviser reliability are:

1   identical errors that are sanctioned in one student version and overlooked in another version or versions;
2   identical errors that are all sanctioned, but the error made by one student is classified differently from that of another student;
3   identical errors that are all sanctioned, but the error weighting differs from one version to another.

Translator trainer ergonomics

As mentioned in the introduction, long-standing notions of quality are presently being challenged. New high-tech realities and forms of collaborative translation seem to call for a broader notion of quality, a notion that includes working environments and working conditions. The interdiscipline that is concerned with the optimization of environmental factors and conditions is ergonomics. The International Ergonomics Association defines "ergonomics" as "the scientific discipline concerned with the understanding of interactions among humans and other elements of a system, and the profession that applies theory, principles, data and methods to design in order to optimize human well-being and overall system performance."[2] Smith (2007: 1530) argues that the main benefit of an ergonomic approach is that it measures the quality of systemic interactions and processes by their effect on "performance, productivity, competitiveness, and safety and health".

In the field of ergonomics, a basic (yet often untenable) distinction is made between physical, cognitive and organizational ergonomics.[3] It is likely that most people are familiar with physical ergonomics: research on physical ergonomics is often aimed at designing a work environment in such a way that the safety, physical health, comfort and performance of the workforce are optimized. Cognitive ergonomics is probably the most popular strand in ergonomics these days, as it deals with topics such as mental workload, work stress, decision-making and ("simple") human-computer interaction. These days, basic insights in cognitive ergonomics are taken into account when user interfaces are being developed. Cases in point are the new interfaces for translators where machine translation, termbases, translation memories and other text corpora are being integrated in the translation process in novel ways (e.g. MateCat, CasMaCAT, Lilt).[4] Organizational ergonomics studies socio-technical systems, which include general organization structures, processes and policies. Topics such as quality assurance, workflow management and cooperative communication can be placed under the umbrella of organizational ergonomics.

In recent years, ergonomics has been elevated to a place of prominence in Translation Studies (see O'Brien 2008; Lavault-Olléon 2011, 2016; Ehrensberger-Dow and Massey 2014; Ehrensberger-Dow and Hunziker Heeb 2016; Cadwell et al. 2016; Moorkens and O'Brien 2017). The surge in interest seems to be a direct consequence of the susceptibility of translation to automation. Translation scholars have mainly sought to investigate the conditions of translators in a technology-driven working environment and the ergonomic effects of technologization and automation on translation practices. In this interdisciplinary subdomain of Translation Studies, little consideration has been bestowed upon ergonomics in translator training. Although it is recommended by some that ergonomic knowledge be integrated into translator training, to date only a small number of strategies seem to have been developed to teach students to adapt to the physical, cognitive and organizational ergonomics of a working environment (see Peters-Geiben 2016; Ehrensberger-Dow 2017; Frérot and Landry forthcoming). This is remarkable, seeing that ergonomic adaptability is listed in the EMT competence framework as one of the personal and interpersonal subcompetences that a student enrolled in a master's degree programme in translation should acquire (European Master's in Translation Network 2017: 10 [C25]).

Although there have been investigations into the role of the trainer in translation education that seem to border on ergonomics (research on human factors in assessment, curriculum design and academic performance), trainer ergonomics has remained an under-researched niche in Translation Studies (see also Van Egdom et al. 2018a, 2018b; Van Egdom et al. forthcoming 2020). However, it is possible for trainers to draw on insights in educational ergonomics, which covers: (1) learning ergonomics, (2) instructional ergonomics, (3) ergonomics of educational facilities, (4) ergonomics of educational equipment and (5) ergonomics of the educational environment (Kao 1976: 667). In recent years, more and more reports have been published on the "cut-throat mentality" that holds sway in academic institutions (e.g. O'Brien and Guiney 2018). Academics have difficulty managing diverse responsibilities, such as teaching, researching, assessing, administering, obtaining funding and publishing. It can be assumed that these responsibilities also place a serious strain on translator trainers. By drawing on insights in educational design, they too can benefit from research-informed ergonomic applications and principles that contribute to the overall well-being of educators and help improve educational performance and system design (see Smith 2007; Kao 2007). Still, there are also some translation-specific training tasks and settings that seem to warrant further research.

In the context of translator trainer ergonomics, the three-pronged distinction (physical, cognitive and organizational ergonomics) can be maintained. In this chapter, cognitive ergonomics will receive most of our attention. When assessing a software product, like translationQ, the criteria for deciding whether a product meets the threshold of ergonomic quality are mostly of a cognitive nature. Poor ergonomic design of a product results in a sense of inconvenience, inefficient mental processing, increased cognitive load and, in the long run, health issues. In a recent study, O'Brien et al. (2017) have shown that this "unease" is triggered in CAT tool use through complex user interfaces, system failures (bugs) and technical problems (formatting and segmentation issues). These CAT tool features mainly take a cognitive toll on translators, but they can also have physical effects (formatting issues, for example, can force a CAT tool user to spend more time at their computer, often sitting in the same position) and organizational effects (as a part of company policy, translators can be forced to accept matches in a translation memory, even when solutions provided by the tool are not appropriate). Despite the emphasis that is being placed on ergonomics, bear in mind that some ergonomic criteria for software design will cut across the demarcation lines between the various domains of ergonomics.

In order to assess the ergonomic quality of translationQ, a set of criteria for interactive interfaces will be used. The set was formulated by Bastien and Scapin (1993), and the framework seems to have "aged" fairly well: after its publication, it proved its worth in the context of website design (Scapin et al. 2000), in both traditional and virtual environments (Bach and Scapin 2003; Bastien and Scapin 2001). Eight main criteria are believed to cover "all software aspects which have an influence on the users' task completion". Each criterion has been clearly defined and is accompanied with a clear rationale. The criteria and definitions are:

1. Guidance: "User guidance refers to the means available to advise, orient, inform, instruct, and guide the users throughout their interactions with a computer (messages, alarms, labels, etc.)."
2. Workload: "Workload concerns all interface elements that play a role in reducing the users' perceptual or cognitive load, and in increasing the dialogue efficiency."
3. Explicit control: "Explicit control concerns both the system processing of explicit user actions, and the control users have on the processing of their actions by the system."
4. Adaptability: "Adaptability refers to [a system's] capacity to behave contextually and according to the users' needs and preferences."
5. Error management: "Error management refers to the means available to prevent or reduce errors and to recover from them when they occur."
6. Consistency: "Consistency refers to the way interface design choices (codes, naming, formats, procedures, etc.) are maintained in similar contexts, and are different when applied to different contexts."
7. Significance of codes: "Significance of codes qualifies the relationship between a term and/or a sign and its reference."
8. Compatibility: "Compatibility refers to the match between users' characteristics (memory, perceptions, customs, skills, age, expectations, etc.) and task characteristics on the one hand, and the organization of the output, input, and dialogue for a given application, on the other hand."

(Bastien and Scapin 1993: 9–41)

Taken together, these criteria will determine whether the ergonomic design of translationQ truly reaches the quality threshold for user interfaces and whether it is likely to lead to more efficient and sustainable trainer-to-trainee revision practices.

2. Improving revision quality with translationQ

Existing CAT tools can be of some use in a didactic setting: the tools have functionalities and features that allow for quick detection of terminological inconsistencies and spelling issues. Still, one would be hard pressed to find a tool that is tailored to practices in translator training. With the launch of translationQ, there is now a tool that has been developed *by* translator trainers and *for* translator trainers (see Van Egdom et al. 2018a, 2018b). This section begins with a brief overview of the main objectives of this joint initiative of Televic and KU Leuven, and the most important functionalities and features of translationQ. The overview will provide a rationale for the development of the tool and will illustrate how ergonomic quality and revision quality have served as points of departure in the assessment of this software. In the remainder of this section, translationQ will be scrutinized more closely.

Introducing translationQ

The plans for an evaluation and revision tool originated at KU Leuven, where Winibert Segers and Hendrik Kockaert were looking for a way to make lighter work of translation evaluation and trainer-to-trainee revision (Kockaert et al. 2016). Their teaching experience had revealed that they were often correcting and revising the same errors in student versions and, what was worse, that it was often difficult to ensure the consistency of corrections and feedback across versions. Working with Televic, they developed a tool that would reduce the repetitiveness of evaluation and revision tasks, making these processes more efficient, and that would also help to ensure consistency across versions and across assignments, thus increasing reliability. In 2017, after a beta test with partners in academia and in the language industry, the cloud-based tool translationQ was officially launched.

The tool currently consists of a revision module. In this module, a reviser uploads a source text (in DOC, PDF or XLIFF format) onto the platform. The tool will automatically start segmenting texts at sentence level, but the reviser can also choose to merge sentences to form bigger text units. Once the text is uploaded, the reviser (in translator training, the instructor) can publish an assignment by formulating a brief (prospective text sender and audience, deadline, etc.), providing reference material, and assigning the task to a number of users (in translator training, students). The users receive a notification e-mail with a direct link to the assignment in the translationQ portal. The translators produce their translation on the platform or upload their translation to the input interface. In this interface, alignment issues are flagged and can be solved by the users. In case of technical problems, the translations can also be sent to the commissioner, who can then upload them onto the platform. Once the versions have been submitted, the reviser can start revising by reading the versions, highlighting errors and providing feedback in a feedback window. When the revision process is completed, the user is notified that feedback has been provided. In the translationQ environment, users can look at the results and compare them to those from other assignments as well as those of peers (the "User report" tab will show the average score of the group). The reviser can also compare the task-relevant data of users and groups in the tool, and analyse error data in a spreadsheet file.

Thus far, the revision processes seem very straightforward. The true cleverness of the system lies in the storage and constant updating of error data in an "error memory". While correcting student versions, the reviser can draw on error data that have been produced in other translation assignments as well as in the versions under review. An algorithm goes in search of, detects and flags identical errors (in corresponding segments of other students' versions) and similar errors (in different segments of the same translation assignment), and suggests corrections and feedback automatically. The same algorithm can also flag potential errors based on similar errors made in earlier assignments. It is up to the reviser to decide whether computed errors and feedback are to be accepted. When the reviser accepts an error and feedback suggestion, the program automatically copies and pastes earlier feedback in one or more student versions. This is why the software developers contend that, by working in translationQ, the trainer-reviser can keep a tight rein on consistency while speeding up the revision process.

TranslationQ: revision standards

It is naive to think that a tool can by itself ensure that revision quality standards are being upheld: revision quality will always be dependent on human factors. Still, a closer look at the functionalities and features of translationQ can tell us something about the likelihood that the tool will contribute to revision quality. Table 11.1 provides an overview of indicators of revision quality and the potential contribution of translationQ.

First, the tool should allow for a bilingual examination of translations. As illustrated in Figure 11.1, the source and target texts are displayed alongside each other, both in the translator interface and in the reviser interface. In most cases, the instructor-reviser will direct most of their attention to the translation. When in doubt, however, the reviser is always encouraged to cast a glance at the ST, which is permanently displayed in the left column.

ISO 17100 (2015a) also clearly states that the purpose of the translation should always be kept in mind. In the translator interface, the translation brief is always displayed. The same cannot be said for the reviser interface. In a didactic context, this seldom poses a problem, as the reviser is often the person who has formulated the brief. However, in case of extensive briefing or of multiple reviser revision, a direct link to the translation brief would be useful.

Another revision task in the ISO standard is the correction of errors in the translation or the recommendation of corrections. In translator training, the instructor-reviser is seldom responsible for corrections; correction is something that is often required in a summative context (e.g. evaluation). Instead of setting things right immediately, Van Egdom and Segers (2019: 64) recommend that the

TABLE 11.1 Indicators of revision quality in translator training

Indicator	tQ
Examining quality of the translation	+
Bearing the source text in mind	+
Checking suitability for purpose	±
Correcting errors/recommending implementation of corrections	+
Providing constructive feedback	+
Repeating the process until translation quality is acceptable	−

FIGURE 11.1 Two-column lay-out

attention of the student be drawn to the error and its nature, and that "plans for improvement" be suggested (see also Carless 2006; Omer and Abdulahrim 2017: 46). As can be seen in Figure 11.2, the translation feedback sheet does allow for the immediate correction of errors, but it also encourages the reviser to provide formative feedback. TranslationQ seems to check all the relevant boxes for constructive translation feedback (see Van Egdom and Segers 2019: 62):

- Upon detection, the error is highlighted in the target segment as well as in the feedback sheet ("item").
- Information is provided on the nature of the error ("category", highlighting of corresponding source-text unit).
- Information is provided on the severity ("score").
- Suggestions for corrective actions are made ("correction").
- Information is provided on the cause of the error ("feedback").

On the translation feedback sheet, the reviser has ample room to refer the student to authoritative sources that discuss the error ("feedback").[5]

A field on the feedback sheet that is particularly worthy of note is "category". TranslationQ makes revision processes authentic through the use of error categories that are common in the language industry: the Dynamic Quality Framework (DQF) categories (O'Brien et al. 2011).[6] The DQF categories are broadly in line with the "aspects" of translation and revision that ought be taken into account according to ISO 17100 (e.g. accuracy, syntax, spelling) (2015a: 10).

By employing the analytical categories of DQF, the translationQ engineers also wanted to provide an impetus to more "objective" revision practices. As error

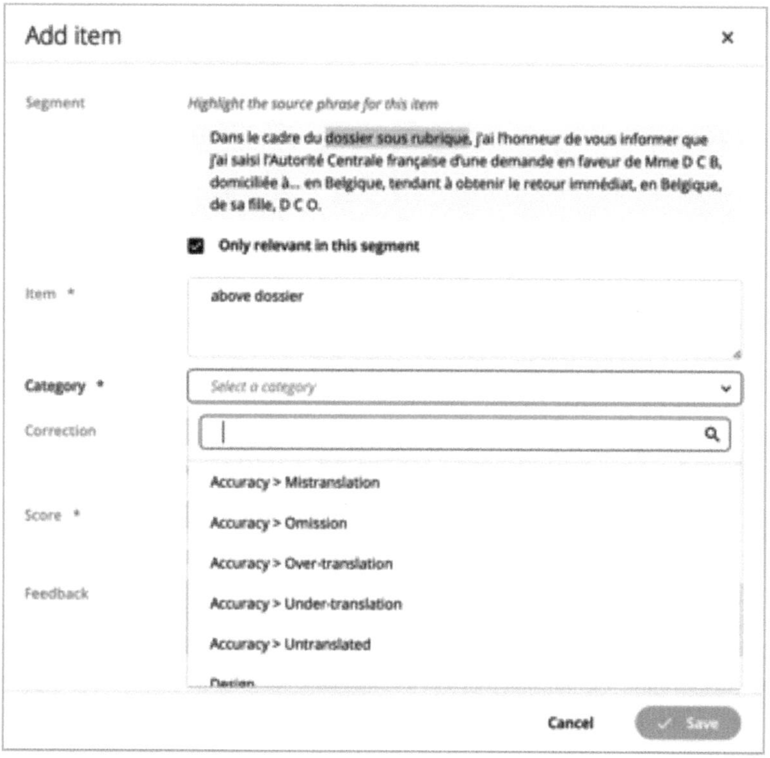

FIGURE 11.2 Pop-up translation feedback sheet

categories are predefined, all users will be inclined to employ the same metalanguage and to refer to textual problems in the same way.

While it is true that using a common framework is a good way to reduce subjectivity in revision, it is impossible to ensure complete objectivity. In recent years, some criticism has been levelled at analytical categories: despite clear definitions, "it is often a matter of subjective judgement . . . whether an error falls into one category or another" (Saldanha and O'Brien 2014: 101–2; see Van Egdom et al. 2018a).

The translation feedback sheet also asks the reviser to penalize (or reward) the translator for a translation solution in the "score" field. Subjective influences loom large in error weighting: in professional practices, the evaluator/reviser decides whether an error is minor, major or critical (see Van Egdom et al. 2018a, 2018b). In translationQ, the situation is similar: it will be up to the reviser to decide on the category and the severity of an error.

Still, the tool seems to provide an adequate solution to problems with reviser reliability.[7] A problem recognizable for every trainer is related to repetitiveness in trainer-to-trainee revision: it is difficult, if not impossible, to remember all revisions of a single assignment, let alone of earlier assignments, when revising on paper or

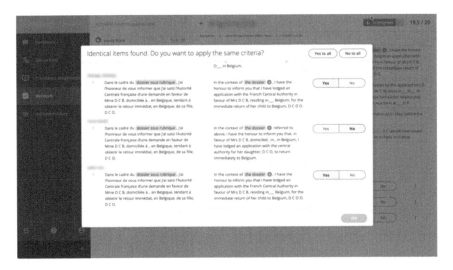

FIGURE 11.3 TranslationQ algorithm flagging potential identical errors

in a word processor. The error memory of translationQ provides a solution for the reviser's limited memory capacity. As mentioned, the tool detects identical errors and similar errors and copies the information from earlier feedback sheets onto the flagged fragments. The error memory also contains error data from other assignments and can flag identical errors and similar errors from earlier assignments (Figure 11.3). Provided that the reviser is familiar with the system and is able to manage error data well, it is likely that, by working in translationQ, trainer-to-trainee revisions will become more consistent—which can be considered a positive step toward objectivity.

The only relevant quality issue that has remained unaddressed in this discussion is the "revision loop": in the translation industry, revision is not necessarily completed when the reviser has examined the translation a single time; revision ought to be repeated until the LSP and the reviser agree on the quality of the product (ISO 17100, p. 11). At the time of writing, translationQ does not allow for the amendment of a revised version by the student. The reason for this might be that translator trainers seldom ask their students to resubmit their translations.

3. TranslationQ: ergonomic quality criteria

In most research on the ergonomic quality of translation tools and applications, the human interacting with them is factored into the assessment. Although some exploratory research has been conducted with a view to assessing human–computer interaction with translationQ (Van Egdom et al. 2019), the following discussion, based on the eight criteria outlined previously, will be of an analytical nature, with a view to shedding light on the likelihood of translationQ contributing to the efficiency and effectiveness of operations and interactions between instructor-revisers and student translators. Table 11.2 provides an overview of the ergonomic criteria and the potential contribution of translationQ.

TABLE 11.2 Ergonomic criteria for user interfaces

Criteria	tQ
Providing guidance	+
Reducing workload	±
Allowing for explicit control	±
Being adaptable	±
Reducing errors and allowing for error recovery	±
Having consistent coding	+
Having significant coding	±
Being compatible	+

Guidance

In a technological context, effective and efficient practices are heavily dependent on the so-called "ease of use" and "ease of learning" of a system (see also Venkatesh and Davis 2000). Bastien and Scapin state that "good guidance facilitates learning and use" (1993: 9). If translationQ users know where they are in the accomplishment of a revision task, what actions are required and how additional information can be obtained, this would indicate that the tool provides good guidance.

The steps the reviser must follow in translationQ are logically structured. The project preparation procedure is straightforward: having opened the "Source Texts" tab in the Back Office, the reviser is asked to categorize the new project in the database (for instance, in the folder "Medical Translation EN-NL") and to upload the source material. In the next tab, "Translation Assignment", situated right under the "Source Text" tab, the reviser can publish the assignment by formulating a translation brief and selecting the pool of translators (individual users or user groups).

The revision procedure is also well structured. When opening the "Revisions" tab, the reviser must select an assignment. Before opening an assignment, the reviser is asked to select the revision memory that is to be used for the assignment (for instance, the memory "Medical Texts EN-NL"). The reviser can now start revising. In the revision mode, all relevant submissions are numbered and listed on the left side of the page. The first submitted translation is immediately shown alongside the source text. The reviser starts making corrections to the first translation by selecting fragments with the click of a mouse. Every time an error is selected, the translation feedback sheet pops up. Having filled in the fields on the sheet, the reviser can confirm ("save") the error and feedback. When the error is confirmed, the algorithm will flag potential errors (see Figure 11.3) and ask the reviser to indicate whether the same criteria can be applied to all the highlighted units.

Although it is possible to switch between different students' versions, the reviser will normally start with "Translator 1" and end with the final submission. What is perhaps less evident when working in the revision interface is the fact that "error feedback" can be edited using a right-click, and that changing the "status" of a submission (from "in progress" to "completed") is not equal to publishing the results. When all submissions have been revised, the reviser must click the "complete revision" button at the top right. The results are now published and accessible in the "Reporting" module.

Unfortunately, the reviser is not automatically directed to the "Reporting" module. The reviser must find out how to get to the user and assignment reports. Some guidance is sometimes required in these situations. TranslationQ always displays a question mark (icon) at the top right. By clicking, the user is directed to a well-organized support page at the translationQ website. There they will often find the information that is needed to overcome the obstacle (for instance, information on open "User reports"). When needed information is not available at the website, the user is invited to send feedback about an FAQ page and to formulate a query (see Figure 11.4). All in all, the tool seems to offer good guidance to the reviser.

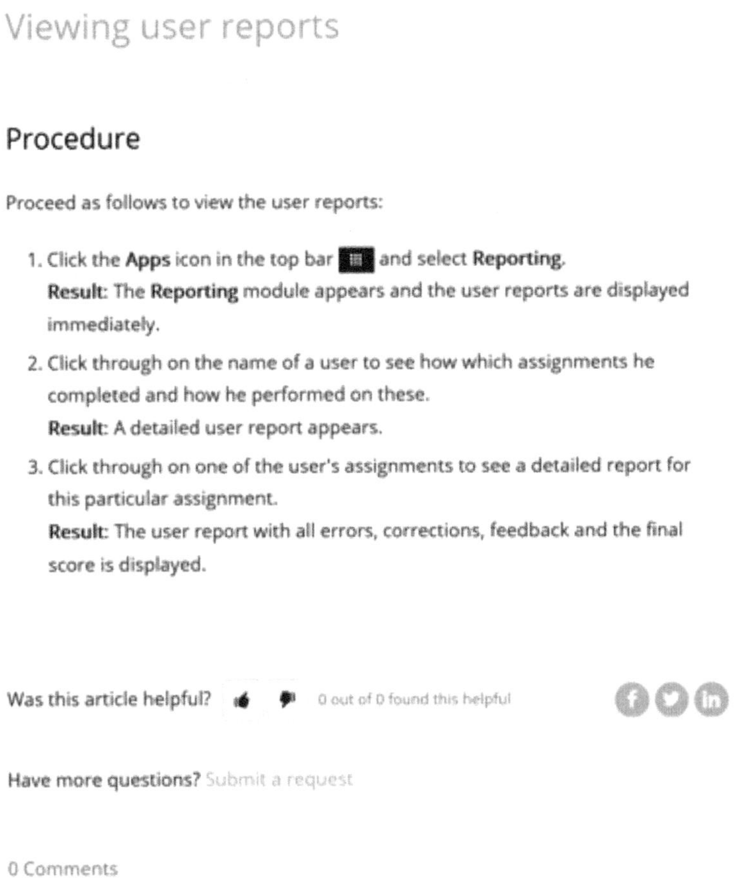

Viewing user reports

Procedure

Proceed as follows to view the user reports:

1. Click the **Apps** icon in the top bar ▦ and select **Reporting**.
   Result: The **Reporting** module appears and the user reports are displayed immediately.

2. Click through on the name of a user to see how which assignments he completed and how he performed on these.
   Result: A detailed user report appears.

3. Click through on one of the user's assignments to see a detailed report for this particular assignment.
   Result: The user report with all errors, corrections, feedback and the final score is displayed.

Was this article helpful? 👍 👎 0 out of 0 found this helpful   🇫 🇾 🇮🇳

Have more questions? Submit a request

0 Comments

FIGURE 11.4 TranslationQ support page ("Viewing user reports")

Workload

One of the ergonomic criteria that seems most difficult to meet is the workload criterion. Complaints that tools are too complicated, complex and far from intuitive are often reported in the literature on CAT tools (e.g. O'Brien et al. 2017). The tools have too many functionalities which are often difficult to find and tend to display redundant information on the screen. The perceptual and cognitive load in CAT tools affects task efficiency in a negative way (with users being distracted by "unnecessary" information), increases the probability of errors being made by the user and increases the likelihood that the user will become hesitant to use the tool (see Bastien and Scapin 1993: 18, 24).

The translationQ engineers attempted to design a tool that contains all the information needed to execute the task at hand. At the top right, there is always an "app" icon, which allows the user to navigate across the four main modules (the "Administration" module, the "Back Office" module, the "Portal" module and the "Report" module). All the key features of the modules are displayed on the left side of the screens. The number of key features per module is always limited and they are summed up in a succinct manner (e.g. "Source Texts", "Translation Assignment", "Revisions", "Revision Memory"), thereby reducing reading effort. Clicking on one of the features does not seem to display more than the information that is relevant to a subtask. As a result, it seems unlikely that users will experience serious cognitive strain. However, there may be cognitive issues with what seems to be the most demanding subtask: the revision task itself. In the "Revision" tab, the screen is often a bit crowded with information: it displays (1) subtasks in the Back Office, (2) a list with the names or number of students who have submitted a translation, (3) the source text, (4) a student translation, (5) status information and (6) either text item information, scoring information or general feedback for the task at hand. Findings in a recent exploratory study suggest that filling in the translation feedback sheet that pops up during revision is also seen as a tedious activity (Van Egdom et al. 2019). The tediousness can be indicative of cognitive strain.

Workload has also been demonstrated to decrease when the number of action steps for a task is limited. In this regard, some ergonomic concerns can be raised: it does not seem possible to simply "drag a file" to translationQ and publish an assignment in two or three mouse clicks, or to create entire project templates that can be used and reused (it is, however, possible to "clone" source texts).

Fast interaction is not something the translationQ user can expect (see Van Egdom et al. 2019). Still, the cognitive strain and the number of action steps for trainer-to-trainee revision tasks are reduced when working in translationQ, in that potential errors in students' versions are flagged and the reviser is allowed to reuse feedback from earlier versions or assignments.

Explicit control

Explicit control is the third ergonomic quality criterion listed by Bastien and Scapin (1993). Users should be allowed to define their input and be able to exert control over the processing of actions throughout the program. In translationQ, tasks are generally divided into subtasks, which all require an explicit command on the part of the user ("Save", "Submit"). To increase awareness of the consequences of an explicit command, especially one with irreversible consequences, dual activation is required (see Bastien and Scapin 1993: 25). In translationQ, two-step activation is required to start processes like submitting a translation and publishing the revised translations.

According to ergonomic guidelines, users should also be allowed to pace their data entry. In the preparation phase as well as in the revision phase, input can always be saved. Translators can also save their translation anytime. Revisers can navigate between modules and subtasks throughout the process.

Essential in explicit user control is the possibility of interrupting and cancelling transactions or processes. TranslationQ allows users to cancel and edit macro-processes (e.g. creation of a source folder) and micro-processes (e.g. acceptance of errors). There are, however, a few commands that are irreversible. Once the reviser has published the revision results, it is no longer possible to:

- add, edit or delete errors in the assignment at hand;
- change the status of an error (accepted/rejected);
- change the general task feedback;
- overwrite the task score;
- import additional translations for the assignment.[8]

This can pose problems in a didactic context. In many cases, there will be an in-class discussion of the assignments. It sometimes happens that a student can prove that a translation solution that has been marked as an error by the instructor-reviser is in fact a correct solution. In these cases, the reviser should be allowed to change the status of an error and to override the task score.

Adaptability

The fourth criterion, adaptability, is frequently mentioned in research on translation ergonomics. In more traditional translation tools, human and organizational requirements were addressed only in an ad-hoc manner (Lagoudaki 2008; Olohan 2011). As mentioned in section 1, more consideration seems to be paid to human interaction and to tools' customizability in the designing of modern translation tools. The adaptability of tools to different situations and different users is of critical importance. Some content and processes in translationQ can be adapted to fit users' needs. For example, revisers can choose to merge segmented sentences; this will allow trainee translators and revisers to work at paragraph level. A recent study on translation ergonomics has shown that segmentation is often a major source of irritation in professional practice (O'Brien et al. 2017; for a discussion of the effects of sentence-level segmentation, see Bédard 2000; Mossop 2006; LeBlanc 2013).

Users can also choose to adapt error categories: the default categories can be either replaced by institution-specific categories or removed if deemed irrelevant. However, error categories can be modified only by an institutional administrator. The consistency and exchangeability of error memories would be compromised if individual users were to be allowed to customize error categories themselves.

Flexibility of processes has also been prioritized by Televic: a user can choose to reuse source texts, select different error memories, revise anonymously, divide up the work (among multiple revisers), opt for extensive revision (by filling out all the fields in the feedback sheet) or concise revision (by filling out only mandatory fields), override scores and so on. With its wide array of optional features, processes in translationQ seem to be fitted to the needs of inexperienced users (who usually prefer a simple project set-up) as well as experienced users. Still, there are some situations in which the adaptability of the program is limited. For example, a reviser might prefer revision by segment instead of revision by version: translationQ does not have a functionality that allows a reviser to look at all translations of one particular segment at one glance. Furthermore, the workflow cannot be adapted to all didactic situations: for example, as it is impossible to form a revision loop, students cannot be asked to amend their version themselves in translationQ.

Error management

The fifth determinant of ergonomic quality is error management. Errors are inevitable in software design and software use. System errors, user errors and error messages can disrupt entire processes and have a negative influence on user experience. The principles of error management can be broken down into three subcriteria: error protection, quality of error messages and error correction. To prevent errors from occurring, an error is best detected before validation of an action (Bastien and Scapin 1993: 33). A few measures have been taken by Televic engineers to prevent errors from occurring. For example, translationQ alerts users when mandatory fields, which are always marked with an asterisk (*), have not been filled in (correctly) (see Figure 11.2). It is impossible for the user to proceed with the confirmation of an error without filling in these fields. Another error protection measure is the dual activation required for crucial steps in the preparation and revision process (publishing the assignment and publishing the feedback).

When errors do occur, software engineers should see to it that information about the error is communicated to the user: an error message should be concise and meaningful, and it should give a clear idea of the nature of the error and the action required to correct it (Bastien and Scapin 1993: 34). In translationQ, error messages usually appear immediately and are fairly informative. For instance, when importing Word files of student translations in batch, the reviser is given a warning when the number of segments in the source text and a particular translation do not correspond, and is asked to split or merge segments until both texts appear equally long.

Also essential in error management is correction. Although an error is always disruptive, it can be less disruptive when the user has to correct only the data or command entries that caused the error (Bastien and Scapin 1993: 35). There have been reports of students who have experienced a system error (without error message) that forced them to recommence the assignment, starting with the first segment (Van Egdom et al. 2019). In addition, the principles of ergonomic design dictate that users should be able to correct errors immediately (Bastien and Scapin 1993: 35). In an exploratory study by Van Egdom et al. (2019), two participants (out of five) complained about bugs in the program: while revising a number of student versions, a series of error messages appeared simultaneously, all saying that corrections had not been saved. From an ergonomic point of view, the fact that the error messages appeared is positive, but they should have appeared immediately after the system errors occurred. For the revisers, it was difficult to find out which corrections had been lost due to the system error.

Consistency

An interface is consistent when design choices are maintained everywhere (Bastien and Scapin 1993: 36). In translationQ, procedures, labels and commands are always presented in a recognizable format, location and syntax, except in one case. The label "completed" is used to determine the status of single submissions and is meant to help the reviser keep track of what has been fully revised (and what not), but it is also used to confirm the completion of the entire revision process and to initiate the publication of the results. This means that one term is used to designate two concepts, which is highly undesirable within a domain (see ISO 1087–1 2000). For beginners, this might be particularly confusing, especially because revision status and completion both feature in the same subtask. This issue could be resolved by replacing the "complete" label that is used to confirm the completion of the entire revision task: substitutes for this label could be "publish" or "publish all".

Significance of codes

Such ambiguous labelling affects not only consistency; it can also be seen as a coding issue. For a code to be significant, there has to be a strong semantic relationship between the code and the item/action the code refers to (Bastien and Scapin 1993: 37). Codes ought to be meaningful and distinguishable. In the case of the label "completed", the distinguishability of actions is at stake. One also wonders whether the coding in translationQ is meaningful to all users: "assignment" is sometimes used when the term "project" seems more appropriate; "item" is employed to refer to what is called a "text unit"; "source phrase" is used to refer to a "source text unit". The coding is thus sometimes arbitrary. Still, the software engineers have taken the significance of codes into consideration when designing the tool. Little use has been made of abbreviations. When abbreviations are used, they are based on official abbreviation rules/standards (e.g. ISO 639–1 2002 for language coding). Furthermore, the engineers have sought to increase authenticity by introducing DQF error categories. Authentic didactic practices are looked upon favourably by pioneers in the ergonomics of translation education (Massey 2016; Frérot and Landry forthcoming).

Compatibility

The final criterion listed by Bastien and Scapin is "compatibility". In the translation industry, this term calls to mind struggles with pdf files, figures, tables and the like. At the time of writing, translationQ cannot be used in CAT tools. However, assignments can be exported and imported as XLIFF files: a student can choose to do an assignment in SDL Trados and then upload their version onto the translationQ platform. TranslationQ also accepts Microsoft Word files; the program segments the Word files (be they source texts or translations) in a way similar to CAT tools. Error memories can also be exchanged among revisers; as the configuration of an error memory is similar to that of a termbase, it can be exported as a TBX file (see ISO 30042 2019).

However disruptive incompatible programs and file types may be, Bastien and Scapin do not give an overly "technical" spin to compatibility: a tool is deemed compatible when the organization of output, input and dialogue is consistent with user characteristics and task characteristics (1993: 38). It seems superfluous to mention that it is impossible to paint a comprehensive picture of user characteristics. For one thing, the characteristics of trainers (revisers) differ markedly from those of trainees (translators). Profiling of users requires an in-depth study of user types and personalities. However, some information on users can be inferred from their core activities (teaching, learning) and the tasks that are to be executed in the tool.

Trainees, for example, would benefit from a tool that has a professional "look and feel", a tool that reflects professional practices. In educational theory, authentic experiential learning (AEL) is seen as a key to student participation and successful preparation for the market (for a discussion of AEL, see Kiraly 2016; Massey 2016; Buysschaert et al. 2017, 2018). Working in a tool that bears a resemblance to a professional working environment would enhance authentic practices in the classroom. In translationQ, the two-column layout is a good example of authenticity: the page layout is somewhat similar to that of CAT tools; the environment is familiar (see Bastien and Scapin 1993: 38). Another stride in the direction of AEL is the implementation of professional error categories: in-class use of these categories can help reduce the gap between training and the profession. Another feature that is built in to foster AEL is the "dashboard" in the "Report" module. Through the user reports, a student can glean an idea of task-specific performance, track progress and compare their performance with that of the group (see Figure 11.5). Finally, there is the need for constructive feedback. This matter was addressed in section 2; the only drawback seems to be that students are not allowed to process the feedback by producing a final version.

Trainers also have a keen interest in using authentic revision processes and constructive feedback. Given the workload in translator training, however, they would

FIGURE 11.5 User report showing the translation assignments, scores and average scores of the group

also expect a tool that is efficient: general didactic practices, and revision practices in particular, should require less time and energy when the tool is used. Using an error memory seems to be a good way of doing away with repetitive revision. Still, the results of our exploratory user study suggest that revision remains very time-consuming, because the set-up of an assignment is sometimes difficult and filling in the feedback fields tends to be a tedious task (Van Egdom et al. 2019). What was not taken into account in the exploratory study is the fact that certain subtasks are automated in translationQ; calculating scores for formative assessment, distributing feedback among students, archiving assignments and translations, and registering scores are automated in translationQ.

Despite the fact that the revision task itself seems to remain time-consuming, the tool has great organizational benefits. From an organizational point of view, the data in the error memory can also be very helpful: the data can be exported as an Excel file and experimented with in pivot tables. By pivoting the data in the tables, learning trends can be visualized that seem outside the trainer's grasp in traditional didactic practices. The tables offer insight into: general error and error type frequency, error (type) frequency per group, error (type) frequency per student and score distribution per error type. After careful examination, the reports and error data might enable a trainer or a team of trainers to address the needs, abilities and limitations of student groups and individual students, steering didactic practices in the direction of "tailored" learning (see Hofmann and Miner 2009). In terms of organizational ergonomics, this is highly desirable: not only does didactics come to inform assessment, but also assessment comes to inform didactics (see Pym 1992: 283).

4.   Conclusion, limitations and future research

In this chapter, trainer-to-trainee revision practices have been observed through the prism of technology. Today, technological solutions that are fully geared to revision practices in the classroom are hard to come by. Still, customized revision tools can stand the translator trainer (as well as the trainee) in good stead. A technological solution worthy of its name would do away with the repetitiveness of revision practices in translator training and would enhance feedback consistency across revision tasks.

A tool that promises to meet these conditions is translationQ. In order to assess whether this tool truly lives up to the expectations, translationQ has been critically reviewed. The two focal points in the review were standards for high-quality trainer-to-trainee revision and ergonomic criteria for sustainable computer-aided processes. On the whole, the review suggests that translationQ meets the requirements for high-quality revision. TranslationQ's error memory, which allows for consistent feedback, seems to mark a great stride forward toward more "objective" trainer-to-trainee revision. Furthermore, the tool encourages trainers to provide students with extensive feedback. The only negative aspect, noted in section 2, is the fact the tool does not allow for interactive feedback loops.

Slightly less positive is the judgement that can be passed on the ergonomic quality of the program. Some serious concerns have been raised with regard to the following aspects:

- the perceptual load in the revision interface;
- the tediousness of filling in the feedback sheet;
- the possibility of rectifying revision input and scores after publication;
- the absence or untimely appearance of error messages.

Still, translationQ has quite a few redeeming ergonomic qualities that may convince translator trainers to use the program. The most important of these have to do with organizational ergonomics. Although filling in feedback sheets is reported to require a bit of energy on the part of the reviser, the error memory allows for the "reuse" of error input across assignments. This means that revision practices become less repetitive. The tool is also technically compatible with the most frequently used tools in translator training. What is more, translationQ seems highly compatible with user expectations: students can work in a learning environment that is "authentic" and also allows them to glean an idea of their learning progress and of their strengths and weaknesses. Meanwhile, trainers can manage a database for translation assignments, a translation repository, download error memories and look up task-specific and user-specific data that are relevant to the assessment of students and can inform didactic practices.

Is translationQ likely to improve the quality of trainer-to-trainee revision? So long as the tool manages to overcome its growing pains (especially the problems with error messages), the results of our analytical review suggest a promising future. However, the review has abstracted from the realities in which trainer-to-trainee revision practices are embedded. Empirical research is warranted in order to formulate a conclusive statement about the quality of trainer-to-trainee revision practices in translationQ. Direct observations, keystroke logging data and eyetracking data may allow us to develop a deeper understanding of revision processes in translationQ. Information on user experience can also shed light on the quality of revision practices. Such information can be obtained through interviews, questionnaires and focus group discussions. What is also lacking in our review is a baseline with which the quality of translationQ can be compared. In other words, no research has been published yet on the revision quality and ergonomic quality of existing revision methods and tools. Revision practices in translationQ should be pitted against the way revisers currently work. Time and extensive research will tell whether translationQ can set new qualitative standards in trainer-to-trainee revision.

Notes

1 www.televic-education.com/en/translationq (accessed 09/08/2019).
2 www.iea.cc/whats/ (accessed 11/11/2018).
3 This threefold distinction is also made at the IAE website: www.iea.cc/whats/ (accessed 11/11/2018).
4 https://matecat.com; https://casmacat.eu; https://lilt.com.
5 No direct reference is made to Omar and Abdulahrim; some of their criteria for constructive feedback do not seem to apply in this context (e.g. frequent), and others are dependent on the concrete input of the reviser (e.g. understandable).
6 In some respects, the pop-up feedback sheet can even be said to resemble the "old" LISA QA form, which lists roughly the same error categories but also urges the reviser/reviewer to provide information on the severity of an error, etc. The LISA QA form can be found at https://slideplayer.com/slide/4705/1/images/54/Use+of+Quality+Assurance+Forms.jpg.
7 For the sake of completeness, it should be noted that reviser reliability can also be compromised when the names of students are shown during revision. TranslationQ has functionalities for double-blind revision to neutralize bias.
8 https://support.televic-education.com/hc/en-us/articles/115004358289-8-Completing-your-revision.

12

THE MT POST-EDITING SKILL SET

Course descriptions and educators' thoughts

Clara Ginovart Cid and Carme Colominas Ventura

This chapter explores the findings of a mixed-methods study based on an online questionnaire, an analysis of syllabi[1] and one-on-one interviews with educators[2] in European Master's in Translation (EMT) or related programmes where the students learn and practise machine translation post-editing (MTPE). The decision to consider master's programmes only (and to exclude undergraduate MTPE courses) was made in order to delimit the study, given the time constraints faced by the researchers. Furthermore, the fact that MTPE has been more present in postgraduate programmes (O'Brien 2002: 105; Plaza Lara 2019: 276) means that master's courses probably benefit from a stable body of knowledge about such training. The present study belongs to a larger research project that involves two other questionnaires: one directed at language service companies (LSCs)[3] and another at individual translators (Ginovart et al. 2020; Ginovart 2020). The findings of the three surveys are presented by Ginovart and Oliver (2020).

With all three data collection instruments (questionnaire, syllabus analysis and interviews), we had a general research question: How do postgraduate educators train MTPE in Europe nowadays?

In section 1, the relevant literature is summarized to introduce our field of study. In section 2, the methodology used for the three instruments is described. We then present the quantitative outcomes of the online questionnaire in section 3. Section 4 explores the qualitative outcomes: first the syllabi, and then the more prominent topics covered during the interviews. Finally, in section 5 we set out the concluding thoughts and suggestions for further work.

1. Relevant literature

The conviction that familiarity with translation technology is crucial to a successful professional career is shared by industry stakeholders (Transperfect as reported by Zaretskaya 2017: 123; SDL in their Corporate Translation Technology Survey,

2017: 12) and translator educators (O'Brien 2002: 100; Bowker 2002; Doherty et al. 2012; Doherty and Kenny 2014; Kenny and Doherty 2014). More recently, the improved performance of MT, with its neural networks technology, and the expanding presence of MT in the industry are posing a new challenge to translator training programmes. As Cid-Leal et al. (2019) point out, there is a shift from computer-assisted human translation to human-assisted machine translation. Colominas and Oliver (2019) present a survey showing that, at Spanish universities, there is a significant mismatch between the real use of MT by students and the use understood (or recommended) by educators. This gap between the educators' beliefs and the actual practice of the students certainly leads to a misalignment between learning objectives and outcomes.

In fact, for some time researchers have generally agreed (O'Brien 2002; Şahin 2011) that post-editing is different from conventional human translation and consequently requires specific skills. Gaspari et al. (2015) observed that training programmes lacked MT, translation quality assessment, and post-editing (PE) skills in their syllabi. The proposed skill sets found in the literature (O'Brien 2002: 102–3; Rico and Torrejón 2012: 169–70; Nitzke et al. 2019: 247–50) can be broadly classified into two different types depending on the function (either more limited or more extensive) attributed to the post-editor. One perspective assumes that the function of the post-editor consists merely in editing and validating the translation suggestions obtained with an MT system, this being referred to as a 'downward migration' (Kenny 2018: 66) or a 'limited or reductive role' (Kenny and Doherty 2014: 290). This definition is applied by a considerable number of stakeholders in both the industry and the research community (Joscelyne and Brace 2010: 24; KantanMT 2014; Pym 2013; Absolon 2018). At the other extreme, authors such as Rico and Torrejón (2012), Sánchez-Gijón (2016), Rico (2017: 80), Blagodarna (2018: 4), Moorkens (2018b: 4) and Pym (2019a) assume a more extensive job profile. In addition to editing MT segments, a professional post-editor performs other functions: linguistic pre-processing, augmenting systems with customized glossaries and managing MT systems and the overarching workflows. It is clear that new professional skills are needed, but neither the industry nor the research community seem to have reached consensus on their specific definition or delimitation. Furthermore, the question has been raised of when such training should be introduced and to what extent (basic introduction or advanced specialized knowledge) (Plaza Lara 2019: 261–2; Nitzke 2019: 45).

The lack of agreement on the skills involved is observed, for example, in ISO 18587 (2017). There the training perspective is added as an Annex to the standard. The Annex states the potential benefits of MTPE training in a general way and briefly describes the five topics training may cover (advanced use of translation memory and MT, advanced terminology work, advanced text-processing skills, practice in both light and full PE, and use of Quality Assessment tools). The need for consensus has already led to the emergence of survey-based research to learn more about the current profile of the post-editor in general (Gaspari et al. 2015), and particularly from the perspective of the industry (Ginovart et al. 2020).

2.   Methodology

Participants

We e-mailed more than 200 educators in translation schools drawn from the EMT list of members, but also from other resources so as to include the non-EMT schools. For instance, a shared unpublished database of translation and interpreting schools in Europe is available on the Translation Commons' Learn/Resources Hub,[4] and there is the list of approved schools published by the American Translators Association (ATA n.d.). Alternatively, the Internet was browsed by country (European Union 2020) to find the relevant schools. The method used for dissemination of the questionnaire was therefore convenience sampling. One possible limitation of or bias in our preselected list of universities is that some translation schools were unknown to the authors and were therefore not contacted.

   We sent the 53 educators who agreed to participate a consent form for signature and the link to the online questionnaire. After filling it in, they could agree to take part in an interview with the lead researcher, and 48 did so.

Data collection instruments

The quantitative aspect of our study stems from the data collected via the online questionnaire. We obtained 54 submissions from 53 educators (one of them filled it out twice, as she taught at two institutions)[5]. They have different job profiles: while the majority have full-time positions as professors, some of them come from the industry, that is, they work at an LSC and are guest instructors of the MTPE course (on a more or less regular basis).

   The online questionnaire, entitled 'Survey for MTPE training providers'[6] was available only in English, and was designed in Jotform.[7] It was open for submissions from May to August 2019. To keep it as short as possible, we focused on three core topics:

1   PE training elements;
2   PE skills;
3   PE tasks.

However, a series of short questions also broached general or related matters such as PE briefs and guidelines, PE feedback and translation technology tools (11 items in total; see section 3).

   To design those parts of the online questionnaire where we present our three core topics (15 training elements, 11 PE skills and 14 PE tasks), we relied on previous work by researchers in the field. To name just a few, the list of 15 training elements was mainly inspired by PE training courses developed by SDL, Trágora (n.d.), DigiLing (n.d.), ASAP Translations (n.d.), TAUS (Van der Meer 2015) and fellow researchers (for instance, Guerberof and Moorkens 2019). The list of 11 PE skills stems from a reading of work by the Post-editing Training network (Tradumàtica Research Group n.d.), Rico and Torrejón (2012), Guerberof (2013), Doherty and Kenny (2014), Koponen (2015, 2018), Moorkens and O'Brien (2017) and Pym (2011c, 2013), among others. The list of 14 PE tasks was created thanks to the following publications: Krings (2001), Allen (2003), Temizöz (2016), Sánchez-Gijón (2016), Gaspari et al. (2015), do Carmo (2017), Vintar et al. (2017), Vieira and Alonso (2018) and Blagodarna (2018), among others.

The questionnaire contained 32 questions of different types: multiple-choice with radio button, checkbox (either with or without limited choices), free text, and matrix (a multiple-choice question/answer formed by a set of columns and rows). Even though we did not run a pilot for this specific questionnaire, the design benefited from the lessons learned from the questionnaire submitted to LSCs (Ginovart et al. 2020). For that questionnaire, we not only had a pilot, but we also requested a report on it from the Applied Statistics Service of the Universitat Autònoma de Barcelona. This report helped us improve the types and order of questions and possible answers in order to avoid bias and drop-out as far as possible.

The qualitative aspect of our mixed-methods research stems in the first instance from our reading of the syllabi. But, more importantly, the qualitative data are found in the 49 interviews with the 48 educators who agreed to discuss their course and syllabus with the lead researcher (the same person who filled out the questionnaire twice provided two separate interviews). The interviews allowed the detailed views of the participants to be collected in order to help explain the initial quantitative survey responses. The interviews were conducted by e-mail, telephone or the Internet (chat or, most often, videoconference), and one was a personal interview.

In the next section, the data collected via the online questionnaire are investigated. To analyse the data, we used the pivot tables function in Microsoft Excel. We first present the outlook for master's training in MTPE in Europe by probing the respondents on general and related topics: the weight of PE in MTPE-related courses; training materials and aids used in class; methods for MT output evaluation; whether the source text or the target text is read first; the pricing models; PE levels; PE risks; deontological issues; PE briefs and PE guidelines (studied in more detail by other researchers such as Flanagan and Christensen 2014). Then, in the last part of section 3, we delve into the core topics of the questionnaire: PE training elements, PE skills and PE tasks.

3.   Quantitative results

A total of 61 questionnaires were submitted, of which 54 were considered valid for the present study. Seven submissions were excluded because they concerned courses at the undergraduate level or had another type of audience (such as 'Train the trainer' courses).[8]

A total of 53 educators engaged in MTPE courses in 17 different countries responded to the survey. As already mentioned, one educator taught two different courses, so we had 54 submissions from the following countries: Austria (1), Belgium (4), Croatia (1), Czech Republic (1), Finland (3), France (6), Germany (8), Greece (1), Ireland (1), Italy (5), Latvia (1), Malta (1), Poland (2), Portugal (1), Spain (8), Switzerland (2) and the United Kingdom (8).

General or related matters

We investigated the following eleven general or related matters in order to contextualize our three main topics (PE training elements, PE skills and PE tasks):

- weight of PE in the syllabus;
- teaching methods and materials;
- evaluation of MT output;
- source or target text first;
- pricing models;
- PE levels;
- relation between raw output and final quality;
- PE risks;
- ethical and deontological practices;
- PE briefs;
- PE guidelines.

Weight of PE in the syllabus: On Table 12.1, the weight of PE in the syllabi of the courses studied is displayed. However, one limitation must be acknowledged: the possible interpretation of 'syllabus' as either a whole course or part of a course. To deal with this ambiguity, more precise information was gathered when we analysed the syllabi (see section 4).

Teaching methods and materials: We included a set of multiple-choice questions (checkbox type, with 9 possible answers, a free-text field and no limit on the number of answers to be selected). The average respondent selected 5.2 answers. Slide presentations, hands-on PE, and MT output evaluation are the materials used most often in PE courses (see Figure 12.1, which shows the absolute number of times each item was selected and the percentage relative to the total of 277 selections by all respondents).

TABLE 12.1 What percentage of the syllabus focuses on PE?

Weight of PE in syllabus	% of participants agreeing
25% or less	51%
26% to 50%	20%
More than 51%	29%

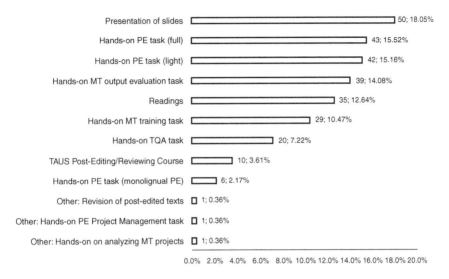

FIGURE 12.1 What training support(s) do you use for your MTPE training?

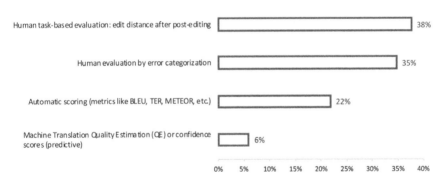

FIGURE 12.2 What two methods would you choose as the most important to be presented to MTPE students, regarding the evaluation of MT output?

Evaluation of MT output: As shown in the previous item, the evaluation of the MT output seems to be an important activity (selected 39 times). Regarding methods for MT output evaluation, respondents could select one to four options. The average respondent selected 1.83 methods (nine respondents chose only one method, and two used the 'Other' field to enter their own method). The content introduced in the 'Other' free-text field by these two educators was 'TAUS DQF'[9] and 'Productivity measurement', which, in our opinion, are represented by 'Human task-based evaluation' even though the parameters of speed and quality should be added to the equation along with the editing distance. The findings are shown in Figure 12.2.

Quality estimation (QE), as a method with which users can evaluate MT output, is represented by only 6% of the total 101 selections by respondents. It would seem that QE is still a work in progress, and that no major use of it has been reported in the industry or within academia so far. A change of paradigm can be deduced from Figure 12.2: from automatic scoring (22%) to more human-centred methods such as error categorization (35%) and task-based evaluation (38%).

Source or target text first: We asked the respondents if they discuss what should be read first, the source or the target segment (radio button type of question). Among these educators, 33% advise reading the source segment first; 18%, the target first; and 49% do not hold a definite position on this: they give their students the opportunity to explore both approaches and discuss with them the advantages and disadvantages of both.

Pricing models: We asked the educators whether they discuss with students how to apply a rate for MTPE projects. Out of the 7 available options, the average respondent chose 1.33 types of rate.

In Figure 12.3, it can be seen that 18 respondents do not discuss rates; 22 said that price per hour is the recommended model (this corresponds to 30% of the total 72 selections); 17 respondents selected 'Price per source word (pre-analysis)'; and only a few checked the post-analysis (5) or the target word option (3). It should be emphasized that 7 educators used the 'Other' free-text option to explain that they discuss various possible pricing scenarios and that the pros and cons of each approach are debated. For instance, one respondent said they present the possibility of having a 'price per project'. The possibility of having mixed-model pricing

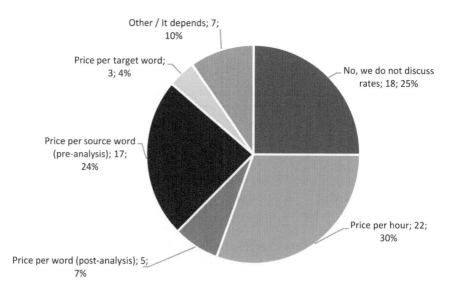

FIGURE 12.3 Do you discuss with the students how to apply a rate on MTPE projects?

with a fixed rate (source words) and a variable rate (editing distance), as proposed by Bammel (2019), was not mentioned by anyone.

PE levels: When asked 'Which PE levels do you show[10] to your PE students?', given that it was a multiple-choice question, almost all the respondents chose both light and full PE. Indeed, the average respondent selected 1.83 answers. Of the total 99 answers selected, 'light PE' represented 43%, 'full PE' 52% and 'Other' 5%. This corresponds closely to the hands-on full PE task and the hands-on light PE task seen in Figure 12.1.

Relation between raw output and final quality: To provide a more detailed response than the light–full PE dichotomy discussed in the previous item, we also asked which of the three relations of Figure 12.4 the respondents explicitly mention during their course. Alternatively, the respondents could choose 'Other/It depends'. The average respondent chose two of these options (total answers = 108).

PE risks: To deal with the varied correlations between MT output quality and the expected quality of the PE discussed in the previous item, several authors (Mossop 2014b; Nitzke et al. 2019) have highlighted the need for problem-solving strategies and the trade-off between necessary changes and over-editing. Since this also seemed to be important to understanding the general situation at translation schools, we asked the respondents in a radio-button type of question which of the three PE errors (under-editing, over-editing or pseudo-editing) they believe the students are more likely to commit. About half (49%) believe it is over-editing. Some interviewees would justify this at the interviewing stage. According to them, it could partially be explained by the fact that translation schools continue to stress

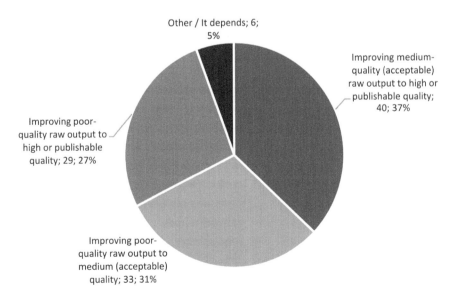

FIGURE 12.4 Which of the following relations between the raw MT output and the final quality expected do you explicitly mention during the training?

the quality factor in their human translation classes as a general principle. However, 40% of the respondents say that under-editing is also quite often a problem. This percentage might be increasing with the advent of neural MT, as fluency is misleadingly improved (Castilho et al. 2017) and some accuracy errors can go unseen by translators in training. The remaining respondents either do not have an opinion (7%) or believe their students tend to introduce errors into the MT output, or perform pseudo-editing (4%).

Ethical and deontological practices: We asked the educators whether they discuss the implications of using MT without informing the requester of the translation that it is being used. Only ten of them do not discuss it, and among those who do, one respondent used the free-text 'Other' field to specify that students are advised not to use MT without the agreement of the client.

PE brief: Another important aspect that has not been considered in previous research is how the translation brief may vary with the advent of neural MT, adaptive MT, predictive writing, QE, etc. In answering the radio-button question whether they present a PE brief to the students that is different from a translation brief, 43 (80%) respondents answered 'Yes' and 11 (20%) 'No'. We asked the 43 who answered affirmatively which elements should be present in a PE brief. Out of the ten available options (including 'Other'), the average respondent selected 5.76 in this multiple-choice question. In Figure 12.5, we present the absolute number of times an option was chosen and the percentage this represents of the total 248 responses. The responses ranged from 'PE level' (38 responses) to 'Examples of scenarios indicating when to discard a segment' (16 responses).

PE guidelines: As shown in the discussion of the previous item, PE guidelines seem to be an important element in briefs (with 37 selections, guidelines received the second highest number of votes). Out of seven possibilities (including 'None' and 'Other'), we asked the respondents which PE guidelines they present to

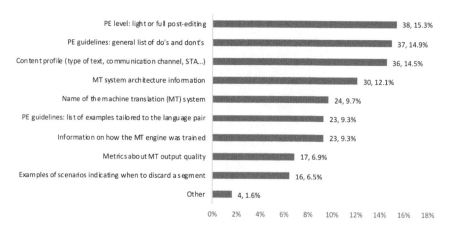

FIGURE 12.5 Which of the following elements do you present to your students as being necessary or interesting in a MTPE assignment or brief?

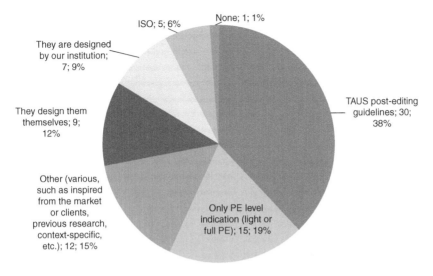

ISO; 5; 6%

None; 1; 1%

They are designed by our institution; 7; 9%

TAUS post-editing guidelines; 30; 38%

They design them themselves; 9; 12%

Other (various, such as inspired from the market or clients, previous research, context-specific, etc.); 12; 15%

Only PE level indication (light or full PE); 15; 19%

FIGURE 12.6 Which PE guidelines do you present to your students?

the students (see Figure 12.6). It was a multiple-choice question and the average respondent selected 1.5 answers (total answers = 79). The most selected was 'TAUS post-editing guidelines' (30), followed by 'Only PE level indication' (15) and 'Other' (12). In this last free-text field, the educators explained that various types of guidelines may be presented: inspired by the market/clients or by previous research, or context-specific guidelines. Nine respondents design PE guidelines themselves.

Core topics

We will now discuss the core questions of the survey (PE training elements, PE skills and PE tasks).

PE training elements: We enquired, via a multiple-choice question, which topics were covered in the course (see Figure 12.7). With 15 options available, the average respondent chose 9.07 (total answers = 490).

As seen in Figure 12.7, the most popular choice is 'MT systems' (51); only three participants failed to select it. The next most popular choices were 'PE levels: light and full post-editing' (48), 'Practical PE exercises in the relevant language pair' (48), 'MT evaluation: human (scoring, ranking, error categorization)' (46), and 'Integration between CAT and MT system' (44).

PE skills: We then asked the respondents to rate the listed 11 PE skills according to their importance to a professional post-editor on a scale from 1 (slightly important) to 5 (very important); each skill could be left unrated (not important). Figure 12.8 shows the average score for each of the 11 skills, with the 'Capacity to post-edit up to human quality (full PE)' included only for reference.

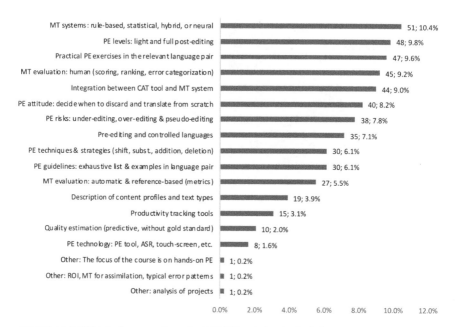

FIGURE 12.7 Which elements does the MTPE training include?

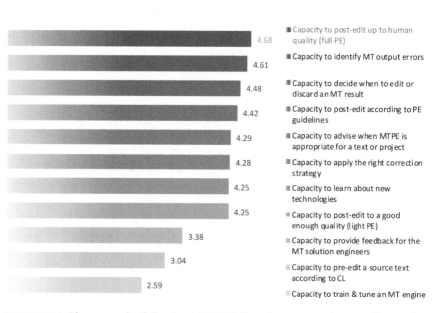

FIGURE 12.8 Please rate the following MTPE skills and competencies according to the importance

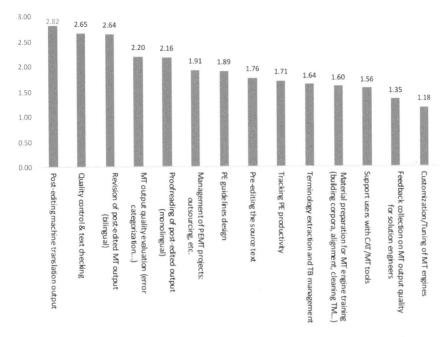

FIGURE 12.9 What workload do you think the following PE-related tasks might carry in the everyday work of a professional post-editor?

As can be observed from the scores in Figure 12.8, MTPE educators claim that identifying MT output errors (4.61), decision-making about editing or discarding MT results (4.48) and applying PE guidelines (4.42) are the three most important PE skills, considering that the 'Capacity to PE up to human quality' (4.68) was present only to give focus to the question. It may be surprising that the 'Capacity to post-edit to a good enough quality (light PE)' is the fourth least selected capacity, considering that 'PE levels' was the second training element covered in the courses (Figure 12.7).

PE tasks: We asked the educators' opinion about the load that PE-related tasks constitute in the everyday work of a professional post-editor. Each of the 14 tasks listed could be rated as main task (3), secondary (2), occasional (1) or not applicable (0). In Figure 12.9, the average score for each PE-related task is displayed. MTPE itself, which has the highest score (2.82), is shown only as a reference.

According to the educators surveyed, the tasks of 'Quality control & text checking' (2.65), 'Revision of post-edited MT output (bilingual)' (2.64), and 'MT output quality evaluation' (2.20) are the most practised by professional post-editors.

To conclude the questionnaire, we wished to elicit the thoughts and determine the needs of the educators regarding PE courses: 20% said that current PE courses are adequate for meeting needs, 36% are of the opposite opinion, and 44% do not know. This may suggest that there is some uncertainty among educators about industry requirements or, at least, about the needs of their trainees. When asked if they would like to have access to a third-party platform where their students could practise real MTPE assignments, 76% of the respondents responded positively and 15% negatively, while 9% said their choice would depend on the specifics of the platform and the assignments provided.

4. Qualitative results

The syllabi

After the educators had been contacted and they had expressed their interest in taking part in this study by signing the consent form, we requested their syllabus outline if it was not available at their institution's website. The 49 syllabi available at the time enabled us to gain insight into the way PE is currently being taught in translation master's programmes in Europe. We were interested in:

- the name of the course;
- whether it is compulsory or an elective module;
- the number of contact and study hours;
- the number of ECTS;
- whether it includes an examination;
- the language pair(s) that it covers;
- prerequisites for enrolling;
- whether it has or allows for a distance-learning mode.

First, more than one-half the syllabi are for EMT programmes. Second, the written outlines contain highly varied levels of information. While some of them are rich in content (name of instructor, teaching mode, teaching language, training activities, methodology, competences and subcompetences, learning outcomes and objectives, evaluation system, calendar), others contain general information only.

Course name: A total of 20 out of the 49 syllabi mention 'post-editing' in their title. The remainder mention 'computer-assisted translation', 'translation tools' or 'translation technology'; others focus on localization, project management, the translation profession or the relevant language pair of the corresponding revision or editing course.

Compulsory or elective: Slightly more than 25% are elective; the remainder are compulsory. Some courses are taught in more than one postgraduate programme, and one possibility is that the same course was compulsory in one programme but elective in another.

Contact and study hours: According to the syllabus outlines, five modules offer 60 contact hours or more; the other 44 typically range from 12 to 50 hours of contact time. However, as was shown on Table 12.1, the hours dedicated exclusively to PE constitute, more often than not, less than half of the syllabus. For two courses, the study time is more than 300 hours; for the other 47, it ranges considerably, from 160 hours to 8 hours, and in these courses, the study time on PE in particular presumably varies accordingly.

ECTS credits: The syllabi mostly range from 2 to 10 ECTS; only two syllabi are worth 1 ECTS, three are worth 14 ECTS, and one is a quarter of the master's (22.5 ECTS).

Examination: Thirty-nine syllabi do not involve passing an examination or a test. For evaluation, other tools such as assignments, an essay or a portfolio are used. Ten syllabi include an examination but only four include PE in the examination. With or without an examination, we wondered whether the students' grades take into account to any extent the final quality of the post-edited texts they deliver, which is why we included this question in the interviews (discussed later).

Language pairs: Since PE has traditionally been more linked to courses on computer-assisted translation (CAT) tools, project management or localization, some of the syllabi are (or try to be), as some interviewees put it, 'language agnostic'. Two syllabi enable up to 14 language pairs to be handled. This may depend on the year and the students a course attracts but, in general, the syllabi and the subsequent interviews revealed that the educators have groups of students representing anything from three to eight language pairs. It should be noted, however, that approximately 20 syllabi cover one single language pair, either uni- or bi-directional. The fact that the population of students enrolled can be international either made it impossible to evaluate the quality of the post-edited text (if the educator had not mastered the target language) or led the students to post-edit languages in which they are not native.

Prerequisites for enrolling: Approximately 35 of the courses do not have any formal prerequisites, especially those that are compulsory, since the fact of being enrolled in the master's programme, for example, or having successfully completed the first year of the master's, should mean that the students have the basics (of translation, CAT tools or any field that is needed for the given syllabus) necessary to undertake the PE-related course. For the remaining courses, there is usually a recommendation, such as being able to use an MS Office suite (word processing, spreadsheet and presentation software), being familiar with CAT tools or possessing other information and communication technology (ICT) skills. For a couple of courses, the completion of another, less advanced course is a prerequisite.

Distance learning: Thirty-seven courses require the presence of the student at the university. This can probably be explained largely by the need for a laboratory equipped with licensed software and tools. Even if the students could be connected via a virtual private network (VPN), the educators would probably still need to give hands-on on-site support. For example, students may have technical issues with the VPN or the translation technology tools. Also, considering the content of the class, an answer to one student's question could be useful for the rest of the class, and the oral debate about the quality of different translation solutions probably is (or should be?) a major part of the course.

The interviews[11]

The 49 interviews, which lasted between 15 and 25 minutes, were held mostly in English, but also in French, Spanish and Catalan. They took place between September and November 2019 and provided qualitative insights into a number of interesting matters. The interviews allowed the lead researcher to become acquainted with the educator's profile and background, which by itself provided important information.

During the interviews, the lead researcher asked the educators:

1   how long PE has been included in their course ('Age of syllabus');
2   which tools and software they present to the students, and if they have a hands-on class about MT engine training ('Tools and software');
3   if they had or knew at the time of the interview of any plans to increase the PE presence in the curriculum ('Plans to increase MTPE');
4   if their colleagues encourage the use of MT in 'traditional' translation courses ('Use of MT in regular translation courses');
5   if they use the task-based or project-based approach as a pedagogical method in the course ('Teaching methods');
6   whether or not their students have hands-on practice in error categorization and, independently, what is their opinion of the error typologies with neural MT outputs ('Error categorization of the MT output');
7   if they think trainee post-editors should be encouraged to read the source or the target segment first ('Source or target segment first');
8   if they include pre-editing of the ST in their course, and if they think this is useful to obtain a higher NMT output quality ('Pre-editing of the source text');
9   if they consider the final quality of the post-edited product in the students' assessment ('Evaluation of the PE text');
10 if deontological issues with MTPE are discussed in class and what their views are on this topic ('Deontological issues with MTPE');
11 whether they know the so-called 'split principle' as a training method for MTPE ('Split training').

Age of syllabus: In which year was the course first given? Since when has it included PE? Even though two courses go back to 2000 and 2005, the majority are more recent, and the most pioneering syllabi started tackling the matter of PE between 2012 and 2014. Especially in the past five years, from 2015 to 2020, PE has shown a clear growth trend: either new courses are being created from scratch, or PE is gaining more weight in existing courses about CAT tools, MT, project management or related fields. This probably has to do with the introduction of standards such as ISO 18587 and the inclusion of PE-related skills in EMT, reflecting the reality of the market.

Tools and software: It is common practice to use more than one CAT tool during the course. The four most used are Memsource, SDL Trados Studio, MateCat and MemoQ. Microsoft Excel and Word are used by six of the educators to practise the PE skill set in their courses. Finally, some mentioned Across, STAR Transit and Lilt. On the topic of MT providers, the most used is Google Translate, followed by DeepL. The remaining educators mentioned Microsoft and/or Bing, KantanMT,

Tilde, e-Translation and SDL Language Cloud. The vast majority do not train MT systems in their courses.

Plans to increase MTPE: At the time they were responding to the online questionnaire (from May to August 2019), more than half of the participants surveyed already knew that their course would undergo modifications. Most changes would be to dedicate more ECTS and hours to PE; some would entail splitting a course and making one stand-alone course in revision and PE. A couple of participants said that PE would now be included in the undergraduate programme.

Use of MT in regular translation courses: We wanted to ascertain whether PE practice and the PE skill set are present throughout the whole programme and not only in one single course. There seems to be an ongoing effort to increase the use of CAT and MT tools in regular translation classes. Half of the respondents either do not know about their colleagues' use of MT in their classic translation courses, or know that they do not introduce MT at all. The other half know at least one traditional translation course where the educator includes some practice with translation technologies. However, it is more often CAT tools than MTPE. Little research has focused on the evolution of traditional translation courses to include MTPE, and the authors are convinced that 'Train the trainer' courses would be helpful in moving in that direction.

Teaching methods: The project-based approach, in which the students perform 'multi-facetted learning activities in real (and not just realistic) working environments', held promise in the past decade (Kiraly 2012: 84). The interviewees were asked whether they favoured a task-based or a project-based approach, or another teaching method. A significant number of educators claim that their course as a whole is not project-based, but rather task-based. Nonetheless, one of these tasks is to work on a CAT-tool project to some extent. Even when some interviewees first said that their syllabus had a project-based approach, in further discussion about Kiraly's model, we agreed that it is somewhere in between: one exercise that has the shape and appearance of a real translation project may last over two weeks, but this is only *one* part of the course; before or after this specific assignment, there are other exercises or activities on MT and/or PE which are task-based. Approximately ten of the studied syllabi are structured according to the project-based approach.

Error categorization of the MT output: Almost half of the interviewees do not currently have a structured exercise or one that involves comparing neural MT errors to other types of MT errors (rule-based, statistical or hybrid). Even if an exercise about error categorization is not present in a course, we asked the interviewees if they had an opinion about the similarities and differences between the NMT outputs nowadays compared to other MT systems in the past. All except one agreed that the error typology has changed since the advent of NMT. One, for instance, says "we dedicate almost an entire class to the typical errors and advantages of RBMT, SBMT and NMT". In general, they also observed the "improvements regarding target language fluency that had already been reported in the research community, such as an increased quality of morphology and syntax", to quote one educator. Approximately 20 educators went further to state explicitly that the challenge now lies in the capacity to spot accuracy errors.

Source or target segment first: This seems to be a controversial topic. We asked the educators who had not chosen one or the other in the online questionnaire (49%) what would determine a preference for one method over the other, in their opinion, or whether they observed a tendency among the students. One explained:

> I would say I'm a bit 'old school' in the sense I tend to focus on the source text: in my opinion, ultimately, an MTPE task has the same basic goal of a 'traditional' translation task: to convey the meaning of the ST. Therefore, I tend to start reading the ST and only then the TT, trying to make the most of the MT output in order to convey the ST meaning. In my personal experience, reading first the TT can easily influence the way we understand the ST, thus leading to a more error-prone state of mind of the post-editor. However, I try not to influence my students, and I try to make it clear to them that both approaches have merits and flaws. And, despite the fact that I do not have the 'scientific' data to support my theory, I would say the students that have a stronger background in 'traditional' translation tend to focus more on the ST. The less experienced students are generally more open to try both approaches, and some of them prove the TT-focus to work nicely as well.

Pre-editing of the source text: Most respondents do not include any assignment or activity on pre-editing in their course. A few do have practice in controlled language or pre-editing, but those who said on the survey that they cover it in their class were mostly referring to a theoretical presentation of the concept or a mention of the possibility of doing it in the industry, not actual hands-on experience. This was clarified during the interview. It has to be emphasized that for the three cases (pre-editing not present, mentioned only, or practised too), there was the possibility, confirmed by some educators, that pre-editing is more extensively covered in another syllabus. We also questioned the participants about their opinion of the usefulness of controlled language and pre-editing with neural MT outputs, and the general reaction was hesitant and sceptical. Predominantly, their feeling is that the need for pre-editing may be less significant with neural than with statistical MT (as has been suggested in Nitzke et al. 2019), but that it can still be useful or necessary, depending on the style and genre of the text and mainly to ensure high-quality originals. Some mentioned how difficult it can be to introduce pre-editing in a real scenario in the translation industry, when sometimes the LSC does not know who wrote the source text, or when the producer of the source text cannot anticipate that it is going to be machine-translated later. However, for those who still consider that pre-editing will, to some extent, benefit the MT output quality, it is striking that formatting corrections came up quite often as factors that could have an impact on the quality of the MT output. Some educators also referred to the profitability of pre-editing only when there are a certain number of target languages into which a text must be translated.

Evaluation of the PE text: We asked whether the final delivered quality of the post-edited text was considered when calculating a student's grade. One of the interviewees commented:

> The quality of the final texts is not (directly) evaluated, as we're more focused on checking if the students are able to identify the usual features of MT, its typical advantages and errors, and if they are able to properly take advantage of MT in a MTPE task. However, we do discuss how different approaches to MT influence the final quality of the text: for instance, we compare versions of the same texts where a student tried to use as much as possible of the MT output and other student chose to translate most of the text from scratch, and we discuss, with the whole class, if we can clearly state that one is better than the other, taking into account several factors that can influence that result (the translator him/herself, the type of text, the technology used, the intended purpose of the text, etc.).

There are more instances of courses in which the quality of the post-edited text is not graded than courses where it is. Still, in 15 of the courses, the quality of the product is taken into account for the purposes of evaluation. In some cases, even when quality cannot be a consistent variable for grading, a compromise is found: it is evaluated only for the target languages that the educator can competently correct; colleagues help with evaluating other target languages, or groups or pairs of students review their peers' post-edited texts.

Deontological issues with MTPE: When asked about the ethical question of whether to inform a customer that MT is being used, some of the educators clearly regarded not informing as being intrinsically a violation of the code of ethics; a professional translator should always inform the customer about the tools they use. More often, the view among the educators was that MT tools should be available to translators without the prior agreement of the client, as long as they are used as one more resource for providing a product whose quality is not inferior to the one that would have been provided with human translation (which nowadays assumes the use of CAT tools). Adopting a similar position, some interviewees stated that they show their students how the use of an MT system remains embedded in the metadata of each translation unit or segment in a CAT environment. Only a couple of interviewees mentioned the potential dangers of sending confidential data to the MT providers. Confidentiality is still an important aspect of MTPE, one that providers such as Google seem to take seriously (Google Cloud n.d.). However, the community of users still express doubts (Gheorghe 2019), which probably means that educators should tackle these issues more often in their courses. Likewise, we enquired about the possibility of a translator post-editing the MT output in a language in which the translator is not native. It seems that the 'mother-tongue principle', which has already been progressively abandoned in the industry

(Wagner et al. 2014: 103), is also not so important in MTPE training: more than half of the respondents have to 'accept' more than one language pair in their PE hands-on practice. This is just one more reason to start researching the best way to include MTPE in regular translation classes.

Split training: To conclude, we asked the interviewees about their knowledge of 'split training' (Absolon 2019) because it appeared to be a quite unknown recent proposal. Only one of our interviewees knew about it. The lead researcher explained her understanding of it: it consists in dividing skills into subskills to a more or less granular level and in attributing a tailored practical exercise to each subskill. Once introduced to the concept, their opinions were diverse, ranging from a minority of positive views through a majority who did not express a view either way, to some interviewees who expressed their conviction that it would not be useful in their courses.

Finally, some educators introduced new topics that had not been foreseen in the interview but that are certainly of current interest in the MTPE field. One mentioned that, instead of focusing so much on classifying errors, it would be better to show the students processes from real scenarios—for instance, how to prepare good feedback after PE, so that engineers of MT systems can continuously improve their algorithms with sound training data and linguistic insights.

5. Concluding remarks

Recently, the master's programmes in translation or related studies have been updated, especially regarding their MTPE content. Some of the educators in our study have found the same trend is affecting undergraduate programmes too.

In this chapter, we have discussed the outcomes of a survey-based study mixed with qualitative data from syllabi outlines and interviews with the relevant educators. In general, the customization or training of MT engines is excluded from MTPE courses in European postgraduate programmes. We have also learned that it is common practice to present more than one tool (CAT environment or MT system), which calls for task-based activities rather than a project-based methodology. According to our interviewees, few colleagues include practice in MTPE in their 'traditional' or 'regular' translation courses. This lack of intertwining of traditional translation techniques with the use of technologies may partially explain why 76% of our respondents say they would benefit from an online platform where their students could have PE hands-on practice, as this would allow them to further combine these two skill sets, traditionally separated at translation schools. Only in a few cases is the final translation quality evaluated, since it is commonly understood that this is a competence to be learned in regular translation courses; the emphasis in MTPE classes is mostly placed on procedures and processes, the features of software, and maybe the techniques for efficient keyboard use. The interviews with the educators also highlighted their scepticism about the use of controlled language or pre-editing for MT.

Whereas our interviewees often expressed their wish for a more holistic pedagogical approach, this seems difficult to put it into practice. Indeed, ICT skills for translators, especially with regard to MTPE, are taught as a completely separate competence from translation techniques aiming at quality deliverables. One remarkable observation by two interviewees was that PE is trying to be regarded as a different skill, distinct from translation, but for them it is not so different: the MT engine is just one more resource that, in the end, is similar to other translator resources, such as translation memory.

The concept of 'split training' elicited positive interest among a number of the educators, whereas others thought it was too 'mechanical'. However, we believe that further research into split training should not exclude the possibility of eventually integrating it into a holistic teaching methodology. In particular, it is possible that the greater the level of granularity to which split training in PE skills is researched, the easier it will be to build up modules tailored to any specific audience or context. For this reason, the next step in our work will consist of an experimental pre-test/post-test study similar to the one conducted by Dede (2019). In it, we will evaluate online split training built around the three main PE skills identified in this chapter and in the larger research project mentioned in our introductory remarks: the capacity to identify MT output errors, to decide when to post-edit or translate from scratch, and to apply PE guidelines (see Figure 12.6 in section 3).

We expect that professionals who successfully master core PE skills will be able to build their careers eventually to practise what Pym (2019a) has described as "[an] 'authorizing' activity, somewhat akin to that of a notary in the field of official documents or a good copy editor in publishing". Such mastery may enable all stakeholders to devise a consensual definition of job descriptions so that *human-assisted* MT may be assimilated to 'a post-editing service' (assuming a good-quality MT output) and *machine-aided* human translation could in turn be assimilated to 'a translation service'.

Acknowledgements

This chapter has been written within the framework of the Government of Catalonia's Industrial Doctorates Plan. The authors thank the 53 educators who kindly shared their views and working methods with us. We are especially grateful to the 48 who made themselves available for interviews with the lead researcher. We express our gratitude to Isabelle S. Robert and Brian Mossop, two of the editors of this book, for their interest in our work. Finally, our thanks go to the anonymous reviewers for their constructive feedback, which enabled us to improve this chapter significantly.

Notes

1 We understand 'syllabus' to mean the 'summary outline of a course of study', and 'course' as 'a number of lectures or other matter dealing with a subject' (following the definitions of Merriam-Webster's dictionary). We acknowledge that in certain places in the questionnaire and during interviews, the meanings might overlap.

2 Following Massey et al. (2019: 212–13), the term 'educator' has been used in this chapter, even if in some cases (unfortunately, in our opinion), MTPE is still regarded as an isolated, purely practical activity.

3 According to ISO 18587, Translation Service Provider (TSP) and Language Service Provider (LSP) include single freelance professionals. We use 'LSC' as a more restricted term than TSP or LSP, but one that is more comprehensive than 'translation agency'.

4 Prepared by a Lille 3 student for the EUATC during his Master's 2 (TSM) internship at Nancy Matis SPRL. Available at http://xl8.link/List.

5 The fact that she agreed to fill in the questionnaire twice, and to have two distinct interviews, shows that she was aware of reporting about two different courses. In the case of the more subjective questions, that is, those that pertain to the instructor and were not course-related, we have excluded her answers (53 submissions).

6 https://form.jotformeu.com/82844920241354.

7 www.jotform.com.

8 A short professional course provided by an expert in a specific field to update the knowledge and practices of university educators.

9 Data Quality Framework of the Translation Automation User Society.

10 The word 'show' in the questionnaire was chosen on purpose to include, as far as possible, those courses in which time or other constraints may prevent actual practice, but the two levels of PE are still defined theoretically.

11 Since the views shared by the educators were sometimes nuanced, vague modifiers such as 'majority' or 'some' are at times used when reporting the qualitative results.

BIBLIOGRAPHY

Abdallah, Kristiina (2012) *Translators in Production Networks. Reflections on Agency, Quality and Ethics.*

Abercrombie, Nicholas et al., eds. (2006) *The Penguin Dictionary of Sociology.*

Absolon, Jakub (2018) 'The need for competency-based selection and training of post-editors'. ASAP-translation.com.

Absolon, Jakub (2019) 'Human Translator 4.0 Manual of effective use of machine translation for a modern translator'. ASAP-translation.com.

Aikawa, Takako et al. (2012) 'The impact of crowdsourcing post-editing with the collaborative translation framework'. *Advances in Natural Language Processing*, 1–10.

Akaike, Hirotugu (1974) 'A new look at the statistical model identification'. *IEEE Transactions on Automatic Control* 19:6, 716–23.

Alabau, Vicent et al. (2013) 'CASMACAT: an open source workbench for advanced computer aided translation'. *The Prague Bulletin of Mathematical Linguistics* 100:1, 101–12.

Alabau, Vicent et al. (2016) 'Learning advanced post-editing'. In *New Directions in Empirical Translation Process Research* (Carl et al., eds.), 95–110.

Allain, Jean-François (2010) 'Repenser la révision. Défense et illustration de la relecture croisée'. *Traduire* 223, 114–20.

Allen, Jeffrey (2003) 'Post-editing'. In *Computers and Translation* (Somers, ed.), Benjamins Translation Library, 35.

Allman, Spencer (2006) 'Acknowledging and establishing the hierarchy of expertise in translator-reviser scenarios as an aid to the process of revising translation'. www.birmingham. ac.uk/documents/college-artslaw/cels/essays/translationstudiesdiss/allmandissertation. pdfs.

Allman, Spencer (2007) 'Negotiating translation revision assignments'. In *Proceedings of the Translation Conference, 2007: Translation as Negotiation*, 35–47.

Allport, Gordon Willard (1954) 'The historical background of social psychology'. In *The Handbook of Social Psychology, Vol. I* (Lindzey, ed.), 3–56.

Alonso, Elisa and Lucas Nunes Vieira (2017) 'The Translator's Amanuensis 2020'. *Journal of Specialised Translation* 28, 345–61.

Alves, Fábio et al. (2010) 'Translation units and grammatical shifts: towards an integration of product and process-based translation research'. In *Translation and Cognition* (Shreve and Angelone, eds.), 109–42.

Alves, Fábio et al. (2016) 'Analysing the impact of interactive machine translation on post-editing effort'. In *New Directions in Empirical Translation Process Research: Exploring the CRITT TPR-DB* (Carl et al., eds.), 77–94.

Andújar Moreno, Gemma (2019) 'El papel de la revisión editorial en la autoría múltiple del texto traducido: la versión española de Beautiful Children, de Charles Bock, como estudio de caso'. *Sendebar* 30, 35–60.

Angelelli, Claudia (2019) 'Assessment'. In *A History of Modern Translation Knowledge* (D'Hulst and Gambier, eds.), 435–42.

Angelone, Erik (2010) 'Uncertainty, uncertainty management, and metacognitive problem solving in the translation task'. In *Translation and Cognition* (Shreve and Angelone, eds.), 17–40.

Antonini, Rachele et al. (2017) 'Introducing NPIT studies'. In *Non-professional Interpreting and Translation: State of the Art and Future of an Emerging Field of Research* (Antonini et al., eds.), 1–26.

Aranberri, Nora et al. (2014) 'Comparison of post-editing productivity between professional translators and lay users'. In *Proceedings of the Third Workshop on Post-Editing Technology and Practice (WPTP-3)*, 20–33.

Arevalillo Doval, Juan José (2005) 'The EN-15038 European quality standard for translation services: What's behind it?' www.translationdirectory.com/article472.htm [consulted 18 December 2018].

Arthern, Peter J. (1983) 'Judging the quality of revision'. *Lebende Sprache* 2, 53–7.

Arthern, Peter J. (1991) 'Quality by numbers: assessing revision and translation'. In *Fifth Conference of the Institute of Translation and Interpreting* (Picken, ed.), 85–94.

ASAP Translations (n.d.) 'English—Slovak MTPE course'. Nitra: ASAP-translation.com. http://mtposteditors.com/tests/test_EN_SK_01.html.

ATA (n.d.) 'Schools approved for voting membership applications'. www.atanet.org/certification/eligibility_approved.php#.

Austermühl, Frank (2013) 'Future (and not-so-future) trends in the teaching of translation technology'. *Tradumàtica: tecnologies de la traduciò* 11, 326–37.

Austrian Standards (2015) 'Certification Scheme S06 Translation Service Provider according to ISO 17100'. www.iso17100.net/fileadmin/user/bilder/downloads-produkte-und-leistungen/S-07.106-ISO17100_EN.pdf [consulted 29 December 2018].

Austrian Standards (2019) 'Zertifizierung: was sind die Vorteile einer Zertifizierung?'. www.austrian-standards.at/produkte-leistungen/zertifizierung/ [consulted 18 December 2018].

Austrian Standards Institute (2014) 'Normung insight' (K. Grün, orator) *Ausbildungsmodul Austrian Standards. Austrian Standards Meeting Center*, Vienna.

Aziz, Wilker et al. (2014) 'Sub-sentence level analysis of machine translation post-editing effort'. In *Post-Editing of Machine Translation: Processes and Applications* (O'Brien et al., eds.), 170–99.

Bach, Cédric and Dominique Scapin (2003) 'Ergonomic criteria adapted to human virtual environment interaction'. In *Proceedings of the 15th French-Speaking Conference on HCI*, 24–31.

Bakkes, Christiaan (2004a) *Die lang pad van Stoffel Mathysen.*

Bakkes, Christiaan (2004b) *Stoffel by die afdraaipad.*

Bakkes, Christiaan (2006) *Stoffel in die wildernis.*

Bakkes, Christiaan (2007) *Stoffel se veldnotas.*

Bakkes, Christiaan (2008) *In bushveld and desert: A game ranger's life.*

Ballou, Janice (2008) 'Open-ended questions'. In *Encyclopedia of Survey Research Methods* (Lavrakas, ed.), 548–9.

Bammel, Steven S. (2019) '2019 Korean > English revising/post-editing'. http://bit.ly/revising-post-ed.

Bastien, Christian and Dominique Scapin (1993) *Ergonomic Criteria for the Evaluation of Human-Computer Interfaces.*

Bastien, Christian and Dominique Scapin (2001) 'Évaluation des systèmes d'information et critères ergonomiques'. In *Systèmes d'information et interactions homme-machine. Environnements évolués et évaluation de l'IHM. Interaction homme-machine pour les SI, Vol. 2* (Kolski, ed), 53–79.

Bates, Douglas et al. (2015) 'Fitting linear mixed-effects models using ime4'. *Journal of Statistical Software* 67:1, 1–48.

Bédard, Claude (2000) 'Mémoire de traduction cherche traducteur de phrases'. *Traduire* 186, 41–9.

Benfield, John R. and Christine B. Feak (2006) 'How authors can cope with the burden of English as an international language'. *Chest* 129:6, 1728–30.

Bennett, Karen (2013) 'English as a Lingua Franca in Academia'. *The Interpreter and Translator Trainer* 7:2, 169–93.

Bennett, Karen (2014a) 'The political and economic infrastructure of academic practice: the "semi-periphery" as a category for social and linguistic analysis'. In *The Semi-periphery of Academic Writing: Discourses, Communities and Practices* (Bennett, ed.), 1–12.

Bennett, Karen (2014b) 'Conclusion: combating the centripetal pull in academic writing'. In *The Semi-periphery of Academic Writing: Discourses, Communities and Practices* (Bennett, ed.), 240–6.

Bennett, Karen. (2015) 'Towards an epistemological monoculture: mechanisms of epistemicide in European research publication'. In *English as an Academic and Research Language* (English in Europe Vol. 2) (Ramón Plo and Carmen Pérez-Llantada, eds.), 9–35.

Bentivogli, Luisa et al. (2016) 'Neural versus phrase-based machine translation quality: a case study'. In *Proceedings of the 2016 Conference on Empirical Methods in Natural Language Processing*, 257–67. Association for Computational Linguistics, Austin, Texas.

Berman, Antoine (1985) 'La Traduction comme épreuve de l'étranger'. *Texte* 4, 67–81.

Bertaccini, Franco and Sara Di Nisio (2011) 'Il traduttore e il revisore nei diversi ambiti professionali'. *inTRAlinea*, Issue: Specialised Translation II.

Bicchieri, Cristina (2000) 'Words and deeds: a focus theory of norms'. In *Rationality, Rules, and Structure* (Nida-Rümelin and Spohn, eds.), 153–84.

Bicchieri, Cristina (2006) *The Grammar of Society: The Nature and Dynamics of Social Norms.*

Bicchieri, Cristina (2017a) *Norms in the Wild: How to Diagnose, Measure and Change Social Norms*, Kindle edition.

Bicchieri, Cristina (2017b) 'Social norms, social change'. Lectures convened by the University of Pennsylvania/UNICEF, March. www.coursera.org/learn/norms/home/welcome [consulted 24 November 2018].

Bicchieri, Cristina et al. (2018) 'Social norms'. In *The Stanford Encyclopedia of Philosophy* (Zalta, ed.).

Biel, Łucja (2011) 'Training translators or translation service providers? EN 15038:2006 standard of translation services and its training implications'. *Journal of Specialised Translation* 16, 61–76.

Bisiada, Mario (2018) 'The editor's invisibility: analysing editorial intervention in translation'. *Target* 30:2, 288–309.

Blagodarna, Olena (2018) 'Enhancement of post-editing performance: introducing machine translation post-editing in translator training'. PhD dissertation, Universitat Autònoma de Barcelona.

Bogic, Anna (2010) 'Uncovering the hidden actors with the help of Latour: the "making" of the second sex'. *MonTI. Monografías de Traducción e Interpretación* 2, 173–92.

Bojar, Ondřej (2011) 'Analyzing error types in English-Czech machine translation'. *The Prague Bulletin of Mathematical Linguistics* 95, 63–76.

Bowker, Lynne (2000) 'A corpus-based approach to evaluating student translation'. *The Translator* 6:2, 183–210.

Bowker, Lynne (2001) 'Towards a methodology for a corpus-based approach to translation evaluation'. *Meta* 46:2, 345–64.

Bowker, Lynne (2002) *Computer-aided Translation Technology: A Practical Introduction*.

Bowker, Lynne and Jairo Buitrago Ciro (2015) 'Investigating the usefulness of machine translation for newcomers at the public library'. *Translation and Interpreting Studies* 10:2, 165–86.

Breuer, Esther Odilia (2015) *First Language Versus Foreign Language: Fluency, Errors and Revision Processes in Foreign Language Academic Writing*.

Broekkamp, Hein et al. (1996) 'Attention strategies in revising a foreign language text'. In *Theories, Models and Methodology in Writing Research* (Rijlaarsdam G et al., eds.), 170–81.

Bruce, Steve and Steven Yearley, eds. (2006) *The SAGE Dictionary of Sociology*.

Brunette, Louise (1997) *Contribution à la pédagogie de la révision anglais-français en pays bilingue: le cas du Canada*.

Brunette, Louise (1998) 'L'enseignement de la révision pédagogique'. In *Traduction et langues de spécialité. Approches théoriques et considérations pédagogiques* (Guével and Egan, eds.), 25–43.

Brunette, Louise (2000) 'Towards a terminology for translation quality assessment'. *The Translator* 6:2, 169–82.

Brunette, Louise (2002) 'Normes et censure: ne pas confondre'. *TTR: traduction, terminologie, rédaction* 15:2, 223–33.

Brunette, Louise (2003) 'Révision pédagogique et interférences linguistiques'. In *La formation à la traduction professionnelle* (Mareschal et al., eds.), 141–51.

Brunette, Louise and Chantal Gagnon (2013) 'Enseigner la révision à l'ère des wikis: là où l'on trouve la technologie alors qu'on ne l'attendait plus'. *Journal of Specialised Translation* 19, 96–121.

Brunette, Louise et al. (2005) 'The GREVIS Project: revise or court calamity'. *Across Languages and Cultures* 6:1, 29–45.

Budin, Gerhard (2007) 'Entwicklung internationaler Normen im Bereich der Translationsqualität bei ISO/TC 37'. In *Translationsqualität* (Schmitt, ed.), 54–65.

Bundgaard, Kristine (2017a) '(Post-)editing—a workplace study of translator-computer interaction at Textminded Danmark A/S'. PhD Dissertation. Aarhus University, Denmark. http://vbn.aau.dk/files/261592757/PhD_thesis_Kristine_Bundgaard.pdf [consulted 7 November 2018].

Bundgaard, Kristine (2017b) 'Translator attitudes towards translator-computer interaction—findings from a workplace study'. *Hermes—Journal of Language and Communication in Business* 56, 125–44.

Bundgaard, Kristine and Tina Paulsen Christensen (2019) 'Is the concordance feature the new black? A workplace study of translators' interaction with translation resources while post-editing TM and MT matches'. *Journal of Specialised Translation* 31, 14–37.

Burgess, Sally et al. (2014) 'Affordances and constraints on research publication: a comparative study of the language choices of Spanish historians and psychologists'. *Journal for English for Academic Purposes* 14, 72–83.

Buysschaert, Joost et al. (2017) 'Professionalising the curriculum and increasing employ-ability through authentic experiential learning: the cases of INSTB'. *Current Trends in Translation Teaching and Learning E (CTTL-E)* 4, 78–111.

Buysschaert, Joost et al. (2018) 'Embracing digital disruption in translator training: tech-nology immersion in simulated translation bureaus'. *Revista Tradumàtica: tecnologies de la traducció* 17, 125–33.

Buzelin, Hélène (2005) 'Unexpected allies: how Latour's network theory could comple-ment Bourdieusian analyses in translation'. *The Translator* 11:2, 193–218.

Buzelin, Hélène (2007) 'Translations in the "making"'. In *Constructing a Sociology of Transla-tion* (Wolf and Fukari, eds.), 135–69.

Buzelin, Hélène (2011) 'Agents of translation'. In *Handbook of Translation Studies Online* (Gambier and van Doorslaer, eds.).

Bywood, Lindsay et al. (2017) 'Embracing the threat: machine translation as a solution for subtitling'. *Perspectives: Studies in Translatology* 25:3, 492–508.

Cadwell, Patrick et al. (2016) 'Human factors in machine translation and post-editing among institutional translators'. *Translation Spaces* 5:2, 222–43.

Cadwell, Patrick et al. (2018) 'Resistance and accommodation: factors for the (non-) adop-tion of machine translation among professional translators'. *Perspectives: Studies in Trans-latology* 26:3, 301–21.

Callegaro, Mario (2008) 'Social desirability'. In *Encyclopedia of Survey Research Methods* (Lavrakas, ed.), 825–6.

Carl, Michael (2012) 'Translog-II: a program for recording user activity data for empirical reading and writing research'. In *Proceedings of the Eighth International Conference on Lan-guage Resources and Evaluation* (Calzolari et al., eds.), 4108–12.

Carl, Michael and Arnt Lykke Jakobsen (2009) 'Towards statistical modelling of translators' activity data'. *International Journal of Speech Technology* 12:4, 125–38.

Carl, Michael and Moritz Jonas Schaeffer (2017) 'Why translation is difficult: a corpus-based study of non-literality in post-editing and from-scratch translation'. *Hermes—Journal of Language and Communication in Business* 56, 43–57.

Carl, Michael and M. Cristina Toledo Báez (2019) 'Machine translation errors and the transla-tion process: a study across different languages'. *Journal of Specialised Translation* 31, 107–32.

Carl, Michael et al. (2011) 'On the systematicity of human translation processes'. In *Tralogy 2011. Translation Careers and Technologies: Convergence Points for the Future.*

Carl, Michael et al. (2014) 'Post-editing machine translation—a usability test for professional translation settings'. In *Psycholinguistic and Cognitive Inquiries in Translation and Interpreta-tion Studies* (Ferreira and Schwieter, eds.), 145–74.

Carl, Michael et al. (2016a) 'The CRITT translation process research database'. In *New Directions in Empirical Translation Process Research* (Carl et al., eds.), 13–54.

Carl, Michael et al., eds. (2016b) *New Directions in Empirical Translation Process Research.*

Carless, David (2006) 'Differing perceptions in the feedback process'. *Studies in Higher Edu-cation* 31, 219–33.

Castilho, Sheila and Sharon O'Brien (2016) 'Evaluating the impact of light post-editing on usability'. In *Proceedings of the 10th International Conference on Language Resources and Evalu-ation, LREC 2016*, 310–16.

Castilho, Sheila et al. (2017) 'Is neural machine translation the new state of the art?'. *The Prague Bulletin of Mathematical Linguistics* 108:1, 109–20.

Catford, J.C. (1965) *A Linguistic Theory of Translation.*

CEFR (2019) 'Common European framework of reference for languages'. www.coe.int/en/web/common-european-framework-reference-languages/table-1-cefr-3.3-common-reference-levels-global-scale.

CEN (2006a) see European Committee for Standardization 2006a.

Chakhachiro, Raymond (2005) 'Revision for quality'. *Perspectives: Studies in Translatology* 13:3, 225–38.

Chesterman, Andrew (2016) *Memes of Translation. Revised.*

Chesterman, Andrew and Emma Wagner (2014) *Can Theory Help Translators? A Dialogue Between the Ivory Tower and the Wordface*, 2nd edition.

Christensen, Tina Paulsen (2011) 'Studies on the mental processes in translation memory-assisted translation—the state of the art'. *Trans-kom* 4, 137–60.

Cid-Leal, Pilar et al. (2019) 'Traducción automática y posedición: perfiles y competencias en los programas de formación de traductores'. *MonTI: monografías de traducción e interpretación* 11, 187–214.

Ciobanu, Dragoş et al. (2019) 'Speech synthesis in the translation revision process: evidence from error analysis, questionnaire, and eye-tracking'. *Informatics* 6:4, 51.

Cohen, A.R. (1964) *Attitude Change and Social Influence.*

Colominas, Carme and Antoni Oliver (2019, unpublished) 'Use of MT on regular translation courses'. Presentation at the Conference *Translation Technology in Education—Facilitator or Risk?* at the University of Nottingham, 5 July 2019.

Coppers, Sven et al. (2018) 'Intellingo: an intelligible translation environment'. In *Proceedings of CHI*, 1–13.

Cordingley, Anthony and Chiara Montini (2015) 'Genetic translation studies: an emerging discipline'. *Linguistica Antverpiensia, New Series: Themes in Translation Studies* 14, 1–18.

Corrius, Montse et al. (2016) 'Situated learning and situated knowledge: gender, translating audiovisual adverts and professional responsibility'. *The Interpreter and Translator Trainer* 10:1, 59–75.

Costa, Angela et al. (2015) 'A linguistically motivated taxonomy for machine translation error analysis'. *Machine Translation* 29:2, 127–61.

Council of Europe (2001) *Common European Framework of Reference for Languages: Learning, Teaching, Assessment.*

Council of the European Union. (1993) 'Council Directive 93/42/EEC of 14 June 1993 concerning medical devices'. *Official Journal of the European Union L* 169, 1–60.

Čulo, Oliver and Jean Nitzke (2016) 'Patterns of terminological variation in post-editing and of cognate use in machine translation in contrast to human translation'. *Baltic Journal of Modern Computing* 4:2, 106–14.

Čulo, Oliver et al. (2014) 'The influence of post-editing on translation strategies'. In *Post-Editing of Machine Translation: Processes and Applications* (O'Brien et al., eds.), 200–18.

Daems, Joke and Lieve Macken (2019) 'Interactive adaptive SMT versus interactive adaptive NMT: a user experience evaluation'. *Machine Translation* 33, 117–34.

Daems, Joke et al. (2013) 'Quality as the sum of its parts: a two-step approach for the identification of translation problems and translation quality assessment for HT and MT+PE'. In *Proceedings of MT Summit XIV Workshop on Post-editing Technology and Practice* (O'Brien et al., eds.), 63–71.

Daems, Joke et al. (2017a) 'Translationese and post-editese: how comparable is comparable quality?'. *Linguistica Antverpiensia New Series-Themes in Translation Studies* 16, 89–103.

Daems, Joke et al. (2017b) 'Identifying the machine translation error types with the greatest impact on post-editing effort'. *Frontiers in Psychology* 8, 1282.

Daems, Joke et al. (2017c) 'Translation methods and experience: a comparative analysis of human translation and post-editing with students and professional translators'. *Meta* 62:2, 245–70.

Damerau, Fred J. (1964) 'A technique for computer detection and correction of spelling errors'. *Communications of the ACM* 7:3, 171–6.

Dam-Jensen, Helle and Carmen Heine (2013) 'Writing and translation process research: bridging the gap'. *Journal of Writing Research* 5:1, 89–101.

Darity, William (2008) *International Encyclopedia of the Social Sciences*, Volume 1.

Da Silva, Igor A. Lourenço et al. (2017) 'Translation, post-editing and directionality: a study of effort in the Chinese-Portuguese language pair'. In *Translation in Transition: Between Cognition, Computing and Technology* (Jakobsen and Mesa-Lao, eds.), 108–34. Benjamins Translation Library 133.

De Almeida, Giselle (2013) 'Translating the post-editor: an investigation of post-editing changes and correlations with professional experience across two Romance languages'. PhD dissertation, Dublin City University. http://doras.dcu.ie/17732/ [consulted 12 November 2018].

De Almeida, Giselle and Sharon O'Brien (2010) 'Analysing post-editing performance: correlations with years of translation experience'. In *Proceedings of the 14th Annual Conference of the European Association for Machine Translation*.

Dede, Volkan (2019) 'Does a formal post-editing training affect the performance of novice post-editors? An experimental study'. https://doi.org/10.13140/RG.2.2.23578.08643.

Delisle, Jean, Hannelore Lee-Jahnke and Monique C. Cormier (1999) *Terminologie de la traduction / Translation terminology / Terminología de la traducción / Terminologie der Übersetzung*.

Densmer, Lee (2014) '6 Reasons to stop preferential changes from ruining your QA process'. *Moravia's Global Blog*. https://info.moravia.com/blog/bid/351122/6-Reasons-to-Stop-Preferential-Changes-from-Ruining-Your-QA-Process [consulted 24 November 2018].

Depraetere, Ilse (2010) 'What counts as useful advice in a university post-editing training context? Report on a case study'. In *EAMT 2010: Proceedings of the 14th Annual Conference of the European Association for Machine Translation*.

D'Hulst, Lieven and Yves Gambier, eds. (2019) *A History of Modern Translation Knowledge*.

DigiLing (n.d.) 'Post-editing machine translation'. https://learn.digiling.eu/.

do Carmo, Félix (2017) 'Post-editing: a theoretical and practical challenge for translation studies and machine learning'. PhD dissertation, Universidade do Porto. https://repositorio-aberto.up.pt/handle/10216/107518 [consulted 31 August 2019].

Doherty, Stephen and Dorothy Kenny (2014) 'The design and evaluation of a statistical machine translation syllabus for translation students'. *The Interpreter and Translator Trainer* 8:2, 295–315.

Doherty, Stephen et al. (2012) 'Taking statistical machine translation to the student translator'. In *Tenth Biennial Conference of the Association for Machine Translation in the Americas*.

Dörnyei, Zoltán (2007) *Research Methods in Applied Linguistics*.

Dorr, Bonnie et al. (2010) 'Part 5: machine translation evaluation'. In *Handbook of Natural Language Processing and Machine Translation* (Olive et al., eds.), 801–94.

Drugan, Joanna (2013) *Quality in Professional Translation: Assessment and Improvement*.

Dubois, Lise (1999) 'La traduction officielle au Nouveau-Brunswick: sa place et son rôle'. PhD dissertation, Université Laval. https://www.collectionscanada.gc.ca/obj/s4/f2/dsk1/tape9/PQDD_0007/NQ43065.pdf [consulted 7 September 2018].

Dunne, Keiran J. (2011) 'From vicious to virtuous cycle. Customer-focused translation quality management using ISO 9001 principles and agile methodologies'. In *Translation and Localization Project Management: The Art of the Possible* (Dunne and Dunne, eds.), 153–87.

Ehrensberger-Dow, Maureen and Andrea Hunziker Heeb (2016) 'Investigating the ergonomics of a technologized translation workplace'. In *Reembedding Translation Process Research* (Muñoz Martín, ed.), 69–88.

Ehrensberger-Dow, Maureen and Gary Massey (2014) 'Cognitive ergonomic issues in professional translation'. In *The Development of Translation Competence: Theories and Methodologies from Psycholinguistics and Cognitive Science* (Schwieter and Ferreira, eds.), 58–86.

Ehrensberger-Dow, Maureen et al., eds. (2015) *Interdisciplinarity in Translation and Interpreting Process Research.*

Ehrensberger-Dow, Maureen (2017) 'An ergonomic perspective of translation'. In *The Handbook of Translation and Cognition* (Schwieter and Ferreira, eds.), 332–34.

ELIA et al. (2019) 'Expectations and concerns of the European language industry 2019'. https://ec.europa.eu/info/sites/info/files/2019_language_industry_survey_report.pdf.

EMT Expert Group (2009) 'Competences for professional translators, experts in multilingual and multimedia communication'. https://ec.europa.eu/info/sites/info/files/emt_competences_translators_en.pdf [consulted 21 November 2018].

Ende, Anne-Kathrin et al., eds. (2013) *Alles hängt mit allem zusammen. Translatologische Interdependenzen.*

Englund Dimitrova, Birgitta (2005) *Expertise and Explicitation in the Translation Process.*

Englund Dimitrova, Birgitta (2010) 'Translation process'. In *Handbook of Translation Studies,* Volume 1 (Gambier and Van Doorslaer, eds.), 406–11.

European Commission (2018a) '2018 Language industry survey—expectations and concerns of the European language industry'. https://ec.europa.eu/info/sites/info/files/2017_language_industry_survey_report_en.pdf [consulted 5 November 2018].

European Commission (2018b) 'Medical devices—European Commission'. https://ec.europa.eu/growth/sectors/medical-devices_en [consulted 24 November 2018].

European Commission (2019a) 'List of EMT members 2019–2024'. https://ec.europa.eu/info/resources-partners/european-masters-translation-emt/list-emt-members-2019-2024_en.

European Commission (2019b) 'Medical devices—European Commission'. https://ec.europa.eu/growth/sectors/medical-devices_en [consulted 12 June 2019].

European Committee for Standardization (2006a) *EN 15038 Translation Services—Service Requirements.*

European Committee for Standardization (2006b) *EN 15038 Übersetzungs-Dienstleistungen—Dienstleistungsanforderungen.*

European Communities (2008) *The European Qualifications Framework for Lifelong Learning (EQF).*

European Master's in Translation Network (2017) 'European master's in translation competence framework 2017'. https://ec.europa.eu/info/sites/info/files/emt_competence_fwk_2017_en_web.pdf [consulted 11 November 2018].

European Parliament, Council of the European Union (2007) 'Directive 2007/47/EC of the European Parliament and of the Council of 5 September 2007 Amending Council Directive 90/385/EEC on the Approximation of the Laws of the Member States Relating to Active Implantable Medical Devices, Council Directive 93/42/EEC'. *Official Journal of the European Union, Series L* 169, 21–55.

European Union (2020) 'Countries. In About the EU'. https://europa.eu/european-union/about-eu/countries_en.

Farahzad, Farzaneh (1992) 'Testing achievement in translation classes'. In *Teaching Translation and Interpreting 2: Insights, Aims, Visions* (Dollerup and Loddegaard, eds.), 121–32.

Feinauer, Ilse and Harold M. Lesch (2013) 'Health workers: idealistic expectations versus interpreters' competence'. *Perspectives* 21:1, 117–32.

Feinauer, Ilse and Amanda Lourens (2017) 'The loyalty of the literary reviser: author, source text, target text or reader?'. *Stellenbosch Papers in Linguistics Plus* 53, 97–118.

Fernández Polo, Francisco Javier and Mario Cal Varela (2009) 'English for research purposes at the University of Santiago de Compostela: a survey'. *Journal of English for Academic Purposes* 8:3, 152–64.

Fernández-Torné, Anna (2016) 'Machine translation in audio description? Comparing creation, translation and post-editing efforts'. *SKASE Journal of Translation and Interpretation* 9:1, 64–87.

Field, Andy (2013) *Discovering Statistics Using IBM SPSS Statistics*.

Flanagan, Marian and Tina Paulsen Christensen (2014) 'Testing post-editing guidelines: how translation trainees interpret them and how to tailor them for translator training purposes'. *The Interpreter and Translator Trainer* 8:2, 257–75.

Fleck, Christian (2015) 'Attitude: history of concept'. In *International Encyclopedia of the Social & Behavioral Sciences* (Wright, ed.), 175–7.

Flowerdew, John (2001) 'Attitudes of journal editors to nonnative speaker contributions'. *TESOL Quarterly* 35:1, 121–50.

Forcada, Mikel L. and Felipe Sánchez-Martínez (2015) 'A general framework for minimizing translation effort: towards a principled combination of translation technologies in computer-aided translation'. *Proceedings of the 18th Annual Conference of the European Association for Machine Translation*, 27–34.

Fraser, Janet (1996) 'Professional versus student behaviour'. In *Teaching Translation and Interpreting 3: New Horizons* (Dollerup and Appel, eds.), 243–50.

Frérot, Cécile and Aurélie Landry (forthcoming) 'Multi-analysis of translators' work: an interdisciplinary approach by translator and ergonomics trainers'. *The Interpreter and Translator Trainer* 16.

Garcia, Ignacio (2008) 'Translating and revising for localisation: what do we know? What do we need to know?'. *Perspectives* 16:1, 49–60.

Garcia, Ignacio (2010) 'Is machine translation ready yet?'. *Target* 22:1, 7–21.

Garcia, Ignacio (2011) 'Translating by post-editing: is it the way forward?'. *Machine Translation* 25:3, 217–37.

Garcia, Ignacio (2012) 'A brief history of postediting and of research on postediting'. *New Directions in Translation Studies. Special Issue of Anglo Saxonica* 3:3, 292–310.

Gaspari, Federico et al. (2015) 'A survey of machine translation competences: insights for translation technology educators and practitioners'. *Perspectives: Studies in Translatology* 23:3, 333–58.

Germann, Ulrich (2008) 'Yawat: yet another word alignment tool'. In *Proceedings of the 46th Annual Meeting of the Association for Computational Linguistics on Human Language Technologies: Demo Session*, 20–3.

Gheorghe, A. (2019) 'Google Translate: privacy and confidentiality concerns'. www.linkedin.com/pulse/google-translate-privacy-confidentiality-concerns-alex-gheorghe.

Gile, Daniel (2004) 'Integrated problem and decision reporting as a translator training tool'. *Journal of Specialised Translation* 2, 2–20.

Gile, Daniel (2006) 'Do respondents to surveys tell the truth?'. www.est-translationstudies.org/resources/research_issues/Do respondents.htm [consulted 24 November 2018].

Ginovart, Clara (2020) 'The Professional Profile of a Post-editor according to LSCs and Linguists: a Survey-Based Research'. *HERMES-Journal of Language and Communication in Business*, 60, 171–190.

Ginovart, Clara and Antoni Oliver (2020) 'The post-editor's skill set according to industry, trainers and linguists'. In Portsiel, Jörg (ed.) *Maschinelle Übersetzung für Übersetzungsprofis*, 305–322.

Ginovart, Clara et al. (2020) 'Language industry views on the profile of the post-editor'. *Translation Spaces*. https://doi.org/10.1075/ts.19010.cid.

Giroux, Sylvain and Ginette Tremblay (2002) *Méthodologie des sciences humaines*, 2nd edition.

Giroux, Sylvain and Ginette Tremblay (2009) *Méthodologie des sciences humaines*, 3rd edition.

Google Cloud (n.d.) 'Data Usage FAQ'. In *AI and Machine Learning Products*. https://cloud.google.com/translate/data-usage.

Göpferich, Susanne (2009) 'Towards a model of translation competence and its acquisition: the longitudinal study TransComp'. In *Behind the Mind. Methods, Models and Results in Translation Process Research* (Göpferich et al., eds.), 11–37.

Gouadec, Daniel (2007) *Translation as a Profession.*

Goulet, Marie-Josée et al. (2017) 'La traduction automatique comme outil d'aide à la rédaction scientifique en anglais langue seconde: résultats d'une étude exploratoire sur la qualité linguistique'. *Anglais de Spécialité (ASp)* 72, 5–28.

Graham, Mark et al. (2011) *Geographies of the World's Knowledge.*

Green, Spence et al. (2014) 'Predictive translation memory: a mixed-initiative system for human language translation'. In *Proceedings of the 27th Annual ACM Symposium on User Interface Software and Technology (UIST '14).*

Groves, Declan and Dag Schmidtke (2009) 'Identification and analysis of post-editing patterns for MT'. In *Proceedings of MT Summit*, 429–36.

Guerberof Arenas, Ana (2008) 'Productivity and quality in the post-editing of outputs from translation memories and machine translation'. *Localisation Focus* 7:1, 11–21.

Guerberof Arenas, Ana (2013) 'What do professional translators think about post-editing'. *Journal of Specialised Translation* 19, 75–95.

Guerberof Arenas, Ana (2014a) 'Correlations between productivity and quality when post-editing in a professional context'. *Machine Translation* 28, 165–86.

Guerberof Arenas, Ana (2014b) 'The role of professional experience in post-editing from a quality and productivity perspective'. In *Post-editing of Machine Translation: Processes and Applications* (O'Brien et al., eds.), 51–76.

Guerberof Arenas, Ana (2017) 'Quality is in the eyes of the reviewer: a report on post-editing quality evaluation'. In *Translation in Transition: Between Cognition, Computing and Technology* (Jakobsen and Mesa-Lao, eds.), 188–206.

Guerberof Arenas, Ana and Joss Moorkens (2019) 'Machine translation and post- editing training as part of a master's programme'. *Journal of Specialised Translation* 31, 217–38.

Hagemann, Susanne (2019) 'Directionality in translation and revision teaching: a case study of an A-B teacher working with B-A students'. *Interpreter and Translator Trainer* 13:1, 86–101.

Halliday, M.A.K. and J.R. Martin (1993) *Writing Science: Literacy and Discursive Power.*

Hanauer, David I. and Karen Englander (2011) 'Quantifying the burden of writing research articles in a second language: data from Mexican scientists'. *Written Communication* 28:4, 403–16.

Hansen, Gyde (2006) 'Retrospection methods in translator training and translation research'. *Journal of Specialised Translation* 5, 2–41.

Hansen, Gyde (2008) 'A classification of errors in translation and revision'. In *CIUTI-Forum 2008 Enhancing Translation Quality. Ways, Means, Methods*, 313–26.

Hansen, Gyde (2009) 'The speck in your brother's eye—the beam in your own. Quality management in translation and revision'. In *Efforts and Models in Interpreting and Translation Research: A Tribute to Daniel Gile* (Hansen et al., eds.), 255–80.

Harris, Brian (2017) 'Unprofessional translation'. In *Non-professional Interpreting and Translation: State of the Art and Future of an Emerging Field of Research* (Antonini et al., eds.), 29–43.

He, Yifan et al. (2010) 'Improving the post-editing experience using translation recommendation: a user study'. In *Proceedings of the Ninth Conference of the Association for Machine Translation in the Americas*, 247–56.

Herbig, Nico et al. (2019) 'Multi-modal indicators for estimating perceived cognitive load in post-editing of machine translation'. *Machine Translation* 33:1, 91–115.

Hermans, Theo (1999) *Translation in Systems: Descriptive and System-Oriented Approaches Explained.*

Hernández-Morin, Katell (2009) 'Pratiques et perceptions de la révision en France'. *Traduire* 221, 58–78.

Hine, Jonathan (2003) 'Teaching text revision in a multilingual environment'. In *Beyond the Ivory Tower: Rethinking Translation Pedagogy* (Baer and Koby, eds.), 135–56.

Hofmann, Jennifer and Nanette Miner (2009) *Tailored Learning: Designing the Blend That Fits.*

Hokamp, Chris and Qun Liu (2015) 'Handycat: the flexible CAT tool for translation research'. In *Proceedings of the 18th Annual Conference of the European Association for Machine Translation,* 216.

Holmes, James S. (1972) 'The name and nature of translation studies'. In *Translation section of the Third International Congress of Applied Linguistics,* 66–79.

Hönig, Hans (1998) 'Positions, power and practice: functionalist approaches and translation quality assessment'. In *Translation and Quality* (Schäffner, ed.), 6–34.

Horguelin, Paul (1978) *Pratique de la révision.*

House, Juliane (2003) 'English as lingua franca and its influence on discourse norms in other languages'. In *Translation Today: Trends and Perspectives* (Anderman and Rogers, eds.), 168–179.

House, Juliane (2013) 'English as a lingua franca and translation'. In *Handbook of Translation Studies* (Gambier and van Dooerslaer, eds.), 59–62.

Hu, Ke and Patrick Cadwell (2016) 'A comparative study of post-editing guidelines'. In *Proceedings of the 19th Annual Conference of the European Association for Machine Translation, EAMT 2016,* 346–53.

Huang, Jin (2018) 'Working styles of student translators in self-revision, other-revision and post-editing'. In *Eye Tracking and Multidisciplinary Studies on Translation* (Walker and Federici, eds.), 145–84.

Huertas-Barros, Elsa and Julliet Vine, eds. (2019) *New Perspectives on Assessment in Translator Education.*

Huertas-Barros, Elsa et al., eds. (2018) *Quality Assurance and Assessment Practices in Translation and Interpreting.*

Hurtado Albir, Amparo, ed. (2017) *Researching Translation Competence by PACTE Group.*

International Organization for Standardization (2000) *ISO 1087–1 Terminology Work -Vocabulary- Part 1: Theory and Application.*

International Organization for Standardization (2002) *ISO 639–1 Codes for the Representation of Names of Languages.*

International Organization for Standardization (2012) *ISO TS 11669 Translation Projects—General Guidance.*

International Organization for Standardization (2015a) *ISO 17100 Translation Services—Requirements for Translation Services.*

International Organization for Standardization (2015b) *DIN EN ISO 17100 Übersetzungsdienstleistungen—Anforderungen an Übersetzungsdienstleistungen (ISO 17100:2015).*

International Organization for Standardization (2017) *ISO 18587 Translation Services—Post-Editing of Machine Translation Output—Requirements.*

International Organization for Standardization (2019) *ISO 30042 Management of Terminology Resources—TermBase eXchange (TBX).*

International Organization for Standardization (2020) 'Catalogue de normes'. www.iso.org/iso/fr/home/store/catalogue_tc/catalogue_tc_browse.htm?commid=654486 [consulted 6 February 2020].

Ipsen, A. Helene and Helle V. Dam (2016) 'Translation revision: correlating revision procedure and error detection'. *Hermes—Journal of Language and Communication in Business* 55, 143–56.

Jakobsen, Arnt Lykke (2002) 'Orientation, segmentation, and revision in translation'. In *Empirical Translation Studies: Process and Product* (Hansen, ed.), 191–204.

Jakobsen, Arnt Lykke (2019) 'Moving translation, revision, and post-editing boundaries'. In *Moving Boundaries in Translation Studies* (Helle V. Dam et al., eds.), 64–80.

Jia, Yanfang et al. (2019) 'How does the post-editing of neural machine translation compare with from-scratch translation? A product and process study'. *Journal of Specialised Translation* 31, 60–86.

Jiménez-Crespo, Miguel A. (2018) 'Crowdsourcing and translation quality: novel approaches in the language industry and translation studies'. In *Translation Quality Assessment* (Moorkens et al., eds.), 69–93.

Jones, Francis R. (2006) 'Unlocking the black box: researching poetry translation processes'. In *Translation and Creativity: Perspective on Creative Writing and Translation Studies* (Pertecheggla and Loffredo, eds.), 59–74.

Joscelyne, Andrew and Colin Brace (2010) *Postediting in Practice. A TAUS Report.* TAUS. http://xl8.link/TAUS2010.

Juhel, Denis (1982) *Bilinguisme et traduction au Canada. Rôle sociolinguistique du traducteur.*

KantanMT (2014) 'Post-editing machine translation'. https://kantanmtblog.com/2014/08/20/post-editing-machine-translation/.

Kao, H.S.R. (1976) 'On educational ergonomics'. *Ergonomics* 19:6, 667–81.

Karwacka, Wioleta (2015) 'Medical translation'. In *Ways to Translation* (Bogucki et al., eds.), 271–98.

Kenny, Dorothy (2018) 'Sustaining disruption? On the transition from statistical to neural machine translation'. *Tradumàtica: tecnologies de la traducció* 16, 59.

Kenny, Dorothy and Stephen Doherty (2014) 'Statistical machine translation in the translation curriculum: overcoming obstacles and empowering translators'. *Interpreter and Translator Trainer* 8:2, 276–94.

Killman, Jeffrey (2016) 'Introducing machine translation in translator training: comparing "information mining" with post-editing'. *EntreCulturas* 7:8, 179–93.

Kim, Mira (2009) 'Meaning-oriented assessment in translations'. In *Testing and Assessment in Translation and Interpreting Studies* (Angelelli and Jacobson, eds.), 123–58.

Kiraly, Don (2012) 'Growing a project-based translation pedagogy: a fractal perspective'. *Meta* 57:1, 82–95.

Kiraly, Donald, ed. (2016) *Towards Authentic Experiential Learning in Translator Education.*

Ko, Leong (2011) 'Translation checking: a view from the translation market'. *Perspectives: Studies in Translatology* 19:2, 123–34.

Kockaert, Hendrik J. and Julia Makoushina (2008) 'Zen and the art of quality assurance. Quality assurance automation in translation: needs, reality and expectations'. In *Proceedings of the Thirtieth International Conference on Translating and the Computer*, no pagination.

Kockaert, Hendrik J. et al. (2016) 'TranslationQ, EvaluationQ & RevisionQ: Automated translation process with real-time feedback & evaluation/revision with Preselected Items Evaluation (PIE)'. Workshop at the Translating Europe Workshop, Brussels, February, 5.

Koehn, Philipp (2009) 'A process study of computer-aided translation' machine translation'. *Machine Translation* 23:4, 241–63.

Koehn, Philipp et al. (2015) 'Final report on interactive editing'. https://cordis.europa.eu/docs/projects/cnect/6/287576/080/deliverables/001-deliverable33Ares20152495853.pdf [consulted 31 August 2019].

Koglin, Arlene and Rossana Cunha (2019) 'Investigating the post-editing effort associated with machine-translated metaphors: a process-driven analysis'. *Journal of Specialised Translation* 31, 38–59.

Kolb, Waltraud (2013) 'Who are they? Decision-making in literary translation'. In *Tracks and Treks in Translation Studies* (Way et al., eds.), 207–21.

Konttinen, Kalle et al. (2017) 'Multilingual translation workshop—developing professionals in a simulated translation market'. *MikaEL—Electronic Journal of the KäTu Symposium on Translation and Interpreting Studies* 10, 150–64.

Koponen, Maarit (2012) 'Comparing human perceptions of post-editing effort with post-editing operations'. In *7th Workshop on Statistical Machine Translation*, 181–90.

Koponen, Maarit (2013) 'This translation is not too bad: an analysis of post-editor choices in a machine translation post-editing task'. In *Proceedings of MT Summit XIV Workshop on Post-Editing Technology and Practice* (O'Brien et al., eds.), 1–9.

Koponen, Maarit (2015) 'How to teach machine translation post-editing? Experiences from a post-editing course'. In *Proceedings of the 4th Workshop on Post-Editing Technology and Practice (WPTP4)*, 2–15.

Koponen, Maarit (2016) 'Is machine translation post-editing worth the effort? A survey of research into post-editing and effort'. *Journal of Specialised Translation* 25, 131–48.

Koponen, Maarit (2018) 'Learning to post-edit: an analysis of post-editing quality and processes of translation students'. *Presentation at International Association for Translation and Intercultural Studies (IATIS) 6th International Conference*, Hong Kong, 5 July 2018.

Koponen, Maarit and Leena Salmi (2015) 'On the correctness of machine translation: a machine translation post-editing task'. *Journal of Specialised Translation* 23, 118–36.

Koponen, Maarit et al. (2012) 'Post-editing time as a measure of cognitive effort'. In *Proceedings of the AMTA 2012 Workshop on Post-Editing Technology and Practice*, 11–20.

Koponen, Maarit et al. (2019) 'A product and process analysis of post-editor corrections on neural, statistical and rule-based machine translation output'. *Machine Translation* 33:1, 61–90.

Koskinen, Kaisa (2008) *Translating Institutions. An Ethnographic Study of EU Translation.*

Krings, Hans P. (2001) *Repairing Texts: Empirical Investigations of Machine Translation Post-Editing Processes* (Koby, ed.).

Künzli, Alexander (2005) 'What principles guide translation revision? A combined product and process study'. In *Translation Norms: What Is 'Normal' in the Translation Profession? Proceedings of the Conference Held on 13th November 2004 in Portsmouth* (Kemble, ed.), 31–43.

Künzli, Alexander (2006a) 'Die Loyalitätsbeziehungen der Übersetzungsrevisorin'. In *Übersetzen—Translating—Traduire: Towards a "social turn"?* (Wolf, ed.), 89–98.

Künzli, Alexander (2006b) 'Teaching and learning translation revision: some suggestions based on evidence from a think-aloud protocol study'. In *Current Trends in Translation Teaching and Learning* (Garant, ed.), 9–23.

Künzli, Alexander (2006c) 'Translation revision—a study of the performance of ten professional translators revising a technical text'. In *Insights into Specialized Translation* (Gotti and Šarčević, eds.), 195–214.

Künzli, Alexander (2007a) 'The ethical dimension of translation revision. An empirical study'. *Journal of Specialised Translation* 8.

Künzli, Alexander (2007b) 'Translation revision. A study of the performance of ten professional translators revising a legal text'. In *Doubts and Directions in Translation Studies, Selected Contributions from the EST Congress, Lisbon 2004* (Gambier et al., eds.), 115–26.

Künzli, Alexander (2009) 'Qualität in der Übersetzungsrevision—eine empirische Studie'. In *Translation zwischen Text und Welt: Translationswissenschaft als historische Disziplin zwischen Moderne und Zukunft* (Kalverkämper and Schippel, eds.), 291–303.

Künzli, Alexander (2014) 'Die Übersetzungsrevision—Begriffsklärungen, Forschungsstand, Forschungsdesiderate'. *Trans-kom* 7:1, 1–29.

Kuo, Szu-Yu (2014) 'Quality in subtitling: theory and professional reality'. PhD dissertation, Imperial College London.

Kurz, Christopher (2016) *Translatorisches Qualitätsmanagement: Eine Untersuchung der Übersetzungsdienstleistungsnormen DIN EN ISO 17100 und DIN EN 15038 aus übersetzungspraktischer Sicht.* tekom-Hochschulschriften, Band 24. Stuttgart: tekom.

Kuznetsova, Alexandra et al. (2017) 'lmerTest package: tests in linear mixed effects models'. *Journal of Statistical Software* 82:13, 1–26.

Lacruz, Isabel (2018) 'An experimental investigation of stages of processing in post-editing'. In *Innovation and Expansion in Translation Process Research* (Lacruz and Jääskeläinen, eds.), 217–40. American Translators Association Scholarly Monograph Series 18.

Lacruz, Isabel, and Gregory M. Shreve (2014) 'Pauses and cognitive effort in post-editing'. In *Post-Editing of Machine Translation: Processes and Applications* (O'Brien et al., eds.), 246–72.

Lafeber, Anne (2012) 'Translation skills and knowledge—preliminary findings of a survey of translators and revisers working at inter-governmental organizations'. *Meta* 57:1, 108–31.

Lafeber, Anne (2017) 'The skills required to achieve quality in institutional translation: the views of EU and UN translators and revisers'. In *Institutional Translation for International Governance: Enhancing Quality in Multilingual Legal Communication* (Ramos, ed.), 63–80.

Laflamme, Caroline (2009) 'Les modifications lexicales apportées par les réviseurs professionnels dans leur tâche de révision: du problème à la solution'. PhD dissertation, Université Laval, Québec, Canada. http://hdl.handle.net/20.500.11794/20833 [consulted 7 November 2018].

Lagoudaki, Elina (2008) 'Expanding the possibilities of translation memory systems: From the translator's wishlist to the developer's design'. Unpublished PhD dissertation. Imperial College London.

Läubli, Samuel et al. (2013) 'Assessing post-editing efficiency in a realistic translation environment'. In *MT Summit XIV Workshop on Post-Editing Technology and Practice*, 83–91.

Lauscher, Susanne (2000) 'Translation quality assessment: where can theory and practice meet?'. *The Translator* 6:2, 149–68.

Lavault-Olléon, Elisabeth (2011) 'L'ergonomie, nouveau paradigme pour la traductologie'. *ILCEA* 14, 1–16.

Lavault-Olléon, Elisabeth (2016) 'Traducteurs à l'oeuvre: une perspective ergonomique en traductologie appliquée'. *ILCEA* 27, 1–9.

Lawson, Tony, and Joan Garrod, eds. (2001) *Dictionary of Sociology.*

LeBlanc, Matthieu (2013) 'Translators on Translation Memory (TM). Results of an ethnographic study in three translation services and agencies'. *The International Journal for Translation and Interpreting Research* 5:2, 1–13.

LeBlanc, Matthieu (2014) 'Language of work in the federal public service: what is the situation today?'. In *Fifty Years of Official Bilingualism: Challenges, Analyses and Testimonies* (Clément and Foucher, eds.), 69–76.

Lee, Hyang (2006) 'Révision: définitions et paramètres'. *Meta* 51:2, 410–19.

Lemaire, Nathalie (2018) 'Écrire, traduire, réviser les textes expographiques: vers une assurance qualité à six mains'. *Forum. Revue internationale d'interprétation et de traduction/International Journal of Interpretation and Translation* 16:1, 76–102.

Lesch, Harold Michael and Bernice Saulse (2014) 'Revisiting the interpreting service in the healthcare sector: a descriptive overview'. *Perspectives: Studies in Translatology* 22:3, 332–48.

Levenshtein, Vladimir I. (1966) 'Binary codes capable of correcting deletions, insertions and reversals'. *Soviet Physics Doklady* 10:8, 707–10.

Li, Shuangyu et al. (2017) 'Interaction—a missing piece of the jigsaw in interpreter-mediated medical consultation models'. *Patient Education and Counseling* 100:9, 1769–71.

Llitjós, Ariadna F. et al. (2005) 'A framework for interactive and automatic refinement of transfer-based machine translation'. In *Proceedings of the EAMT Conference 2005*, 87–96.

Lommel, Arle (2018) 'Where's my translation jet pack?'. In *Proceedings of Translating and the Computer 40*.

Lommel, Arle and Donald Depalma (2016) 'Europe's leading role in machine translation—how Europe is driving the shift to MT'. http://cracker-project.eu/wp-content/uploads/Europes_Leading_Role_in_MT.pdf [consulted 31 August 2019].

Lommel, Arle et al. (2014) 'Multidimensional Quality Metrics (MQM): a framework for declaring and describing translation quality metrics'. *Revista Tradumàtica* 12, 455–63.

López-Navarro, Irene et al. (2015) 'Why do I publish research articles in English instead of my own language? Differences in Spanish researchers' motivations across scientific domains'. *Scientometrics* 103, 939–76.

Lorenzo, María Pilar (2002) 'Competencia revisora y traducción inversa'. *Cadernos de tradução* 2:10, 133–66.

LRQA (Lloyd's Register Quality Assurance) (2016) 'Ablauf einer Zertifizierung'. www.lrqa.de/unsere-services/zertifizierung/ablauf-einer-zertifizierung/ [consulted 29 December 2018].

Lüdecke, Daniel (2018) 'sjPlot: Data Visualization for Statistics in Social Science'. https://doi.org/10.5281/zenodo.1308157, R package version 2.6.2, https://CRAN.R-project.org/package=sjPlot.

Macken, Lieve et al. (2011) 'Dutch Parallel Corpus: a balanced copyright-cleared Parallel Corpus'. *Meta* 56:2, 374–90.

Magris, Marella (1999) 'Il processo della revisione e la qualità del testo finale: alcune riflessioni basate su un manuale di infermieristica'. *Rivista internazionale di tecnica della traduzione* 4, 133–56.

Maier, Beate and Isabel Schwagereit (2016) 'Ein Jahr ISO 17100—lohnt sich die Zertifizierung?'. *Forum ATICOM* 2, 13–19.

Major, George and Jemina Napier (2012) 'Interpreting and knowledge mediation in the healthcare setting: what do we really mean by "accuracy"?' *Linguistica Antverpiensia* 11, 207–25.

Marashi, Hamid and Mehrnaz Okhowat (2013) 'The comparative impact of editing texts translated into Farsi with and without the original English texts'. *Perspectives: Studies in Translatology* 21:3, 299–310.

Marin-Lacarta, Maialen and Mireia Vargas-Urpi (2019) 'Translators revising translators: a fruitful alliance'. *Perspectives: Studies in Translation Theory and Practice* 27:3, 404–18.

Marshall, Gordon, ed. (2003) *Oxford Dictionary of Sociology*.

Martin, Charles (2012) 'The dark side of translation revision'. *Translation Journal* 16:1.

Martín, Pedro et al. (2014) 'Publishing research in English-language journals: attitudes, strategies and difficulties of multilingual scholars of medicine'. *Journal of English for Academic Purposes* 16, 57–67.

Martin, Tim (2007) 'Managing risks and resources: a down-to-earth view of revision'. *Journal of Specialised Translation* 8, 57–63.

Massardo, Isabella et al. (2016) 'TAUS MT post-editing guidelines'. Amsterdam. www.taus.net/think-tank/articles/postedit-articles/taus-post-editing-guidelines.

Massey, Gary (2016) 'Incorporating ergonomics into the translation curriculum: why, where and how'. *Paper Presented at the 8th EST Congress*, Aarhus.

Massey, Gary (2017) 'Translation competence development and process-oriented pedagogy'. In *The Handbook of Translation and Cognition* (Schwieter and Ferreira, eds.), 496–518.

Massey, Gary et al. (2019) 'Training the translator trainers: an introduction'. *Interpreter and Translator Trainer* 13:3, 211–15.

Matthews, Bob and Liz Ross (2010) *Research Methods: A Practical Guide for the Social Sciences*.

McDonough Dolmaya, Julie (2015) 'Revision history: translation trends in Wikipedia'. *Translation Studies* 8:1, 16–34.

McElhaney, Terrence and Muriel Vasconcellos (1988) 'The translator and the postediting experience'. *Technology as Translation Strategy* (Vasconcellos, ed.), 140–8.

Mellinger, Christopher D. (2017) 'Translators and machine translation: knowledge and skills gaps in translator pedagogy'. *The Interpreter and Translator Trainer* 11:4, 280–93.

Mellinger, Christopher D. (2018) 'Re-thinking translation quality. Revision in the digital age'. *Target* 30:2, 310–31.

Mellinger, Christopher D., and Gregory M. Shreve (2016) 'Match evaluation and over-editing in a translation memory environment'. In *Reembedding Translation Process Research* (Muñoz Martín, ed.), 131–48.

Mendoza Garcia, Inmaculada and Nuria Ponce Márquez (2013) 'The relevance of the reviewer's role: a methodological proposal for the development of the translation competence'. *Skopos* 2, 87–110.

Mertin, Elvira (2006) *Prozessorientiertes Qualitätsmanagement im Dienstleistungsbereich Übersetzen*.

Mitchell, Linda (2015) 'The potential and limits of lay post-editing in an online community'. In *Proceedings of the 18th Annual Conference of the European Association for Machine Translation*, 67–74.

Mitchell, Linda et al. (2014) 'Quality evaluation in community post-editing'. *Machine Translation* 28:3–4, 237–62.

Montalt, Vicent (2011) 'Medical translation and interpreting'. In *Handbook of Translation Studies Online* (Gambier and van Doorslaer, eds.).

Moorkens, Joss (2018a) 'Eye tracking as a measure of cognitive effort for post-editing of machine translation'. In *Eye Tracking and Multidisciplinary Studies on Translation* (Walker and Federici, eds.), 55–69. Benjamins Translation Library 143.

Moorkens, Joss (2018b) 'What to expect from neural machine translation: a practical in-class translation evaluation exercise'. *Interpreter and Translator Trainer* 12:4, 375–87.

Moorkens, Joss and Sharon O'Brien (2017) 'Assessing user interface needs of post-editors of machine translation'. In *Human Issues in Translation Technology: The IATIS Yearbook* (Kenny, ed.), 109–30.

Moorkens, Joss and Ryoko Sasamoto (2017) 'Productivity and lexical pragmatic features in a contemporary cat environment: an exploratory study in English to Japanese'. *Hermes— Journal of Language and Communication in Business* 56, 111–23.

Moorkens, Joss and Andy Way (2016) 'Comparing translator acceptability of TM and SMT outputs'. *Baltic Journal of Modern Computing* 4:2, 141–51.

Moorkens, Joss et al. (2016) 'Developing and testing Kanjingo: a mobile app for post-editing'. *Tradumàtica: Tecnologies de la traducció* 14, 58–66.

Moorkens, Joss et al., eds. (2018) *Translation Quality Assessment: From Principles to Practice*.

Morin-Hernández, Katell (2009) 'La révision comme clé de la gestion de la qualité des traductions en contexte professionnel'. PhD dissertation, University of Rennes. http://tel. archives-ouvertes.fr/docs/00/38/32/66/PDF/TheseMorinHernandez.pdf [consulted 29 December 2018].

Mossop, Brian (1982) 'A procedure for self-revision'. *Terminology Update* 15:3, 6.

Mossop, Brian (1990) 'Translating institutions and "idiomatic" translation'. *Meta* 35:2, 342–55.

Mossop, Brian (1992) 'Goals of a revision course'. In *Teaching Translation and Interpreting: Training, Talent, and Experience* (Dollerup and Loddegaard, eds.), 81–90.

Mossop, Brian (2001) *Revising and Editing for Translators*.

Mossop, Brian (2006) 'Has computerization changed translation?'. *Meta* 51:4, 787–93.

Mossop, Brian (2007a) 'Empirical studies of revision: what we know and need to know'. *Journal of Specialised Translation* 8, 5–20.

Mossop, Brian (2007b) *Revising and Editing for Translators*, 2nd edition.

Mossop, Brian (2011) 'Revision'. In *Handbook of Translation Studies, Volume 2* (Gambier and Van Doorslaer, eds.), 135–39.

Mossop, Brian (2014a) *Revising and Editing for Translators*, 3rd edition.

Mossop, Brian (2014b) *Revising and Editing for Translators. Translation Practices Explained, 1* Online Resource, 244.

Mossop, Brian (2020) *Revising and Editing for Translators*, 4th edition.

Munday, Jeremy (2012) *Evaluation in Translation: Critical Points of Translator Evaluation-making.*

Nakanishi, Chiharu (2007) 'The effects of different types of feedback on revision'. *The Journal of Asia TEFL* 4:4, 213–44.

Navarro, Ignasi (2012) 'La postedició de continguts en publicacions diàries'. *Tradumàtica* 10, 185–91.

Neather, Robert (2012) '"Non-expert" translators in a professional community'. *The Translator* 18:2, 245–68.

Nida, Eugene Albert (1964) *Toward a Science of Translating.*

Niño, Ana (2008) 'Evaluating the use of machine translation post-editing in the foreign language class'. *Computer Assisted Language Learning* 21:1, 29–49.

Nitzke, Jean (2019) *Problem Solving Activities in Post-editing and Translation from Scratch: A Multi-method Study.*

Nitzke, Jean and Katharina Oster (2016) 'Comparing translation and post-editing: an annotation schema for activity units'. In *New Directions in Empirical Translation Process Research* (Carl et al., eds.), 293–308.

Nitzke, Jean et al. (2019) 'Risk management and post-editing competence'. *Journal of Specialised Translation* 31, 239–59.

Nord, Britta (2018) 'Die Überzetzungsrevision—ein Werkstattbericht'. *Trans-kom* 11:1, 138–50.

Nord, Christiane (1997) *Translating as a Purposeful Activity: Functionalist Approaches Explained.*

Nord, Christiane (2005) *Text Analysis in Translation: Theory, Methodology, and Didactic Application of a Model for Translation-oriented Text Analysis.*

Notaristefano, Maristella (2010) 'La revisione di una traduzione specializzata: interventi e profilo del revisore'. *Rivista internazionale di tecnica della traduzione* 12, 215–25.

O'Brien, Sharon (2002) 'Teaching post-editing: a proposal for course content'. In *Proceedings of the 6th EAMT Workshop Teaching Machine Translation*, 99–106.

O'Brien, Sharon (2005) 'Methodologies for measuring the correlations between post-editing effort and machine translatability'. *Machine Translation* 19:1, 37–58.

O'Brien, Sharon (2008) 'Processing fuzzy matches in translation memory tools: an eye tracking analysis'. In *Looking at Eyes: Eye-Tracking Studies of Reading and Translation Processing* (Göpferich et al., eds.), 79–102.

O'Brien, Sharon (2010) 'Introduction to post-editing: who, what, how and where to next?'. In *The Ninth Conference of the Association for Machine Translation in the Americas.*

O'Brien, Sharon (2012) 'Translation as human computer interaction'. *Translation Spaces* 1:1, 101–22.

O'Brien, Sharon et al. (2011) 'Translation quality evaluation framework'. www.taus.net/component/rsfiles/download?path=Reports%252FFree%2BReports%252Ftausdynamic quality.pdf.

O'Brien, Sharon et al. (2014) 'Kanjingo: a mobile app for post-editing'. In *Third Workshop on Post-Editing Technology and Practice*, 125.

O'Brien, Sharon et al. (2017) 'Irritating CAT tool features that matter to translators'. *Hermes: Journal of Language and Communication in Business* 56, 145–62.

O'Brien, Sharon et al. (2018) 'Machine translation and self-post-editing for academic writing support: quality explorations'. In *Translation Quality Assessment: From Principles to Practice* (Moorkens et al., eds.), 237–62.

O'Brien, Tim and Dennis Guiney (2018) *Staff Wellbeing in Higher Education: A Research Study for Education Support Partnership.*

O'Curran, Elaine (2014) 'Machine translation and post-editing for user generated content: an LSP perspective'. In *Proceedings of the 11th Conference of the Association for Machine Translation in the Americas, Vol. 2: MT Users Track*, 50–4.

Olohan, Maeve (2011) 'Translators and translation technology: the dance of agency'. *Translation Studies* 4:3, 342–57.

Omer, Ahmad A. and Mohamed E. Abdulahrim (2017) 'The criteria of constructive feedback: the feedback that counts'. *Journal of Health Specialties* 5, 45–8.

Ortiz-Boix, Carla and Anna Matamala (2017) 'Assessing the quality of post-edited wildlife documentaries'. *Perspectives: Studies in Translatology* 25:4, 571–93.

Ortiz-Martínez, Daniel et al. (2016) 'Integrating online and active learning in a computer-assisted translation workbench'. In *New Directions in Empirical Translation Process Research* (Carl et al., eds.), 57–76.

Oster, Katharina (2017) 'The influence of self-monitoring on the translation of cognates'. In *Empirical Modelling of Translation and Interpreting* (Hansen-Schirra et al., eds.), 23–39.

Ottmann, Angelika, ed. (2017) *Best practices—Übersetzen und Dolmetschen Ein Nachschlagewerk aus der Praxis für Sprachmittler und Auftraggeber.*

Parra Escartín, Carla et al. (2017) 'Machine translation as an academic writing aid for medical practitioners'. In *Proceedings of the MT Summit XVI, vol 1: Research Track*, 254–67.

Parra-Galiano, Silvia (2001) 'La revisión de traducciones en la didáctica de la traducción: cara y cruz de una misma moneda'. *Sendebar* 12, 373–86.

Parra-Galiano, Silvia (2006) 'La revisión y otros procedimientos para el aseguramiento de la calidad de la traducción en el ámbito profesional'. *Turjuman* 15:2, 11–48.

Parra-Galiano, Silvia (2007a) 'La revisión como procedimiento para el aseguramiento de la calidad de la traducción: grados, tipos y modalidades de revisión'. *SENEZ* 32, 97–122.

Parra-Galiano, Silvia (2007b) 'Propuesta metodológica para la revisión de traducciones: principios generales y parámetros'. *TRANS* 11, 197–214.

Parra-Galiano, Silvia (2011) 'La revisión en la norma europea EN-150038 para "servicios de traducción"'. *Entreculturas: revista de traducción y comunicación intercultural* 3, 165–87.

Parra-Galiano, Silvia (2015) 'El conocimiento experto (pericia) en la revisión de traducciones: clave en la gestión y propuestas de investigación'. In *VI Congreso Internacional sobre Traducción e Interpretación organizado por la Asociación Ibérica de Estudios de Traducción e Interpretación (AIETI), celebrado en la Universidad de Las Palmas de Gran Canaria, 23–25 de enero de 2013.* (Extremera, ed.), 587–603.

Parra-Galiano, Silvia (2016) 'Translations revision: fundamental methodological aspects and effectiveness of the EN 15038:2006 for translation quality assurance'. In *Interchange between Languages and Cultures: The Quest for Quality* (Zehnalova et al., eds.), 39–52.

Parra-Galiano, Silvia (2017) 'Conceptos teóricos fundamentales en la revisión de traducciones y su reflejo en el Manual de revisión de la DGT y en las normas ISO 17100:2015 y EN 15038:2006'. *Hermeneus: Revista de la Facultad de Traducción e Interpretación de Soria* 19, 270–308.

Pérez-González, Luis and Şebnem Susam-Saraeva (2012) 'Non-professionals translating and interpreting. participatory and engaged perspectives'. *The Translator* 18:2, 149–65.

Pergnier, Maurice (1990) 'Comment dénaturer une traduction'. *Meta* 35:1, 219–25.

Peters-Geiben, Lucia (2016) 'La prévention comportementale et contextuelle: intégrer une approche ergonomique dans la formation des traducteurs'. *ILCEA* 27, 1–22.

Pietrzak, Paulina (2014) 'Towards effective feedback to translation students'. *inTRAlinea Special Issue: Challenges in Translation Pedagogy*, 1–9.

Piller, Ingrid (2015) 'Language ideologies'. In *The International Encyclopedia of Language and Social Interaction* (Tracy et al., eds.), 1–10.

Plaza Lara, Cristina (2019) 'SWOT analysis of the inclusion of machine translation and post-editing in the master's degrees offered in the EMT network'. *Journal of Specialised Translation* 31, 260–80.

Plitt, Mirko, and François Masselot (2010) 'A productivity test of statistical machine translation post-editing in a typical localisation context'. *The Prague Bulletin of Mathematical Linguistics* 93, 7–16.

Pontrandolfo, Gianluca (2017) 'La revisión de traducciones jurídicas y la evaluación de su calidad en el ámbito profesional: un estudio empírico'. In *Between Specialised Texts and Institutional Contexts—Competence and Choice in Legal Translation* (Dullion, ed.), 114–44.

Popič, Damjan (2014) 'Revising translation revision in Slovenia'. In *New Horizons in Translation Research and Education 2* (Mikolič Južnič et al., eds.), 72–89.

Popović, Maja et al. (2014) 'Relations between different types of post-editing operations, cognitive effort and temporal effort'. In *Proceedings of the 17th Annual Conference of the European Association for Machine Translation, EAMT 2014*, 191–8.

Porro Rodríguez, Victoria et al. (2017) 'Study on the use of machine translation and post-editing in Swiss-based language service providers'. *Parallèles* 29:2, 19–35.

Prioux, René and Michel Rochard (2007) 'Economie de la révision dans une organisation internationale: le cas de l'OCDE'. *Journal of Specialised Translation* 8, 21–41.

Province of New Brunswick (2013) *2012–2013 Annual Report: Office of the Commissioner of Official Languages.*

Province of New Brunswick (2015a) 'Official languages. Language of work policy and guidelines'. Finance and Treasury Board. https://www2.gnb.ca/content/gnb/en/departments/finance/human_resources/content/policies_and_guidelines/language_work.html [consulted 4 January 2020].

Province of New Brunswick (2015b) 'Official languages. Language of service policy guidelines'. Finance and Treasury Board. www.welcomenb.ca/content/gnb/en/departments/finance/human_resources/content/policies_and_guidelines/language_service.html [consulted 4 January 2020].

Pym, Anthony (1992) 'Translation error analysis and the interface with language teaching'. In *Teaching Translation and Interpreting: Training, Talent and Experience* (Dollerup and Loddegaard, eds.), 279–88.

Pym, Anthony (2011a) 'Translation research terms: a tentative glossary for moments of perplexity and dispute'. *Translation Research Projects* 3:3, 75–99.

Pym, Anthony (2011b) 'What technology does to translating'. *Translation and Interpreting* 3:1, 1–9.

Pym, Anthony (2011c) 'Training translators'. In *The Oxford Handbook of Translation Studies* (Malmkjær and Windle, eds.).

Pym, Anthony (2013) 'Translation skill-sets in a machine-translation age'. *Meta* 58:3, 487–503.

Pym, Anthony (2019a) *How Automation Through Neural Machine Translation Might Change the Skill Sets of Translators.* Pre-print on Academia.edu xl8.link/Pym2019.

Pym, Anthony (2019b) 'Quality'. In *Routledge Handbook of Translation and Technology* (O'Hagan, ed.), 437–52.

Rabadán, Rosa (2010) 'Applied translations studies'. In *Handbook of Translation Studies—Volume I* (Gambier and van Doorslaer, eds.).

Rasmussen, Kirsten W. and Anne Schjoldager (2011) 'Revising translations: a survey of revision policies in Danish translation companies'. *Journal of Specialised Translation* 15, 87–120.

Rega, Lorenza (1999) 'Alcune considerazioni sul problema della revisione nell'ambito della traduzione'. *Rivista internazionale di tecnica della traduzione* 4, 115–31.

Rico, Celia (2017) 'Training translators in machine translation'. *Tradumàtica: Tecnologies de la Traducció* 15, 75.

Rico, Celia and Enrique Torrejón (2012) 'Skills and profile of the new role of the translator as MT post-editor'. *Revista Tradumática* 10, 166–78.

Rico, Celia et al. (2017) 'The challenge of machine translation post-editing: an academic perspective'. In *Trends in E-Tools and Resources for Translators and Interpreters* (Corpas Pastor and Durán-Muñoz, eds.), 203–18. Approaches to Translation Studies 45.

Rigouts Terryn, Ayla et al. (2017) 'Conceptualizing translation revision competence: a pilot study on the acquisition of the "knowledge about revision" and "strategic" subcompetences'. *Across Languages and Cultures* 18:1, 1–27.

Rike, Sissel (2013) 'Bilingual corporate websites—from translation to transcreation?'. *Journal of Specialised Translation* 20, 68–84.

Risku, Hanna et al. (2016) 'Writing vs. translating. Dimensions of text production in comparison'. In *Reembedding Translation Process Research* (Muñoz Martín, ed.), 47–68.

Risku, Hanna et al. (2017) 'Transcreation as a translation service: process requirements and client expectations'. *Across Languages and Cultures* 18:1, 53–77.

Robert, Anne-Marie (2013) 'Vous Avez Dit Post-Éditrice? Quelques Éléments d'un Parcours Personnel'. *Journal of Specialised Translation* 19, 29–40.

Robert, Isabelle S. (2008) 'Translation revision procedures: an explorative study'. In *Translation and Its Others: Selected Papers of the CETRA Research Seminar in Translation Studies 2007* (Boulogne, ed.). www.arts.kuleuven.be/cetra/papers/files/robert.pdf [consulted 31 January 2020].

Robert, Isabelle S. (2012) 'La révision en traduction: les procédures de révision et leur impact sur le produit et le processus de révision'. PhD dissertation, University of Antwerp.

Robert, Isabelle S. (2013) 'Translation revision: does the revision procedure matter?'. In *Treks and Tracks in Translation Studies* (Bartlomiejczyk et al., eds.), 87–102.

Robert, Isabelle S. (2014a) 'Investigating the problem-solving strategies of revisers through triangulation: an exploratory study'. *Translation and Interpreting Studies* 9:1, 88–108.

Robert, Isabelle S. (2014b) 'La relecture unilingue: une procédure de révision de traduction rapide, fonctionnelle, mais déloyale'. *TTR: traduction, terminologie, rédaction* 27:1, 95–122.

Robert, Isabelle S. (2018) 'La recherche en révision: portrait bibliométrique, questions de recherche et méthodologies'. *Parallèles* 30:2, 129–52.

Robert, Isabelle S. and Louise Brunette (2016) 'Should revision trainees think aloud while revising somebody else's translation? Insights from an empirical study with professionals'. *Meta* 61:2, 320–45.

Robert, Isabelle S. and Aline Remael (2016) 'Quality control in the subtitling industry: an exploratory survey study'. *Meta* 61:3, 578–605.

Robert, Isabelle S. and Luuk Van Waes (2014) 'Selecting a translation revision procedure: do common sense and statistics agree?'. *Perspectives: Studies in Translatology* 22:3, 304–20.

Robert, Isabelle S. et al. (2017a) 'Towards a model of translation revision competence'. *The Interpreter and Translator Trainer* 11:1, 1–19.

Robert, Isabelle S. et al. (2017b) 'Conceptualizing translation revision competence: a pilot study on the "tools and research" subcompetence'. *Journal of Specialised Translation* 28, 293–316.

Robert, Isabelle S. et al. (2018) 'Conceptualizing translation revision competence: a pilot study on the "fairness and tolerance" attitudinal component'. *Perspectives: Studies in Translatology* 26:1, 2–23.

Robin, Edina (2014) 'Explicitation and implicitation in revised translations'. In *Complex Visibles Out There: Proceedings of the 2014 Olomouc Linguistic Colloquium* (Veselovská, ed.), 559–74.

Robin, Edina (2018) 'The classification of revisional modifications'. In *Latest Trends in Hungarian Translation Studies* (Horváth, ed.), 155–63.

Robin, Edina (2019) 'The modification of translation universals in revised texts'. In *Getting Translated* (Sohár et al., eds.), 125–47.

Rochard, Michel (2004) 'La réviseur: Achille ou Mentor ?'. *Traduire* 203, 59–69.

Rodríguez Rodríguez, Beatriz María (2012) 'El enfoque constructivista en el aprendizaje de las competencias de revisión de traducciones'. *Entreculturas* 4, 15–38.

Rokeach, Milton (1968) *Beliefs, Attitudes and Values: A Theory of Organization and Change.*

Rossi, Caroline (2017) 'Introducing statistical machine translation in translator training: from uses and perceptions to course design, and back again'. *Revista Tradumàtica* 15, 48–62.

Rossi, Caroline and Jean-Pierre Chevrot (2019) 'Uses and perceptions of machine translation at the European Commission'. *Journal of Specialised Translation* 31, 177–200.

Sager, Juan (1993) *Language Engineering and Translation: Consequences of Automation.*

Şahin, Mehmet (2011) 'Using MT post-editing for translator training'. In *Proceedings of Tralogy II.* http://xl8.link/Sahin2011.

Sakamoto, Akiko (2019) 'Why do many translators resist post-editing? A sociological analysis using Bourdieu's concepts'. *Journal of Specialised Translation* 31, 201–16.

Saldanha, Gabriela and Sharon O'Brien (2013) *Research Methodologies in Translation Studies*, iBook edition.

Saldanha, Gabriela and Sharon O'Brien (2014) *Research Methodologies in Translation Studies.*

Sánchez-Gijón, Pilar (2016) 'La posedición: hacia una definición competencial del perfil y una descripción multidimensional del fenómeno'. *Sendebar* 27, 151–62.

Sánchez-Gijón, Pilar et al. (2019) 'Post-editing neural machine translation versus translation memory segments'. *Machine Translation* 33:1–2, 31–59.

Sanchis-Trilles, Germán et al. (2014) 'Interactive translation prediction versus conventional post-editing in practice: a study with the CasMaCat workbench' *Machine Translation* 28:3–4, 217–35.

Scapin, Dominique et al. (2000) 'A framework for organizing web usability guidelines'. In *Proceedings of the Sixth Conference on Human Factors and the Web.*

Schaeffer, Moritz et al. (2019a) 'Eye-tracking revision processes of translation students and professional translators'. *Perspectives-Studies in Translation Theory and Practice* 27:4, 589–603.

Schaeffer, Moritz et al. (2019b) 'Cognitive effort and efficiency in translation revision'. In *Quality Assurance and Assessment Practices in Translation and Interpreting* (Huertas-Barros et al., eds.), 226–43.

Schjoldager, Anne et al. (2008) 'Précis-writing, revision and editing: piloting the European Master in Translation'. *Meta* 53:4, 798–813.

Schmitz, Klaus-Dirk, ed. (2017) *Normen für Übersetzer und Technische Redakteure.*

Schneider, Richard (2012) 'UEPO TÜV SÜD stellt Zertifizierung von Übersetzungsbüros nach DIN EN 15038 ein'. https://uepo.de/2012/09/28/tuv-sud-stellt-zertifizierung-von-ubersetzungsburos-nach-din-en-15038-ein/ [consulted 29 December 2018].

Schnierer, Madeleine (2019) *Qualitätssicherung. Die Praxis der Übersetzungsrevision im Zusammenhang mit EN 15038 und ISO 17100.*

Schopp, Jürgen (2007) 'Korrekturlesen—ein translatorisches Stiefkind?'. *Lebende Sprachen* 52:2, 69–74.

Schwartz, Lane (2014) 'Monolingual post-editing by a domain expert is highly effective for translation triage'. In *Proceedings of the Third Workshop on Post-editing Technology and Practice (WPTP-3)*, 34–44.

Schwieter, John W. and Aline Ferreira, eds. (2017) *The Handbook of Translation and Cognition*.

Scocchera, Giovanna (2013) 'What we talk about when we talk about revision: a critical overview on terminology, professional practices and training, and the case of literary translation revision in Italy'. *Forum: International Journal of Interpretation and Translation* 11:2, 141–74.

Scocchera, Giovanna (2014) 'What kind of training for literary translation revisers?'. *inTRAlinea Special Issue: Challenges in Translation Pedagogy*. http://www.intralinea.org/specials/article/what_kind_of_training_for_literary_translation_revisers [consulted 6 September 2018].

Scocchera, Giovanna (2015) 'Computer-based collaborative revision as a virtual lab of editorial/literary translation genetics'. *Linguistica Antverpiensia, New Series: Themes in Translation Studies* 14, 168–99.

Scocchera, Giovanna (2016a) 'Dalla cacofonia all'armonia: il ruolo della revisione collaborativa nella traduzione editoriale'. *mediAzioni* 21.

Scocchera, Giovanna (2016b) 'The sociology of revision: results of a qualitative survey on the professional practice of translation revision for publishing purposes and its agents, and how they relate to what we know (or we think we know) about revision'. *Paper read at the Eighth European Society for Translation Studies (EST) Congress*, 15–17 September, Åarhus, Denmark.

Scocchera, Giovanna (2017a) *La revisione della traduzione editoriale dall'inglese all'italiano. Ricerca, professione formazione.*

Scocchera, Giovanna (2017b) 'Translation revision as rereading: different aspects of the translator's and reviser's approach to the revision process studies in book culture'. *Translators and Their Readers* 9:1, 1–20.

Scocchera, Giovanna (2018) 'Collaborative revision in editorial/literary translation: some thoughts, facts and recommendations'. In *Traduire à plusieurs. Collaborative Translation* (Monti and Schnyder, eds.), 281–94.

Scocchera, Giovanna (2019) 'The competent reviser: a short-term empirical study on revision teaching and revision competence acquisition'. *The Interpreter and Translator Trainer* 14:1, 19–37.

Screen, Benjamin (2017) 'Machine translation and Welsh: analysing free statistical machine translation for the professional translation of an under-researched language pair'. *Journal of Specialised Translation* 28, 317–44.

Screen, Benjamin (2019) 'What effect does post-editing have on the translation product from an end-user's perspective?' *Journal of Specialised Translation* 31, 133–57.

Shih, Claire Yi-yi (2006) 'Revision from translators' point of view. An interview study'. *Target* 18:2, 295–312.

Shreve, Gregory M. et al. (2014) 'Efficacy of screen recording in the other-revision of translations: episodic memory and event models'. In *MonTI Special Issue—Minding Translation* (Muñoz Martín, ed.), 225–45.

Shuttleworth, Mark (2002) 'Combining MT and TM on a technology-oriented translation masters: aims and perspectives'. In *Proceedings of the 6th EAMT Workshop on Teaching Machine Translation*, 123–9.

Silva, Roberto (2014) 'Integrating post-editing MT in a professional translation workflow'. In *Post-Editing of Machine Translation: Processes and Applications* (O'Brien et al., eds.), 24–50.

Simeoni, Daniel (1995) 'Translating and studying translation: the view from the agent'. *Meta* 40:3, 445–60.

Simianer, Patrick et al. (2016) 'A post-editing interface for immediate adaptation in statistical machine translation.' In *Proceedings of COLING 2016, the 26th International Conference on Computational Linguistics: System Demonstrations*, 16–20.

Siponkoski, Nestori (2013) 'Translators as Negotiators: a case study on the editing process related to contemporary Finnish translation of Shakespeare'. *New Voices in Translation Studies* 9, 20–37.

Skelton, John R. and Sarah J. L. Edwards (2000) 'The function of the discussion section in academic medical writing'. *BMJ : British Medical Journal* 320:7244, 1269–70.

Smith, Thomas J. (2007) 'The ergonomics of learning: educational design and learning performance'. *Ergonomics* 50:10, 1530–46.

Snover, Matthew et al. (2006) 'A study of translation edit rate with targeted human annotation'. in *Proceedings of AMTA 2006*, 223–31.

Solum, Kristina (2018) 'The tacit influence of the copy-editor in literary translation'. *Perspectives: Studies in Translation Theory and Practice* 26:4, 543–59.

Somers, Harold (1997) 'A practical approach to using machine translation software'. *The Translator* 3:2, 193–212.

Sosoni, Vilelmini (2017) 'Casting some light on experts' experience with translation crowdsourcing'. *Journal of Specialised Translation* 28, 362–84.

Specia, Lucia (2011) 'Exploiting objective annotations for measuring translation post-editing effort'. In *15th Conference of the European Association for Machine Translation*, 73–80.

Specia, Lúcia et al. (2018) *Quality Estimation for Machine Translation*.

Spies, Carla-Marie (2013) 'Die wisselwerking tussen die agente betrokke by die publikasieproses van literêre vertalings'. Unpublished doctoral dissertation, Stellenbosch University, Stellenbosch, South Africa.

Statistics Canada. www.statcan.gc.ca/

Stoeller, Willem (2011) 'Global virtual teams'. In *Translation and Localization Project Management: The Art of the Possible* (Dunne and Dunne, eds.), 289–317.

Tardáguila, Esperanza (2009) 'Reflexiones sobre la revisión de traducciones'. *Mutatis Mutandis* 2:2, 367–76.

Tatsumi, Midori (2009) 'Correlation between automatic evaluation metric scores, post-editing speed, and some other factors'. In *Proceedings of MT Summit XII*, 332–3.

TAUS (2010) 'Machine translation post-editing guidelines'. www.taus.net/academy/best-practices/postedit-best-practices/machine-translation-post-editing-guidelines [consulted 1 November 2018].

Teixeira, Carlos da Silva Cardoso (2014) 'The handling of translation metadata in translation tools'. In *Post-Editing of Machine Translation: Processes and Applications* (O'Brien et al., eds.), 109–25.

Teixeira, Carlos da Silva Cardoso (2015) 'The impact of metadata on translator performance: how translators work with translation memories and Machine translation'. PhD dissertation, Universitat Rovira i Virgili.

Temizöz, Özlem (2016) 'Postediting machine translation output: Subject-matter experts versus professional translators'. *Perspectives* 24:4, 646–65.

Temizöz, Özlem (2017) 'Translator post-editing and subject-matter expert revision versus subject-matter expert post-editing and translator revision'. *Translator Education and Translation Studies* 4:2, 3–21.

Temnikova, Irina (2010) 'Cognitive evaluation approach for a controlled language post-editing experiment'. In *Proceedings of the 7th International Conference on Language Resources and Evaluation*, 3485–90.

Thaon, Brenda (1984) 'The role of a revision course in a translation program'. In *La Traduction: l'universitaire et le practicien* (Thomas et al., eds.), 297–301.

Thelen, Marcel (2013) 'Translation quality assessment in translator training'. In *Alles hängt mit allem zusammen. Translatologische Interdependenzen* (Ende et al., eds.), 191–202.

Thicke, Lori (2013) 'The industrial process for quality machine translation'. *Journal of Specialised Translation* 19, 8–18.

Toral Ruiz, Antonio (2019) 'Post-editese: an exacerbated translationese'. In *Proceedings of Machine Translation Summit XVII Volume 1: Research Track*, 273–81.

Toral Ruiz, Antonio and Víctor M. Sánchez-Cartagena (2017) 'A multifaceted evaluation of neural versus phraseased machine translation for 9 language directions'. In *Proceedings of the 15th Conference of the European Chapter of the Association for Computational Linguistics: Volume 1, Long Papers*.

Toral Ruiz, Antonio et al. (2018) 'Post-editing effort of a novel with statistical and neural machine translation'. *Frontiers in Digital Humanities* 5, 1–11.

Torrejón, Enrique and Celia Rico (2002) 'Controlled translation: a new teaching scenario tailor-made for the translation industry'. In *Proceedings of the 6th EAMT Workshop on Teaching Machine Translation*, 107–16.

Toury, Gideon (1995) *Descriptive Translation Studies—and Beyond*.

Toury, Gideon (2012) *Descriptive Translation Studies—and Beyond*.

Tradumàtica Research Group. (n.d.) 'POST-IT: Equipo de investigación' [POST-IT: Investigating Team]. http://xl8.link/post-it.

Trágora Formación. (n.d.) 'Curso online (80 h)—Posedición para traductores EN-ES'. www.tragoraformacion.com/cursos/traduccion/curso-online-posedicion-traductores/

TÜV Rheinland DIN CERTCO (2019) 'Registrations and certifications'. www.dincertco. tuv.com/search?locale=en&q=ISO+17100 [consulted 3 and 4 January 2019].

Uotila, Anna (2017) 'Revision and quality assurance in professional translation: a study of revision policies in Finnish translation companies'. Master's thesis, University of Tampere. http://urn.fi/URN:NBN:fi:uta-201712202991 [consulted 26 October 2018].

Valdez, Susana (2019) 'Perceived and observed translational norms in biomedical translation in the contemporary Portuguese translation market: a quantitative and qualitative product- and process-oriented study'. PhD dissertation, University of Lisbon and Ghent.

Van Brussel, Laura et al. (2018) 'A fine-grained error analysis of NMT, SMT and RBMT output for English-to-Dutch'. In *Proceedings of the Eleventh International Conference on Language Resources and Evaluation (LREC 2018)*, 3799–804.

Vandepitte, Sonia and Joleen Hanson (2018) 'The role of expertise in peer feedback analysis: exploring variables and factors in a translation context'. In *Quality Assurance and Assessment Practices in Translation and Interpreting* (Huertas-Barros et al., eds.), 315–25.

Van der Meer, Anne Maj (2015) 'Post-editing course'. Online training course. www.taus. net/academy/taus-post-editing-course.

van der Meer, Jaap and Achim Ruopp (2014) *Machine Translation Market Report*.

Van Egdom, Gys-Walt and Mark Pluymaekers (2019) 'Why go the extra mile? How different degrees of post-editing affect perceptions of texts, senders and products among end users'. *Journal of Specialised Translation* 31, 158–76.

Van Egdom, Gys-Walt and Winibert Segers (2019) *Leren vertalen. Een terminologie van de vertaaldidactiek*.

Van Egdom, Gys-Walt et al. (2018a) 'How to put the translation test to the test? On preselected items evaluation and perturbation'. In *Quality Assurance and Assessment Practices in Translation and Interpreting* (Huertas-Barros et al., eds.), 26–56.

Van Egdom, Gys-Walt et al. (2018b) 'Revising and evaluating with TranslationQ'. *Bayt Al-Hikma Journal for Translation Studies* 2:2, 25–56.

Van Egdom, Gys-Walt et al. (2019) 'Ergonomic quality in trainer-to-trainee revision processes: a pilot study'. *Paper Read at EST Conference*, Stellenbosch.

Van Egdom, Gys-Walt et al. (forthcoming, 2020) 'Ergonomics in Translator and Interpreter Training', special issue of *The Interpreter and Translator Trainer*.

Van Rensburg, Alta (2012) 'Die impak van revisie op vertaalde eksamenvraestelle in 'n hoëronderwysomgewing'. *LitNet Akademies* 9:2, 392–412.

Van Rensburg, Alta (2017) 'Developing assessment instruments: the effect of a reviser's profile on the quality of the revision product'. *Linguistica Antverpiensia, New Series: Themes in Translation Studies*, 16, 71–88.

Van Waes, Luuk and Mariëlle Leijten (2015) 'Fluency in writing: a multidimensional perspective on writing fluency applied to L1 and L2'. *Computers and Composition* 38, 79–95.

Vasconcellos, Muriel (1987a) 'A comparison of MT post-editing and traditional revision'. In *Proceedings of the 28th Annual Conference of the American Translators Association*, 409–15.

Vasconcellos, Muriel (1987b) 'Post-editing on-screen: machine translation from Spanish into English'. In *Proceedings of the Conference Translating and the Computer* 8 (Picken, ed.), 133–46.

Vasconcellos, Muriel and Dale Bostad (1992) 'Machine translation in a high-volume translation environment'. In *Computers in Translation: A Practical Appraisal* (Newton, ed.), 58–77.

Venkatesh, Viswanath and Fred Davis (2000) 'A theoretical extension of the technology acceptance model: four longitudinal field studies'. *Management Science* 46, 186–205.

Vieira, Lucas Nunes (2017a) 'Cognitive effort and different task foci in post-editing of machine translation: a think-aloud study'. *Across Languages and Cultures* 18:1, 79–105.

Vieira, Lucas Nunes (2017b) 'From process to product: links between post-editing effort and post-edited quality'. In *Translation in Transition: Between Cognition, Computing and Technology* (Jakobsen and Mesa-Lao, eds.), 162–86.

Vieira, Lucas Nunes and Elisa Alonso (2018) 'The use of machine translation in human translation workflows: Practices, perceptions and knowledge exchange'. www.iti.org.uk/images/downloads/ITIReport-Lucas.pdf.

Vilar, David et al. (2006) 'Error analysis of machine translation output'. In *Proceedings of the 5th International Conference on Language Resources and Evaluation (LREC'06)*, Genoa.

Vintar, Špela et al. (2017) 'Labour market needs survey and the DigiLing model curriculum'. In *Project DigiLing: TransEuropean e-Learning Hub for Digital Linguistics*. www.digiling.eu/wp-content/uploads/2017/05/DigiLingReport_IO1.pdf.

Von Meck, Anoeschka (2004) *Vaselinetjie*.

Von Meck, Anoeschka (2009) *My Name Is Vaselinetjie*.

Wagner, Emma (1985) 'Post-editing Systran—a challenge for commission translators'. *Terminologie et Traduction* 3.

Wagner, Emma et al. (2014) *Translating for the European Union Institutions*.

Way, Catherine (2009) 'Bringing professional practices into translation classrooms'. In *Proceedings of the Eighth Portsmouth Translation Conference, 'The Changing Face of Translation'*, 131–42.

Wicker, Allan W. (1969) 'Attitudes versus actions: the relationship of verbal and overt behavioral responses to attitude objects'. *Journal of Social Issues* 25:4, 41–78.

Willey, Ian and Kimie Tanimoto (2015) '"We're drifting into strange territory here": what think-aloud protocols reveal about convenience editing'. *Journal of Second Language Writing* 27, 63–83.

Winterbach, Ingrid (2002) *Niggie*.

Winterbach, Ingrid (2007) *To Hell with Cronjé*.

Winterbach, Ingrid (2010) *To Hell with Cronjé*.

Witczak, Olga (2016) 'Incorporating post-editing into a computer-assisted translation course. A study of student attitudes'. *Journal of Translator Education and Translation Studies* 1, 35–55.

Wolfson, Leandro (2004) 'A 10-year retrospective on a distance revision course: most frequent translation problems (part I)'. *The ATA Chronicle*, November/December, 33–6.

Wolfson, Leandro (2005) 'A 10-year retrospective on a distance revision course: most frequent translation problems (part II)'. *The ATA Chronicle*, January, 29–33.

World Health Organization (2017) *Human Resources for Medical Devices: The Role of Biomedical Engineers.* http://apps.who.int/iris/bitstream/10665/255261/1/9789241565479-eng.pdf?ua=1 [consulted 24 November 2018].

World Health Organization (2018) *Biomedical Engineering Global Resources.* www.who.int/medical_devices/support/en/ [consulted 24 February 2018].

Yamada, Masaru (2015) 'Can college students be post-editors? An investigation into employing language learners in machine translation plus post-editing settings'. *Machine Translation* 29:1, 49–67.

Yamada, Masaru (2019) 'The impact of Google neural machine translation on post-editing by student translators'. *Journal of Specialised Translation* 31, 87–106.

Yousif, Elias (2009) 'Revision of institutional documents: in search of a road map'. *Turjuman* 18:2, 11–32.

Zaidan, Omar F. and Chris Callison-Burch (2011) 'Crowdsourcing translation: professional quality from non-professionals'. In *Proceedings of the 49th Annual Meeting of the Association for Computational Linguistics*, 1220–9.

Zaretskaya, Anna (2017) 'Machine translation post-editing at TransPerfect—the "human" side of the process'. *Tradumàtica. Tecnologies de la Traducció* 15, 116–23.

Zaretskaya, Anna (2019) 'Raising the TM threshold in neural MT post-editing: a case-study on two datasets'. In *Proceedings of MT Summit XVII Vol. 2*, 213–18.

Zhechev, Ventsislav (2014) 'Analysing the post-editing of machine translation at Autodesk'. In *Post-Editing of Machine Translation: Processes and Applications* (O'Brien et al., eds.), 2–23.

INDEX

Note: page numbers in *italics* indicate a figure and page numbers in **bold** indicate a table on the corresponding page. Page numbers followed by "n" indicate a note.

ability 190–1; to adapt client specifications 201; to delete MT suggestion 49; to detect errors 7; NMT 52; participants 98; thinking 89; translators 81
academic writing 91; *see also* writing
acceptability 54
accuracy 139; comparative revision 139; consistency and 103; errors 9, 234, 242; semantic 118; translations 54, 156, 171–2
Across (software) 240
actions: editing 44–5; keyboard 42; non-linear 42–3
active learning 47
adaptability/adaptation 59, 210, 219–20
additions 28, **30**, 31, 42, 54, 100
adequacy 54, 66
adequate revision 145
adjectives 102
adverbs 102
Afrikaans 166
agent-driven tasks 181
Akaike's Information Criterion (AIC) 60, 64
A-language 189–90, 198, 200; *see also* language
American Translators Association (ATA) 228
analysis 56–8; of answers 156; case studies based 134; data 91, **97**, *97*, 97–103, *99–103*, 120, 153–4; edit 104; editing efficiency 58–9; empirical 180;

errors 3, 52; human translation 57, **57**; intervention optimality 58–9; investigation results 129; machine-translation (MT) 57, **57**, 190; mixed effects models 59–60; non-professional editing 78–86; post-editing 26–31, 188; quantitative 129; of real-life data 182; revisions 26–31, 58–9, 170, 188; risk 159; sentence-level 60; thematic 154
analytical skills 10
Anglophones 74, 77–8
annotations 54, 58; data *96*; decision tree *105*; edit 95–7, *96*; scale 14
anxiety 90
ArisToCAT project 70
assessment of quality 3–4, 227
attitudes: behaviour 149, 150; concepts of 149; of revisers and translators 148–64; subcompetences 193, **194**
Austria 129, 230
Austrian Economic Chambers (WKO) 119
Austrian Standards International (ASI) 113
authentic experiential learning (AEL) 222
author-revision 181
automatic metric 56
automation of process 87

behaviour(s): attitudes 149–50; editing 32, 45–6; expectations 149; over-editing 33; participants 21; precursors of 149;

reading 45; revision 9; translators 22, 46; typing 31, 45
Belgium 55, 230
beliefs 149–52; about other agents **150**; characterization 149; educators 227; questionnaire 148; reviser 154; translator 154; types of 148–9
bilingualism 15, 74, 126–7, 191
Bing 89, 240
B-language 189–90, 198, 200; *see also* language
briefs: assignments 211; PE 22, 201, 229; revised translation 8; revisers 4, 142; revision training 7; translations 201, 205, 212, 216

Canada 73–4, 80
CasMaCat project 47
Catalan 239
categorization scheme 54
certificate holders, described 117
certification: advantages 113–14; importance 114; process of LICS 115–16; process of LRQA 114–15; quality standards 113–16; registration and 117
challenges: of annotating edits 98; attitudes 37; editing tools 47–8; educators 242; LSP workflows 147; post-editing 15; post-editors 52; real-life 202; translation 170; translators 46; *see also* revision and post-editing
changes: in DIN EN 15038 110; essential 22; grammatical 28, 30; linguistic 11; necessary 54, 58; post-editing 12; preferential 22, 31, 52, 57–8; revisers 8; semantic 103; stylistic 33; text content *140*; unnecessary 21, 54, 57
civil servants 73–4, 77, 80, 82, 84–5
claims, productivity 41
clients 38, 41, 83; enterprise 39; French as language of work with 78–9; specifications 201; translators 79, 84; *see also* briefs
cognitive effort 13–14
cognitive ergonomics 208
cognitive load 47–8
Cohen's Kappa 28
coherence 25
collaborative networks 132
commas 27, 31, 102
comments: on deviations 116; editors 172, 175; inadequate for translation between German 40; inserting 199;

interviewees 80; justifying 98; self-revision 180; translators 177, 189
community, machine-translation (MT) 43
companies: background 136; choices of, certified 126, *126*; classification, by size *120*; operators 136; profile 120–1; service range 136; size of, certified 122, **123**
comparative examination 167
comparative reading 167
comparative revision 139
compatibility 210, 222–3
competences: core 192; defined 190; discursive 87; instrumental 192; instrumental/tool 192; interpersonal 192; metalinguistic-descriptive 193; post-editing 12, 190–5; professional 192; psycho-physiological 192; revision 190–5; skills and 38; strategic 192
complex editing 45
compliance: certified/uncertified companies with EN 15038 **124**, 125; with guidelines of EN 15038 *124*; recommendations for quality standards 123–5
computer-aided translation (CAT) 2–3, 9, 21, 37, 39, 43, 193, 209, 235, 238–41, 243
computer-assisted human translation 227
conflict 46
conjunctions 102
consistency 25, 41, 210, 221; accuracy and 103; of corrections 211; defined 210; errors 25, 220; feedback 224; objectivity and 204; PE 41; translations 118
contact and study hours 237–9
content: editing 133, 139–41; machine-translation (MT) 47; parameters 139
continuum 133–4, *134*, 144–6
controlled language 242
copy-editing 133, 181
copy editor 245
core competences 192
core questions 235–8, *236*–7
Corporate Translation Technology Survey 226–7
corpus approaches 3
correcting: human-translated text 50; identical errors 204; machine-translation output 2, 94; same errors 211; spelling errors 43; translators' errors 131; typographical mistakes 42; *see also* changes
Council of the European Communities 10, 11

course descriptions *see* machine translation post-editing (MTPE)

creative editing 131–47; research design 135–6; revision 132–3; revision continuum 133–4, *134*, 144–6; revision policies 134–5; survey results 136–44; *see also* editing/edit

creativity/creative: editing 141, 145; translation 136, 144; variation 139–42

critical errors 53; *see also* errors

Croatia 230

cross-university collaboration 188

Czech Republic 230

data: analysis 91, **97**, *97*, 97–103, *99–103*, 120; annotations *96*; categorising 33; collection 8–9, 46, 73, 226, 228–9; eyetracking 22, 33; keylogging 22, 26–7; sentence-level 59

debriefing interviews 14

decision-making 8, *142*, 142–4, 237

DeepL 53–4, 56, 89, 240

defective revision 4, 8

degrees: complexity 45; conceptualization 167; parameters and 198

deletions 28, **30**, 31, 42, 44–5, 54, 100

Denmark 10, 24

deontological issues with MTPE 243–4

dependent variables 59–60

Descriptive Translation Studies (DTS) 148

determiners 102

dichotomy 54

didactics 7, 205

DIN CERTCO 117, 121

discursive competence 87

disrupting technology 35

distance learning 189, 239

downward migration 227

draft translation 166

Dutch 54, 207

Dutch Parallel Corpus 53

Dutch-speaking audience 55

Dutch translations 56, 58

Dynamic Quality Framework (DQF) 213–14

ECTS 239, 241

editing/edit 42–3, 188; actions 37, 44–5; analysis 104; annotation 95–8, *96*; behaviour 32, 45–6; cognitive effort 33; content 133, 139–41; defined 37; distribution 99–103, *99–103*; efficiency 58–9; effort 26–8, 33, 39, 70; essential 91–2; of French translations

by non-professionals 80–5; interactive tools 46–8; modes 47; non-professional 86; preferential 91–2; process 22; proofreader 103; rates 43–4, 102, *102*; semantic 103; services 136, 144; stage 133, 147n1; statistics *97*, 97–9, *99*; style 98, 102; threshold 43–4; time and effort **26**, 26–7; tools challenges 47–8; types 44–5; typology 99–100; writing and 47; *see also* non-professional editing

editing effort **26**, 26–7

editors 90; comments 172, 175; non-professional 80; role 92

educators 232; beliefs 227; challenges 242; consent form 238; MTPE 229, 237; opinion 237; profile and background 240

efficiency: editing 58–9; teaching 7; translations 37; translators 39

empirical expectations 150, **150**

empirical research findings 206

empirical studies of post-editing 12–16; participant-oriented studies 14–15; process-oriented studies 13–14; product-oriented studies 12–13; studies in different environments 15–16; *see also* post-editing (PE)

empirical studies of revision 5–11; participant-based studies 9–10; relationship between process and quality of product 7–9; studies in different environments 10–11; studies of product 5–6; studies of revision competence and teaching 6–7

EMT Competence Framework 187

EN 15038 1, 11, 109–11; awareness of 121; quality standards 121; reception 119–20, 122; recommendations of 123–5; registration in *121*; restrictive formulation of 125; revision in 117–19; translation 117–19, 133

end-of-study questionnaire 7

English 78–9, 85, 89, 98, 228, 239; fiction 5; as first or second foreign language 24; into French 75–6; into German 25, 33; gerunds as nouns in 36; as language of work internally 78; non-native speakers 90; novels 5; placement 94; proficiency 102; source texts 5, 22; translation of French text 9; into Turkish 103; word sense problems 54

English as a Foreign Language (EFL) 90–1, 93–4

English–Finnish 197

English-French bilingualism 74

English-to-Afrikaans translations 6
English-to-French 80
enterprise clients 39
ergonomics: cognitive 208; criteria
216; defined 208; in education 209;
instructional 209; learning 209;
organizational 208; physical 208;
translator trainer 208–10
errors: accuracy 9, 234, 242; adequacy
54, 66; analysis 3, 52; categorization
232, 241–2; consistency 25, 220;
correction 46; critical 53; grammatical
32, 54, 85; human translations 25, *55*;
identification 46; introducing 12, 16;
machine-translation (MT) 41, 50–1, *55*;
management 210, 220–1; nature and
distribution 50; ortho-typographic 103;
revisers 51; spelling 43; style and 25,
85; syntactic 32; types 25, 40–1, 54, *55*;
typographic 103; typologies 95, 241;
unnatural 25
essential changes/edits 22, 91–2
ethical and deontological practices 234
e-Translation 241; *see also* translations
European Commission 2, 14–15
European Master's in Translation (EMT)
39, 191, 203
European Qualifications Framework 190
European Union 1
evaluation: human task-based 231–2; of
MT output *231*, 231–2; of PE text 243
examination 206, 239
Excel 60
expectations: behaviour 149; concepts
of 149; described 149; of reader 40;
revision 149
experimental set-up: post-editing human
translations 53–60; post-editors 94, **95**
explicit control 210, 218–19
extralinguistic subcompetences 191
eyetracking/eye-tracking: data 22, 33;
keylogging 9; subjective evaluations
12–13; technology 13–14

failure of translators 40
feasibility, monolingual post-editing 15
feedback: consistency 224; group 189;
high-quality 206; translation 214
Finland 230
Finnish 11, 134–7
fixed rate 233
formatting 117
France 10, 230
Francophones 74, 77–8, 80, 85, 87

French 22, 74, 77, 90, 239; Acadian 85;
Canadian 79; Continental 85; editing
translations by non-professionals 80–5;
into English 75; English translation of 9;
idiomatic administrative 81; as language
of work with clients 78–9; Quebec
85; translations 73, 81; varieties 86;
vernacular 85
French–Finnish 197
full post-edit/edit(ing) (FPE) 23–4, **23–4**,
26, 29, 31

German 4, 22, 90; English into 25, 33;
native speakers 24; newspaper 25;
translations 5
German–Finnish 197
German-to-Italian translations 5
Germany 114, 117, 121, 129, 230
Global Autonomous Language Exploitation
programme 41
Google Translate 23–4, 53–4, 89, 93–4, 240
graduate translators 39
grammar 25, 28, **30**, 94, 117; changes 28,
30; errors 32, 54, 85; metaphor 36
Great Britain 230
Greece 230
GREVIS research group 8
group feedback 189
guidance 210, 216–17

high-quality feedback 206
house style 9, 167, 182n4
human-assisted machine translation 227;
see also machine-translation (MT)
Human-Computer Interaction 47
human task-based evaluation 231–2
human translations (HT) 25, 38,
46; analysis 57, **57**; errors 25, *55*;
participants 55–6, **56**; post-editing 51,
61; predictable errors compared to
50; quality 50; reliability 55; revision
62; text origin 60, *61*, *63–7*; *see also*
machine translation (MT)
Hungarian 5
hyper-revisions 51, 57, 162
hypothesis 53, 168

identification: errors 46; of problems
54–5, *55*
identity crisis 38
idiom: compliance with clients style guide
139; translations 79; word 3
idiomatic administrative French 81
independent variables 59

industrial translation 42
informational explicitness 40
information and communication
    technology (ICT) 239
insecurity 28, **30**
insertions 42, 44–5
instructions: ergonomics 209; full post-
    edit (FPE) 23–4, **23–4**; light post-edit
    (LPE) 23–4, **23–4**; translators 37; *see also*
    pedagogy
instrumental/tool competence 192
instrumental/tools subcompetences
    193–4, **194**
Integrated Problem and Decision
    Reporting 7
intelligibility 54
interactive editing tools 46–8
Interactive Machine Translation (IMT) 47
International Ergonomics Association 208
interpersonal aptitude 50
interpersonal competence 192
interpersonal subcompetences 193, **194**
interpreters 86–7
intervention: optimality 58–9, 67, **68**;
    participants 58
interview(ing) 233
interviews 120, 239–44; debriefing 14;
    questionnaires 120, 134; semi-structured
    77–8; translators 11
intra-reviser reliability 207
introducing errors 12, 16; *see also* errors
Ireland 230
ISO 9001 113
ISO 17100 1–2, 11, 51, 109–11, 113, 127,
    187, 201, 205, 212; certificate holders
    117; quality standards 121; reception and
    use 119–20; recommendations of 118;
    requirements of 126; revision 117–19;
    self-revision in 198; translation revision
    in 117–19; translation workflow 133
ISO 18587 38, 227, 240, 246n3
Italian–Finnish 197
Italian publishing sector 9
Italy 9, 230

job satisfaction 38
justifying corrections 196, 198; *see also*
    correcting

KantanMT 240
keyboard actions 42
keylogging 26; data 22, 26–7; eyetracking
    9; software 46
keystroke logs 45

knowledge 193
Knowledge about Revision 191

language: choice in workplace 78;
    controlled 242; conventions 139;
    creative use 145; experts 9; fluency 241;
    pairs 43, 239; proficiency 197; skills 40;
    specialists 82; technology 15
Language Industry Certification System
    (LICS) 115–16
Language of Service Policy and
    Guidelines 75
language service companies (LSCs) 226,
    228–9
language service providers (LSPs) 131–2,
    203; creative translation 144; editing
    services of 144; revision continuum 145;
    revision policies of 136–7; standardised
    production workflow 133; as translation
    agencies 135; viewpoint of 135;
    workflows 137
Latourian perspective 11
Latvia 230
learners, second language 95
learning: active 47; distance 239;
    ergonomics 209; online 47
lexical choices 80
lexicon 28, **30**
lexis 117
light post-edit/edit(ing) (LPE) 23–4, **23–4**,
    26, 29, 31
Lilt 89, 240
linear translation 46
linear writing process 42
lingua franca 89
linguistic analysis 91
linguistic changes 11
linguistic correctness 138
linguistic minority 74
linguistic skills 192
literacy skills 79
literary publishing 9, 11
literary revisers 11, 165
literary revision 9
literary translation 11; revision in 165–82
Lloyd's Register Quality Assurance
    (LRQA) 114–15
lme4 59
lmerTest 59–61, 64
locale 117
localisation industry 37–8

machine-translation (MT) 187, 189–90;
    age 191; analysis 57, **57**; community 43;

content 47; errors 41, 50–1, *55*, 241–2; online 89; output 2–3, 13, 23, 26–7, 31–2, 41, 43, 46, 50–1, 53–4, 61, 66, 98, 103, 229, 231–2, 234, 237, 241–2; participants 55–6, **56**; post-editing of 2, 12–15; process 36, 40; quality 44, 53; statistical 35, 48, 242; suitability 91; technology 52; text 15, 60, *61*, *63*–7; tools 243; translation memories (TM) and 3; use by translators 38; use in regular translation courses 241; *see also* post-editing human translations; post-editors
machine translation post-editing (MTPE) 226–45; deontological issues 243–4; literature 226–7; methodology 228–9; participants 228; plans to increase 241; qualitative results 238–44; quantitative results 229–38, **230**, *231*–7; training 244; *see also* post-editing (PE)
Malta 230
Mann-Whitney U test 28–9
MateCat 240
matricial norms 42
mechanics 138, 189
MemoQ 240
memory *see* translation memories (TM)
MemSource 9, 240
metalinguistic-descriptive competence 193
metalinguistic knowledge 193
micro processing working style 8
Microsoft: Excel 240; Office suite 239; Word 94, 240
mixed effects models 59–60, 63
monolingual examination 206
monolingual post-editing 15
monolingual revision 126–7
Moses tokenizer 57
motivation: post-editors 91–2; revisers and translators 148
movement 44–5
Multilingual Translation Studies Degree Programme, University of Turku 196–7, **197**
Multilingual Translation Workshop I/II 201

necessary changes 54, 58; *see also* changes
needs: for interactive editing tools 46–8; technological 37
Netherlands 55
neural machine translation (NMT) 33, 35, 41, 200; error typology 241; interactive systems 48; online 53; output 39, 52
New Brunswick Translation Bureau 75–6, 79–80, 84–5; Official Languages Act 74–5

NMT *see* neural machine translation (NMT)
non-linear actions 42–3
non-linear writing process 42
non-native speakers 90; of English 89–90; errors 92, 98
non-official languages 74
non-professional editing/revision 73–88; editors 80; findings and analysis 78–86; French translations by 80–5; sociolinguistics 74–6; work environment and methodology 76–8; *see also* editing/edit
non-professional interpreting and translation (NPIT) 73, 86
non-professional post-editing 12
normative attitudes 150, **150**
normative expectations 150, **150**
norms: attitudes and expectations 149–52; competences and 160; language 82, 85, 156; linguistic 87, 158, 198; professional 87–8; terminological 156, 160; translations 149; typology of reviser interventions 5
Norwegian: literary translators 5; novels 5
nouns 102

omissions 25, 42, 52
online learning 47
online questionnaire 7, 14, 119–20, 135, 153, 226, 228–9, 241
open-ended questions 141
opinion of educators 237
optimality, intervention 58–9
optimisers 37, 40
organizational ergonomics 208
Organization for Economic Cooperation and Development 11
orthography 25, 94
ortho-typographic errors 103
other-revision 178–81; authors changes 175; competence 6; feedback 198; one dimensional and linear 168; PE process 8; quality standards 109; second translator 165; self-revision and 189; by students 7; translation workflow 137
over-edit(ing) 21; as abstract concept 22; behaviour 33; classification of 30–1, **30–1**; instructions to avoid 22; preferential changes 22; quantification of 27–30; translation memories (TM) 21
over-revision 58, 162

PACTE model 191
Pan-American Health Organization 2

parameters 235, 241; content 139; degrees and 198; revisions 118, 127–9, *128*, 137–9, *138*, 145; for translation revision 118

participant(s) 55–6; based studies 9–10; distribution task and text **24**; edit distribution *101*; edit rates 102, *102*; intervention 58; machine translation post-editing (MTPE) 228; oriented studies 3, 14–15; *vs.* proofreader 91, 97, 97–8, *100*; recruitment and profiles 92–3, **93**; for revision quality *65*; scores 59; selection 77; survey 241; for TER scores *62*; variation across 64

PE *see* post-editing (PE)

pedagogy 7

physical environment 132

physical ergonomics 208

Poland 230

Portugal 230

Portuguese: Brazilian 22; European 154

post-editese' 13

post-editing (PE): age of syllabus 240; of audiovisual material 15; brief 234, *234*; challenges 15; changes 12; charges 56; competences 12, 190–5, **194**; defined 2; compared to editing and revision 35–49; compared to revision 50–70; empirical studies of 12–16; evaluation of text 243; guidelines 234–5, *235*; human translations (HT) 51, 61; industry statistics 39; instructions **23**; IT texts 22; levels 233; of machine-translation 2, 12–15, 187; monolingual 15; narratives of resistance to 37–9; non-professional 12, 89–106; output 41; participant-oriented studies 14–15; process 13–14, 36; productivity 14; product-oriented studies 12–13; progression 35; quality 104; reflections 12; research 12–16; revisions 40, 203; risks 233–4; skills 12, 235–7, *236*; as specialised form of translation 40–2; speed 51; studies in different environments 15–16; style 41; tasks *237*, 237–8; teaching 39; technology 3; text origin *61*, *63*–7; theoretical publications 12; traditional 47; training 94, 187–202, 226–46, *236*; translation 8, 12; translator training 39; usability 13; weight in syllabus 230, *230*; *see also* machine-translation (MT)

post-editing human translations 50–70; experimental set-up 53–60; research 50–3; results 60–8

post-edition 36

post-editors 40, 89–104; awareness 50; challenges 52; data analysis **97**, *97*, 97–103, *99–103*; edit annotation 95–7, *96*; experimental set-up 94, **95**; future work 103–4; methodology 92–3; motivation 91–2; non-professional 89–106; professional 235, 237; research 90–1; translators 32; *see also* editors

post-eyetracking questionnaire 9

post-task questionnaire 94, 98

précis-writing 188

precursors of behavior 149

prediction: of editing behaviour 45–6; post-editing (PE) 47; writing 39, 234

pre-editing: skills 192; of source text 242–3; *see also* post-editing (PE)

preferential changes 22, 31, 52, 57–8; *see also* revision and post-editing

preferential edits 91–2

prepositions 102

prerequisites for enrollment, syllabus 239

presentation: certification 129; theoretical 242

pre-task questionnaire 94

pricing models *232*, 232–3

problems, identification of 54–5, *55*

process: automation of 87; DTS 148; editing 22; human translation 46; industrial translation 42; linear writing 42; machine-translation (MT) 36, 40; non-linear writing 42; post-editing 14, 36; of product 7–9; revision 36, 51; translation 11, 27, 33, 36, 44, 52; writing 28

production/productivity: claims 41; improvement 38; measurement 231; segments 42; time 40

product-oriented studies 3, 12–13

professional: competence 192; development 49; post-editor 235, 237; proofreader 89; proofreading 94; revisers 7–8, 79, 86, 90–1; skills 227; translators 9, 12–14, 16, 24, 37, 41–2, 51, 89–92, 103

professionalisation 114

project-based approach 241

project manager 146

pronouns 102

proofreader: edit distribution *101*; edits 103; *vs.* participants 97, 97–8, *100*; participants and 91; physicians and 95; professional 89; revision 181

proofreading: annotation and 92; archival documents 169; monolingual **95**;

professional 94; reviewing and 205;
symbols 11; text 92
pseudo-editing 234
psycho-physiological competence 192
psycho-physiological subcompetences
193, **194**
public service, New Brunswick 79–80
punctuation **23**, 28, **30**, 31, 94, 96

qualitative results, MTPE 238–44
quality **68**; assessment 3–4, 227;
certification 113–16; compliance
recommendations 123–5; criteria 127–9,
128, 207; estimation 43, *231*, 232;
human translation 50; management
systems 112, **113**; MT 44, 53; overview
109–11; post-editing 16, 104; in practice
121; of product 7–9; registration
116–17; revision 7–9, 53, 58–9, 63–7,
64–6, 109–30, 203–25; standards 22,
30–1, 109–30; TM 44; translation 32–3,
37, 51, 53, 111–13; for TSPs **111–12**
quantification of over-editing 27–30
quantitative analysis 129
quantitative results, MTPE 229–38, **230**,
231–7
Quebec 74, 80
questionnaires 92–3, 120, 136, 148–9;
beliefs 148; core 235–8, *236–7*; data
collection 153; design and data analysis
153–4; end-of-study 7; interview 120,
134; online 7, 14, 119–20, 135, 153,
226, 228–9, 241; open-ended 141; pilot
testing 153; post-eyetracking 9; post-
task 94, 98; pre-task 94; revisers 153–4;
translators 153–4

rapid post-edit(ing) 32
rates: editing 43–4, 102, *102*; fixed 233;
variable 233
raw output and final quality 233
RBMT 51, 200, 241
reader expectations 40
reading 36, 40, 42, 45
real-life challenges 202
reception: EN 15038 119–20, 122; ISO
17100 119–20
redundancy 41
registration: advantages of 117; certificates
and 117; in EN 15038 *121*; fee-based
116–17; numbers 117; quality standards
116–17
related and general matters **230**, 230–5,
231–5

reliability: human translations 55; revisers
207; translation 51
replacement 44
research: 1–17; community 227; core
questions 235–8, *236–7*; design 135–6;
hypotheses 53; post-editing human
translations 50–3; post-editors 90–1;
questions 52–3, 60, 92, 168; skills 10
retranslating 8, 191–2, **194**, 198
Reverso 89
reviser-revision 181
revisers 148–63; attitudes 149–64, **150**;
awareness 50; beliefs 149, **150**, 154;
biomedical translation 152–3; changes
8; data collection 153; errors 51;
expectations 149–52, **150**, 156–7;
function 1; interventions 5; literary
11; loyalties 11; methodology 153–5;
motivations of 148; norms 149–52;
overview 148–9; participants 154–5;
professional 7–8, 79, 86, 90–1; profiles
155; proposed changes 5; qualifications
11; questionnaire 153–4; reliability 207;
translators 10, 11, 32
revising 36
revision and post-editing 21–34; analysis
and results 26–31; classification of over-
editing instances 30–1, **30–1**; compared
35–49; 50–70; over-editing 21;
quantification of over-editing instances
27–30; research 3; studies 22–6; time
and editing effort **26**, 26–7; *see also* post-
editing (PE)
revision continuum 133–4, *134*; as
hypothesis 146; language service
providers (LSPs) 145; role and benefits
of 144–6; as service design tool 144–5;
uses 134
revision quality: construct of 205–10;
indicators of **212**; with translationQ
210–15; in translator training 203–25
Revision Routine Activation 191
revision(s) 188; adequate 145; aspects of
118–19; attitudes 149; bilingual 126–7;
charges 56; comparative 139; compared
with PE 40; competences 190–5, **194**;
content editing 141; course 1, 4, 6, 10,
188, 204; defective 4, 8; defined 1–2,
36, 166, 205; empirical studies 5–11; in
EN 15038 117–19; encompassing term
180; expectations 149; history 1; human
translations (HT) *62*; interventions 8;
ISO 17100 117–19; levels 142, *142*;
in literary translation 165–82; methods

118, *126*, 126–7, *127*; monolingual
126–7; objectives of 142, *143*;
parameters 118, 127–9, *128*, 137–9,
138, 145; participant-based studies 9–10;
as part of translation workflow 132–3;
policies 134–5; procedures 8, 11, 136;
process 36, 51; proofreader 181; quality
7–9, 53, 58–9, 63–7, *64–6*, 109–30;
research 3–11; scope of 142, *143*, 144;
service 145; skills 201, 204; source-text
informed 181; studies 5–7, 10–11; text
origin *61*, *67*; time-consuming process
51; trainer-to-trainee 204; training in 7,
187–202; translation 195–202; translator
181; unilingual 181; without exception
125, 125–6; workflow 137
rewriting 174–5, 181
risk analysis 159
rule-based machine translation (MT) 51,
190, 200, 241

satisficers 37, 39–40
SBMT 241
scientific writing 90–1
scores, Translation Edit Rate (TER) 57, **57**,
59–63, *61–3*
SDL 228; Language Cloud 241; Trados
Studio 240; Translation Technology
Insights 58
second language learners 95
second translator 41
selection: participants 77; of text 53–4
self-beliefs 149
self-confidence 4
self-post-editing 89, 91, 98; *see also* post-
editing (PE)
self-revision 2, 8, 36, 40, 93, 132,
163n6–164n6, 165, 168, 175–6, 180;
comparative 157; engage in 180; expert
subtask of translation 203; initial 171,
179; in ISO 17100 198; as part of
translation process 161; of PE 40; for
professional translators 1–2, 165; as root
cause of lack of quality 157; solitary
process 173; students 6; *see also* revision
semantic accuracy 118
semantic change 103
semantic edits 103
semicolons 31
semi-structured interviews 77–8
sentence-level analysis 60
sentence-level data 59
sentence-level models 67–8, **68**
sessions 34n1, 34n4

severity weight 54, *55*
significance of codes 210, 221–2
sjPlot 59
skills **194**; analytical 10; competences
and 38; defined 190–1; language 40;
linguistic 192; literacy 79; post-editing
12; pre-editing 192; professional 227;
reading 42; research 10; revision 201,
204; translation 12; translators 39;
writing 42
slide presentations 230
Slovenia 5
social sciences 148, 149
social workers 79, 84
sociolinguistics 74–6, 85–6
software: keylogging 46; tools and 240–1
source segment 242
Spain 92, 230
Spanish 90, 93–4, 98, 239; L1 writers 91;
researchers 90; speaking physicians 89,
92; universities 92, 227
Spanish–Finnish 197
speakers: non-native 90; non-native-
English 90; of non-official languages 74
spelling 28, **30**, 43
split training 244–5
STAR Transit 240
statistical machine translation (SMT) 35,
48, 52, 200
strategic competence 192
strategic subcompetences 193, **194**
studies: participant-based 9–10; post-
editing 15–16, 22–6; of product
5–6; revision 10–11, 22–6; of revision
competence and teaching 6–7
style 28, **30**; categories 95; changes 33;
choices 80; edits 102; errors and 25, 85;
lexical choices and 32; post-editing (PE)
41; problems 51, 94
stylistic editing 133, *140*, 181
stylistic suitability 138
subcompetences: attitudinal 193, **194**;
bilingual 191; extralinguistic 191;
instrumental/tools 193, **194**; interpersonal
191, 193–4, **194**; psycho-physiological
193, **194**; strategic 193, **194**
subject-matter experts 92, 103
sub-language 138
subtractions 42
survey: open-ended questions 141; results
of 136–44
Switzerland 230
syllabus 230, *230*, 238–40, 245n1;
compulsory or elective 238

syntactic errors 32
syntax 28, 30, **30**, 94, 241

target segment 242
task: distribution 56; evaluation 232; potential 56; translators 55
TAUS 228
TAUS DQF 231
TAUS PE guidelines 23, **23**
teaching: methods and materials 230, *231*, 241; post-editing (PE) 39, 188–90; revision 6–7, 188–90
technology: development 48; eyetracking 13–14; machine-translation (MT) 52; translations 53, 226
TELEVIC/KU Leuven 204, 210, 211
TER *see* Translation Edit Rate (TER)
TERCOM 57
terminology 117
text: content *140*; elimination **26**; human translations (HT) 60, *61*, *63–7*; machine-translation (MT) 15, 60, *61*, *63–7*; production **26**; selection 53–4; type 141
thematic analysis 154
theoretical presentation 242
think-aloud: data collection 8; protocols 3, 6, 13–14; retrospective 9, 15; revision quality and ability 7–8
Tilde 241
time: editing effort and **26**, 26–7; production 40; translations 52
tools: challenges 47–8; interactive editing 46–8; MT 243; software and 240–1; subcompetences 193, **194**
\traditional post-editing *see* machine-translation (MT)
trainer: ergonomics 208–10; oriented ability 192; to trainee revision 204–7; translator 203–4
training: courses 32; MTPE *231*, 244; post-editing 94; in post-editing 187–202, 226–46; in revision 187–202; split 244–5; translation 24; translators 39
transcreation 144, 147n3
transference 40
translate-edit-proofread 187
translating 36, 42–3, 48
Translation and Interpretation Services (AD-1502) 76
Translation Centre for the Bodies of the European Union 11

Translation Commons' Learn/Resources Hub 228
Translation Edit Rate (TER) 43–4, 56, **68**; quantity of text 58; scores 57, **57**, 59–63, *61–3*
'translationese' 13
translation memories (TM) 2, 35, 190; machine translation and 3; optimising work 39; over-editing 21–2; quality 44; translators 15
translationQ: algorithm flagging potential identical errors *215*; ergonomic quality criteria 215–23; ergonomic quality of 209–10; overview 211–12; revision quality with 210–15; revision standards 212–15; support page *218*
translation revision 36, 195–202; aspects of 118–19; defined 1; in EN 15038 117–19; ISO 17100 117–19; methods 118; parameters for 118; source text 2
translation(s): accuracy 54, 156, 171–2; agencies 1, 11, 50, 55–6, 62, 69–70, 126, 135, 189; centralization 87; challenges 170; competence 4; consistency 118; courses 198–201; creative 136; defined 36; efficiency 37; expertise 9; feedback sheet 214–15, *215*; human 25, 38, 46; post-editing 8, 12, 40–2, 195–202; process 11, 27, 33, 36, 44, 52; programmes 39; project managers 14; purpose of 117; quality 6, 32, 33, 37, 51, 53, 111–13, 227; reliability 51; roles in New Brunswick public service 79–80; skills 12; stage 133; students 12–14; target group 117; technology 53, 226, 238; time 52; tools 238; training 24; workflow 132–3; writing 47
translation service providers (TSPs) 38; importance of certification 114; quality management systems 112, **113**; quality standards for **111–12**; revised translation 118
translator education 190; as academic study 195; competences 188; curriculum 188, 195; graduates of 187; post-editing in 188; programme 188; stages of 194–5
translator(s) 1, 81–2; accepting revisers' suggestions 5; advantages 38; argument 40; attitudes 149–64; behaviour 22, 46; beliefs 149, **150**, 154; bilingual 15; biomedical translation 152–3;

challenges 46; clients 79, 84; comments 177, 189; computer interaction 14; data collection 153; education 195; efficiency 39; errors 52; expectations 149–52, 157–60; failure 40; graduate 39; instructions 37; interpreters and 86–7; interviews 11; job satisfaction 38; machine-translation (MT) use by 38; methodology 153–5; motivations of 148; narratives of 37; norms 149–52; overview 148–9; participants 154–5; post-editors 32; productivity 13; professional 9, 12–14, 16, 24, 37, 41–2, 89–92, 103; profiles 155–6; questionnaire 153–4; revisers 10–11, 32; revision 181; skills 39; specialisation 36; task 55; trainer 203–4, 208–10; training 39, 51, 148, 203–25; translation memories 15; *see also* post-editor

translator trainer ergonomics 208–10

translator training 203–24; revision quality 205–7; translationQ 210–23; *see also* quality; training

Translog II (program) 22

t-test 29

turn-around times 38

TUV Rheinland 117

two-column lay-out *213*

typing behaviour 31, 45

typing speed 48

typographic errors 103

under-edit(ing) 28, 33

under-revision 58, 66, *67*

unilingual editor-revision 181

unilingual revision 181

United Nations 1

Universitat Autònoma de Barcelona 229

University of Antwerp 7

University of Mainz 24

University of Santiago de Compostela 90

University of Turku 188, 196, **197**

unnatural errors 25

unnecessary changes 21, 54, 57

user report *223*

variables: dependent 59–60; independent 59

verbs 102

virtual private network (VPN) 239

Wikipedia 5, 10

workload 210, 218, *237*

workplace 78; *see also* non-professional editing

writers: EFL 94; Spanish L1 91

writing 36, 40, 42; academic 91; editing and 47; first language 89; French 80; linear process 42; non-linear process 42; predictive 39, 234; process 28; scientific 90–1; translation 47

YAWAT (alignment tool) 22

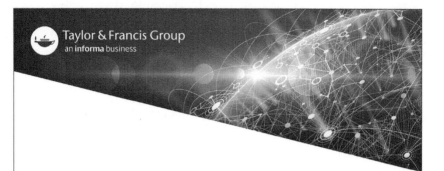